Excommunication for Debt in Late Medieval France

Late medieval church courts frequently excommunicated debtors at the request of their creditors. Tyler Lange analyzes over 11,000 excommunications between 1380 and 1530 in order to explore the forms, rhythms, and cultural significance of the practice. Three case studies demonstrate how excommunication for debt facilitated minor transactions in an age of scarce small-denomination coinage and how interest-free loans and sales credits could be viewed as encouraging the relations of charitable exchange that were supposed to exist between members of Christ's body. Lange also demonstrates how from 1500 or so believers gradually turned away from the practice and toward secular courts, at the same time as they retained the moralized, economically irrational conception of indebtedness we have yet to shake. The demand-driven rise and fall of excommunication for debt reveals how believers began to reshape the institutional Church well before Martin Luther posted his theses.

TYLER LANGE is a lecturer in the Department of History at the University of California, Berkeley, and a historian of the late Middle Ages and the early modern period whose research centers on questions of legal, religious, and social practices between 1400 and 1600. He has previously published *The First French Reformation: Church Reform and the Origins of the Old Regime* (Cambridge, 2014).

Excommunication for Debt in Late Medieval France

The Business of Salvation

Tyler Lange

University of California, Berkeley

CAMBRIDGE
UNIVERSITY PRESS

CAMBRIDGE
UNIVERSITY PRESS

University Printing House, Cambridge CB2 8BS, United Kingdom

Cambridge University Press is part of the University of Cambridge.

It furthers the University's mission by disseminating knowledge in the pursuit of education, learning and research at the highest international levels of excellence.

www.cambridge.org
Information on this title: www.cambridge.org/9781107145795

First published 2016

Printed in the United States of America by Sheridan Books, Inc.

A catalogue record for this publication is available from the British Library

Library of Congress Cataloguing in Publication data
Names: Lange, Tyler, 1981– author.
Title: Excommunication for debt in late medieval France : the business of salvation / Tyler Lange.
Description: New York : Cambridge University Press, 2016. | Includes bibliographical references and index.
Identifiers: LCCN 2015049715 | ISBN 9781107145795 (hardback)
Subjects: LCSH: Excommunication (Canon law)–History. | Catholic Church–France–History. | Debtor and creditor–France–History. | Church and state–France–History.
Classification: LCC KBU3610.D43 L36 2016 | DDC 262.9–dc23
LC record available at http://lccn.loc.gov/2015049715

ISBN 978-1-107-14579-5 Hardback

Contents

Figures

Tables

Map

Prefatory note

The historian speaks the language of his or her age. He or she may stretch readers' historical awareness but can only go so far without risking incomprehensibility. Speaking of the business of salvation with respect to excommunication for debt is meaningful in terms both of present and of past intersections of the logic of the "market" and the logic of "religion." Through the late medieval economy of salvation, a believer could transact (if not exclusively monetarily) his or her way to salvation through meritorious acts and the intercession of saintly protectors; at the same time, through the procedures of church courts, a despairing creditor could bar a debtor from the sacraments that offered a chance of salvation.[1] Today, when even the most intimate tasks and relationships can be purchased, it should not shock that late medieval borrowers obligated themselves on pain of excommunication, offering their salvation as a pledge.[2] George Lakoff has observed that we speak in metaphors: argument is war, time is money, virtue is up and depravity is down.[3] Achieving salvation was a business in the medieval sense – a *commercium* or exchange, ideally not a *mercatura* or bargain – and in the modern sense. If metaphors of life

[1] On devotional indulgences and counting piety, see R. N. Swanson, *Indulgences in Late Medieval England: Passports to Paradise* (Cambridge University Press, 2007); Thomas Lentes, "Counting Piety in the Late Middle Ages," in Bernhard Jussen (ed.), *Ordering Medieval Society: Perspectives on Intellectual and Practical Modes of Shaping Social Relations*, P. Selwyn (trans.) (Philadelphia: University of Pennsylvania Press, 2001), 55–91; Eamon Duffy, *The Stripping of the Altars: Traditional Religion in England 1400–1580* (New Haven: Yale University Press, 1992). I make no approving reference to the perverse thesis of Robert B. Ekelund, Robert D. Tollison, Gary M. Anderson, Robert F. Hébert, and Audrey B. Davidson, *Sacred Trust: The Medieval Church as an Economic Firm* (New York: Oxford University Press, 1996), that the medieval Church behaved like a firm seeking to maintain "market dominance"; as Swanson (*Indulgences*, 420) observes of the thesis: "The driving premisses are fundamentally unsound."

[2] Arlie Russell Hochschild, *The Outsourced Self: Intimate Life in Market Times* (New York: Metropolitan Press, 2012). This commodification or securitization of salvation troubled theologians and canonists, especially as we shall see below in the context of priests who pledged their capacity to perform divine service, that is, who in effect pledged their parishioners' salvation.

[3] George Lakoff, *Metaphors We Live By* (University of Chicago Press, 1980).

and career as battle or war were common before the end of the Cold War ("hostile takeover" springs to mind), in the 2000s and 2010s metaphors of entrepreneurship and advertising appear to be common. We – even academics, as my profiles on LinkedIn or academia.edu illustrate – are entrepreneurs of ourselves, "branding" and "selling" our identities, constantly marketing ourselves so that others will consume, will "buy" our skills, our blogs, our handicrafts, our apps, or our books. Appropriately, we entrepreneurs of the self consume to create these identities, often on credit.[4] Thus, and especially in the United States, those living in our neoliberal age prefer to imagine society as constituted primarily by market relations between entrepreneurs and consumers.[5] Our categories of analysis encourage us to weigh the financial costs and benefits, the potential profits of every action, every relationship, every institution. This study explores the meaning and operation of ordinary credit in an age when society was imagined as the Body of Christ, when "religion" meant a particular religious order (e.g., of Saint Benedict), and when a "market" was a legally established time and place for commerce. What follows offers, if not an overt critique of the present, then at least an implicit comparison with an age when actions, relationships, and institutions could be and often were appraised by measures other than economic, an age when the tension between power and transcendence, between net worth and salvation, had not collapsed into the constant monetary appraisal of self-worth.

Although the following work may strike some readers as being too hard on the Church, to me it is quite the opposite. Excommunication for debt provided an economic and, in a way that is initially difficult for us to comprehend, a religious service by sanctioning real failures of charity and trust. We should not imagine the creditor seeking to excommunicate a delinquent debtor as a usurer manipulating the sanctions of the Church. We should imagine him or her as a seller on credit seeking payment or a purchaser seeking the delivery of items already paid for. Debt is not only "a promise corrupted by both math and violence."[6] It can also be a source of power for the borrower, when it enables the realization of his or her "capabilities."[7] The Church does not need our pity, nor

[4] Joseph Stiglitz has observed that growth in the United States in the decade before 2007 was "reliant on the bottom 80 percent consuming about 110 percent of their income": "Inequality is Holding Back the Recovery," *The New York Times*, January 20, 2013.

[5] Rather than between laborers: Corey Robin, "Nietsche's Marginal Children: On Friedrich Hayek," *The Nation* (May 27, 2013): www.thenation.com/article/174219/nietzsches-marginal-children-friedrich-hayek?page=full#

[6] David Graeber, *Debt: The First 5,000 Years* (Brooklyn: Melville House, 2012), 391.

[7] Amartya Sen, "Equality of What?" in *McMurrin S. Tanner Lectures on Human Values* (Cambridge University Press, 1980), I: 195–220.

the white-washing of its history. Those who lament a lost premodern or pre-Reformation age when social norms were securely anchored in religion and arrayed according to religious categories fail to consider that, when religion was everywhere, it was spread more thinly (if not more lightly). Not only was religious content banalized, but it could appear even at what strike us to be less than grave moments.[8] In other words, excommunication sanctioned minor debts because salvation was at stake everywhere, every day, in every act. Isn't it, though? Every moment can be evaluated as it pertains to salvation, just as every moment can be subjected to cost–benefit analysis.

This book implies that today's Market might be as much a church as the late medieval Church, for its norms and its values structure our thought to the extent that it requires great effort even to think as a Christian.[9] What has been called "Scottish Theology" is often unexamined and near inescapable. Neoliberal modes of thought directed at the maximization of profit, like Christian modes of thought directed at the pursuit of salvation through the institutional Church, promise untold benefits to those who believe but intolerance and exclusion to those who do not believe or cannot join. Just as the hope of salvation brought solace and hope to many at the cost of great suffering for a few, the wish to consume has improved living standards enormously since 1800 at the cost of a sense of relative deprivation that insults the human dignity of those left behind, who are often driven to despair or to violence. What follows cannot explain fully modern market society, for the transformation of Christ's faith-based body into the faith-based Market was mediated by the experience of the early modern states that accounts for evident European and global disparities in degrees of market orientation. "When powerful financiers, politicians, and economists tell billions of humans that they should adopt the market as sole social regulator, anthropologists [and historians, I would add!] are well placed to show that what is presented as a logical necessity is actually a choice ... We can expose the historical and cultural specificity of this new faith."[10] Excommunication for debt

8 As Pope John XXIII observed to the Second Vatican Council: "the deposit of faith is one thing ... the way it is expressed is another," quoted by Pope Francis, "Evangelii gaudium," §41, p. 36.

9 As observed by Michel de Certeau, tr. Tom Conley, "The Inversion of What Can Be Thought: Religious History in the Seventeenth Century," and "The Formality of Practices: From Religious Systems to the Ethics of the Enlightenment (The Seventeenth and Eighteenth Centuries)," in *The Writing of History* (New York: Columbia University Press, 1988), 125–146 and 147–205. Hence our difficulty in conceiving of liberalism in noneconomic terms: Larry Seidentop, *Inventing the Individual: The Origins of Western Liberalism* (Cambridge, MA: Belknap Press, 2014), 362–363.

10 Michel-Rolph Trouillot, *Global Transformations: Anthropology and the Modern World* (New York: Palgrave Macmillan, 2003), 138–139.

helps us to understand a perplexing aspect of the new faith: widespread, persistently irrational, and uneconomic attitudes to debt. We believe that it is just (and not just economically rational) to repay debts because the conceptual universe of credit was secularized in the sixteenth century without losing any of the morality that accompanied obligations between Christ's members. If we cannot materially escape our *stahlhartes Gehäuse*, perhaps we can rethink its moral valence.

Acknowledgments

My debts of honor are many. This book could not have been written without the generous scholarly sociability and material support offered by colleagues in the New and the Old Worlds. Foremost among these are Laurent Mayali and Albrecht Cordes, who afforded me nearly four years of research and writing. At Professor Mayali's invitation, the Robbins Collection in Civil and Religious Law provided a two-year postdoctoral fellowship. At Professor Cordes's invitation, the Research Focus on Extrajudicial and Judicial Conflict Resolution at the Goethe-Universität invited me to Frankfurt for six months, a stay later much extended thanks to fellowships from the Goethe-Universität's GO-IN Program, the European Union's Marie Curie Program, and the Alexander von Humboldt Foundation.

I thank wonderful colleagues in three countries. In Berkeley, Mary Elizabeth Berry, Thomas A. Brady, Jr., Robert Harkins, Carla Hesse, Laurent Mayali, Maureen Miller, Jeffrey Miner, Ethan Shagan, and Jesse Torgerson provided helpful comments. In Frankfurt, I am indebted to Albrecht Cordes, Wim Decock, Thomas Duve, Guido Pfeiffer, and Margrit Schulte-Beerbühl. In Paris, I thank Frédéric Gabriel and Patrick Arabeyre. Audiences in Berkeley, Frankfurt, Aspen, Montréal, at the American Society for Legal History Conference in 2012, at Amherst College, and at Wesleyan University offered helpful feedback. I thank especially warmly Tom Brady, Albrecht Cordes, Wim Decock, and Jesse Torgerson, who took the time to read all or part of various stages of the manuscript. Finally, I offer this book as *piaculum* to Rebecca, who moved our whole menagerie internationally that it be completed.

As to errors and infelicities, I repeat the words of Innocent III once quoted by the great Brian Tierney: *feci diligenter ut potui, non sufficienter ut volui.*

Note on names, dates, and currency

Quantifying the records of late medieval courts is difficult for three reasons: nomenclature, dating, and currency. How do we translate the name given in Latin as *Jacobus Fabri*? Was the man called Jacques Lefèvre, Jacques Febvre, Jacques Faur, Jacques Du Faur, or even Jacques Fabri? Was he called Jacquet? More than one individual could be concealed under the same Latin name. Homonymy is a great worry: were there four or two Guillaume Le Telliers in early-sixteenth-century Montivilliers? There were an elder and a younger Guillaume, but was Guillaume Le Tellier, *clericus*, later ordained, becoming Sire Guillaume Le Tellier, priest? In my databases, I have only assimilated such names into one individual when unities of time (years active), place (parish of residence or activity), and transactions (the same persons sanctioned or were sanctioned) merited this. Another problem concerns officers of the court, who sometimes excommunicated under their own names, rather than as *Dominus Sigillifer* and so on. Were they then acting on official business, on their own behalf, or were they then out of office? For all these reasons, and because economic cells were excommunicated together at the same time as some individual excommunications were listed together (as when householders of a parish were excommunicated for withholding tithes or levies by the churchwardens), my quantifications are probably not precise to the tenth of a percent. In gross, however, they are accurate and indicative. That the core of the following study rests on databases containing more than 11,000 sanctions lessens the risk of grossly distorted and misleading quantification.

Dates are less fraught. Until 1564 in Northern France (in a royal edict adopted by 1567), the year began on Easter.[1] I have not corrected the Paschal years of the documents in my databases. All resulting charts therefore concern Paschal or Old-Style (OS) years and not calendar or New-Style (NS) years. I have not converted liturgical dates to modern

[1] Olivier Guyotjeannin and Benoît-Michel Tock, "'Mos presentis patrie'. Les styles de changement du millésime dans les actes français (XIe-XVIe siècle)," *Bibliothèque de l'École des Chartes* 157:1 (1999), 41–109, esp. 60–61.

dates, for the most part, for two reasons. An excommunication on the "Tuesday after Quasimodo" in a certain year remains as such, both because it is not particularly important to my argument to count the days of the year to determine on which calendar day the Tuesday after the first Sunday after Easter fell in a given year and because the switch from liturgical dating to calendar dating at Montivilliers between the 1433–1463 and the 1499–1530 registers signifies a notable change in mentality, not necessarily a change in religiosity but perhaps more the adoption of dating practices facilitating year-to-year accounting. For the order of the mass prefaces, readers can consult the table given as an appendix to Chapter 2 or any of the missals available on gallica.bnf.fr.

Currency is as knotty a problem as nomenclature. When amounts are given, they are generally given in moneys of account, either pounds of Tours (*livres tournois*, abbreviated as £t rather than lt for legibility) or pounds of Paris (*livres parisis*, £p). 4£p were equivalent to 5£t, though I have tried to give every figure also in *livres tournois* so as to facilitate comparison, even though this can make depreciations of the currency appear to be price or wage increases. Following the model of silver coinage instituted by Charlemagne, each pound was divided into 20 *solidi* or *sous* and each *solidus* or *sou* into 12 *denarii* or *deniers*. An *obole* was a half *denier* and a *pite* a quarter *denier*. Debts were paid out in kind, as the registers examined below often specified the amount of merchandise and gave a monetary value for it (perhaps to indicate quality) in other obligations, or in higher value "white" silver coins or lower value "black" billon coins with little silver content. At times, particularly in the middle of the fifteenth century, sums were sometimes given in gold coins rather than *livres tournois*, for example, as 17 *saluts* or 22 *écus*. Because of the fluctuating bimetallic exchange rates, and the sometimes great disparity between nominal and real value of gold coins, these sums may have at times designated 17 physical *saluts* or 22 physical *écus* but at other times may have concealed an exchange rate diverging too widely from the statutory value to be recorded in silver money of account in a legal document. This was because "in the case of large payments, it was the value of gold coins that determined the manner of payment and potentially prices, as we have seen at Dieppe at the end of the Hundred Years War."[2] The complexity of late medieval currency, and the calculations required to navigate even mundane payments, bear witness to historians' often-repeated reminder that humans of the past were no less clever than we, and may have indeed had to be cleverer.

[2] Philippe Lardin, "Monnaie de compte et monnaie réelle: des relations mal étudiées," *Revue européenne des sciences sociales* XLV:137 (2007), 45–68, at 66.

Abbreviations

ADEM	Archives départementales de l'Eure-et-Loir, Chartres
ADO	Archives départementales de l'Orne, Alençon
ADSM	Archives départementales de la Seine-Maritime, Rouen
ADY	Archives départementales de l'Yonne, Auxerre
AN	Archives nationales de France, Paris
BN	Bibliothèque nationale de France, Paris
C	*Causa* of the *Decretum*
Cod.	*Codex*
D	*Distinctio* of the *Decretum*
Dig.	*Digestum vetus et novum*
Febvre I, II	Lucien Febvre, "L'application du Concile de Trente et l'excommunication pour dettes en Franche-Comté," *Revue historique*, 103 (1910), 225–247, and 104 (1910), 1–39
Inst.	*Institutiones*
Isambert	Isambert, Jourdan, and Decrusy, eds. *Recueil général des anciennes lois françaises, depuis l'an 420 jusqu'à la révolution de 1789*. Paris: Belin-Leprieur/Verdière, 1825. 29 vols.
£t	*livres tournois … sous … deniers …*
£p	*livres parisis … sous … deniers …*
Mansi	Joannes Dominicus Mansi et al., eds. *Sacrorum conciliorum nova et amplissima collectio*. Paris: Hubert Welter, 1902. 57 vols.
NS	New Style, years begin on January 1
OS	Old Style, years begin on Easter
PL	*Patrologiae cursus completus … Series latina*. Ed. J-P Migne. Paris: Garnier, 1878–1904. 382 vols.
VI	*Liber sextus*
X	*Liber extra*

Introduction

Excommunication for debt offers us a privileged window into premodern practices of credit, rebalancing historians' focus on high credit and long-distance trade at the expense of humble, quotidian credit and local trade. It allows us to recover one of the means by which relatively minor but indispensable regional commerce functioned, what Arnold Esch has called trade in "tons of salt" as opposed to rarer, more exotic, and more studied trade in "grams of pepper."[1] Historians of medieval and early modern credit have observed that "the more that lenders dealt with a poor clientele, the more difficult it is to find traces of their lending activity, because the State and its various fiscal organs were uninterested in it and because the amounts at issue were rarely worth the trouble of disputing."[2] Or, "[f]rom the late fifteenth century, we have the first concrete evidence that customers maintained a current account with retailers, settled only from time to time. It is highly likely that this practice had started much earlier."[3] Or, concerning the traces of this "under-recorded credit"[4] before late medieval church courts, "[t]he evidence is there, but unquantifiable in any meaningful terms. Those unconsciously incurring excommunication cannot be numbered; nor can we know how many were officially proclaimed excommunicate and rapidly submitted."[5] This study will demonstrate precisely that there is evidence, and that this evidence can be meaningfully quantified. To do so, I draw on three

[1] Arnold Esch, "Überlieferungs-Chance und Überlieferungs-Zufall als methodisches Problem des Historikers," *Historische Zeitschrift* 240 (1985), 529–570, at 563.

[2] Laurence Fontaine, *L'Économie morale: Pauvreté, crédit et confiance dans l'Europe pré-industrielle* (Paris: Gallimard, 2008), 112. The work is now available as *The Moral Economy: Poverty, Credit, and Trust in Early Modern Europe* (Cambridge: Cambridge University Press, 2014).

[3] Bas Van Bavel, *Manors and Markets: Economy and Society in the Low Countries, 500–1600* (Oxford: Oxford University Press, 2010), 188–189.

[4] Fontaine, 52: "la multitude de ces petits prêts ne passe pas le plus souvent chez le notaire mais se retrouve d'abord dans les livres de compte ou des petits billets privés. Le sous-enregistrement du crédit paysan est noté dans toutes les études."

[5] R. N. Swanson, *Church and Society in Late Medieval England* (Oxford: Blackwell, 1989), 180.

case studies comprising more than 11,000 excommunications from late medieval Northwestern France. My choice of locales reflects my previous research, the focus of existing studies of excommunication, and the availability and quality of surviving records. As I shall show, because the majority of these records were issued explicitly for debt and because an unknowable number of the rest were issued for failure to respond to a summons in cases of debt, quantitative and qualitative study of the records of excommunication illuminates late medieval practices of credit. Yet, because obligations before church courts do not appear to have been systematically recorded (and, if they were, do not survive for the area of study) and because other forms of obligation could be brought before church courts, I cannot count all instances of credit; only those instances can be counted when creditors chose to bring defaulting debtors before an ecclesiastical tribunal. These breaks in the bonds of credit nevertheless tell us something about the frequency, amounts, and nature of premodern informal or privately recorded credit. It is precisely the quantitative aspect of this project that is novel, for it suggests the economic functionality of excommunication for debt, an aspect of the phenomenon unexplored in Véronique Beaulande's otherwise excellent study of excommunication in the province of Rheims.[6] The emphasis of my study will therefore be as much on the economic function of church courts as on their religious significance.

Credit in the premodern period has been the subject of notable studies in the past fifteen years, reflecting the repeated crises of the contemporary economy since the tech bubble of the late 1990s. Some of the most thought-provoking of these are the issue of the *Annales* on early modern credit (1994), Craig Muldrew's *The Economy of Obligation: The Culture of Credit and Social Relations in Early Modern England* (1998), Laurence Fontaine's *L'Économie morale. Pauvreté, crédit et confiance dans l'Europe préindustrielle* (2008; English, 2014), Chris Briggs' *Credit and Village Society in Fourteenth-Century England* (2009), Paolo Prodi's *Settimo non rubare. Furto e mercato nella storia dell'Occidente* (2009), Martha Howell's *Commerce before Capitalism in Europe, 1300–1600* (2010), and David Graeber's *Debt: The First 5,000 Years* (2011). In a sense, all these authors are indebted to Edward P. Thompson's "The Moral Economy of the English Crowd in the Eighteenth Century" (1971), however much they might nuance his contribution, and in dialogue with Karl Polanyi's *The Great Transformation: The Political and Economic Origins of*

[6] Véronique Beaulande, *Le malheur d'être exclu? Excommunication, réconciliation et société à la fin du Moyen Âge* (Paris: Publications de la Sorbonne, 2006).

Our Time (1944). What they share (with the exception of Prodi[7]) is a desire less to seek the origins of contemporary capitalism or capitalisms, as did Polanyi, than to recover the "embedded" logics of economic life in premodern Europe, an economic life embedded, then as now, in social, cultural, religious, and politicolegal life.[8] Each of those had a teleology other than profit through perpetual economic growth. While many historians and economists have studied how the Church's prohibition of usury influenced economic activity, few of these speak of, or are perhaps even aware of, the transitional role of ecclesiastical courts in the functioning of credit from *c.* 1300 to *c.* 1600.[9] Even Graeber's book, at once on a far grander chronological scale and more present-focused, might have benefitted from mentioning the role of the Church's justice in premodern European credit, as it affirms his definition of the Middle Ages. Although more narrowly legal and institutional accounts have long noted this particular function of ecclesiastical tribunals,[10] its significance has neither been appreciated by a wider audience nor investigated for lack of sources and imagination. This function of church courts explains how Thompson's moral economy came to be both a moral quantity and an economy. In other words, those of Deirdre McCloskey's persuasive case for the importance of cultural, intellectual factors in the West's economic take-off, this study examines the mentality that the West shook off around 1800.[11]

[7] *Settimo non rubare* completes a trilogy exploring the origin of the three *fora* of modern Western public life: the political forum in *Il sacramento del potere. Il giuramento politio nella storia costituzionale dell'Occidente* (1992), the legal forum in *Una storia della giustizia: Dal pluralismo dei fori al moderno dualismo tra coscienza e diritto* (2000), and last the economic forum or "market." It is a shame that none of these has been translated into English.

[8] Polanyi argued that the modern economy is by definition "disembedded." On this, see inter alia Mark Granovetter, "Economic Action and Social Structure: The Problem of Embeddedness," *American Journal of Sociology* 91:3 (1985), 418–510.

[9] Chris Briggs is an exception: "The Availability of Credit in the English Countryside, 1400–1480," *Agricultural History Review* 56:1 (2008), 1–24, esp. 19–23.

[10] Inter alia, Anne Lefebvre-Teillard, *Les officialités à la veille du concile de Trente* (Paris: R. Pichon et R. Durand-Auzias, 1973), 222–250, esp. 235–237; Pierre-Clément Timbal, *Les obligations contractuelles dans le droit français des XIIIe et XIVe siècles d'après la jurisprudence du Parlement* (Paris: Éditions du CNRS, vol. 1: 1973, vol. 2: 1977), II:119–124; Beaulande, *Le malheur*; Caroline Bourlet and Julie Claustre, "Le marché de l'acte à Paris à la fin du Moyen Âge: juridictions gracieuses, notaires et clientèles," in Mathieu Arnoux and Olivier Guyotjeannin (eds.), *Tabellions et tabellionages de la France médiévale et moderne* (Paris: École des Chartes, 2011), 51–84; R. H. Helmholz, "Assumpsit and Fidei laesio," in *Canon Law and the Law of England* (London: Hambledon Press, 1987), 263–289; Swanson, *Church and Society*, 140–190, esp. 166–168; H. C. Lea, "Excommunication," in *Studies in Church History* (Philadelphia: Henry C. Lea's Son and Company, 1883), 235–521, esp. 416–478.

[11] Deirdre McCloskey, *Bourgeois Dignity: Why Economics Can't Explain the Modern World* (Chicago: University of Chicago Press, 2010).

Late medieval church courts were primarily involved in relations of credit through the practice of excommunication for debt.[12] Creditors utilized canonical procedure to exert pressure upon debtors, citing them to appear in court or warning them to pay up on pain of exclusion from the sacraments of the Church. If cited debtors failed to show up or to pay up, they would be automatically excommunicated without trial for disobeying the Church's commands. In this way, ecclesiastical tribunals, often depicted as a preeminent site of the abuses of the late medieval Church, provided useful economic services. From the fourteenth century at the latest, excommunication for debt served as an inexpensive mechanism for the enforcement or renegotiation of day-to-day, minor or verbal credit. Yet by 1500 or so, ecclesiastical judges and indulgence sellers were increasingly criticized for making a "*marchandise*" or improper business of the sacraments, for profiting from debtors' sincere desire to receive the sacraments at the times prescribed by ecclesiastical legislation and common practice. Over the period covered by this study, European Christians came more and more to see excommunication for debt as an unholy mixing of the economic and the religious. Of course, such an appraisal requires a distinction of categories that was only incipient at the end of the Middle Ages but became clearer as demand for this remedy fell over the sixteenth century. Until this shift, explored in Chapter 4, the jurists who theorized the Church's law, the judges who administered the Church's justice, and the Christians who sought justice from ecclesiastical tribunals concurred that excommunication for debt served a religious end by sanctioning breaches of faith within the community of believers. When purchasers or borrowers failed to make good on loans or purchases, they failed to act charitably toward fellow members of Christ at the same time as they broke an obligation made as much before God as with the other party. At the core of the notion that simple, verbal promises are binding (*pacta sunt servanda, solus consensus obligat*) is the sacredness of the voluntary obligation of one Christian to another. Excommunication for debt manifested the efforts of church courts to encourage trustworthiness, good faith, and charity, concerns evident also in theologians' and canonists' resistance to any but a voluntarist conception of the marriage bond or to dispensations from religious and other solemn vows.

[12] Excommunication is here to be understood as including other, similar sanctions that separated the sanctioned individual from the sacramental community: minor excommunication or personal interdict (in England recorded as suspension from entering churches), suspension from the capacity to perform the sacraments (for priests), major excommunication barring a believer from the sacraments, and the so-called aggravation (or anathema) and reaggravation of an excommunication.

While not the only form of recourse available to late medieval lenders, the practice conveys the manner in which the late medieval economy was embedded in social and religious life. Contemporaries were aware that excommunication for debt served what to us are both economic and religious purposes, and their judgment of the appropriateness of these purposes shifted over time. The rise and fall of excommunication for debt signals the transformation of religious sensibilities and of practices of credit between 1300 and 1600. Examining the remodeling of ecclesiastical justice in the sixteenth century restores the importance of the Reformation for economic history. However, rather than resuscitating or transposing Max Weber's Protestant Ethic, I would argue that the sixteenth-century Reformations of Christianity still stand at the distant origin of modern capitalisms for their role in secularizing and ethicizing the trust and the moralized conception of debt that facilitate modern market transactions. The path to today's market led through the community of believers via the early modern confessional states. By subjugating autonomous ecclesiastical tribunals and redefining what it meant to be a Christian,[13] the Protestant and Catholic Reformations facilitated the divergence of proto-national or regional political cultures, forms of taxation, and forms of economic life that furnished the long-term confessional foundations of contemporary divergent French, Catalonian, German, Lombard, English, and American capitalisms. Even today, what one might call the Catholic ethic by which even economically irrational debts are to be honored subsists in the reluctance of homeowners to walk away from underwater mortgages, albeit without the accompanying virtue of forgiveness or the restitution of *male ablata* on the part of purchasers of mortgage debt.

The history of credit

Late medieval Europeans swam in a sea of credit. This was necessary, given the lack of formalized credit available to the very poorest and given the chronically scarce and depreciating minor coinage necessary for ordinary transactions.[14] This was also a matter of choice, or at least of a

[13] My Reformation is John Bossy's. It is not limited to the Protestant Reformation but encompasses the transformation of religious practice among all varieties of Western Christianity between 1400 and 1700: John Bossy, *Christianity in the West, 1400–1700* (Oxford: Oxford University Press, 1985).

[14] As Thomas J. Sargent and François R. Velde note in *The Big Problem of Small Change* (Princeton: Princeton University Press, 2002), 124–125, there was less a late medieval "bullion famine" than a famine of the small *billon* coins needed for daily transactions; Martha Howell, *Commerce Before Capitalism in Europe, 1300–1600* (Cambridge University Press, 2010); Fontaine, *L'Économie*; Craig Muldrew, *The Economy of Obligation: The Culture of Credit and Social Relations in Early Modern England* (New York: St Martin's

cultural justification of necessity, as in the *Tiers Livre* of François Rabelais first published in 1546: "'But when,' asked Pantagruel, 'will you be free of debt?' ... Panurge responded: 'God help me from ever being free of debt. I'd never again find anyone to lend me a penny.'" Panurge further justified this choice on a fashionably humanistic basis: "'... all my life, I've imagined debt to be like a bond between Heaven and earth, the sole sustenance of humanity – without which, I say, all humans would die –, perhaps to be the universe's great soul, which the philosophers claim gives life to all things.'" For Rabelais's fictional giant, credit kept the world in motion. It encouraged affection and charity among men: otherwise, Panurge speculated, who but one's creditors would wake each morning to pray to God for one's well-being and success?[15] Credit reconciled self-interest and the greater good, in Panurge's perhaps duplicitously invoked commonplaces. In the sixteenth century, indebtedness played the role assigned in the eighteenth century to the desires for consumption and for profit by Bernard Mandeville and Adam Smith. It did so with the important difference that late medieval society was imagined as the Body of Christ composed of sinful believers striving for salvation, rather than as a market filled with self-interested, consuming citizens. Indebtedness, Fontaine writes of early modern villages, "established one's membership in the community"; conversely, demanding repayment amounted to exclusion from the community.[16] Until the sixteenth century, excommunication for debt made this relationship even more obvious, as failure to repay debts could lead to exclusion not just from the community of the living gathered at the parish mass but from the community of the dead shriven before death, buried in the churchyard, and prayed for by the living.

The accounts of premodern credit mentioned above generally focus on the secular remedies that came to predominate in the sixteenth century and are recognizably cognate to modern forms of constraint. This reflects not a true historical absence, but a problem of sources and a conceptual blindness. For instance, ecclesiastical justice is notably present neither in historical works concerning Ghent nor in other towns of the Low Countries. Even though the act books of the officiality of Tournai burned in 1940, Jacques Toussaert, Monique Vleeschouwers-Van Melkebeek, and

Press, 1998); M. Berthe (ed.), *Endettement Paysan et Crédit Rural dans l'Europe médiévale et moderne: Actes des XVIIes Journées d'Histoire de l'Abbaye de Flaran* (Toulouse: Presses universitaires du Mirail, 1998), esp. François Menand and Jean-Louis Gaulin, "Crédit rural et endettement paysan dans l'Italie communale," 35–68, at 35: "tout le monde vit à crédit."

15 François Rabelais, *Gargantua et Pantagruel*, bk. III, Ch. 3.

16 Fontaine, *L'Économie*, 67, 69.

Véronique Beaulande have demonstrated excommunications for debt in maritime Flanders and in the regions of Cambrai, Tournai, Beauvais, and Corbie.[17] Which is to say, in the ecclesiastical province of Rheims, which covered much of the Southern Netherlands, the practice is attested in the very centuries covered by Howell's *Commerce before Capitalism*. As much as the lack of sources, a failure of imagination must play a role in this omission. For England, Muldrew's *Economy of Obligation* begins in 1530–1550, after the decline of ecclesiastical jurisdiction over credit. The Henrician Reformation certainly shook ecclesiastical justice, but it had been under assault even prior to the Hunne affair of 1515.[18] Indeed, the Hunne case was important precisely because it crystallized an ongoing movement to redefine the competence of English courts christian. As Richard Helmholz has pointed out, since the 1490s, royal courts had been reforming ecclesiastical justice by attracting and by driving debt cases from church courts into royal courts.[19] Chris Briggs has proposed a shift in debt litigation from manorial courts to church courts in mid-fifteenth-century England.[20] The following study will confirm the plausibility of such a movement, although it is difficult to identify any comparable shift on the continent. There, our sources for seigneurial courts and church courts are either scanty or as yet scantily studied. They tend, as in my case studies, to concentrate on towns. For France, Véronique Beaulande's *Le malheur d'être exclu* (*The Misfortune of Exclusion*) senses some of the patterns demonstrated by my study but ventures fewer quantifications and neglects entirely the potential economic importance of procedural excommunications. My intent, particularly in Chapter 3, is to use individual examples to suggest the kinds of economic relationships buried in year-by-year figures of hundreds of excommunications. Beaulande's study nevertheless confirms the frequency of excommunications for debt in late medieval Northern France. Finally, Fontaine's *L'Économie morale* focuses on the

[17] Jacques Toussaert, *Le sentiment religieux en Flandre à la fin du Moyen Âge* (Paris: Plon, 1963); Monique Vleeschouwers-Van Melkebeek, *Compotus sigilliferi curie Tornacensis (1429–1481)* (Brussels: Commission royale d'histoire, 1995), 3 vols; Beaulande, *Le malheur*.

[18] Assault, it seems to me, remains the appropriate word and does not wholly contradict Shannon McSheffrey's observation of the collaboration of ecclesiastical and secular authorities in London during these years (unpublished Discussion at the 2014 Annual Meeting of the American Historical Association). The Hunne case involved the harassment of a merchant who refused to pay a mortuary fee and who was found dead under suspicious circumstances in the Bishop of London's prison: Richard Wunderli, "Pre-Reformation London Summoners and the Murder of Richard Hunne," *Journal of Ecclesiastical History* 33:2 (1982), 209–224.

[19] R. H. Helmholz, "Assumpsit and Fidei laesio," and "Debt Claims and Probate Jurisdiction in Historical Perspective," *American Journal of Legal History* 23:1 (1979), 68–82.

[20] Briggs, "Availability."

seventeenth and eighteenth centuries, when the French state had securely reduced church courts into meek administrators of clerical discipline and registrars of baptisms, marriages, and burials governed by royal laws and surveilled by royal courts.

Historians of credit might be pardoned ignorance of canon law for the small place it holds in existing discussions of premodern credit.[21] Church courts participated in the "judicialization of credit relations," particularly humble ones, evident from the fourteenth century; only in the sixteenth century did the king become "the sole guarantor of private agreements."[22] Early modern moral economies thus emerged from a society in which credit was not regulated only by the State and its courts. Of the two levels of justice identified by Michael Breen in Old Regime France, church courts belonged with seigneurial and municipal tribunals to the lower, popular level, in opposition to the elite justice of the parlements and the presidial or bailiwick courts.[23] Outstanding studies of marital, sexual, and doctrinal cases before church courts can make us forget just how broad a competence late medieval church courts had. Yet Europe did not simply move from a situation in which economic life was embedded in and inseparable from social or religious life to one in which the economy was autonomous. Economic life is never autonomous or disembedded, and the place and content of the economic, the social, and the religious change over time. My study therefore focuses on the period between 1300 and 1600, which saw the rise and fall of excommunication for debt and laid the religious foundations for Thompson's early modern moral economies.

Discussing the religious aspects of credit means engaging with presuppositions about the terms "society" and "Church." When I argue that "medieval society was imagined as being Christ's body," as I shall in the following paragraph, this is equivalent to writing that "the Church was imagined as Christ's body." For the period of which I speak, the Church was human society, with few exceptions.[24] Non-Christians, above all

[21] It is making an entrance into the history of contract law through the history of moral theology: Thomas Duve, "Kanonisches Recht und die Ausbildung allgemeiner Vertragslehren in der Spanischen Spätscholastik," in O. Condorelli, F. Roumy, and M. Schmoeckel (eds.), *Der Einfluss der Kanonistik auf die europäische Rechtskultur, Bd. 1: Zivil- und Zivilprozessrecht* (Cologne/Weimar/Vienna: Böhlau Verlag, 2009), 389–408; Wim Decock, *Theologians and Contract Law: The Moral Transformation of the Ius Commune (ca. 1500–1650)* (Leiden: Martinus Nijhoff, 2013).

[22] The quoted passages are from Julie Claustre, *Dans les geôles du roi. L'emprisonnement pour dette à Paris à la fin du Moyen Âge* (Paris: Publications de la Sorbonne, 2007), 24.

[23] Michael Breen, "Law, Society, and the State in Early Modern France," *Journal of Modern History* 83:2 (2011), 346–386.

[24] Christian authority was imagined to extend in a sense even outside Christendom: James Muldoon, *Popes, Lawyers, and Infidels: The Church and the Non-Christian World, 1250–1550* (Philadelphia: University of Pennsylvania Press, 1979).

Jews, whether already expelled in the thirteenth and fourteenth centuries, as in England (1290) or France (1394), or in the process of exclusion or segregation, as in Spain or Italy, do provide a sort of exception, though one might think of them as enclaves within the Body of Christ, not technically part of it though carried with it and complying with many of its norms. The existence of non-Christians in medieval Europe is less of a problem, however, than our tendency to clericalize the concept of a Church and thereby to interpret the word as signifying only the clergy or the ecclesiastical administration. The word had this sense in the Middle Ages too, particularly when clerics sought to exempt themselves from lay justice or taxation, or when layfolk enunciated anticlerical complaints.[25] The sense of the Church as an institution predominated only after the Council of Trent, as the papalization of the Counter-Reformation Church made it seem to be less the body of Christians than the clerical hierarchy directed by the Bishop of Rome. In the late Middle Ages, the concept of the Church still comprehended all baptized Christians. So in the fifteenth century, the phrase "Gallican church" (*ecclesia gallicana*) referred not just to the bishops of France but to the Christians of the kingdom of France as a component of the universal Church. Only in the mid-sixteenth century did the crystallization of clerical taxation through periodic Assemblies of the Clergy with a permanent administration effectively clericalize the Gallican church. I have elsewhere discussed how the broad conception of the Gallican church served to sacralize the kingdom of France and to preserve a relatively autonomous French church within the Catholic Church.[26] For present purposes, I ask my readers to resist their urges to read "clerical institution" when I write "Church." The word of course is polysemic, and I shall try to be clear about whether I intend "Church" to signify the clerical institution, the clergy as a body, or Christian society as a whole.

This polysemy reflects how medieval society was imagined as being Christ's body on the basis of passages at 1 Cor. 11:3: "But I would have you know that the head of every man is Christ"; Eph. 1:22–23: "And [the Lord] hath put all things under his feet, and gave him to be the head over all things to the church (*supra omnem ecclesiam*), Which is his body, the fulness of him that filleth all in all"; Eph. 5:23: "For the husband is the head of the wife, even as Christ is the head of the church: and he is the saviour of the body"; and Col. 1:18: "And he is the head of the body, the church: who is the beginning, the firstborn from the dead; that in

[25] On clerical immunity, see Robert Génestal, *Le Privilegium fori en France du Décret de Gratien à la fin du XIVe siècle* (Paris: Editions Ernest Leroux, 1921 and 1924).

[26] Tyler Lange, *The First French Reformation: Church Reform and the Origins of the Old Regime* (New York: Cambridge University Press, 2014).

all things he might have the preeminence (*primatum*)."[27] The sense that the Church was Christ's body through a sort of marital union intensified and was reified over the course of the Middle Ages as popes became monarchs and as the Eucharist came to be understood as Christ's body.[28] In the eleventh century, the Eucharist, formerly identified as Christ's "mystical body," came to be described as his "real body." The Church was henceforth seen as Christ's "mystical body" and the metaphor of the marriage of Christ to his Church applied at multiple levels: at the level of the universal Church, where the pope acted Christ's part, at the level of a local church, where the bishop acted Christ's part, and even at the level of a priest "married" to a benefice with care of souls. Christ's mystical body was also a political body, as from the eleventh century, popes acted and portrayed themselves as monarchs, increasingly on the model of Roman emperors and with the aid of elements of Roman law.[29] The vicars of Christ – a term signifying that they acted for Christ on earth – stood in for the Church's spouse, governing Christ's wife and administering her dowry, so to speak. Yet, even as lawyer-popes and lawyer-bishops came to rule an increasingly juridicized Church constructed in terms of an appellate hierarchy and in which doctrinal correctness came by the late fifteenth century to be assimilated to submission to the pope's judgment, the Body of Christ was nevertheless still supposed to be animated by charity, the divine love that surpassed earthly love and bound Christ's members to serve each other selflessly.[30]

John Bossy has emphasized the importance of charity and concord in "communal Christianity."[31] By consuming Christ's "real body" in the

[27] On the multiple meanings of the term in this period, see Miri Rubin, *Corpus Christi: The Eucharist in Late Medieval Culture* (Cambridge: Cambridge University Press, 1991).

[28] Robert Descimon, "Les fonctions de la métaphore du mariage politique du roi et de la république en France, XVe-XVIIIe siècles," *Annales ESC* 47:6 (1993), 1127–1147; Henri de Lubac, *Corpus mysticum. L'Eucharistie et l'Église au Moyen Âge. Étude historique* (Paris: Aubrie, 1944).

[29] Gabriel Le Bras, "Les origines canoniques du droit administratif," in *L'évolution du droit public: Études en l'honneur d'Achille Mestre* (Paris: Sirey, 1956), 395–412; Pierre Legendre, "Du droit privé au droit public: Nouvelles observations sur le mandat chez les canonistes classiques," *Mémoires de la Société pour l'Histoire du Droit et des Institutions des anciens pays bourguignons, comtois et romands* 30e Fascicule (1970–1971), 7–35.

[30] Paolo Prodi, *Una storia della giustizia: Dal pluralismo dei fori al moderno dualismo tra coscienza e diritto* (Bologna: Il Mulino, 2000); Laurent Mayali, "'Duo erunt in carne una' and the Medieval Canonists," in Vincenzo Colli and Emanuele Conte (eds.), *Iuris Historia: Liber Amicorum Gero Dolezalek* (Berkeley, California: Robbins Collection, 2008), 161–175; Frédéric Gabriel, "Qualifications de la communauté et autorité de la Tradition: l'histoire des dogmes comme construction ecclésiale, de Torquemada à Lethmaet (XVe-XVIe siècle)," *Bulletin du centre d'études médiévales d'Auxerre*, Hors-série n°7 (2013): http://cem.revues.org/12901.

[31] Bossy, *Christianity in the West*, and "The Mass as a Social Institution," *Past & Present* 100 (1983), 29–61.

Eucharist, Christians affirmed that they belonged to his "mystical body," the Church. Bossy highlights how the liturgy was directed at establishing concord and social cohesion by allaying conflict through the circulation of the pax, the board that each congregant kissed in lieu of the direct kiss of peace at the end of the Middle Ages, through the distribution of blessed bread and other sacramentals including blessed water, salt, or wax, and through pastoral injunctions to eradicate hatred from the community during Lent prior to the annual confession and communion required since 1215 and conventionally made toward Easter. The fifteenth-century English canonist William Lyndwood (*c.*1374–1446), captures the rhetoric of conciliation in his commentary on English provincial statutes. With respect to a canon commanding "rectors, vicars, and the curates of other churches who are at peace (insofar as possible) with their flocks, to admonish their parishioners that they be one body in Christ unified in faith and in peace; assiduously to pacify enmities if these have arisen in their parishes; to encourage them to join in friendship; and to recall those in conflict to concord," Lyndwood noted that "this truly belongs to the duty of a prelate to urge those in conflict, whether clerics or layfolk, more toward peace than toward litigation."[32] Believers could manifest the charity that was supposed to animate Christ's body through the forgiveness of injuries, the forgiveness of debts, the restitution of unjust gains, or even the repayment of debts. It is evident that late medieval Christians understood this and sought to enforce concord through social pressure. Both Beaulande's and my data reveal a burst of excommunications and absolutions toward the end of Lent, even on Holy Saturday. This *flambée* reflects attempts by creditors to force debtors to honor their promises by blocking them from taking their "rights," that is, from making their "Easter duty" of communion. Toward the end of Lent, excommunicated debtors repaid their creditors, negotiated payment plans, or ceded their property to their creditors so as to secure absolution. Creditors, perhaps goaded by their confessors, forgave debts so as to secure absolution.[33] Those who failed to make peace could be called out in public for this failure. Eamon Duffy cites a telling example from late medieval London of the heavy imperative toward reconciliation:

> In 1529 Joanna Carpenter, of the parish of St Mary Queenhithe, sought to exploit that weight by seizing the arm of her neighbour Margaret Chamber, with whom she was at odds, as Mistress Chamber knelt waiting her turn to receive

[32] *Provinciale (seu Constitutiones Angliae)* (Oxford: H.Hall, 1679), 71–72, 72 note i. J. W. Bennett, "The Medieval Loveday," *Speculum* 23 (1958), 351–370, cites Lyndwood's gloss at 370.

[33] X.5.19.10: "Mutuans ea mente, ut ultra sortem aliquid recipiat, tenetur in foro anime ad illud restituendum."

Easter communion. 'I pray you let me speke a worde with you,' she said, 'for you have need to axe me forgyveness, before you rescyve your rights.'[34]

Mistress Carpenter sought to enforce charity, clearly feeling that Mistress Chamber – and perhaps she too – remained out of communion. Without forgiveness, Christ's body was not whole. This imperative was also pronounced in the courts of the day, where in fact Mistresses Carpenter and Chamber were summoned. Both ecclesiastical and secular courts encouraged out-of-court settlements.[35] Church courts in particular aimed to produce concord among Christians. One argument of this book is that excommunication for debt, a practice that strikes us as anything but charitable, could in fact be seen to fulfill the pastoral and Christian imperative to encourage charity and concord within Christ's body. Accordingly, the posthumous Supplement to Aquinas's *Summa Theologiae* responds to the question of "whether anyone should be excommunicated for inflicting temporal harm?" that, although the punishment should not exceed the fault, "the measure of fault (*culpae quantitas*) is not measured by the extent of the damage (*ex nocumento*) someone does, but by the will with which someone does it, acting against charity. Wherefore, though the punishment of excommunication may exceed the harm done, it does not exceed the measure of fault."[36] Excommunication punished the breach of charity, not the physical harm.

Excommunication for debt could be deemed a charitable, medicinal encouragement of sinners to return to the fold because non-usurious lending was viewed as an act of charity. Here we encounter the much emphasized usury prohibition of the medieval Church. One could find Biblical justification for this, whether in the harsher terms of the Old Testament or in the more generous terms of the New, e.g., Mt. 10:8: "freely ye have received, freely give (*gratis accepistis, gratis date*)" or Lk. 6:35: "lend, hoping for nothing again (*mutuum date, nihil inde sperantes*)," or in an Aristotelian justification predicated on the sterility of money:

Usury (*obolostatikê*) is most reasonably hated, because its gain comes from money itself and not from that for the sake of which money was invented. For money was brought into existence for the purpose of exchange, but interest (*tókos*)

[34] Duffy, *Stripping*, 95.

[35] e.g., Karl S. Bader, "Arbiter arbitrator seu amicabilis compositor. Zur Verbreitung einer kanonistischen Formel in Gebieten nördlich der Alpen," *Zeitschrift der Savigny-Stiftung für Rechtsgeschichte 90, Kanonistische Abteilung* 46 (1960), 239–276, or the immense series of settlements or *accords* registered by the Parlement de Paris from 1300 to 1640: AN X/1c.

[36] *Supplementum ad Summa theologiae*, q. xxi art. iii, in *Thomae Aquinatis Opera Omnia* (Rome: Typographia polyglotta, 1906), XII:43.

increases the amount of the money itself (and this is the actual origin of the Greek word: offspring resembles parent, and interest is money born of money); consequently this form of the business of getting wealth is of all forms the most contrary to nature.[37]

Usury was prohibited, but there was some uncertainty over whether this meant lending at interest or lending at excessive interest.[38] The trend over the Middle Ages was to move from the former to the latter. The eye of the needle was progressively opened to moneylenders and to those who offered forms of interest-bearing loans.[39]

Annuities secured on real property, whether in the form of ground-rents to lords (*census*), mortgages, or *rentes* purchased for cash but tied to a piece of property were acceptable forms of lending as they involved a legitimate exchange. In some regions, religious or secular authorities set acceptable rates of interest for different types of loans. In late medieval Florence, the bishop's synodal statutes accepted rates of five or six percent in certain cases, though in practice the bishop tolerated higher rates.[40] Even the Avignon papacy itself had, during the Great Western Schism, to borrow at interest rates of between 28 and 36 percent per year.[41] With the papal bureaucracy openly admitting that it paid "for profit and interest, for interest, for damages and interest" (*pro lucro et interesse, pro interesse, pro dampno et interesse*) or that it had obliged itself through an "interest-bearing loan" (*mutuum cum usuris* or *sub usura*), the papacy's late and restricted countenancing of certain types of interest-bearing loan

[37] Aristotle, *Politics*, 1258b, translation and original from the *Thesaurus Linguae Graecae*: www.tlg.uci.edu.

[38] John T. Noonan, *Banking and the Early Scholastic Analysis of Usury* (Washington, DC: Catholic University of America Press, 1951); Odd Langholm, *Economics in the Medieval Schools: Wealth, Exchange, Value, Money, and Usury according to the Paris Theological Tradition, 1200–1350* (Leiden: Brill, 1992); Eric Kerridge, *Usury, Interest, and the Reformation* (Aldershot: Ashgate, 2002); Diana Wood, *Medieval Economic Thought* (Cambridge: Cambridge University Press, 2002). John Munro distinguishes more correctly and more subtly between lending at interest, in which the capital is not retained, and participation in an enterprise (*commenda*, *compagnia* or partnership contract, or joint-stock corporation) with retention of capital: "Usury, Calvinism, and Credit in Protestant England: From the Sixteenth Century to the Industrial Revolution," in *Religione e istituzioni religiose nell'economia europea. 1000–1800. Atti della "Quarantatreesima Settimana di Studi" 8–12 maggio 2011* (Florence: Firenze University Press, 2012), 155–184, at 159. Munro concedes a page after introducing the distinction, however, that "the true difference between these two forms of investment returns was the retained ownership of capital proved to be incomprehensible for most people" (160–161).

[39] Jacques Le Goff, *Your Money or Your Life: Economy and Religion in the Middle Ages*, Patricia Ranum (trans.), (New York: Zone Books, 1988).

[40] Richard Trexler, *Synodal Law in Florence and Fiesole, 1306–1518* (Vatican City: Bibliotheca Apostolica Vaticana, 1971), 106–112.

[41] Jean Favier, *Les finances pontificales à l'époque du Grand Schisme d'Occident, 1378–1409* (Paris: Éditions E. de Boccard, 1966), 559, more generally, 556–561.

is something of a surprise.[42] In response to the queries of German bishops, in 1425, 1452, and 1455 popes tardily authorized property-based annuities (*Zinssen, rentes*[43]), provided that they were redeemable when the borrower chose and that the interest was no greater than the tenth penny (10 percent). Such annuities were legally purchases of future income rather than loans at interest. In France, where a royal ordinance had set the maximum interest at 20 percent in 1312, the Parlement of Paris judged in accordance the new principles from 1426.[44] By the early sixteenth century, the common rate had fallen at Paris from the tenth to the twelfth penny (8.33 percent), and the Parlement tended to reduce rates from the tenth to the twelfth penny in its decisions. It could reduce them still further to the fifteenth penny (6.67 percent) if it judged the original rate to have been too high for too long. During the Wars of Religion, the king twice tried to privilege royal as opposed to private debt, commanding in 1567 and 1572 that, while he could access credit at the twelfth penny, his subjects could do so only at the fifteenth penny.[45] Rather than driving borrowers to purchase annuities from the king, the edicts instead depressed private lending at Paris and were abrogated in 1574, when the legal maximum returned to the twelfth penny.[46] In 1601, however, Henry IV reduced the legal maximum to the sixteenth penny (6.25 percent). In 1634, Louis XIII reduced it again to the eighteenth penny (5.56 percent).[47] That this maximum was not general across France, as the legal maximum remained the tenth penny in Normandy, for instance, indicates how the real debates at the end of the Middle Ages concerned in first place whether lending had to be disguised as a property transaction and in second place what the maximum moral interest rate was. The need to lend and to borrow was unquestioned. Debate concerned moral constraints on lending and borrowing.

The scholastic economists, to use an anachronistic term for what were mainly moral theologians and canonists, justified lending at interest for four principal reasons, the so-called extrinsic titles: forbearance (*poena conventionalis*), emergent loss (*damnum emergens*), opportunity cost or cessant gain (*lucrum cessans*), and bottomry and partnership (*periculum sortis*). Only the first two were accepted for cash loans (*mutua*) and the

[42] Favier, *Les finances*, 558.
[43] For which the Latin term was also *census*, highlighting the terminological confusion between *census*-as-ground rents and *census*-as-property-based-annuities. See Bernard Schnapper, *Les rentes au XVIe siècle: Histoire d'un instrument de crédit* (Paris: SEVPEN, 1957), 41–46.
[44] Schnapper, *Les rentes*, 65–78.
[45] Schnapper, *Les rentes*, 169.
[46] Schnapper, *Les rentes*, 170.
[47] Schnapper, *Les rentes*, 279.

last, with capital retained by the investor, did not fall under the usury prohibition.[48] Forbearance concerned payment of a penalty if payment was delayed beyond a term assigned at the outset. This, what was called interest by *titulus morae*, provided a popular cover for usury. It may explain the case before the manor court of West Wratting in 1322, when a creditor claimed damages of 6s 8d on a debt of 20s, that is, damages/interest of 33 percent. However, the debtor's pledge alleged that only 10s of the debt remained, making the damages/interest amount to 67 percent of the smaller sum. The court demanded that the pledge pay 10s and damages of 2s or 20 percent on the smaller sum.[49] Something similar may be concealed in rising amounts of debt in succeeding sanctions at Montivilliers discussed in Chapter 3. Should the penalty for delinquency not have been specified at the outset, the lender could claim interest either through emergent loss, which referred to potential losses from unanticipated emergencies after the loan had been made. Canonists and theologians were less sure about opportunity cost, as it implied that money was not sterile.[50] Bottomry and partnership reflected the risks of business, particularly shipping, in that the lender or investor stood to lose his entire investment. Much academic energy was expended on debating the boundaries between legitimate interest and illegitimate usury.

This debate continued through the Protestant Reformation. Though the theologians Conrad Summenhart (†1502) and John Major (1467–1550) had opened the door to further manners of taking legitimate interest, the Fifth Lateran Council (1515) reiterated the old prohibitions. While the reformers were no kinder to usury than the schoolmen, their justification of the prohibition and their definition of usury changed. Martin Luther certainly decried those who devoured poor folk through usurious loans ("*Zinsjunckern*") but in 1519/20 conceded the taking of interest in cases of need, when borrowers could not burden their property, through purchase contracts:

> If this can be done without violating canon law, which provides for the payment of four, five, or six gulden on the hundred, it may tolerated. But they should always have the fear of God, and be afraid of taking too much rather than too

48 Kerridge prefers archaic terms such as fenory (*foenus*), ocker (*usury*), and cessant gain. See too Munro, "Calvin," 161–162.

49 Chris Briggs, *Credit and Village Society in Fourteenth-Century England* (Oxford: The British Academy, 2009), 65.

50 Hostiensis argued for this in the thirteenth century: Munro, "Usury," 162 n.22; Leonardus Lessius argued for it in the sixteenth and Hugo Grotius in the seventeenth: Decock, *Theologians*, 600 n.1965, and "Leonardus Lessius on Buying and Selling (1605), Translation and Introduction," *Journal of Markets and Morality* 10 (2007), 466–482; also T. Van Houdt, "Money, Time and Labour. Leonardus Lessius and the Ethics of Money-Lending and Interest-Taking," *Ethical Perspectives* 2 (1995), 11–27.

little, so that greed may not become a factor in addition to the security of a reasonable purchase contract. The smaller the percentage, the more godly and Christian the contract.[51]

The emphasis is to be placed on the last sentence. Focusing not on the Scholastics' Aristotelian teleology of money, that is, not on the notion that money was solely a commodity consumed through exchange, Luther emphasized the intention of the contracting parties, in accordance with his voluntarist philosophical origins.[52] John Calvin felt likewise that "if only there were engraved on our hearts, what Christ prescribes, by the rule of equity, To do as we would be done by, then soon lengthy disputations about usuries would serve very little purpose."[53] While good Christians would not take excessive interest, both Calvin and Philip Melanchthon felt that good Christian magistrates should decide what constituted excessive interest.[54] Law was a task for secular rulers, not for the Church, in their Protestant vision of church and polity.

Thus, when in the 1540s, dissatisfied with the speculations of theologians and with the decisions of church courts, the Calvinist-leaning French jurist Charles Dumoulin turned his formidable mind to the problem of usury, he too sought a new definition. For him, usury occurred any time one used another's money but was, however, legitimate. In his words, it was "the reasonable value or compensation for the usage of or the delay in payment of the money owing."[55] Like Calvin, Dumoulin viewed

[51] *D. Martin Luthers Werke* (Weimar: Herman Böhlau, 1888), Schriften, 6:36–60, "(Großer) Sermon von dem Wucher," 58: "Wan nu das geschicht an ubirtretung des geystlichen gesetz, das man auffs hundert 4, 5, 6 gulden gibt, lest sichs tragen, doch soll allzeyt die gottis forcht sorgfeltig seyn, das sie mehr forchte, sie nhem zuvil den zu wenig, das der geytz nit neben der sicherheyt des zimlichen kauffs eynreysse. Ihe weniger auffs hundert, yhe gottlicher und Christlicher der kauff ist." In English, James Atikinson and Helmut Lehman (eds.), *Luther's Works* (Minneapolis: Augsburg Fortress Press, 1959), 45:305.

[52] Heiko Oberman, *The Harvest of Medieval Theology: Gabriel Biel and Late Medieval Nominalism* (Cambridge: Harvard University Press, 1963), and *Luther: Man between God and the Devil* (New Haven: Yale University Press, 1989).

[53] Calvin, cited in Kerridge, 51–52.

[54] Melanchthon, cited in Kerridge, 39: "Iudicium de contractibus et de usuris, ut de alijs rebus politicis, petendum esse a Magistratu civili, hoc est, ab ipsis legibus recte et sane intellectis, et consentientibus cum ratione … Etsi enim alicubi permittunt usuras, non tamen approbant, quia Leges non possunt omnibus vicijs mederi." Kerridge, 48: "Calvin, like Bullinger and other leaders of the Reformed Churches, left mundane commercial and financial matters to the Magistrate and allowed what the Magistrate allowed. And the Magistrate understood usury in the narrow and generally employed sense. In Calvin's Geneva arrêtes made by the city council in 1538 and 1544 expressly forbade usury in the sense of ocker and limited true and legitimate interest on loans of such things as flour, wheat, wine and firewood, to 5 per cent. To take more than the legal limit was to take usury in the narrow sense."

[55] Cited in Jean-Louis Thireau, *Charles du Moulin (1500–1566). Étude sur les sources, la méthode, les idées politiques et économiques d'un juriste de la Renaissance* (Geneva: Droz, 1980), 377.

lending at interest as fundamentally legitimate. Like Luther and Calvin, Dumoulin emphasized the spirit rather than the Scriptural letter ordinarily invoked against lending at interest. The charitable interest rate varied. Because, Dumoulin reasoned, all borrowers were not the needy poor, it was legitimate to charge a reasonable rate of interest when borrowers might realize gains on the basis of the capital lent. The rate would be set by the lay authority, surely in accord with reason and conscience, as it was by the Parlement of Paris.[56] Dumoulin's incipient sense that money was potentially fruitful capital and not an item of consumption provided a novel justification for reasonable interest. While Catholic contemporaries felt Dumoulin's innovation to be tinged with religious and economic heresy, his understanding of money appears to accord with the popular understanding of lending by which most Europeans lived, for below the letters of change, annuities, and notarized obligations that stimulated so much discussion of usury, diverse forms of minor credit proliferated. Some of these rested on written engagements, others on pledges or pawned items, and still others on nothing but the promise of future recompense. Many in fact rested on the informal agreements (*nuda pacta*) that Roman law and lay courts in general were reluctant to enforce.[57] Indeed, Wim Decock has demonstrated how Luther's and Dumoulin's intentionalism foreshadowed the qualified acceptance of the *nudum pactum* into civil law through the work of Catholic moral theologians.[58] Nevertheless, the usury prohibition meant that, even if Europeans borrowed the capital required to set up households, farms, and workshops, and paid interest for use of that capital, that any interest was concealed in judicial records, including those at the basis of this study.

To call this minor credit wholly informal is misleading, because parol contracts and private obligations were enforceable before church courts and were, I will argue, remembered, transferred, and discounted. Day-to-day credit was flexible and easily negotiable but for those reasons nearly invisible to the historian. From an economic perspective, and at

[56] Thireau, *Charles du Moulin*, 348–400.

[57] Baldus' hesitancy about canonists' acceptance of *nuda pacta* is apparent in his discussion of c. Antigonus (X.1.35.1), where he argues that a simple agreement is "vested" after all (*Baldus super decretalibus* (Lyon, 1564), 112 no.5): "Sed ubi habet causam extrinsecam ut liberalitatis pacis et concordie tunc pactum est omnium servandum ut hic. preterea istud non est pactum nudum sed vestitum robore canonice sanctionis unde tu canonista addis ad vestimenta pactorum vestimentum quod appellatur vestimentum roboris. Porro de iure civili est quedam vestimentum quod appellatur legis auxilium quod non est alius nisi specialis favor attributus alicui actui a lege nec habet locum nisi in casibus expressis in iure. sed de iure canonico habet locum similiter in omni pacto bono et equo cuiuscunque generis et forme." The following chapter's section on contracts discusses vested pacts.

[58] Decock, *Theologians*.

the risk of drawing finer distinctions than the sources permit, there are four major categories of minor credit relevant to this story.[59] Investment loans are intended to increase productive assets, for example to set up a household upon marriage, to lease new farmland so as to expand the area under cultivation, or to acquire a wheeled plow permitting the cultivation of heavier, richer, and more productive soils.[60] Since these loans ought to increase productivity, under ideal conditions they would be self-liquidating. Seasonal operations loans, including purchase or sales credits, permit farmers to purchase seed corn or livestock to work their land. These would ideally be paid back after the harvest, in our period frequently at Michaelmas (September 29), when many agricultural leases expired. Of course, this depends on the "external" factors that bedevil farmers and ranchers everywhere. A bad harvest following a wet summer could drive the farmer deeper into debt the next year. A series of bad harvests could drive him into debt peonage or perhaps expropriation. Consumption loans are related to seasonal operations loans but are directed at survival rather than at cultivation. In the modern world, these are often used to increase the consumption power of an economic cell. In the premodern world, irregular work patterns for wage laborers, unsustainably small farms, slow technological progress, and predatory leases and loans led to a condition of "structural overindebtedness" in which many borrowed less to buy consumer goods than to eat.[61] Finally, cash-flow loans are credit extended for a term – whether quarterly, semi-annual, or annual – to distribute cash into a local economy. In the late Middle Ages, such credit smoothed the notably discontinuous revenue streams of the premodern economy.[62] In the premodern world, one might

[59] Fontaine (32) instead differentiates loans (i) to sow or to eat before the harvest, (ii) to pay taxes, (iii) to marry or to set up a household, and (iv) to eat in the absence of work.

[60] A classic example of the entrepreneurial use of loans secured on land: Jan Luiten van Zanden, Jaco Zuijderduijn, and Tine De Moor, "Small is Beautiful: The Efficiency of Credit Markets in Late Medieval Holland," *European Review of Economic History* 16 (2012), 3–22.

[61] On "structural overindebtness," see Fontaine, *L'Économie*, 59, 302; Jacques Bottin, *Seigneurs et paysans dans l'Ouest du pays de Caux (1540–1650)* (Paris: Éditions Le Sycomore, 1983); Olwen Hufton, *The Poor of Eighteenth-Century France* (Oxford: Clarendon Press, 1988); Jean Jacquart, "L'endettement paysan et le crédit dans les campagnes de la France moderne," in Berthe, *Endettement paysan*, 283–298; Nicole Lemaître, *Le scribe et le mage: Notaires et société rurale en Bas-Limousin aux XVIe et XVIIe siècles* (Ussel: Musée du pays d'Ussel, 2000).

[62] The problem of discontinuous revenue afflicted even monarchs, who turned to venality and expensive short-term loans, and to their servants, who smoothed the king's revenue-stream with their own money (and vice versa, providing a basis for periodic prosecutions for the malversation that was virtually a condition of the State's financial functioning): Philippe Hamon, *L'argent du roi: Les finances sous François Ier* (Paris: Comité pour l'histoire économique et financière de la France, 1994), and *'Messieurs des finances': Les grands officiers de finance dans la France de la Renaissance* (Paris: Comité pour l'histoire économique et financière de la France, 1999).

imagine these as being given less often in specie than in material – material nevertheless appraised by its monetary value.[63] Craftsmen might receive the raw materials of their trade on credit, with the expectation that the supplier would be repaid upon the sale of the finished product.[64] In England, wool merchants or broggers might only pay for part of the wool they delivered to market in cash and receive the rest on credit until settlement after the wool had been sold.[65] Participants in rural industry might receive the wool or flax they were to process on credit with the expectation of repayment upon sale of the materials back to the vendor or merchant.[66] All types of loan mentioned here created or confirmed an existing relationship and could put the borrower at a distinct disadvantage vis-à-vis his or her creditors. As Antoni Furiò has noted, credit "doubled the relation of lord and peasant with that of creditor and debtor" and, in contrast to a prevalent view, sought not "the expropriation of the peasantry [or] tenurial conquest, but a greater share of the agricultural surplus."[67]

Taxes, judicial fines, and tithes also necessitated cash loans that could reinforce prior relations of subordination. Taxes seldom resulted in excommunication, it seems, although there are two possible cases from late medieval Normandy: on the Thursday after Cantate 1437 (OS) two curés were suspended from the capacity to celebrate divine service at the request of Sire Guillaume de La Haye, "receiver of a certain aide (*receptor cuiusdam subsidii*)" for 80 *saluts d'or* (90£t), with the two curés presumably acting as collectors for this large sum; on December 13, 1456 Robert Cuvier of Harfleur was excommunicated at the request of Jean Toustain "receiver of the king's aides (*receptor subsidii regii*)" for 6 *écus d'or* (9£t), presumably his share of the levy.[68] These were eventually absolved, the arrears forgiven or paid. By the fifteenth century, church courts less frequently imprisoned or flogged, and instead assigned monetary fines or commuted corporal punishments such as floggings to monetary fines. When unpaid, the latter led to excommunication at the request of a court's receiver of fines. Tithe cases did give rise to numerous

[63] Luca Clerici, "Fonctions de la monnaire et formes de paiements en Italie du nord dans la seconde moitié du XVe siècle," *Histoire et Mesure*, 12:1–2 (1997), 5–36.

[64] See the examples in Claire H. Crowston, *Fabricating Women: The Seamstresses of Old Regime France, 1675–1791* (Chapel Hill: Duke University Press, 2001), and *Credit, Fashion, Sex: Economies of Regard in Old Regime France* (Chapel Hill: Duke University Press, 2013).

[65] Christopher Dyer, *A Country Merchant, 1495–1520: Trading and Farming at the End of the Middle Ages* (Oxford: Oxford University Press, 2012).

[66] On the putting-out system, see Jan de Vries, *The Industrious Revolution: Consumer Demand and the Household Economy, 1650 to the Present* (Cambridge University Press, 2008).

[67] Furiò, "Endettement paysan et crédit dans la Péninsule Ibérique au Bas Moyen Âge," in Berthe, *Endettement paysan*, 139–167, at 167.

[68] Archives départementales de Seine-Maritime, Rouen (hereafter ADSM), G 5271.

excommunications. While church courts often reduced fines on account of a delinquent's poverty, they treated laxity in the payment of tithes and other ecclesiastical dues with less mercy. In the famous Hunne case of 1515, a London merchant died under suspicious circumstances while imprisoned for a cascade of actions that began with his refusal to pay a mortuary fee. In such cases, debt manifested prior subjection: to the king for taxes, to the lord or owner for dues or rent, to a court for fines, and to a tithe-holder or tithe-farmer for tithes.

We know that these types of "hidden" credit existed, but the records for it are notably thin and notably late.[69] What if today's records of the billing for small services and of the activity of collections agencies vanished? Historians have had difficulty grasping the extent of minor, quotidian credit. We can nevertheless gauge it obliquely through the records of those debts that creditors chose to bring before church courts. The study of excommunication for debt illuminates a level of otherwise nearly invisible credit unrecorded either by notaries public or by court clerks before it entered the judicial record. From Raymond De Roover's pioneering work on banking, to Pierre-Clément Timbal's, Jean Yver's, or Bernard Schapper's on contracts, obligations, and forms of property-based lending in France, to the more recent contributions of, for instance, W. J. Zwalve or the authors in the *Cahier de Flaran* on rural credit, existing works focus on larger and therefore better documented obligations.[70] One can be forgiven for believing that there must have been little recourse to minor credit in late medieval Northern France, in contrast to England or Southern Europe, where the records of manorial courts and of notaries testify to credit practices.

There are brief flashes of illumination, however: Enguerran Martel, early-fifteenth-century Norman peasant and small merchant sold wine, horses, cloth, woad, wool, clothing, and bacon on credit or for differed

[69] e.g., Justin Colson, Review of Dyer's *A Country Merchant*, *Reviews in History* n.1339 (2012), www.history.ac.uk/reviews/review/1339: "Intriguingly, there is no evidence of instruments recording the many small debts to which Heritage [the wool brogger who is Dyer's subject] was party, indicating that the majority of the small merchant's activities were carried out on trust. Pessimistic assessments of the volume of trade in the 15th century, such as those of [Pamela] Nightingale, based on records of large debts, inevitably ignore this 'hidden economy' of small-scale unrecorded debt."

[70] Raymond De Roover, *Business, Banking, and Economic Thought in Late Medieval and Early Modern Europe: Selected Studies of Raymond de Roover*, Julius Kirshner (ed.) (University of Chicago Press, 1976); Timbal, *Les Obligations*; Jean Yver, *Les contrats dans le très ancien droit normand (XIe-XIIIe siècles)* (Domfront: Imprimerie du Publicateur, 1926); Schnapper, *Les rentes*; W. J. Zwalve, "*Sola scriptura*, An essay in comparative legal history on 'obligacions' in thirteenth-century France and England," *Tijdschrift voor Rechtsgeschiedenis* 80 (2012), 95–128.

payment in amounts ranging from 1 to 60£t but averaging 5£t.[71] The simple parol contract or the credit privately recorded in a bill (*cédule*) or a ledger (*cahier*, *compte*) seldom appear in notarial records, cartularies, formularies, or any of the habitual sources of economic and financial history. They appear only obliquely in the records even of church courts and almost never in the records of the higher lay jurisdictions. This is because parol contracts and private acts were not generally or easily enforceable in the higher lay courts whose records survive. The commonness of excommunication for debt has been acknowledged by many authors (Pierre-Clément Timbal, Anne Lefebvre-Teillard, Richard Helmholz, R. N. Swanson, and Véronique Beaulande), without drawing sustained attention. It is easier to track the relatively few letters of *nisi* issued by church courts, so called for the clause providing for the excommunication of the obligee in case of default, than to collate the meager evidence for massive recourse to ecclesiastical tribunals in cases of debt at the end of the Middle Ages. It is not simply a matter of counting debts registered before church courts, which are scarce, but of understanding how the canonical procedure permitted excommunication in cases of debt and how and where such cases might be recorded.

Legal history, social history, and canon law

In 1957, Bernard Schnapper concluded his study of *rentes* in sixteenth-century Paris by advising his readers: "I think … that it is time to use statistical analysis in writing the history of private law."[72] Yet, neither during the subsequent tsunami of cliometrics nor the retreat of quantitative social history before the linguistic turn have many legal historians, certainly French legal historians of the period concerned, taken up the statistical analysis of private law, though most would concede that this is the only way to penetrate the enormous preserved caseloads of appellate courts such as the Parlement of Paris or *Reichshammergericht*. On account of the relatively small corpora of surviving documents, we have good studies of the Parlement's jurisprudence on obligations or on its civil and criminal procedure in the thirteenth and fourteenth centuries.[73] For later periods historians have of necessity retreated

[71] Cited in Theiller, "Comptabilité et réalité financière: quelques observations autour d'un registre comptable de l'abbaye Saint-Amand de Rouen (1387/8-1397)," *Tabularia "Études"* 5 (2007), 51–73, at 63–64 n.24; Mathieu Arnoux and Laëtitia Renault, "Enguerran Martel et ses clients. Quelques remarques sur crédit et justice en Normandie à la fin du Moyen Âge," in Julie Claustre (ed.), *La dette et le juge. Juridiction gracieuse et juridiction contentieuse du XIIIe au XVe siècle (France, Italie, Espagne, Angleterre, Empire)* (Paris: Publications de la Sorbonne, 2006), 151–167.

[72] Schnapper, *Les rentes*, 287.

[73] Timbal, *Les obligations*; Louis de Carbonnières, *La procédure devant la chambre criminelle du Parlement de Paris au XIVe siècle* (Paris: H. Champion, 2004).

either to the history of legal doctrine, to the normative prescriptions and reverse-engineered rationales of the *arrêtistes*, or to skimming the political froth on the surface of the ocean of the court's civil competence, as I have.[74] Criminal matters are better studied,[75] but the best statistical or textual usage of legal sources has been by social or cultural historians seeking to answer questions of social or cultural history rather than of legal or economic history. This distorts our understanding of what courts did, as Michael Breen has estimated that the ratio of civil to criminal litigation in Old Regime France was something along the lines of fifteen to one and as Isabelle Mathieu has shown that almost eighty percent of cases before the Angevin seigneurial courts she studied were civil matters.[76] This study is in part an attempt to open the history of private law to statistical analysis and thereby to give civil justice the prominence in historical literature that it enjoyed in practice. The availability of data sets will structure but not unduly circumscribe my investigation of the civil competence of late medieval Church, so as to avoid, I hope, fruitless or meaningless database-making and number-crunching.[77] My statistical analysis will be informed by the cultural context of litigation, as in Daniel Smail's study of civil justice in late medieval Marseille.[78] This author's temerarious hope is one day to carry this type of investigation over into the civil justice of the fifteenth- and sixteenth-century Parlement of Paris.

This is to minimize neither the place of traditional legal history, as so many conflicts in this period were articulated and disputed in a legal idiom, nor the place of social history in the following account. I wish only to emphasize that statistical analysis has something to tell us about legal change, since law is not a self-referential, autonomous system,[79] above all in a period when legal doctrine could be eight decades behind developments in judicial practice.[80] With respect to credit, church courts began to lose business to

[74] Lange, *First French Reformation*, beginning with Le Nain's tables then simply scanning entire registers.

[75] Claude Gauvard, *'De grâce especial': Crime, état et société en France à la fin du Moyen Âge* (Paris: Publications de la Sorbonne, 1991); Natalie Davis, *Fiction in the Archives: Pardon Tales and Their Tellers in Sixteenth-Century France* (Stanford: Stanford University Press, 1987); Alfred Soman, *Sorcellerie et justice criminelle: Le parlement de Paris, XVIe-XVIIIe siècles* (Brookfield, VT: Variorum, 1992).

[76] Breen, 354; Isabelle Mathieu, *Les Justices seigneuriales en Anjou et dans le Maine à la fin du Moyen Âge* (Rennes: Presses universitaires de Rennes, 2011), 254: 79 percent were civil, 15 percent criminal, 2 percent mixed, 4 percent were uncategorized.

[77] Tony Judt, "A Clown in Regal Purple: Social History and the Historians," *History Workshop Journal* 7 (1979), 66–94.

[78] Daniel Lord Smail, *The Consumption of Justice: Emotion, Publicity, and Legal Culture in Marseille, 1264–1423* (Ithaca: Cornell University Press, 2003).

[79] Decock, *Theologians*, 1–20.

[80] For example, until the end of the first third of the sixteenth century French jurists rejected the practice of appeals from church courts to parlements evident in the Parlement of Paris from about 1440, and lamented by churchmen in lower jurisdictions

secular courts from the middle of the fifteenth century and in earnest after 1500, well before the Ordinance of Villers-Cotterêts of 1539 circumscribed their competence legislatively.[81] This development was not purely legal; it was also religious, reflecting the broader sixteenth-century Reformations of European Christianity. The shift in legal practice, by which church courts lost much of their civil competence, and in legal doctrine, by which jurists denied bishops or their officials' jurisdiction over property matters, manifested changing ideas about the role and place of clergy, the Church, and royal authority in late medieval France and in Europe more broadly.

Legal history can only be understood in a purely formal manner without some social and intellectual or cultural history. Conversely, historians have neglected the legal context and indeed the legal content of the Ordinance of Villers-Cotterêts. Legal historians focus less on the Ordinance's prescription of the vernacular for legal documents and more on its reorganization of civil procedure, criminal appeals, and the competence of ecclesiastical tribunals. Politically, culturally, or socially minded historians, for their part, may not fully appreciate the context of the ordinance's cryptic prescriptions. Article 1 provides that "we have prohibited and prohibit any of our subjects to have cited or to summon layfolk before ecclesiastical judges in purely personal actions on pain of the loss of their case and a discretionary fine." Article 2 that "we have prohibited all ecclesiastical judges from sending or delivering any written or verbal citations to cite our lay subjects in purely personal cases also on pain of a discretionary fine."[82] These and following articles stripped church courts of virtually any but a moral competence over layfolk. They aimed to suppress use of excommunication in matters of debt. With respect to the first article, the parol or privately recorded contracts enforced by citation and excommunication were personal debts that gave rise to personal actions.[83] With respect to the second, I suspect that many if not most verbal citations in matters of debt had been delivered not personally but "to the house or to the parish church … or to the kin."[84] Although canon

since the early fourteenth century: Tyler Lange, "The Birth of a Maxim: 'A Bishop Has No Territory,'" *Speculum* 89:1 (2014), 128–147.

81 Léon Pommeray, *L'officialité archidiaconale de Paris et sa compétence criminelle* (Paris, 1933), 440–441; Lefebvre-Teillard, *Les officialités*, 70; Swanson, *Church and Society*, 182–190.

82 Isambert, XII: 600–640, at 601.

83 The causes of action were contumacy, perjury, or delay in paying. Concerning the last, Johannes Salicetus (†1412) invoked the extrinsic title of *poena conventualis*: "mora est delictum culpabile in differendo promissum," cited in Ferdinand Elsener, "Die Exkommunikation als Prozessuales Vollstreckungsmittel. Zur Geschichte des Kirchenbanns im Spätmittelalter," in *Tübinger Festschrift für Eduard Kern* (Tübingen: J. C. B. Mohr, 1968), 69–85, at 79.

84 Hostiensis, *Summa aurea* ad X.2, De contumacia, s.v. Qualiter deprehendatur: "mitti debet citatio ad domum vel ad ecclesiam propriam, vel citandus est procurator. Si ipsum dimisit, alias cognati, vel affines de quibus est verisimile quod ipsum defendant." That

law required that citations be announced to the accused, his proctor, his family, or his neighbors, it appears that these prescriptions were commonly flouted, one fears with a small monetary gratification to the summoner. For instance, statutes of *c.* 1529 from Saint-Brieuc in Brittany reiterate that priests were to publish citations during the bidding of the bedes or *prône*[85] of the mass, certify this to the official, and post the citations on a placard. No citations were to be delivered before sunrise or after sundown, and only in cases of pressing need were they to be delivered to neighbors rather than to family members or domestics of the cited or excommunicated person.[86] The care taken by excommunicates to be absolved suggests that, whereas some ignored summonses, others never learned that they had been cited until the priest read out their names in the list of excommunicates at the parish mass. If they delayed, it was surely for lack of funds, for pressing business reasons, or because Easter and their required participation in the Eucharist remained distant. Recognizing the civil competence of church courts illuminates the neglected context for what is probably the most important item of sixteenth-century French royal legislation after the Edict of Nantes.

A balance between quantitative and normative history is thus necessary to untangle the intertwined histories of society and the law. Quantitative methods can help to convey, for example, the place of women or the poor in legal history. They can unlock a layer of legal practice inaccessible through the normative documents of more elevated judicial entities. While this study will only venture beyond church courts for the comparisons

this only concerned those who could not be found or who threatened to harm the summoner was probably generously interpreted.

85 Or prayers of the faithful. The *prône* took the place of the contemporary sermon or homily before the offertory. *Prône* is derived from the Latin *prothyrum* or roodscreen, whence the explications of the Gospel and familiar prayers and the publication of episcopal and royal statutes, banns of marriage, excommunications, and feasts and fasts in the vernacular. Bidding of the bedes refers to the English prayers likewise read out before the offertory.

86 BN Latin 1458, "Modus exequendi citaciones," 114r-v: "(vii) Executores citacionum … dicant cuius ecclesie sunt rectores vel capellani et si excommunicacio vel aliud mandatum contineatur in citatione vel sint alicui parochiani exequatur modo sequenti Ego N. rector vel capellanus curatus talis parrochie executus fui presentes in prono misse dominicalis dicti loci die dominica tali juxta formam supra talem vel tales parrochianos dicti loci et ulterius publicavi presentes in prono dicte misse et apponatur tanta carta in citatione … (viii) Item si execucio fiat ad domicilium apponatur qua die ad quam personam cuius et qualiter nec fiat execucio ante solis ortum vel post solis occasum … (ix) Item exequantur citaciones et moniciones ad propriam personam vel ad personam procuratoris in causa fundati aut ad bannum ecclesie pro citati vel moniti vel ad domicilium illium per familiares servitores domesticos et commensales vel si ita fieri non possit et de qui executor fidem facere tenebitur si casus celeritatem requirit non alias per proximos vicinos."

necessary to understanding any court system in a situation of legal pluralism, awareness of the functioning and logic of coexisting tribunals is crucial to our understanding of debt in the late Middle Ages. Studies of debt only before the Parlement, or only before the Châtelet, or only before the archidiaconal officiality give an incomplete picture of the world of obligations in late medieval Paris, for instance. This book aims there to complement the already-cited works of Pierre-Clément Timbal on the Parlement and of Julie Claustre on the Châtelet. It suggests the potential place of church courts in the enforcement of credit, a potential realized in varying intensities across late medieval Western Europe.

Lack of awareness of the role of ecclesiastical tribunals in matters of credit is a consequence of legal *Dogmengeschichte*'s tendency to treat established traditions as distinct, stable fields of analysis. The consecration of separate chairs to each tradition, the exclusion of some traditions (usually canon law) from a particular university, or the separate publication of the *romanistische*, *kanonistische*, and *germanistische Abteilungen* of the *Zeitschrift der Savigny-Stiftung für Rechtsgeschichte* illustrate the institutional stickiness of such arrangements. This columnar tendency has distorted our understanding of how the plural fora of the Middle Ages functioned, for scholars of each tradition are in some sense imperialists. Historians of canon law tend to make canon law predominate in the history of European law, those of civil law the same for Roman law, and those of customary or Germanic law likewise until the reception of Roman law in different European countries.[87] In truth, Roman, canon, or "customary" law were not impermeable and stable quantities: under the theoretical framework of the learned laws there was a place for *lex*, for *canon*, and for *consuetudo*. In France, for instance, if there was a long-term tendency toward the Romanization of the law, the fundamental categories of property-holding remained based on the alliance of the late Roman concepts of possession and title with early medieval practices of seisin through canonical procedure.[88] "Germanic law" existed more as a polemical concept than as a late antique or early medieval reality.[89] Still later,

[87] For example, Manlio Bellomo, *The Common Legal Past of Europe, 1000–1800*, Lydia G. Cochrane (trans.), (Washington, DC: Catholic University of America Press, 1995); Paul Vinogradoff, *Roman Law in Medieval Europe* (Oxford: Clarendon Press, 1929); André Castaldo, "Pouvoir royal, droit savant et droit commun coutumier dans la France du Moyen Âge. À propos de vues nouvelles: le roi est-il le maître du droit privé, via le droit romain?" *Droits* 46 (2007), 117–158, and "Le droit romain est-il le droit commun?" *Droits* 47 (2008), 173–248.

[88] Emanuele Conte, "Gewere, vestitura, spolium: un'ipotesi d'interpretazione," in Condorelli, *Einfluss*, I:169–191; Lange, "Droit canon et droit français à travers l'activité du Parlement de Paris à l'époque des Réformes," *Revue historique de droit français et étranger* 91:2 (2013), 243–261.

[89] Laurent Waelkens, "Droit germanique: la fin d'un mythe? À propos d'un ouvrage récent?" *Revue historique de droit français et étranger*, 87:3 (2009), 415–426.

Roman law often influenced French law through the medium of a canon law itself constructed after a Justinianic model and with Roman materials, as is evident from procedures such as the *réintegrande* or the inquest. Medieval Roman law was neither the Roman law of the Twelve Tables, nor that of the Republic, nor that of the Principate, nor that of sixth-century Byzantium or Beirut, nor that, for that matter, of nineteenth-century *Pandektenrecht*, but a particular, time-bound, dynamic creation. Although the source texts of medieval Roman law remained relatively stable after their gradual rediscovery, its practical content varied according to its interpreter's period, person, and purposes. It is this structural and shifting Roman law, through which customary, canonical, and properly Roman elements circulated, that set the baseline for all medieval laws. In England, the influence of the learned laws was greater before and to a degree even after the Reformation than autochthonist accounts would have it.[90] The English Reformation, which expanded the scope of the common law from the law of devolution of freehold property into a constitutional law that underlay and dominated all other laws within the kingdom of England, has obscured this more complex history of English law.[91] In France, the triumph of Romanized customary law has likewise tended to discount Roman and canonical elements in French law.[92] Conversely, just as the common laws of England and of France were not exempt from civilian or canonist influences, so canonical procedure was not immune to the influence of local legal practice: consider the role of jurors in English, German, or Swedish church courts.[93]

That historians of credit do not look to church courts reflects a widespread retrojection of the scope of their operation during the early

[90] Charles Donahue, "Roman Canon Law in the Medieval English Church: Stubbs vs. Maitland Re-Examined after 75 Years in the Light of Some Records from the Church Courts," *Michigan Law Review* 72:4 (1974), 647–716; R. H. Helmholz, *Roman Canon Law in Reformation England* (Cambridge: Cambridge University Press, 1990).

[91] Alan Cromartie, *The Constitutionalist Revolution: An Essay on the History of England, 1450–1642* (Cambridge: Cambridge University Press, 2006).

[92] Gérard Giordanengo, "*Roma nobilis, orbis et domina*. Réponse à un contradicteur," *Revue historique de droit français et étranger*, 88:1 (2010), 91–150; Jean-Louis Halpérin, "La détermination du champ juridique à la lumière de travaux récents d'histoire du droit," *Droit et société* 81 (2012), 405–423.

[93] R. Helmholz, "Canonical 'Juries' in Medieval England," in M. Ascheri et al. (eds.), *'Ins Wasser geworfen und Ozeane durchquert'. Festschrift für Knut Wolfgang Nörr* (Cologne/Weimar/Vienna: Böhlau, 2003), 403–418; L. R. Poos, *Lower Ecclesiastical Jurisdiction in Late-Medieval England: The Courts of the Dean and Chapter of Lincoln, 1336–1349, and the Deanery of Wisbech, 1458–1484*, Records of Social and Economic History, New Series 32 (Oxford: The British Academy, 2001), lx–lxi; Eugen Baumgartner, *Geschichte und Recht des Archidiakonates der oberrheinischen Bistümer mit Einschluss von Mainz und Würzburg*, Kirchliche Abhandlungen 39 (Stuttgart: Ferdinand Enke, 1907; repr. Amsterdam: P. Schippers N.V., 1965), 153–154; concerning Sweden, I thank Mia Korpiola for an illuminating conversation in Wetzlar in 2013.

modern period. Paolo Prodi has offered a penetrating analysis of the shifting composition and tenor of canon law in this period.[94] His account redresses the neglect and ghettoization consequent upon its two-stage decline, initially in the sixteenth century, when its scope and applicability were curtailed and clericalized during the Reformations of Christianity, and again in the nineteenth and twentieth centuries, when the codifications of canon law and of European national laws narrowed its intellectual allure. In the late Middle Ages, however, much of the intellectual energy that had in the eleventh and twelfth centuries been devoted to theology was channeled toward canon law. From the thirteenth to sixteenth centuries, canonists claimed to be scientists of "practical theology," arbiters of the correct application of theological precepts to daily life. Although secular courts and theologians struggled against the imperialism of canon law, canon law was the privileged site for reflecting on the shape of the just society at the end of the Middle Ages. It was, as Patrick Arabeyre has put it, a site not of "covert" but of "undeclared political thought."[95] Indeed, how could it be other? Was not political society simply another facet of Christ's body or a portion thereof? As a result of this situation, according to Prodi, the individual's conscience was racked between three fora: (i) the court of conscience or internal forum, that is, the dialogue of confessor and penitent; (ii) the external forum of church courts, in which private plaintiffs as well as court officials prosecuted criminalized sins; and (iii) the additional external forum of secular courts, which likewise tended to criminalize sin. If "the Church does not judge matters of conscience" (*ecclesia non iudicat de occultis*, from the gloss to D.32 c.11), it did judge crimes and civil wrongs. Yet different laws judged on different criteria and provided different remedies or punishments. Canon law did not agree with civil law. Canon law did not agree with customary law. Civil law did not agree with customary law. These dissonances gave rise to treatises on the *differentiae* of canon and civil law. They forced ordinary Christians to choose whether to obey an unjust law or, more commonly, to choose among conflicting laws, as in the case of the canonical and common-law positions on bastardy in medieval England. Differences between courts also permitted forum-shopping for the cheapest, most expeditious justice.

[94] Prodi, *Una storia*.

[95] Patrick Arabeyre, "Un enseignement de science politique dans les facultés de droit canonique françaises de la fin du XVe et au début du XVIe siècle (Paris: Cosme Guymier; Cahors: Guillaume Benoît; Toulouse: Jean d'Ayma)," in M. Stolleis et J. Krynen (eds.), *Science politique et droit public dans les facultés de droit européennes (XIIIe – XVIIIe siècle)* (Frankfurt-am-Main: Max-Planck-Institut für europäische Rechtsgeschichte, 2008), 299–324.

This is less true of the later sixteenth, seventeenth, or eighteenth centuries, when the diminution of the scope of canon law redirected intellectual energy toward theology and, crucially, toward political thought, as the path of voluntarist contract theory from canon law to neo-Scholastic moral theology to seventeenth-century international law traced by Wim Decock illustrates.[96] Much as the clericalization of canon law diminished the subject's intellectual allure, the Reformation shook the confidence that the social body and Christ's body were identical and that the visible, institutional Church bore any relation to the Church of true believers as it would be revealed at the Last Judgment. Even before the Protestant Reformation, a changing sense of the proper role of the institutional Church drove Christians away from using church courts in matters of debt and that encouraged their secular rulers to restrict the competence of ecclesiastical tribunals in civil matters. In the following chapters, I argue that excommunication for debt was mainly a demand-driven process. Supply may have played a role only very briefly during the fifteenth century, when the late medieval slump in landed incomes made prelates more reliant on judicial income than before or after. The rise of excommunication for debt reflects the commercial, legal, and religious developments of the thirteenth and fourteenth centuries. Its decline reflects sixteenth-century changes in religious and legal sympathy, whereby Europeans came to view debt as a matter for lay courts. Even if excommunication for debt was not the primary cause of the Protestant Reformation, some of the bitterness toward the institutional Church and widespread hopes for its reform evident in the Protestant Reformation may well have originated in the role of church courts in credit relations.

This project began with an accusation against the Bishop of Orléans that I read while researching my dissertation. In 1496 the king's attorney told the Parlement of Paris how "a sergeant found a certain person in the environs of Orléans with a full basket of blank citations with which to vex and trouble a bunch of poor winemakers. When he seized the citations, he was cited and then excommunicated," joining what the duke of Orléans's attorney believed to be "twelve or fourteen thousand" excommunicates from whom the bishop sought to profit through the fees for sealing their absolutions.[97] Later I encountered further accusations that bishops had made a "business" or *marchandise* of ecclesiastical justice, notably against the Bishop of Angers in the mid 1520s and against the Archbishop of

96 Paul Ourliac, "Souveraineté et lois fondamentales dans le droit canonique du XVe siècle," in *Études d'histoire du droit médiéval* (Paris: A. et J. Picard, 1979), 553–565; Decock, *Theologians*.

97 AN X^{2a}61, 256v, 250v. The case originated in a jurisdictional squabble between the duke and the bishop.

Besançon in the 1570s.[98] These drew my attention to a nearly imperceptible practice that falls into the interstices of the beaten paths of legal and social history. Although my sources come from Northwestern France, the practice appears to have existed in varying intensities across Europe.

From the thirteenth to the sixteenth century, excommunication for debt offered ordinary people an economical, efficacious mechanism for the enforcement of minor credit. During the difficult fifteenth century, the practice gave holders of ecclesiastical jurisdiction an opportunity to round out their incomes. From one perspective, excommunication for debt was a grave abuse by which the Church sold its salvific magic to creditors. From another, it facilitated charitable, ostensibly interest-free lending within the Body of Christ by providing a mechanism of enforcement for unwritten or privately recorded debts or sales on credit. Indeed, the credit that most often gave rise to excommunications for debt is often visible in the historical record only through this practice, in contrast to the letters of change, annuities secured on real property, or notarized obligations beloved of economic historians and historians of banking. This transitional practice illuminates the religious, social, and economic transformations of the sixteenth century. It demonstrates how the Reformation changed practices of credit and how the circumscription of ecclesiastical civil justice facilitated the emergence of early modern juridically sovereign territories.

[98] The phrase is from the *avocat du roi*'s accusation against the Bishop of Angers in 1525: AN X^{1a}4876, 148v-149v, and Lange, *First French Reformation*, 167–172; for Besançon, see Lucien Febvre, "L'application du Concile de Trente et l'excommunication pour dettes en Franche-Comté," *Revue historique*, 103 (1910), 225–247, and 104 (1910), 1–39.

1 Church courts and credit

On September 2, 1513, Jean Magnart was excommunicated at the request of Sire Guillaume Le Tellier, priest and executor of the late Jean Mesegnel.[1] He was excommunicated in virtue of a warning or monition issued by the ecclesiastical court of the Abbess of Montivilliers in Normandy to pay the sum of 42s 6dt he owed the deceased. Jean Magnart did not pay, and on September 17 his excommunication was "aggravated" and on October 1 "reaggravated."[2] The efficacy of such sanctions presupposed (i) belief in an afterlife that could only be attained through the sacraments of Holy Mother Church and (ii) the omnipresence of credit in the late Middle Ages. This chapter explores how such sanctions could be issued in such cases by such an authority. An excommunicated debtor might have borrowed or bought on credit seed corn, grain for subsistence, the raw materials of his craft, or perhaps hard cash to pay taxes, seigneurial dues, or tithes. How did the institution that was supposed to provide the means of salvation come to withhold them from those who borrowed to live? How did the Church come to have a system of courts with such power? How did church courts come to be competent with respect to testamentary debt or debt not secured on real property? The following chapter accordingly describes the network of church courts, their jurisdiction over matters of contract, their procedure, and the cultural significance of their rituals.

[1] Late medieval French priests were called "sire" (*dominus*), just as late medieval English priests were called "Sir."

[2] ADSM G 5273, Saint-Sauveur: "Johannes magnart excommunicatus pro judicato xlij s vj dt contra dominum guillermum tellier presbiterum commissarium execucionis defuncte johanne mesengnel de ij^{da} septembris … Idem magnart aggravatus pro judicato dicte somme xlij s vj dt contra eundem tellier de xvij^{a} septembris … Idem magnart reaggravatus pro hujusmodi judicato contra prefatum tellier de prima octobris." Entries are easily located by year under the rubric for each parish in the nonpaginated register.

Ecclesiastical jurisdiction

The distant origins of church courts lie in the "fraternal correction (*fraterna correctio*)" and "evangelical denunciation (*denunciatio evangelica*)" demanded by the Gospel (Mt. 18:15–17): "Moreover if thy brother shall trespass against thee, go and tell him his fault between thee and him alone: if he shall hear thee, thou hast gained thy brother. But if he will not hear thee, then take with thee one or two more, that in the mouth of two or three witnesses every word may be established. And if he shall neglect to hear them, tell it unto the church (*dic ecclesiae*)." One might depart from the Authorized Version and here translate *ecclesia* as assembly. In any case, these procedures were aimed to encourage peaceable settlements among Christians and to ensure that their disputes did not come before heathen judges: Paul asked (1 Cor. 6:1, 6): "Dare any of you, having a matter against another, go to law before the unjust, and not before the saints?" and further lamented that "brother goeth to law with brother, and that before the unbelievers" rather than before the "saints." The third-century *Didascalia apostolorum* likewise admonished believers "not to bring [a dispute] immediately before a tribunal of pagans."[3] The shift away from "Christian law (*lex christiana*)" as alternative dispute resolution (ADR) and toward its judicialization pivoted on the preeminent role of bishops within the assembly (*ecclesia*) of believers. This is evident as early as the *Didascalia*: "be mindful, bishops, not to sit in judgment too quickly, lest you be forced to condemn someone; rather admonish them and make peace among them before they come into court." Then, as judge, "if it shall indeed be found that some believers come to litigation, you [the bishop] should entreat them to make peace."[4] "*Dic ecclesiae*" was thus understood relatively early to mean "tell the bishop," the supervisor (*antistes*) and spouse of the local church.

The legalization of Christianity by Constantine I's Edict of Milan (313) opened the door to the enforcement of arbitrated agreements in the bishop's tribunal (*episcopalis audientia*). Theodosius I's declaration of Christianity as the Empire's official religion (380) made possible an even greater role for bishops by assimilating the political community to the community of those baptized in the orthodox, Catholic faith.[5] Later Roman

[3] Cited in Paul Caspers, *Der Güte- und Schiedsgedanke im kirchlichen Zivilgerischtsverfahren. Eine kirchenrechtliche Untersuchung über das Wesen der episcopalis audientia* (Düsseldorf: Triltsch-Verlag, 1954), 9.

[4] Cited in Caspers, *Der Güte- und Schiedsgedanke*, 9.

[5] Theodosius's Edict, Codex Theodosianus XVI, I.I.2 beginning "Cunctos populos ..." was taken as the first law of Justinian's Codex (1.1.1).

law gave bishops competence over clergy and church property, the right to supervise schools and the care of prisoners, the right to challenge the decisions of imperial officials and to appeal to the emperor against them, and the right to hear cases by delegation.[6] The senatorial bishops of late antiquity, who administered towns and acted as royal officials, must have been able to exert considerable force by throwing their personal influence and the threat of exclusion from the community behind their efforts as arbiters. The rhetoric of concord and peaceable settlement nevertheless survived down to millenium, when, as Laurent Jégou has observed, bishops documented the resolution of disputes so as to showcase a process of amicable concord and to conceal any coercion: "the restitution of a usurped property became a donation, the abandonment of illegitimate claims an act of piety, the admission of guilt an act of humility, punishment a penance." In this way, by emulating the merciful Christ and by mobilizing their worldly status, bishops were doubly mediators: "mediators among men, they averred themselves capable of mobilizing their social and political capital to drive rivals towards negotiation and peace; mediators between God and men, they invested their decisions with spiritual significance by submitting them to God's protection."[7] Legislation and judgment were intimately connected with pastoral concerns, and not only because bishops had a role in each. As Patrick Wormald has argued, some Anglo-Saxon legislation is better understood as a type of sermon or

[6] On the early history of the *episcopalis audientia*, see Giulio Vismara, *Episcopalis audientia: l'attività giurisdizionale del vescovo per la risoluzione delle controversie private tra laici nel diritto romano e nella storia del diritto italiano fino al secolo nono* (Milan: Società 'Vita e Pensiero,' 1937), "Ancora sulla 'Episcopalis audientia' (Ambrogio arbitro o giudice?)," *SDHI* 53 (1987), 53–73, and, *La giurisdizione civile dei vescovi (secoli I–IX)* (Milan: Giuffré, 1994); Vratislav Busek, "Episcopalis audientia, eine Friedens- und Schiedsgerichtsbarkeit. Zugleich eine Auseinandersetzung mit Vismara, Episcopalis audientia," *Zeitschrift der Savigny-Stiftung für Rechtsgeschichte, Kanonistische Abteilung* 28/59/72 (1939), 453–492; Caspers, *Der Güte- und Schiedsgedanke*; Walter Selb, "Episcopalis Audientia von der Zeit Konstantins bis zur Nov. XXXV Valentinians III," *Zeitschrift für Rechtsgeschichte* 84 (1967), 162–217; Francisco José Cuena Boy, *La 'Episcopalis audientia'* (Valladolid: Universidad de Valladolid, 1988); Maria Rosa Cimma, *L'Episcopalis Audientia nelle costituzioni imperiali da Constantino a Giustiniano* (Turin: Giappichelli, 1989); W. Hartmann, "Der Bischof als Richter nach den Kirchenrechtlichen Quellen des 4. bis 7. Jahrhunderts," in *La giustizia nell'alto medioevo (secoli V–VIII)* (Spoleto: Centro italiano di studi sull'alto medioevo, 1995), 805–840; John Lamoureaux, "Episcopal Courts in Late Antiquity," *Journal of Early Christian Studies* 3 (1995), 143–167; Robert Parker, *Contra potentium iniurias: The Defensor Civitatis and Late Roman Justice* (Munich: C. H. Beck, 2001), 195–229; A. J. B. Sirks, "The *episcopalis audientia* in Late Antiquity," *Droit et cultures* 65 (2013), 79–88; in brief, Prodi, *Una storia*, 29–57.

[7] Laurent Jégou, *L'évêque, juge de paix. L'autorité épiscopale et le règlement des conflits entre Loire et Elbe (milieu VIIIe–milieu XIe siècle)* (Turnhout: Brepols, 2011), 478. Similarly, documents or objects denoting property transactions were kept with relics upon altars or in cathedral treasuries: Michael Clanchy, *From Memory to Written Record: England 1066–1307* (Oxford: Blackwell, 1993; 1st ed. 1979), 154–162, 254–260.

pastoral exhortation than as efficacious law-giving.[8] The same might be said for portions of Carolingian capitularies.

After the millenium, European bishops held considerable powers of jurisdiction, having gained feudal jurisdiction as lords over their vassals and seigneurial jurisdiction over their peasant subjects. This is evident in the twelfth- and thirteenth-century interpretation of late antique laws on bishops' arbitral sentences. The law *Episcopale iudicium* of Justinian's Codex (1.4.8) provided that: "judgment by a bishop is approved for all who choose to be heard by priests, and we command that their judgments be respected as yours, from which there is no appeal. Lest the episcopal decision be without effect, it is to be executed by our officials." In the Middle Ages this law, then located at Cod. 1.7.9, was accompanied by the *authentica* or loose translation of a Greek constitution subsequent to the Codex,[9] *Si quis litigantium*: "If any of the litigants should appeal the decision within ten days, then the local magistrate will examine the case: and if he should find the judgment founded, and confirm it by his own sentence, and execute the judgment himself, then appeal from his sentence is permitted. If, however, the bishop judged at the Emperor's command or in virtue of a judicial commission, between any persons whomsoever, appeal is to the Emperor or to him who issued the commission." Whether or not the Latin *Authenticum* was transmitted to Italy in the sixth as opposed to the twelfth century,[10] this translated abridgment of Nov. 123 c.21 conveys how the twelfth-century glossators reinterpreted a law originally providing for episcopal judgment of cases concerning clerics into a justification for episcopal judgment of any matters that litigants brought before them.[11] Bishops could accordingly wield a twofold civil jurisdiction, by litigants' choice when they sat as spiritual judges and with respect to their temporal subjects when they sat as secular judges.

By the millenium many bishops were at once lord and pastor.[12] Whether the Bishop of Mainz, lord of a vast territory, or the Bishop of Le Puy, lord

8 Partick Wormald, *The Making of English Law: King Alfred to the Twelfth Century. Volume I: Legislation and Its Limits* (Oxford: Blackwell, 1999).

9 Tammo Wallinga, "*Authenticum* and *authenticae*: What's in a name? References to Justinian's Novels in Medieval Manuscripts," *Tijdschrift voor Rechtsgeschiedenis* 77 (2009), 43–59.

10 Wallinga, "Authenticum *and authenticae*," 45.

11 For the Greek text, C. E. Zachariae von Lingenthal, *Imperatoris Iustiniani Novellae quae vocantur constitutiones extra codicem* (Leipzig: Teubner, 1881), Const. XLV, III: 310–311.

12 Lange, "Birth"; Jean-François Lemarignier, "De l'immunité à la seigneurie ecclésiastique: Les 'territoires coutumiers' d'églises en Île-de-France et dans les régions voisines d'après les diplômes des premiers Capétiens (987–1108)," in *Études d'histoire du droit canonique dédiées à Gabriel Le Bras*, 2 vols. (Paris: Sirey, 1965), 1: 619–630; Reinhold Kaiser, *Bischofsherrschaft zwischen Königtum und Fürstenmacht: Studien zur bischöflichen Stadtherrschaft im westfränkisch-französischen Reich im frühen und hohen Mittelalter*

of a tiny territory, bishops often stood at the summit of two jurisdictional hierarchies, at the head of the clergy and the Christian people of their diocese and at the head of their vassals and lay subjects. In the case of lordship and vassalage, the fiefs given in return for homage established a jurisdictional relationship. In the case of the Church, the pursuit of reform tended to emphasize that the Church was a jurisdictional hierarchy culminating in a legislating, monarchical pope. Gregorian emphasis on the Church's autonomy from the *saeculum* and on the distinctiveness of the clergy from the laity served to drive apart lay and ecclesiastical justice in terms of personnel, procedure, case material, and punishment. From the millenium ecclesiastical power was understood to operate in two manners, to flow through two different channels: the power to judge (*potestas jurisdictionis*) and the power to administer the sacraments (*potestas ordinis*).[13] Jurisdictional power flowed downward from the "vicar of Christ" to his delegates. With respect to the sacramental power common to all priests in virtue of their participation in the sacrament of holy orders, by the fourteenth century extreme papalists had come to assert that even bishops exercised their sacramental power in virtue of papal commission rather than by apostolic succession, since the pope was the source of all powers and the "universal bishop."[14] This papal dominance was manifested by judges' delegate, churchmen whom popes from the twelfth century had commissioned to try specific cases locally. Judicial power was, however, usually wielded by "ordinary judges," principally bishops but also chapters, capitular officials, archdeacons, rural deans, and abbots (or abbesses, one of whom we shall encounter in Chapter 3), in the case of monasteries whose territories had been exempted from the jurisdiction of the local ordinary or bishop. Appeals rose from deans to archdeacons, archdeacons to bishops, bishops to the appropriate metropolitan, and from archbishops to Rome or to a judge delegate, or directly (*omisso medio*) to the pope or judge delegate. Nicholas of Lyra's fourteenth-century gloss to Matthew 18:17 consequently explains the

(Bonn: Rohrschaft, 1981); Olivier Guyotjeannin, *Episcopus et Comes: Affirmation et déclin de la seigneurie épsicopale au nord du royaume de France (Beauvais-Noyon, Xe-début XIIIe siècle)* (Geneva: Librairie Droz, 1987); Jan K. Bulman, *The Court Book of Mende and the Secular Lordship of the Bishop: Recollecting the Past in Thirteenth-Century Gévaudan* (Toronto: University of Toronto Press, 2008).

[13] Laurent Villemin, *Pouvoir d'ordre et pouvoir de juridiction: Histoire théologique de leur distinction* (Paris: Editions de Cerf, 2003).

[14] Michele Maccarrone, *Vicarius Christi: Storia del titulo papale* (Rome: Facultas Theologica Pontificii Athenaei Lateranensis, 1952); on mandates: Laurent Mayali, "Procureurs et représentation en droit canonique médiéval" *Mélanges de l'École Française de Rome* 114 (2002), 41–57; on the pope's *potestas administrationis*: Michael Wilks, *The Problem of Sovereignty in the Later Middle Ages: The Papal Monarchy with Augustinus Triumphus and the Publicists* (Cambridge: Cambridge University Press, 1964).

phrase "tell it unto the church": "that is, to the prelate through public denunciation: and then must the witnesses be introduced to establish the facts of the case, which led to the brother [in Christ]'s previous, private correction."[15] Of the last clause of the Gospel passage, "but if he neglect to hear the church, let him be unto thee as an heathen man and a publican," Lyra remarked: "that is, be he cast out from the other believers through excommunication and ecclesiastical censure." Evangelical denunciation and fraternal correction intersected with the power of the keys, founded on Matthew 18:18: "Verily I say unto you, whatsoever ye shall bind on earth shall be bound in heaven: and whatsoever ye shall loose on earth shall be loosed in heaven," through the procedures of church courts.[16] These passages were understood to provide a basis for prelates' capacity to judge and to assign spiritual penalties in judgment.

By the early thirteenth century in most places, not the ordinary but his so-called judge or official (*officialis*) judged.[17] The bureaucratized tribunals that administered the justice of bishops, archdeacons, and other holders of jurisdictional power are therefore called officialities. The official, to whom bishops or other holders of ecclesiastical jurisdiction had confided the power to judge cases concerning clerics or ecclesiastical property and matters concerning participation in and exclusion from the sacraments, could be substituted by or supplemented by additional auditors. As many different prelates possessed judicial power within a given late medieval diocese, church courts proliferated. Within the late medieval diocese of Paris the bishop, the cathedral chapter, the archdeacons of Paris, Josas, and Brie, and the abbots of Saint-Germain-des-Prés, Sainte-Geneviève, and Saint-Denis had their officials dispensing justice

[15] "Dic ecclesiae. Id est, praelato per denunciationem publicam: et tunc sunt testes inducendi ad facti probationem, qui prius fuerunt inducti ad fratris secretam correptionem."

[16] Like the translators of the Authorized Version, many medieval listeners (in accordance with popular Pelagianism) probably understood the future perfects of this passage as simple futures such that prelates opened and closed the gates of Heaven rather than revealing what God had already established: "Amen dico vobis, quaecumque alligaveritis super terram, erunt ligata et in coelo: et quaecunque solveritis super terram, erunt soluta et in coelo."

[17] Even though officials are attested at Amiens as early as 1178, at Beauvais in 1179, at Rheims in 1182, and at Mainz in 1209, Olivier Guyotjeannin states that "l'officialité classique, dans le domaine de la juridiction gracieuse – le contentieux nous est pratiquement inconnu – n'a pu opérer dans des conditions régulières que peu avant 1220" cited in "Juridiction gracieuse ecclésiastique et naissance de l'officialitè à Beauvais (1175–1220)," in Michel Parisse (ed.), *À propos des actes des évêques: Hommage à Lucie Fossier* (Nancy, Presses universitaires de Nancy 1991), 295–310. See too, for Germany, Louis Carlen, "Zum Offizialat von Sitten im Mittelalter," *Zeitschrift der Savigny-Stiftung für Rechtsgeschichte 90, Kanonistische Abteilung* 46 (1960), 222–238. See too Paul Fournier, *Les officialités au Moyen Âge* (Paris: E. Plon, 1880), Pommeray, Lefebvre-Teillard, or Beaulande.

and ratifying contracts. Not far away at Pontoise the Archbishop of Rouen had an official for those territories of his diocese subject to the Parlement of Paris. In the diocese of Grenoble, there were two diocesan officials, with an *official foraine* judging cases from rural deaneries belonging to the duke of Savoy. The Bishop of Hildesheim likewise had a separate officiality at Brunswick for the territories of its duke.[18] Archbishops sometimes had separate officials for their diocesan and their metropolitan jurisdictions. These judges were the gatekeepers to the sacraments, because the faithful who sought security in this world and salvation in the next were members of the institution organized in terms of a jurisdictional hierarchy that could open and close the gates of Heaven.

Yet, even as the post-Gregorian Church sought to differentiate ecclesiastical lordship from worldly lordship, bishops retained their secular jurisdiction, forcing jurists to justify the coincidence of two conceptually distinct hierarchies in the same person. In France, an ordinance of 1287 aimed to keep the hierarchies distinct by ensuring that the bishop's justice as diocesan and his justice as secular lord be administered by different personnel.[19] There are indications as late as the fifteenth century that bishops' secular and ecclesiastical jurisdictions were not always so neatly separated: in 1434, a man who was both the secular and ecclesiastical subject of the Abbess of Montivilliers was excommunicated for failure to testify before the abbess's lay judge; a few years later the Bishop of Nantes excommunicated one of his temporal subjects in what was originally a tenurial dispute.[20] The French canonist Cosme Guymier (†1504) therefore observed that, when examining whether to appeal a case to a parlement or to an ecclesiastical superior:

> One must consider the quality in which [a clergyman] judged. Thus if a cleric judges not as an ecclesiastical judge but as a lay [judge], there is then no appeal to a bishop, as [there would be] from an ecclesiastical [judge] ... Since the bishop holds feudal jurisdiction of a secular prince, there is no appeal from him to the archbishop but rather to the secular prince who conferred the fief.[21]

Guymier's response glosses over a crucial difficulty of the medieval solution, in that ecclesiastical tribunals judged civil cases, and not just those

[18] Gerhard Schrader, "Die bishöflichen Offiziale Hildesheims und ihre Urkunden im späten Mittelalter (1300–1600)," *Archiv für Urkundenforschung* 13 (1935), 91–176.

[19] AN J 945 no. 119, or Isambert, II: 678.

[20] Guillaume Enguerrand was twice excommunicated during Lent 1434 by the Abbess of Montivilliers for failure to testify before her seneschal, a temporal officer, in the Pleas of Rouelles, a temporal court: ADSM G 5271, Rolleville; for the Nantes case, see Lange, *First French Reformation*, 91–93.

[21] Cosme Guymier, *Pragmatica Sanctio cum Concordatis. Cosme Guymier Clarissimi Senatus Parisiensis. Consiliarii solennis et eruditus Commentarius ad Pragmaticam Sanctionem* (Lyon: Benoît Bonnyn, 1532), 157r.

concerning clerics. It was acceptable that the bishop-duke of Langres have an ecclesiastical tribunal in his capacity as bishop and a secular tribunal as duke of Langres, but what if the former court heard "mixed" cases that touched on both spiritual and secular matters?

The question, of course, concerned what exactly was spiritual and what was secular, particularly in matters of property and of contract. Church courts could claim a broad competence because so many cases potentially involved a clergyman, church property, or morality in some way. Broken contracts implied, as we shall learn below, perjury, whereas "real" disputes concerning property rather than persons (as their origin in the Latin noun *res* or object and the derived adjective *realis* suggests) raised the questions of what sort of jurisdiction church courts had over church property, including tithes, for instance, and whether or not, as suggested by the glossators' interpretation of late antique imperial legislation, church courts could judge property disputes brought to them by layfolk. Property rights could be claimed against a person, in which case they were personal, or against a piece of property, in which case they were real. Issues of legal title tended to be personal, giving rise to civil litigation for damages against the donor or the seller. Issues of possession were real, giving rise to civil litigation for reinstatement with the disputed piece of property or the disputed revenue-stream. Debts could be personal or real. Larger debts secured on property were real. In Paris, even at the end of the sixteenth century, the owners of property-based annuities (*rentes*) in arrears could sue the new owner of the property on which the annuity had been secured. Smaller debts, written and unwritten obligations were personal. By 1500 in the Paris region, increasing numbers of contracts obligated the body of the debtor without an express clause of "obligation of body and property (*obligation corps et biens*)."[22] The obligee could be imprisoned should he fail to pay. In church courts, contracts rather obligated the soul, often through a clause providing for excommunication in case of default. Because late medieval French church courts had only the barest jurisdiction over real property, judging matters of title rather than of possession,[23] the question remained of whether they had territorial jurisdiction over contracts concerning the movable property of layfolk. Were personal actions against laymen or laywomen in church courts an illicit infringement of lay justice?

The answer to that question shifted over the period of this study. Just as the Gregorian reforms of the millenium had helped to distinguish

[22] Claustre, *Dans les geôles*, 243–309.

[23] R. Naz's articles on "possession en droit canonique" and "en droit français" are brief and clear: *Dictionnaire du droit canonique*, R. Naz (ed.) (Paris: Letouzey et Ané, 1949–1965), VII: 44–67, esp. 54–58.

ecclesiastical from lay justice, so late medieval reforms aimed to restrict the scope of ecclesiastical tribunals to matters concerning clerics (*ratione personae*) and to sacramental or religious matters concerning layfolk (*ratione materiae*). Late medieval monarchs contested ecclesiastical competence over layfolk (in personal actions) and over real property (in real actions). In France, from the fourteenth century royal officials argued that ecclesiastical judges had no power over the bodies of layfolk or over the possession of land.[24] Victory was slow to come: still in 1387, when the Archdeacon of Paris threw a Parisian merchant into the Chapter of Paris's prison for a debt of 200 *francs* (200£t) and refused to litigate in a royal court, the king's solicitor in the Parlement of Paris had to argue that "the said archdeacon had no power to arrest or to detain our subjects, above all our lay subjects, in the town of Paris";[25] still in 1451 was it argued before the Parlement of Toulouse that "the Church cannot judge cases concerning real property, because it has no territory; moreover, possession is a matter of fact and thus an ecclesiastical judge cannot award possession in a case involving layfolk."[26] Such arguments reflected a manner of conceiving personal, real, and mixed actions based on canonically inflected interpretations of Roman law that centered on the question of whether or not bishops had "a territory," that is, the question of whether they had territorial jurisdiction.[27]

The lack of clarity about the nature of ecclesiastical jurisdiction was possible in that the Church's jurisdiction was and was not territorial. Ecclesiastical provinces, dioceses, archdeaconries, rural deaneries, and exemptions were defined territorially, just like parishes. Gratian's *Decretum* provided that subjects were to be tried by the ordinaries of their domiciles (C.3 q.6 c.2): "an accused person is not to be tried except within his own court," while implying that (C.3 q.6 c.3) "where the crime is admitted, there shall the case be tried." The abbesses of Montivilliers

[24] François Olivier-Martin, *L'assemblée de Vincennes de 1329 et ses conséquences. Étude sur les conflits entre la juridiction laïque et la juridiction ecclésiastique au XIVe siècle* (Paris: A. Picard, 1909); Jean-Pierre Royer, *L'Église et le royaume de France au XIVe siècle d'après le "Songe du Vergier" et la jurisprudence du Parlement* (Paris: LGDJ, 1969); Jean-Louis Gazzaniga, *L'Église du Midi à la fin du règne de Charles VII (1444–1461) d'après la jurisprudence du Parlement de Toulouse* (Paris: Éditions A. et J. Picard, 1976); Patrick Arabeyre, "Les deux justices. Les deux pouvoirs. La production doctrinale des juristes méridionaux sur les rapports entre justice ecclésiastique et justice royale, de Bernard de Rosier à Guillaume Benoît (deuxième moitié du XVe siècle)," *Les justices d'Église: Cahiers de Fanjeux* 42 (2007), 373–397; Lange, *First French Reformation*.

[25] Cited in Claustre, *Dans les geôles*, 324.

[26] Gazzaniga, *L'Église du Midi*, 247.

[27] Peter Landau, "Zum Ursprung des 'Ius ad Rem' in der Kanonistik," in Stephan Kuttner (ed.), *Proceedings of the Third Annual Congress of Medieval Canon Law: Strasbourg, September 3–6, 1968* (Vatican City, 1971), 81–102; Conte, "Gewere"; Lange "Birth"; idem, "Droit canon."

seized this last justification to excommunicate nonresidents for breaking contracts passed in their territory. Yet while ecclesiastical jurisdiction was defined territorially, it was not competent in all matters concerning all persons within a given territory. As the canonist Panormitanus (†1443/5) noted (of X.2.2.8): "the Church has no territory except with respect to clerics."[28] In other words, ecclesiastical jurisdiction was only territorial or comprehensive over the clergy of a given area. Within its circumscription, an officiality exercised personal jurisdiction over members of the clergy and casual jurisdiction (that is, in certain cases) over members of the laity.

What were these cases? Bernard Lauret (†1495), professor of canon and civil law, *avocat du roi* and then first president in the Parlement of Toulouse, discussed these in his popular work, *Cases in which a secular judge can arrest a cleric without fear of excommunication*, which decisively invoked the principle that bishops had no territory sometime after 1491.[29] Lauret argued that "according to the former laws, bishops had no territory and thus did not execute their own sentences. Temporal judges executed their sentences, according to Cynus and Baldus in the law *Episcopale*."[30] Cynus of Pistoia (1270–1336/7) and Baldus de Ubaldis (1327–1400), had raised the question of whether or not bishops had a territory with reference to the previously mentioned law *Epicopale iudicium* and authentic *Si quis litigantium*. Cynus permitted ecclesiastical judges to rule on civil matters submitted to them, but observed that there was no appeal from such an arbitrative sentence. He also provided that civil magistrates had to command the execution of an ecclesiastical judgment.[31] Baldus clarified Cynus's rationale with respect to the law *Episcopale*: "the sentence of those who do not govern a territory, like the regents and rectors of universities and (some say) bishops according to this law, is to be executed by him who governs a territory," because, "concerning jurisdiction, a bishop had no territory assigned to him according to this law."[32] One could therefore appeal an episcopal sentence to a secular court, when the bishop judged a temporal matter.[33] Late medieval judges could draw two conclusions from these commentaries: first, bishops had no territorial jurisdiction as bishops, which is to say that they had no jurisdiction over real or property matters except

[28] Cited in Lange, "Birth," 139.

[29] On Lauret, see P. Arabeyre, J.-L. Halpérin, and J. Krynen (eds.), *Dictionnaire historique des juristes français, XIIe-XIXe siècle* (Paris: PUF, 2007), 472–473, and Arabeyre, "Les deux justices."

[30] Cited in Lange, "Birth," 140.

[31] Cynus ad Cod.1.7.9, cited in Lange, "Birth," 140 n.41.

[32] Baldus ad C.1.7.9, cited in Lange, "Birth," 139 n.38.

[33] Baldus ad auth. Si quis, cited in Lange, "Birth," 139 n.39.

as delegates of secular authorities; second, and consequently, one might appeal putatively temporal cases to lay judges.

For this reason, at least in customary France, excommunications for debt appear to have originated mainly in unwritten or privately recorded personal obligations, rather than notarized or authenticated real, property-based obligations. This reflected both regimes of landholding in the part of France governed by customary law and the manner in which debt came before church courts. In first place, in the regions of my case studies, the plain of the Beauce around Chartres, the Paris basin, and Upper Normandy at the mouth of the Seine, real property devolved not by testament but by customary succession and marriage contract. As soon as France's nascent *coutumes* became visible in the historical record, real property was governed by the conventions that emerged within a given territory through the negotiations of the territorial ruler, local lords, and peasants.[34] Real property was litigated in seigneurial courts, as were real obligations burdening that property. In the area around Montivilliers, such jurisdictions had two faces: *plaids à héritage* recorded property transfers and litigation over real obligations, whereas *plaids à meuble(s)* dealt with transfers of and litigation concerning movable property, primarily large, mercantile debts such as the equipage of commercial enterprises from Norman ports. Much credit that did not involve real property or concerned small amounts appears to have escaped either registration by a notary or tabellion or authentification by ecclesiastical or lay justice.[35] Furthermore, because real property devolved by custom, it did not come before church courts during the execution of testaments that concerned movables. In second place, church courts could claim competence over personal debts either via the *condictio ex canone* (X.1.35.1)[36] against indebted clerics or via the *denunciatio evangelica* by which layfolk

[34] Customary law becomes visible earlier in the territories of stronger regional magnates, such as Normandy or Anjou, in which public authority did not devolve or devolved late to the castellans. Elsewhere, it comes to view toward 1200 as it crystallizes through the action of royal provosts responsible to the judicial sessions of the king's council that would in the following century become the Parlement of Paris: Paul Ourliac, "Législation, coutumes et coutumiers au temps de Philippe Auguste," in R.-H. Bautier (ed.), *La France de Philippe Auguste: Le temps des mutations* (Paris: Éditions du CNRS, 1982), 471–487. The classic on the geography of customary France is Jean Yver, *Égalité entre héritiers et exclusion des enfants dotés: Essai de géographie coutumière* (Paris: Sirey, 1966).

[35] Laëtitia Renault argues that notaries in late medieval Upper Normandy did not yet play their early modern role of intermediaries in private credit markets: "Tabellions et crédit dans les campagnes normandes au XVe siècle. Quelques hypothèses," in Arnoux and Guyotjeannin, *Tabellions*, 121–143.

[36] The canon *Antigonus* provides that: "Aut inita pacta suam obtineant firmitatem, aut conventus (si se non cohibuerit) ecclesiasticam sentiat disciplinam. Universi dixerunt, pax servetur, pacta custodiantur." The edition of the Correctores Romani there quotes in margin Panormitanus: "iudex ecclesiasticus providet servanti pactum contra non servantem." On Panormitanus's models, Laurentius Hispanus and Johannes Teutonicus,

denounced the sins of other layfolk, in this case the breaking of a promise made implicitly before God.[37] A defaulter has broken faith, as we still say in accordance with references to "lesion" or "breach of faith (*fidei lesio*)" in the records of English church courts. The fundamental principle was that "the Lord wishes there to be no difference between our word and an oath" (C.22 q.5 c.12).[38] Defaulting debtors were sinners to be corrected by fellow Christians and, when that failed by the Church, they were contumacious perjurers deserving of excommunication. This changed at the end of the Middle Ages, when lay justice expanded its definition of what was "real" and territorial so as to contest ecclesiastical jurisdiction over contracts and when litigants took their credit disputes to secular courts. In the early modern period, secular authorities registered nonreligious contracts. Church courts then regulated sacramental life, registering baptisms and marriages, and disciplined the clergy.[39] By the eighteenth century it was even argued that church courts could not assign pecuniary fines except as alms, because fines were "real."[40] The end of excommunication for debt is not only the story of how expansionist, reforming lay jurisdictions redefined the competence of ecclesiastical tribunals but also of how litigants who took their credit disputes elsewhere participated in the reformation of ecclesiastical justice.

Contracts

Recognizing the place of ecclesiastical sanctions in minor credit demands a revision of the received history of contracts: minor, informal extensions of credit were treated as enforceable promises by church courts. The great legal historian Pierre-Clément Timbal asked at the beginning of his study of fourteenth-century contract law before the Parlement of Paris: "can one say that customary law, acknowledging that social life is impossible without respect for the binding character of a promise, was influenced by canonical teaching?" He responded: "it is impossible to

whom Peter Landau identifies as the creators of the *condictio ex canone* on the model of the *condictio ex lege* (Dig. 13.2), see Peter Landau, "Pacta sunt servanda. Zu den kanonistischen Grundlagen der Privatautonomie," in Ascheri, *Ins Wasser*, 457–474, at 467–469, and Durand, *Speculum iudiciale*, IV:2.

37 Hostiensis ad X.2.1.13: "iudex ecclesiasticus potest per viam denunciationis evangelice seu iudicialis procedere contra quemlibet peccatorem etiam laicum maxime ratione periurii vel pacis fracti," cited in Kenneth Pennington, "Panormitanus' Additions to *Novit ille* [X 2.1.13] in his Commentary on the Decretals," in Ascheri, *Ins Wasser*, 697–707, at 701 n.21.

38 "Dominus inter iuramentum et loquelam nostram nullam vult esse distantiam."

39 Prodi, *Una storia*; Bernard d'Alteroche, *L'officialité de Paris à la fin de l'Ancien Régime (1780–1790)* (Paris: LGDJ, 1994); Lange, "Droit canon," 253–261.

40 Lange, "Droit canon," 260.

resist serious doubt in the matter: only few decisions are known, even before church courts, that invoke the principle 'an action arises from a bare promise' (*Ex nudo pacto oritur actio*)."[41] Yet this is exactly what their practice demonstrates. The principle that "an action arises from a bare promise" was crucial not in that it led to definitive judgments but in that the allegation of a broken contract such as a dishonored sale on credit justified the citations and monitions that gave rise to procedural excommunications for debt. Debt cases almost never gave rise to a full canonical trial in which further proof would be demanded.[42] Timbal's answer also reflects the fact that the sentences in the few cases that came to final judgment are unmotivated, citing neither canonical principles nor precedents. Like the king of France's parlements, church courts judged on equity.[43] And it was equitable that a promise be enforced because, as the canonist Antonius de Butrio (1338–1408) wrote, "it is binding in the eyes of God."[44]

Contracts were a particularly weak spot in medieval French law and in medieval law more generally.[45] The formalism and archaism of available legal remedies did not parallel what must often have been a considerable diversity of contractual arrangements. In the high Middle Ages, scholars of canon law and scholars of civil or Roman law disputed whether a simple agreement was binding. From the twelfth century, canonists argued that "consent alone creates a binding obligation (*solus consensus obligat*)," as they did for marriage in the absence of diriment impediments to the formation of the marriage pact.[46] Civilians, in contrast, asserted that "an unformalized agreement does not create an enforceable obligation

[41] Timbal, *Les obligations*, I: 14.

[42] Truly exceptional are complex cases like the "duos processos sumptuosos" opposing Claude Bonvalet and Pierre Hanoude before the archidiaconal officiality of Paris: we know nothing of the first, as the relevant register is lost, but the second involved depositions, the examination of disputed account books, and monitions and excommunications in the commercial parishes of Saint-Nicholas des Champs and Saint-Jacques de la Boucherie: AN $Z^{1o}8$, f.9 to 77v, from December 23, 1499 through a final judgment on August 28, 1500 (NS), from which Bonvalet appealed, to his proctor's acceptance of the sentence on December 5, 1500 (NS), and request to pay court costs.

[43] Donahue, "Roman Canon Law," 699–708; On non-motivation, see Marguerite Boulet-Sautel's introduction to the *Questiones Johannis Galli* (Paris: Éditions de Boccard, 1946), and Bernadette Auzary-Schmaltz and Serge Dauchy, "Le Parlement de Paris," in A. Wijffels (ed.), *Case-Law in the Making* (Berlin: Duncker und Humblot, 1997), I: 199–223.

[44] Cited in Decock, *Theologians*, 129 n.477: "secundum ius canonicum pactum habet firmitatem, quantumcumque nudum, quia habet quantum ad Deum."

[45] Paul Ourliac and Jehan de Malafosse, *Histoire du droit privé, 1. Les obligations* (Paris: PUF, 1957), is incomparable; see too Jean-Louis Gazzaniga, *Introduction historique au droit des obligations* (Paris: PUF, 1992); David Deroussin, *Histoire du droit des obligations* (Paris: Economica, 2007).

[46] Landau, "Pacta."

(*ex nudo pacto non nascitur actio*)." Even though civil lawyers created the notion of "vestments (*vestimenta*)" so as to legitimate unwritten obligations before witnesses, and even though the Parlement of Paris other royal courts recognized "agreements (*convenances*)" before witnesses that fulfilled certain formal criteria, the Parlement seldom ruled on the basis of witnesses' testimony alone.[47] It is not clear that lower French courts were more open to executing verbal contracts than higher courts.[48] Regional variations in France's contract laws as well as strict standards of written proof and asymmetries of power made it difficult to recover some debts in secular courts. Litigation was costly, and the powerful could bend courts to their will through the sheer weight of social superiority backed up by economic force and ultimately by force of arms.[49] Promises of the sort that facilitated many daily transactions could be effectively unenforceable before lay courts.

The usury prohibition may have encouraged the use of simple promises for quotidian credit. It certainly channeled the demand for major credit into expensively drawn-up obligations of doubtful legality and morality with variously concealed interest: fictive sales of property (mortgages, *rentes constituées à prix d'argent*), repurchase agreements (*ventes à réméré*), letters of change, even leases of animals (*baux à cheptel*) that could be proven in a lay court without incurring accusations of usury.[50] With respect to minor credit, it would be cheaper and safer not to resort to a notarial device or sealed instrument, for, even as church courts' posterior jurisdiction over contracts expanded in the fourteenth century, procedural handbooks were careful to describe the minor debt that came before church courts as originating in purely gratuitous issues of credit. For instance, the only monition formula concerning debt in a formulary compiled in the Breton diocese of Tréguier around 1312 1315, prescribes restitution of unjustly taken interest on pain of excommunication, not restitution of the principal, implicitly distinguishing between

[47] Decock, *Theologians*, 109–114; Conte, "Gewere," revises the history of *vestimenta*; Timbal, *Les obligations*, I: 14–36, 394–396.

[48] Mathieu, *Les justices seigneuriales*, 218–220.

[49] Perhaps this was easier for French lords, who could simply fire their judges or give pensions to royal judges, than for English lords, who by this period had to "labor" jurors or those who might become jurors.

[50] On *rentes*: Schnapper; on *ventes à réméré*: Jean Bart, "La vente a réméré en Mâconnais (1450–1560, environ)," *Mémoires de la Société pour l'Histoire du Droit et des Institutions des anciens pays bourguignons, comtois et romands*, 23 (1962), 137–161; on *baux à cheptel*: Pierre Masson, "Le bail à cheptel d'après les actes notariés bourguignons du XIVe siècle jusqu'à la première moitié du XVe siècle," *Mémoires de la Société pour l'Histoire du Droit et des Institutions des anciens pays bourguignons, comtois et romands*, 2 (1935), 77–140. Like repos, *ventes à réméré* were a less than ideal response to a real need.

unjust interest-taking and just repayment.[51] Later formularies specify interest-free cash loans (*mutua*) or sales credit. The "Protocol of Letters in Church Courts" from Le Mans of 1429 provides a template, "letter of citation in a financial dispute (*litera citatoria in causa pecuniaria*)," for the recovery of money lent "as a cash loan (*ex causa mutui*)" through the assignation of a term within which to pay on pain of automatic excommunication.[52] Another template concerns the recovery of "money [given] for the purchase of some bread or other item (*quamdam pecuniam … occasione panis vel alterius rei*)."[53] The formulary of the monastic officiality of Corbie from *c.*1488 likewise provides a "recognizance of a debt (*instrumentum recognitionis debiti*)" of money lent "in a friendly loan (*ex amicabili mutuo*)."[54] At Montivilliers in the first third of the sixteenth century, a debt leading to excommunication could be recorded as a cash loan (*mutuum*) or a sales credit extended by a tavernkeepers, neither of which permitted the charging of interest.[55] Transactions on credit are uniformly described in the records of church courts as the charitable, interest-free obligation of one Christian to another.

As David Graeber's 5,000-year history of debt reminds us, it is a myth that medieval Europeans at any time lived in a noncommercial or nonmonetized society. Markets and money had different origins. In Deirdre McCloskey's pithy formulation, "markets had in fact already arisen anciently, in the twentieth and nineteenth centuries BCE, as Jean Baechler put it, or for that matter in the seven-hundredth century BCE outside the caves of people in southeastern Africa speaking full language."[56] The ever-present needs for exchange of even local commerce led to the creation of numerous solutions: in the words of Marshall Sahlins, "economic activity … [is] the expression, in a material register, of the values and relations of a particular form of life."[57] This was no less the case in medieval Europe than in "Stone-Age" societies: church

[51] BN NAL 426, 6, reflecting practice under St. Ives, diocesan official from 1284 to his death in 1303?

[52] BN Latin 10930, 7. See too Febvre II, 5–8.

[53] BN Latin 10930, 21v.

[54] BN Latin 17766, 2v.

[55] e.g., ADSM G 5273, 34v (1520): "Nicolaus lescolier nepos magistri nicolay excommunicatus pro judicato somme xii^{im} solidorum turonensium pro expensis taberne contra Johannem des preez in domo eiusdem facto de die xxvi^{a} mensis octobris." Apparently this reflected a credit crisis or the spendthrift habits of a well-placed young clerk, as Lescolier was excommunicated on fos. 34v and 35 for debts of 3s on August 3, 14s on September 21, 48s on October 4, and 7s 6d on January 19 (1521, NS).

[56] Deirdre McCloskey, "The Poverty of Boldizzoni: Resurrecting the German Historical School," *Investigaciones de Historia Económica – Economic History Research* 9 (2013), 2–6 at 3.

[57] Cited in McCloskey, "Poverty," 3.

courts did not offer the sole path to debt collection or renegotiation, though their activity structured all credit. In thirteenth-century customary France there were three types of written obligation: *lettres de baillie*, *lettres de chrétienté*, and *lettres scellées*. The first were drawn up by clerks, tabellions, or notaries and sealed by a royal bailiff. These are ancestors of later "authentic" or "public" letters. The second were sealed by a prelate's official. The last were sealed by a nobleman or woman and are the ancestors of "private" letters. The preponderance of *lettres de chrétienté* receded over the course of the thirteenth century as the proportion of acts passed before royal tabellions or notaries grew.[58] At Paris, to judge by the records of the Temple, the officialities of the bishop and archdeacon of Paris dominated the issuance of written credit until the 1280s, when the Châtelet, the lowest royal court of Paris, becomes predominant. Acts ratified before the officialities disappear after 1300.[59] In Normandy, letters of the officiality disappear from the cartulary of the Chapter of Coutances by 1330.[60] In fourteenth-century Paris the "sworn notaries" of the Châtelet dominated the market for written obligations. The city's various officialities continued to authenticate contracts, if rarely, into the sixteenth century. They did this through simple *lettres de chrétienté*, which required one to three monitions before a defaulter was excommunicated, through *lettres de nisi*, by which the borrower explicitly conceded that he would be immediately excommunicated should he default, and *a posteriori* through monitions with respect to verbal or unofficially drafted obligations.

Ecclesiastical tribunals enforced obligations ultimately on pain of excommunication. In contrast, after 1303 contracts passed at the Châtelet obligated either a borrower's property alone or his property and his person.[61] The operative distinction concerned rather authentic acts ("public" or "quasi-public" acts, if one assumes the teleology by which the early modern state became the sole enforcer of contracts) and private acts (*actes sous seing privé*, *cédules*, and so on). Debts authenticated by the notaries of the Châtelet or pursued by royal officials in the course of their duties led to 95 percent of imprisonments for debt in

[58] Zwalve, "*Sola scriptura*"; Mathieu Arnoux, "De la charte à l'acte de tabellion. Formes locales, régionales ou nationales d'une transition: Réflexions à partir du cas normand," in Arnoux and Guyotjeannin, *Tabellions*, 7–27; Bourlet and Claustre, "Le marché"; Ghislain Brunel, "Du tabellion de l'évêque au tabellion du roi. Le cas de la Picardie méridionale aux XIIIe-XIVe siècles," ibid., 85–98.

[59] Bourlet and Claustre, "Le marché," esp. 56.

[60] Arnoux, "De la charte," 14.

[61] The obligation *corps et biens* was officially generalized in 1566, though it had been assumed in practice since the end of the fifteenth century: Claustre, *Dans les geôles*, 193–195.

1488–1489.[62] Private acts had to be proved through a secular court's *juridiction contentieuse*, even if only through a judgment by default against a contumacious defendant, or had to be formalized before a notary or judicial officer. For this reason, the debts authenticated or disputed at the Châtelet were larger than those postpositively ratified or disputed before officialities: 71 percent of debts pursued before the Châtelet in 1488–1489 concerned amounts greater than 50sp, 47 percent amounts greater than 100sp, and 4 percent amounts greater than 1000sp. This means that 43 percent were for an amount between 5 and 50£p (6£ 10st and 62£ 10st), a range of 50 to 500 days' wages for a building laborer and 25 to 250 days' wages for a mason.[63] In comparison, the average before the archdiaconal officiality, where an authentic debt was not necessary to initiate an action, was only 6sp (7.5st) and the median 4sp (5st) in 1426–1439.[64]

The situation appears to have been similar elsewhere in Northern France, and across Europe, where from England to Germany church courts directed spiritual sanctions against recalcitrant debtors, often for relatively small debts. The Church was involved in economic affairs, and not only as a landowner or investor. Contracts were not purely economic devices, though they were that too. Because the market was not seen as disengaged from Christian ethics or society, the failure to pay loans and purchase or sales credit at once damaged the trust on which commerce functioned and revealed a lack of the charity that was supposed to animate relations within the Body of Christ. From the earliest examples in the late twelfth century, when popes threatened illustrious borrowers with excommunication and when officialities began to authenticate contracts, the practice spread downwards and outwards. Even as secular courts took over the authentification of written contracts, credit retained its religious valence. We can see this in the procedure of the *cessio bonorum*, one path to absolution. This procedure borrowed from Roman law permitted a debtor to be provisionally absolved of his debts by renouncing his property to his creditors.[65] The absolution did not wholly expunge the debt, for the *cessiones* recorded in the registers of the audiences of the archdiaconal officiality of Paris specify, in the exact words of Hostiensis – affirming the currency of learned jurists' teachings in officialities –, that the debtor in question was only absolved "until the

[62] Claustre, *Dans les geôles*, 164–165.

[63] Claustre, *Dans les geôles*, 211–213.

[64] The averages for Montivilliers were greater, though not so great as those at the Châtelet: the average was 71.5st and the median 30st in 1499–1530.

[65] Adolf Berger, "Encyclopedic Dictionary of Roman Law," *Transactions of the American Philosophical Society*, New Ser. 43:2 (1953), 387.

he should come to a fatter fortune."[66] Even after he had renounced his property and secured absolution, his creditors retained a claim to any future income or property. Should the absolved debtor escape his misery, he would perjure himself if he failed to make good his debt, once more breaking a promise made implicitly before God.

The formal aspects of excommunication for debt reveal a perverse aspect of late medieval economic life. The most minor and the most common debts incurred the most serious sanctions. The debtor who owed something like $1,000 in today's money, could be forced to mortgage his future to his creditors and ruin the credit with which he purchased his daily bread to preserve his access to the sacraments and to the hope of salvation that they guaranteed. Larger debts, those secured on real property, were instead brought before royal or other secular courts. For those, analogous in value and function to a present-day home mortgage, say, in the range from $500,000 to $2,000,000, a defaulting borrower might risk his property and possibly his freedom, but not his soul. Julie Claustre has demonstrated that imprisonment for debt at the end of the Middle Ages was most often for a day or two and at the creditor's expense in rooms graded according to the debtor's social position.[67] Excommunication for debt was, like rackrenting, sharecropping, and foreclosing on mortgaged property, a means of keeping the lower classes dependent on the rich. At the same time, it offered a cheap, effective remedy to poor creditors confronting long-standing debts or a pressing need for cash with which to pay taxes and tithes or seigneurial dues commuted to cash payments. In the passage cited in the introduction, Rabelais's Panurge described debt as that which bound the human race together in relations of charity. Excommunication for debt allowed creditors to break those relations and to reconstitute them as relations of malediction. Rather than praying for the health and welfare that would enable debtors to repay their debts, frustrated creditors could have them expelled from the community in this world and potentially in the next. Whether this reflected more malice or pressing need is inscrutable in the record.

Although at times it surely reflected both malice and pressing need, this situation shows how credit is, to use the psychoanalytic term reprised by Pierre Legendre, the "bond that separates."[68] According to Legendre's

66 e.g., AN Z^{1o}8, f.10 (Dec. 30, 1499); Hostiensis, Lectura ad X.5.40.23, cited in Helmholz, "Excommunication," 207 n.22: "Caveat quod satisfaciat cum pervenerit ad pinguiorem fortunam."

67 Claustre, *Dans les geôles*, 313–369; on the duration of stays in "*prison fermée*": 338–339; on the graded tariffs of *gîtes* and *gêolages*: 332–333.

68 Pierre Legendre, *Leçons IX: L'autre Bible de l'Occident: Le monument romano-canonique: Étude sur l'architecture dogmatique des sociétés* (Paris: Fayard, 2009), 224.

psychoanalytic interpretation of "the edifice of Romano-canonical law (*le monument romano-canonique*)," the West is certainly a "civilization of belief (*civilisation de croyance*)," though an etymological play might extend "*croyance* (belief)" into "*créance* (loan)" to emphasize that we are equally a civilization of credit. Between the period studied by Timbal, when lay courts provided only imperfect remedies for unwritten obligations, and that studied by Wim Decock, when confessors across Europe urged believers to honor "bare promises," – that is, from the fourteenth century to the sixteenth century – church courts upheld the binding character of voluntary obligations.[69]

Verbal and privately recorded debts were of course only one species of the voluntary obligations that together wove together the fabric of European society. Until the Council of Trent's much disputed decree *Tametsi*, a decree not received in France, in England, or even in the United States until 1908,[70] sacramental marriage was constituted by nothing more than the simple exchange of consent, to the despair of parents, families, and State authorities. Relations of vassalage and patronage were couched in terms of faith, fidelity, and trust, in terms of promises of loyalty. Villages and towns assiduously observed collective vows to saints invoked during droughts or epidemics:[71] from my window I see a chapel built on the hill above Hofheim am Taunus in exchange for the Virgin Mary's intercession to end a plague in 1666. There and at other shrines, to this day individuals fulfill vows when they climb stairs on their knees or deposit ex votos in recognition of cures. At the end of the Middle Ages, promises obliged everyone, even saints: the images of saints who failed to fulfill their obligations were humiliated. We can forget neither the young Martin Luther's entry into the monastery in response to a vow made to St. Anne during a thunderstorm nor his mentor Johann von Staupitz's actualization of God's implicit promise of salvation: "I'm yours, save me (*tuus sum, salvum me fac*)".[72] God too was bound by his covenant with Israel and by the promise of salvation manifested in the

[69] Timbal, *Les obligations*; Decock, *Theologians*.

[70] Gerald P. Fogarty, SJ, "The Historical Origin of the Excommunication of Divorced and Remarried Catholics Imposed by the Third Plenary Council of Baltimore," *The Jurist* 38 (1978), 426–433.

[71] William Christian, *Local Religion in Sixteenth-Century Spain* (Princeton: Princeton University Press, 1981).

[72] Heiko Oberman, *Masters of the Reformation: The Emergence of a New Intellectual Climate in Europe* (Cambridge: Cambridge University Press, 1981), 123–124, notes that for Staupitz the phrase "had ceased to be a petitionary prayer as it had been for his order's spiritual master Augustine, and had become a demand, claiming the faithfulness of God and holding him to his promise of election that he complete the process of salvation begun in justification." Even Luther's teachers could not escape the mentality of contract!

person of his son. If the pope could dispense from vows in virtue of his divine vicariate, a capacity sardonically likened by a French Franciscan to a magic password,[73] the Church otherwise enforced the binding character of voluntary obligations.[74] For, if promises could not be trusted, how could the blood and the wine become the Eucharist *ex opere operato* every day, everywhere, at the hands of every priest? How could God's offer of salvation be trusted? By enforcing simple unwritten obligations, church courts contributed to the confidence in contracts that underlay not just commercial trust but surely also the confidence in God and his Church that underlay religious faith, a point to which I shall return in the last chapter. In the end, was not the Eucharist Christ's "pledge of future glory" (*futurae gloriae … pignus*)?[75] Without binding promises, commerce was as unsure as salvation. If God had to keep his word, surely a parol contract obliged the believer?

Canonical procedure

Because the Church's jurisdiction over contracts operated through the threat of exclusion from the sacraments, it stood at the intersection of two modalities of ecclesiastical authority, jurisdictional power (*potestas jurisdictionis*) and sacramental power (*potestas ordinis*). The former flowed downward from the "vicar of Christ" to his delegates. The latter was common to all ordained priests. Through its monopoly of the administration of the sacraments, the hierarchical Church was the necessary intermediary for Christians seeking salvation. The first gatekeeper to the sacraments was the parish priest who administered baptism, the annual confession and the Eucharist required since 1215, and the *viaticum* or Last Rites that guaranteed a dying believer's chance at salvation. While the believer had to have recourse to a priest for the sacraments, both the priest and the believer had nevertheless to be authorized to administer and to receive them. The second gatekeeper was consequently the official or whoever had jurisdiction over a given territory. However, other officials could exercise their "extraterritorial jurisdiction" (*extranea jurisdictio*) with respect to crimes committed or promises made by nonsubjects

[73] Michel Menot, cited in Larissa Taylor, *Soldiers of Christ: Preaching in Late Medieval and Renaissance France* (Oxford: Oxford University Press, 1992), 124: "Don't you know the magic word (*mot de guet*)? The lord pope has dispensed us."

[74] Unless certain preconditions prohibited the contract's formation in the first place, such as the diriment impediments to marriage or the use of improper substances for the celebration of baptism or the Eucharist.

[75] From antiphon to the Magnificat in the office for Corpus Christi attributed to Aquinas. cp *Summa theologiae* III, 60, 3: "sacramentum est … prognosticum, id est, praenuntiativum futurae gloriae."

within their territories by barring them from the sacraments through excommunications *per placet*. Though this technically violated the principle that subjects be judged by the territorial ordinaries (*ordinarii locorum*), we shall see that this type of jurisdiction was particularly important for the spiritual subjects of the Abbess of Montivilliers in Normandy. Exceptionally, when the archdeacon, episcopal vicar, or the bishop himself inspected and judged parishes, priests, and parishioners on visitation, he became the gatekeeper. This was nevertheless relatively rare, despite the increasing frequency of visitations at the end of the Middle Ages.[76] Ordinarily, ecclesiastical judges wielded the power of the keys, excluding and including Christians among the number of the saved by denying access to the sacraments. Whereas the parish priest wielded this power in confession, in "the internal forum" or "the court of conscience," ecclesiastical judges wielded this all-important power in "the external forum" or "judicial forum" of ecclesiastical tribunals. The official captured the essence of the late medieval Church, a juridical organization in which, to use the words of Pierrette Paravy, receiving the Eucharist was less a sign of membership in a community than a "privilege" granted by a legal authority.[77] This is not to minimize the significance of penitential practice between confessors and believers, only to emphasize that we must not underestimate the influence of the Church's judiciary on late medieval sacramental practice.

Officials assigned fines, banished, and imprisoned, but it was their power to exclude from the sacraments that constituted the Church's most potent tool for social control. For those who sought salvation, and who believed it was only to be had through the Church, being barred from the sacraments was a fearsome threat. Death without the sacraments meant burial in unconsecrated ground in this world and damnation in the next, as well as a fine for the parish if an excommunicate were interred in consecrated ground. So, in 1446, the parishioners of Rives in the Dauphiné had to pay the diocesan official of Grenoble 50 florins (66£ 12s 8dt) to absolve their cemetery of its pollution by an excommunicate's body.[78] Such fines were not uncommon and, as we shall see

[76] See the charts in J. Michael Hayden and Malcom R. Greenshields, *Six Hundred Years of Reform: Bishops and the French Church, 1190–1789* (Montreal: McGill-Queen's University Press, 2005); also Marc Venard, "Les visites pastorales françaises du XVIe au XVIIIe siècle," in Marc Venard (ed.), *Le catholicisme à l'épreuve dans la France du XVIe siècle* (Paris: Éditions du Cerf, 2000), 27–63, based on the CNRS's ongoing *Répertoire des visites pastorales de la France* begun by Gabriel Le Bras, François de Dainville, Jean Gaudemet, and André Latreille.

[77] Pierette Paravy, *De la chrétienté romaine à la Réforme en Dauphiné. Évêques, fidèles et déviants (vers 1340-vers 1530)* (Rome: École française de Rome, 1993), 484, 751.

[78] Paravy, *De la chrétienté romaine*, 464–465; see too Adhémar Esmein, "Débiteurs privés de sépulture," *Mélanges d'archéologie et d'histoire* 5 (1885), 223–245.

in the next chapter, were counted with the proceeds from fines in the accounts of the Archbishop of Rouen. The Church's social control operated through the officialities in two ways: first, through litigation initiated by one believer against another, the so-called instance cases (*ad instantiam*), to which the promotor of justice or prosecutor could join himself as a litigant, as the king of France's *procureur* did in royal courts; secondly, through litigation pursued by the official in virtue of his office (*ex officio*) in response to rumor (*fama*) or vehement suspicion (*notorium*), the so-called office cases.[79] The model of the second path is the *inquisitio* or inquest, carried out by inquisitors commissioned ad hoc, a procedure later adapted by lay jurisdictions across the continent for its perhaps excessive efficacy. In this way, church courts facilitated a participatory social control: if your neighbor, for instance, suspected you of committing adultery with his wife, he could charge you before the local ecclesiastical tribunal. He could do this maliciously, but faced a fine if this were discovered. If he were correct, however, he was simply fulfilling his gospel duty to correct fraternally and to denounce evangelically obdurate sinners. Likewise, if the official strongly suspected you of adultery with your neighbor's wife – perhaps a rumor had come to his attention or perhaps he too wished you ill – he could charge you himself. In either case, you were cited before the official or his delegate by a summoner or *apparitor* to appear on pain of excommunication.[80] Litigation was not, however, the only path to social control.

Church courts (and courts more generally) exercised a not inconsiderable optional, "gracious" or "voluntary" jurisdiction over contracts and civil settlements. As a sort of a posteriori ratification of a verbal or private agreement, excommunication for debt illuminates an aspect of canon law and of the operation of church courts often absent from histories of canon law and church courts. Litigation or "contentious jurisdiction" looms large in works of legal doctrine. Ratification, arbitration, and "gracious jurisdiction" may have loomed larger in practice and may have provided a more effective, customary bridge between canon-law principles and social practice. A study of excommunication for debt shows us how the weight of canonical practice diverged from the focus of canonical doctrine. As the Roman jurist Paulus observed, an observation included in

[79] On canonical procedure, see Fournier, Pommeray, Lefebvre-Teillard, or the relevant titles of the Decretals and Durand's *Speculum iudiciale*.

[80] On summoners, see Louis A. Haselmayer, "The Apparitor and Chaucer's Summoner," *Speculum* 12:1 (1937), 43–57; Wunderli, "Pre-Reformation London Summoners"; and, in the absence of a comparable study, Esther Cohen's portrayal of the sergeants of the Châtelet evokes the mediatory and potentially predatory activities of Parisian summoners: *Peaceable Domain, Certain Justice: Crime and Society in Fifteenth-Century Paris* (Hilversum: Verloren, 1996).

the Liber Extra: "custom is the best interpreter of the laws" (Dig. 1.3.37, X.1.4.8). Canonical procedure was the crucial link between the practice of church courts and the words of jurists. With respect to the canon-law principle that contracts were to be honored, Innocent IV wrote that "he who observes not agreements shall be excommunicated"; Panormitanus that "agreements however informal are to be observed, otherwise the ecclesiastical judge is to aid him who observes the agreement against him who does not?"[81] Canon law ran close to the tracks of legislation, but canon law in practice was not canon law-in-books in any mechanical way. Patrick Wormald has pertinently observed of Anglo-Saxon law that "the development of English *law* from Alfred to Cnut and beyond did not run along the tracks that *legislation* marked out, but it did run in parallel with them. However constricted the ultimate effects of Mosaic or Roman example on the legislative tradition, its impact on the law enforced was profound."[82] Custom, in the sense of how litigants habitually chose to avail themselves of the possibilities of canonical procedure and how ecclesiastical judges habitually chose to implement legal provisions, mediated between canonical doctrine and the practice of ecclesiastical tribunals.

Church courts were not simply instruments of evangelization by citation. Rather, they operated in response to very real demand on the part of believers, particularly in civil matters. What those believers demanded was authentification of written and unwritten contracts! Excommunication may have remained a "medicinal or rehabilitative penalty (*poena medicinalis*)" in judges' eyes,[83] but for creditors it was also a tool of coercion. The precedent for using excommunication to coerce debtors was set at the summit of the Church. Around 1181, for instance, Lucius III asked the Archbishop of Canterbury to command his chancellor to make good on a debt to Bolognese lenders incurred during the Third Lateran Council on pain of excommunication; when in 1203 the Bishop of Utrecht disregarded his first excommunication by the papal legate for an enormous debt of 1,250 marks to Roman and Sienese bankers Innocent III commanded the Bishop of Liège to anathematize him with solemn liturgical curses and finally to depose him if he failed to pay; in 1262 Urban IV excommunicated the Archbishop of Salzburg

[81] Innocent IV ad X.1.35.1: "nisi pacta servet, excommunicabitur," cited at Landau, "Pacta," 470; Panormitanus ad X.1.35.1: "pacta quantumque nuda servanda sunt; vel aliter sic iudex ecclesiasticus providet servanti pactum contra non servantem."

[82] Wormald, *The Making of English Law*, 483.

[83] R. H. Helmholz, "Excommunication as a Legal Sanction: The Attitudes of the Medieval Canonists," *Zeitschrift der Savigny-Stiftung für Rechtsgeschichte, Kanonistische Abteilung* 68 (1982), 202–218.

for a debt of 4,000 marks, who consequently remained unburied for twenty-three years after his death in 1265.[84] High medieval popes did not hesitate to excommunicate even bishops at the request of wronged bankers. Nor did fourteenth-century papal collectors hesitate to excommunicate those who defaulted on their ecclesiastical taxes.[85] Papal actions stoked demand for excommunication for debt. Clever creditors who had heard papal excommunications and anathemas fulminated against prelates during the mass would have quickly grasped that such sanctions might be useful against their debtors. Ecclesiastical judges simply opened a papal prerogative to ordinary believers through the procedure of church courts.

We should not be surprised that church courts were "used" by layfolk, given subjects' skill at repurposing to their own ends (or even soliciting the construction of) the structures of lordship, State, and Church. Robert-Henri Bautier and Olivier Guyotjeannin have observed that officialities crystallized as bureaucratic institutions in the years around 1200 in response to lay demand for the authentification of written contracts with the seal of the officiality.[86] This demand for the *juridiction gracieuse* of church courts is manifested in the documentary record by "seals of jurisdiction (*sceaux de juridiction*)" or "seals for contracts (*sceaux aux contrats*)." Though the use of church courts to seal contracts swiftly declined at the end of the thirteenth century, the practice survived into the sixteenth century. In each of my case studies, and in probate inventories from late-fifteenth-century Paris, I have encountered monitions and contracts sealed in officialities retained as proof of otherwise unrecorded debts.[87] Monitions were warnings to pay on pain of excommunication, a penalty

[84] Lea, "Excommunication," 140–141. Original documents are at X.3.22.3; PL 215, *Innocentii III Opera omnia*, Regestum Lib. VI, ep. 215, vol. II, col. 242–243; Florian Dalham (ed.), *Concilia Salisburgensia* (Augsburg: sumptibus Matthei Rieger, 1788), 98–99.

[85] We await the forthcoming study of Amandine Le Roux on this point.

[86] Robert-Henri Bautier, "Origine et diffusion du sceau de juridiction," *Comptes rendus des séances de l'Académie des Inscriptions et Belles-Lettres* (1971), 204–221; Guyotjeannin, "Juridiction gracieuse."

[87] e.g., AN MC XIX 67 (inventaire-après-décès of November 18, 1493): "Item unes lectres de monicion de monsieur lofficial de paris datees du xxiiij[e] jour de fevrier iiij[xx] et xij/ signees Jo nourry/par lesquelles appert ... amoneste messire Richart de titreculle prebstre de paier/audit deffunct dedans trois jours apres estienne La somme de dix francs restans de la somme de xvj l et quatre solz parisis en laquelle somme ledit debteur estoit tenu envers Iceluy deffunct par lectres auctenticques soubz le scel de ladite officialite pour les causes contenues en icelles lesdites lectres demourez invent/au doz B"; ADSM 5273, Extranea jurisdictio, 1505 (OS), "Allanus buyllet clericus parrochie de buglisia juridictionis Rothomagensis excommunicatus per clausulam de nisi pro judicato ix s restantium ex maiori somma contra charlotam relictam executricem et causam ac jus successionis habentem deffunti jacobi de nerval dum viverit eius mariti de die xx[ma] mensis marcii ante pascha." No absolution is recorded in this last case.

contained in clauses of *nisi* that gave their name to one class of contract ratified by an officiality. Though officialities sealed fewer contracts at the end of the Middle Ages, their competence over contracts by no means disappeared. Anne Lefebvre-Teillard, Véronique Beaulande, Caroline Bourlet, and Julie Claustre have noted that this posterior jurisdiction of officialities over contracts authentificated elsewhere if anywhere constituted a popular and cheap recourse for creditors, particularly in the second half of the fifteenth century.[88] Whereas excommunication came immediately upon default in the case of letters of *nisi*, the posterior jurisdiction of church courts over verbal or privately recorded contracts came in response to citations and monitions.

Two entries from the register of excommunications of the archdiaconal officiality of Paris and two from that of the exemption of Montivilliers explain how excommunication for debt occurred. Under the rubric for the parish of Saint-Germain-l'Auxerrois in the year 1427 Yves Krahan, keeper of the register, noted that:

Excommunicatus est philibertus de ulmo pro johanne novel Re tasse

Excommunicata est jaqueta de bray alias la courtilliere pro symoneta la boularde contumacia R. tasse.[89]

Just after Easter (since the Paschal year had just changed and the register began on the Feast of the Purification of the Virgin), Philibert de l'Orme was excommunicated for debt at the request of Jean Nouvel by the summoner Raoul Tasse. Not long after, Jacquette de Bray alias la Coutellière was excommunicated at the request of Simonnette la Poularde for contumacy also by Tasse. At Montivilliers we get more information. We learn that in 1500 (NS) in the parish of Saint-Sauveur:

Guillelmus telier excommunicatus pro judicato xij s vj d contra martinam relictam deffuncti guillelmi ducis alias verette de die viij aprilis ante pascha anno nonagesimo nono

Parvus johannes celle excommunicatus pro judicato iiij s iij d contra chrestien durant de die xvj aprilis.[90]

Easter 1500 came on April 19. Guillaume Le Tellier was thus excommunicated for a debt of 12s 6dt to Martine, widow of the late Guillaume Le Duc alias Verette on the Wednesday before Palm Sunday. Petitjean Celle was excommunicated for a debt of 4s 4dt to Chrétien Durant on Holy Thursday.

[88] Lefebre-Teillard's chronology (187–190) of demand for separations of habitation parallels that for excommunications for debt.

[89] AN Z[1o]17. [90] ADSM G 5273.

We have here one excommunication "*pro re*," one "*pro contumacia*," and two "*pro judicato*." It is nevertheless possible that all four were consequences of a debt. The three different terms here are misleading, as there were essentially two causes of excommunication in matters of debt. Véronique Beaulande has recently demonstrated that the great bulk of excommunications were procedural.[91] In other words, the late medieval Church rarely sentenced guilty individuals to excommunication as a punishment, preferring fines and physical chastisement. Instead, the gravest of ecclesiastical sanctions – which deprived the believer of access to the sacraments and thus potentially of salvation – punished those who disobeyed court orders to appear in court or to pay a debt. One could consequently argue, as did the Parisian canonist Cosme Guymier (†1504), that there was really only one cause of excommunication: contumacy.[92]

Because breaking a simple promise was a cause of action in canon law, the first path to excommunication for debt was consequently through excommunication for failure to respond to a summons to appear before a church court on a specified day. Because many summons in disputes concerning minor debts would have been issued verbally in response to a verbal accusation, no record of the excommunication would ordinarily appear in the audience books of a court. The only traces would be in the registers of excommunicates and in the court's financial accounts. Financial accounts recorded the proceeds from fees for citations, as they did those from monitions and absolutions. Registers of excommunicates only recorded the plaintiff and the amount if the cited debtor failed to respond. Citations were short and cheap. A ten-centimeter scrap of parchment from the archdiaconal officiality of Paris provides a heavily abbreviated aide-mémoire for a verbal summons in what is presumably a case of debt claimed against a decedent's estate:

91 Beaulande, *Le malheur*, 185–211; Elsener, "Exkommunikation," esp. at 84 with respect to debt.

92 Guymier, *Pragmatica Sanctio*, 217, ad tit. De pignorantibus cultum divinum, v. abolentes: "Dic quod nemo potest se obligare sub pena excommunicationis vel interdicti per viam pacti: ita quod pactum sit sola causa immediata excommunicationis: quia nemo debet excommunicari sine cause cognitione et contumacia … sed bene potest se obligare sub pena excommunicationis: non quod pactum sit causa immediata excommunicationis: sed contumacia vera vel presumpta. ut quia debitor confitetur debitum coram iudice: et iudex extunc condemnat eum ad solvendum creditori: consentienti debitore fert excommunicationem sub conditione nisi satisfaceret in termino erit excommunicatus sine alia monitione. et hoc casu non ipsum pactum sed ipsa contumacia vera vel presumpta in non solvendo in tempore debito est causa excommunicationis." Guymier was concerned to justify the suspension of defaulting priests, because, if the cause of their suspension were the underlying contract, then those promising to pay on pain of suspension from divine service had effectively pledged their capacity to celebrate the mass. Priests would in effect have pledged their parishioners' salvation, so violating the decree of Basel.

Cite Jean [*blank*], executor of Jean de Croix, dwelling in the rue Saint-Honoré, in the court of the Lord Archdeacon of Paris on Wednesday at the request of Gérard Raundat, OP, to respond in justice/[*signed*] Germanet.[93]

The auditor who issued the citation did not know the surname of Jean de Croix's executor. Nor presumably did the Dominican who purchased the citation. The accusation that gave rise to the summons is not specified. The roughly contemporary Procedural Style of the officiality of Corbie provides a similar model:

The Official of Corbie greets all sworn notaries of our court. We command you to summon before us on such a day John N at the request of Peter N to respond to the charges. Given, etc.[94]

It is likely that summoners disposed of these small aides-mémoire after enrolling their result in a court book, register of excommunications, or perhaps a personal account book. Richard Helmholz has remarked on the absence of such mandates from the documentary record.[95] Surviving evidence indicates that such citations were issued verbally in response to verbal solicitations, certainly in minor cases. According to synodal statutes of *c.*1529 from Saint-Brieuc in Brittany, only in cases of debt exceeding 32s 6dt was a *libellus* or written statement of the case in articles required; in cases involving less than 10st the plaintiff had "only briefly (*etiam breviter*)" to explain the case to get a citation, and the judge could give a verbal sentence in such a case.[96] Judges sometimes noted the details of verbal charges on a single sheet declaring that "the plaintiff intends to prove before us ... (*Intendit probare coram nobis* ...)."[97] One could therefore be excommunicated for failure to respond to a citation stemming from a creditor's verbal accusation.[98]

93 Insert in AN $Z^{1o}4$: "Citetis in curia domini archidiaconi parisiensis ad diem mercurij/johannem [blank] executorem johannis decrois/commorantem in vico sancti honorati super requestam girardi/raundati ordinis fratrum predicatorum quod justum responsurus/germanet."

94 BN Latin 18371, f.7: "Et primo citacio communis: Officialis corbeiensis omnibus notariis curie nostre juratis salutem Mandamus vobis quatinus citetis coram nobis ad diem talem post festum tale infra primam nisi dies etc Johannem N contra Petrum N ad obicienda responsurum Datum etc."

95 Richard Helmholz, "Records and Reports: The English Ecclesiastical Courts," in Wijffels (ed.), *Case-Law*, 91.

96 BN Latin 1458, 116r-v: "(xiv) IN CAUSIS excedentibus valorem sive estimacionem unius mutonis auri veteris sommam triginta duorum solidorum et sex denariorum monete usualis valentium edatur libellus ... In aliis vero non excedentibus sommam decem solidorum sufficiat tangere causam petendi etiam breviter quid petitur et a quo ... (xvi) Item quod in minoribus causis dictam sommam decem solidorum non excedentibus semel solvendis valeat verbalis sententia absque scriptis."

97 Such a list of positions survives among the *minutes* of sentences at Montivilliers: ADSM G 5317.

98 Febvre II, 8 n.2.

Citations were cheap, costing 4 or 5dt in Northern France during the period studied, an amount to be compared with the daily wage of 1st paid to male and 6dt to female agricultural laborers in early-sixteenth-century rural Normandy.[99] If the worst accusations are to be believed, summoners sometimes sold blank citations or mumbled citations into their sleeves.[100] Although citations were supposed to be delivered to the person in question and failing that to his house, neighbors, or parish, many summoned individuals appear only to have discovered this when they were denounced as excommunicates during Sunday mass and asked to leave the church.[101] The statutes of Saint-Brieuc cited above imply abuses in reiterating that priests were to publish citations containing excommunications or other mandates during the mass, to certify this to the official, and to post the citations on a placard. Summoners were not to cite before sunrise or after sundown, and only in cases of pressing need to neighbors rather than to family members or domestics of the cited or excommunicated person.[102] Probably reflecting rather flexible fifteenth-century French practice, Cosme Guymier allowed for excommunications to be published "in the Sunday parish mass *or* in sermons, *or* in any other gathering frequented by the people, *or* by posting the sentence on a placard." He allayed the consciences of scrupulous summoners: "do not think that [the excommunication] must be known to all in the city; it is enough that it come to the notice of the neighborhood or greater part of those where it is published."[103] Failures of communication may have been common, and were obviously desirable to creditors, as an excommunication was a stronger bargaining chip than a citation.

The second path to excommunication was through failure to pay a debt authenticated by the court. Verbal, privately recorded, and even

[99] Guy Bois, *Crise du féodalisme* (Paris: Presses de la Fondation Nationale des Sciences Politiques, 1976), 107, figure from the Cistercian grange ofValasse. Women were generally paid half-wages.

[100] The Bishop of Orléans was accused of selling blank citations in 1496; in 1512 the Council of Toledo, forbade the issue of blank mandates. On this, see the conclusion of Chapter 3.

[101] Hostiensis, *Summa aurea* ad X.2, De contumacia, s.v. Qualiter deprehendatur: "mitti debet citatio ad domum vel ad ecclesiam propriam, vel citandus est procurator. Si ipsum dimisit, alias cognati, vel affines de quibus est verisimile quod ipsum defendant." That this only concerned those who could not be found or who threatened to harm the summoner was probably generously interpreted.

[102] BN Latin 1458, "Modus exequendi citaciones," 114r-v.

[103] Guymier, *Pragmatica Sanctio*, ad tit. De excommunicatis non vitandis, v. Publicata, 247: "in civitate loco aut parochia excommunicati in publica missa populosa/vel in sermonibus/vel in alio actu frequentato per populum: aut per affitionem sententie in locis publicis ita quod facile transeat in notitiam populi ... non tamen intellige ut omnibus de civitate debeat esse manifestum. sed satis est quod transeat in notitiam vicinie seu maioris partis in qua actus geritur. sicut de notorio dicitur."

debts authenticated by a court but without clause of *nisi* could have been confirmed with a canonical monition or warning to pay on pain of excommunication. Creditors could purchase monitions for 4dt at Corbie at the end of the fifteenth century:

The Official of Corbie greets all notaries of our court. We command you to warn Pierre N that within five days he should pay Antoine N the sum of twenty sous etc for which he is obligated and ought to have paid before the interval specified in the letters of our court shall have elapsed. Failing that, we excommunicate him and you shall denounce him as having been excommunicated and faithfully certify us of this. Given etc.[104]

In Southern France, the underlying contract was likely to have been notarized:

The Official of Marseille etc to our beloved in Christ, chaplain So-and-So or his lieutenant, greetings. At the request of So-and-So of such a place, we wish and command you that on our behalf you should admonish Hugo So-and-So once, twice, thrice, and peremptorily, personally if you can find him at his house or publicly in church lest he pretend ignorance of this monition, that we, sitting in justice, by the tenor of these present letters warn him that … unless he pay to Peter So-and-So ten gold florins, which he owes in virtue of a sworn public instrument of the hand of Master So-and-So, notary, and exhibited to us in judgment, within six days of this monition … or otherwise amicably settles … [and] unless he shall appear before us at Marseille to allege good and just cause why he should not observe the previous … we shall proceed against him by sentence of excommunication as justice requires and his contumacy demands.[105]

In the North, Caroline Bourlet and Julie Claustre observe that "officialities validated many verbal or non-notarized debts of small value *a posteriori* through monitions, as did seigneurial courts."[106]

The posterior jurisdiction of church courts over verbal or privately recorded obligations came through the confession of debts before an

[104] BN Latin 18371, 55: "Monicio simplex: Officialis corbeiensis omnibus notariis curie nostre juratis salutem Mandamus vobis quatinus moneatis Petrum N ut infra quinque dies reddat et solvat Anthonio N sommam viginti solidorum etc inquibus eidem tenetur et solvisse debuisset Termino iam elapso prout in litteris curie nostre continetur Alioquin ipsum excommunicamus et excommunicatum denuncietis Et de hoc nobis fideliter rescripbatis Datum etc." As to cost, in the same (176): "De monicionibus … statuimus et ordinamus quod pro sigillo monicionis communis sigillum habebit duos denarios et scribus tantumdem Caveat tamen sigillifer ne sigillet aliquam monicionem quousque viderit aut sciverit recognitoriam litteram per prius sigillatam et grossatam." In practice, recognitory letters appear not to have been demanded for minor debts, though they may well have been destroyed upon payment or forgiveness of the debt.

[105] Roger Aubenas, *Recueil de lettres des officialités de Marseille et d'Aix (XIVe-XVe siècle)* (Paris: Auguste Picard, 1937), I: 26–28: "litera monitoria de observando juramentum."

[106] Bourlet and Claustre, "Le marché," 70.

ecclesiastical judge and through debts confirmed by his sentence. In the late-fifteenth-century civil register of the archdiaconal officiality of Paris, such recognizances were marked in the margin with "Oblig[ation]" or "Cond[emnation]." The obligation ostensibly came of the free will of the borrower, who agreed upon a payment plan with the creditor:

Today Jacques Jolin, farmer of Chennevières confessed that he owed Master Guillaume Le Lorrain, priest and curate of the parish of Saint-Pierre aux Boeufs in the city of Paris the sum on 12 *francs* 2sp on account of a true cash loan made many times over the past two years, which sum Jolin promised to pay, that is, 40sp by the Feast of the Assumption of the Virgin, 40sp by Martinmas, 40sp by the following Feast of the Assumption in the year 1478, and the rest on the following Martinmas on pain of excommunication etc. He was warned as required etc. and established his domicile in the aforesaid place. Paid by the creditor: 2sp.[107]

The condemnation came in response to a citation, when the borrower appeared in court and confessed rather than denied his debt and agreed upon term of payment with the creditor:

On the Saturday after the Feast of St. Mark 1477 Henri Planche, cited at the request of Luquin de Fouchères, plaintiff, confessed that he owed the amount contained in the plaintiff's petition and promised to pay before Pentecost.[108]

Both condemnations and obligations resulted in a verbal monition to pay on pain of excommunication. These short notices from late-fifteenth-century Paris omit the warning to pay on pain of excommunication or bury it in the "He was warned as required etc." Similarly, in a case of unpaid tithes at Chartres in 1415 the obligation to pay on pain of excommunication was not recorded.[109] However, obligations in the civil register of the diocesan officiality of Paris for 1384–1387 published by Joseph Petit in 1919 conclude "and he was thrice warned to pay on pain of immediate, retroactive excommunication (*et fuit ter monitus de solvendo sub pena excommunicationis*

[107] AN Z^{1o}4, f.7, "Oblig.": "Hodie Jacobus Jolin laborator apud chanveriacum confessus fuit debere magistro guillelmo de lorrano presbytero curato ecclesie parrochialis sancti petri ad boves in civitate parisiis summam duodecim francorum ii s p/Racione veri mutui per dominum creditorem eidem johanni facti diversis vicibus a duobus annis citra/quam summam promisit solvere videlicet quadraginta s infra festum assumcionem beate marie virginis/quadraginta solidorum in festo sancti martini/xl^{ta} s in festo assumpcionis inde sequenti anno lxxviii^{o} et residuum in sequenti festo sancte martini hyemali sub pena excommunicacionis etc Et fuit monitus ut in forma Et eligit suum domicilium in loco predicto/ii^{o} s/cred."

[108] AN Z^{1o}4, f.6v, "Cond.": "Hodie henricus planche citatus ... ad requestam luquini de fucheres actoris confessus fuit debere contenta in peticionem alias redacta/quam sommam promisit solvere infra festum penthecostes."

[109] ADEL G 816, 11v: "Mercurii post sanctum clementem ... [monicio, in margin] De J ponnette contra J le harengier reum monitus est de solvendo xxii s vi d pro decima in quatenorum vinee de tribus annis."

ex nunc prout ex tunc)."[110] The warning, so banal as to be omitted from later records, rolled the first, second, third, and peremptory citations into one. Beware the notary's "*et coetera*!"[111] In the case of written debts with clause of *nisi*, excommunication was immediate upon the arrival of the specified term of payment, for the official provided for immediate excommunication upon default through a judgment recorded "*pro judicato de nisi*."[112] In the diocese of Séez around 1500 the Official's formulary specified the inclusion of the clause: "unless (*nisi*) [the borrower] should satisfy his creditor with the specified sum within the specified term he shall be by us and by our authority excommunicated with no other prior monition."[113] Although this type of contract drove the institutionalization of officialities, letters "of nisi" grew increasingly rare over the last two centuries of the Middle Ages.[114]

Frequent excommunications "*pro judicato* [*summe*]" at the officiality of Montivilliers probably originate not in formal letters of nisi but in confessed obligations or summary judgments. At Paris, these are scattered throughout the late-fifteenth-century civil registers.[115] Such obligations

110 Joseph Petit (ed.), *Registre des causes civiles de l'officialité épiscopale de Paris, 1384–1387* (Paris: Imprimerie nationale, 1919), 294.

111 Auguste Dumas, "Dieu nous garde de l'"et coetera' du notaire," in *Mélanges Paul Fournier* (Paris: Recueil Sirey, 1929), 153–169.

112 For the last phrase, see Esmein, 238–240, citing G. Dupont (ed.), "Registre de l'officialité de Cerisy, 1314–1457," *Mémoires de la Société des antiquaires de Normandie* 30 (1880), 271–662.

113 ADO 1 G 35, f.15v: "Omnibus visuris Officialis Sagiensis salutem in domino notum facimus Ex die date presencium in nostra presencia personaliter constitutis Johannes de Rane de parrochia de N Sagiensis diocesis Qui sua mera ac spontanea voluntate non coactus gagiavit ac reddere et solvere promisit infra festum N honesto viro Johanni le Ralle curie nostre notario sommam decem librorum turonensium racione puri veri et legitimi mutui per dictum le Ralle sibi facti in peccunia numerata prout ipse Joannis N coram nobis confessus fuit et legitime recognovit Et promisit eamdem sommam x lt eidem Johanni le Ralle reddere et solvere termino antedicto Se et heredes suos ac omnia bona sua mobilia et immobilia presencia et futura quo ad hoc penitus obligando ac voluit et expresse consenciit ipse Joannes quod nisi satisfecerit de dicta somma infra dictum terminum sit a nobis et auctoritate nostra vinculo excommunicacionis innodari nulla alia monitione precedente Et nos hiis auditus dictum Jo N coram nobis presentem et consencientem in permissis juxta eius confessionem sentencialiter condempnamus et per presentes condampnamus ipsumque monimus primo secundo tercio et quarto ex habundanti unaque monicione canonica pro omnibus de reddendo et solvendo dicto Johanni le Ralle infra predictum terminum sommam antedictam ix lt racione qua supra Alioquin dicto termino elapso ipsum ex nunc prout ex tunc et ex tunc prout ex nunc decernimus et declaramus sentenciam excommunicacionis incurrisse In cuius rei testimonii Sigillum curia nre etc."

114 Mathieu Arnoux, "De la charte à l'acte de tabellion. Formes locales, régionales ou nationales d'une transition: Réflexions à partir du cas normand," in Arnoux and Guyotjeannin, *Tabellions*, 7–27; Bourlet and Claustre, "Le marché"; Ghislain Brunel, "Du tabellion de l'évêque au tabellion du roi. Le cas de la Picardie méridionale aux XIIIe-XIVe siècles," ibid., 85–98.

115 This was not the case in the 1420s and 1430s: a fragmentary list of citations and of condemnations giving rise to letters of *nisi* (or perhaps only verbal warnings *nisi*) was reused as a pastedown for the rear cover of AN Z[1o]17.

are virtually absent from the record at Montivilliers, however, apart from three folios of brief early-fifteenth-century obligations jotted at the end of a register of court business used between 1406 and 1485.[116] There are four reasons for this documentary absence. It may be that obligations were recorded in a separate, lost or discarded series of "registers of condemnations."[117] The second, more likely cause is that there was no systematic register of obligations and that documents were returned to the parties to be destroyed upon the cancellation of or payment of debts.[118] Thus was Sire Robert Toustain suspended in 1528 for "failing to return a contract and quittance to François Marcis."[119] The third cause is that many of the obligations that that gave rise to excommunications reflect debts either drawn up by a summoner or confessed to him, for summoners were often notaries of the officiality. Ecclesiastical notaries could be appointed with the capacity to pass contracts accompanied by a verbal monition to pay on pain of excommunication "as if they had been made in the presence of the said Lord Official."[120] Even lacking the monition, the defaulter on an obligation confessed to a summoner may have been excommunicated ipso facto. As Julie Claustre notes, reflecting the jurist

[116] ADSM G 5268, 167v-170v. e.g., 169v: "Simon thomas de espouvilla recognovit et confessus fuit debere et teneri johanni dez roques de dicta parrochia iij s t xxiij.a februarij [1410, OS]." This presumably came with a warning to pay on pain of excommunication.

[117] As in fourteenth century York: Swanson, *Church and Society*, 180.

[118] This common practice to prevent creditors from demanding double payment appears in synodal statutes: e.g., *Concilium Avenionense ... Anno Domini MCCCXXXVII celebratum*, in Mansi, XXV, 1094: "xxvii. De instrumenti debitorum soluto debito restituendis, et si apud debitores remaneant, cancellandis." It appears also in sentences for the restitution of documents (*in causa resitutionis scripturarum*): e.g., ADSM G 5274: "In nomine domini Amen In quadam causa restitutionis scripturarum ... inter ricardum mesegnel parrochie de mannevilletae jurisdictionis Rothomagensis actorem ex una et clementem viard de facto hugueti dyacre oneratum reum ex altera partibus Visis per nos actoris propositis / contestatione sive responsione rei quatuorque scripturarum petiis cuiusdam processus inter ipsas partes et coram decano sancti romani ventilati mentionem facientibus apud nos repositis / conclusionibus partium / aliisque ad causam facientibus mature pensatis / reo contumace / Dicimus atque decernimus nullo habito respectu ad declinationem fori / dictas quatuor scripturarum petias nobis exhibitas esse dicto mesegnel restituendas prout restitui sentenciamus ... Lata die lune xiiij^{a} Junij [1530]."

[119] ADSM G 5273, Saint-Sauveur, 1528: "Idem toustain presbyter suspensus a divinis pro judicato ob defectum tradendi et deliverandi francisco marcix litteram contractionis et exonerationis denariorum ... de die xx^{a} mensis decembris." Another priest had suspended Toustain for 6s 8dt earlier that year.

[120] e.g., ADY H 2161, 205-205v: on the front of the page is a commission of the vicar-general of the Bishop of Langres of 1503 permitting a tabellion and sworn notary of the officiality to ratify contracts outside of Langres "ac si in dicti domini officialis presentia acta et gesta fuisset"; on the reverse is a contract of 1503 by which a farmer promised to pay arrears of rent of 37£t to the Abbot of Saint-Michel above Tonnerre in two terms, for which he was "monitus viva voce et condempnatus auctoritate domini officialis lingonensis."

Paulus's prescription (Dig. 42.2.1) that "he who has confessed is as if convicted (*confessus pro iudicato est*)," "a notary's contract was considered to be equivalent to a judicial decision."[121] The fourth cause is that Northern officialities executed obligations sealed by royal and seigneurial tabellions (as Southern officialities executed notarized obligations) or recorded in private ledgers and bills when both parties appeared and consented and possibly even upon a creditor's request alone.[122]

The cited party rarely chose to contest the charges: in the early sixteenth century the officiality of Montivilliers issued three to five final judgments in debt cases each year against an annual average of 160 excommunications (of which 65 percent or 104, on average, were explicitly for debt).[123] The final judgments could reflect what appear to be verbal or privately recorded debts asserted in a *libellus* and proven through the testimony of witness and the plaintiff's oath on the Gospels, as in an early-sixteenth-century case concerning two debts, one of 34st and the other of only 5st.[124] Officialities could accept or reject the value of private bills (*cedulae*) or contracts (*obligationes*), though mostly on the basis of the testimony of the litigants and their witnesses.[125] Thus, the officiality of Corbie required that simple paper IOUs be acknowledged by the

121 Claustre, *Dans les geôles*, 191.

122 Petit, *Registre des causes civiles*, 484: Christophe d'Auxerre was excommunicated at the request of Colin de Grandchamp for an unpaid debt of 4fr 14sp (5£ 16s 10dt) authenticated by the Châtelet, the lowest level of royal justice in Paris, and for court costs of 15sp (18s 9dt). On June 19, 1387 Christophe came before the official of Paris with a payment plan, paying 12dp (15dt) for a conditional absolution.

123 Compare the register of excommunications from 1499 to 1530, ADSM G 5273, with the register of definitive sentences from 1507 to 1574, G 5274.

124 ADSM G 5317: (i) "In nomine domini amen. Cognito per nos decanum et officialem monasterijvillaris de quadam causa pecuniaria mota et pendente coram nobis inter honestum virum guillermum fourmeilly actorem ex una et johannem thiboutot armigerum clericum reum partibus ex alia viso libello a parte ipsius actoris contra dictum reum in scriptis tradito contestacione per dictum reum super contentis in libello dicti actoris negative facta testium a parte dicti actoris contra dictum reum coram nobis productorum et per nos examinatorum dictis et depositionibus concluso per nos in dicta causa de consensu dictarum partium et aliisque in processu dicti actoris coram nobis reposito contineri videntur que nos et animum nostrum tam de jure quam de facto movere possunt et debent mature consideratis attento juramento per nos et ex officio nostro eidem actori in supplementum probacionis delato et per ipsum actorem ad suum intentum coram nobis ad sancta dei euvangelia prestito asserentem dictum reum sibi fideliter teneri in sommam triginta iiij.or solidorum turonensium ex una et 5 solidorum ex alia pro causis libellatis per hanc sententiam nostram diffinitivam … pronunciamus dictum actorem sufficienter et legitime suam probavisse intencionem … ". It does not seem that this oath was the *iuramentum calumniae*.

125 ADSM G 5317: (ii) "In nomine domini Amen. In causa pecuniaria mota et pendente coram nobis decano et officiali monasterijvillaris Inter aluinum oursel actorem et exceptatum ex una et dominum guillermum le febvre presbiterum reum et excipientem ex alia partibus Visis per nos cedula seu obligacione eiusdem rei instante dicto

issuer to be valid proof of a debt.[126] The last sentence from Montivilliers (iii), accompanied by a monition, and probably the first sentence (i), reflecting an oath in court, would have entailed immediate execution upon default. Monitions accompanied at least some judgments in litigated financial disputes, although, like the warnings that accompanied recognitions or condemnations of debts at Paris, they may often have been omitted from the documentary record. Even so, true litigation remained an infrequent path to excommunication.

It is worth noting here that priests were first suspended from the capacity to perform divine service and only in second place excommunicated, with aggravation and reaggravation following. This clearly troubled some theologians and canonists, as it was condemned at the Council of Basel in 1435 for in effect pledging the mass and menacing the defaulting priest's parishioners with an interdict.[127] Down to 1530 at Montivilliers we find priests suspended in first instance and excommunicated in second

actore coram nobis Recognita peticione eiusdem actoris Exceptione eiusdem rei Contestatione dicti actoris ac recognitione et confessione illius facta super sua contestatione ad instantiam eiusdem rei Conclusionibus dictarum partium Aliisque in processu eiusdem rei contentis actore nichil apud nos producere curante Dicimus et decernimus dictam cedulam cassam et nullam declarari debere prout declaramus dictum reum ab impetitione actoris absolventes Condamnantes ulterius dictum actorem ad solvendum ipsi reo sommam quinque solidorum novem denariorum restantium ex obolo aureo in processu motu Et salvis eiusdem rei expensis Ipsarum taxatione nobis reservata/Lata die lune quinta novembris"; (iii) "... in causa pecuniaria ... inter magistrum petrum brilli presbiterum et guillermum de houllemare executores testamenti defuncti magistri joannis de houlemare dum viveret presbiteri actores ex una et joannem lheureus alias calles deffendentem ex alia ... visis per nos cedulam et obligationem dicti deffendentis coram nobis astantibus dictis actoribus recognita die lune xxvi mensis octobris novissime preteriti Rationibus et petitionibus dicti deffententis factis ad impediendum condemnationem contentorum in dicto cedula conclusionibus partium aliisque contentis in processu actorum deffendente contumace ... Dicimus et decernimus dictum deffendentem esse condemnandum prout condamnamus ad solvendum ipsis actoribus xl librarum turonensium Et ob deffectum solutionis litteram monitoriam decernendam esse prout etiam decernimus Salva tamen actione eiusdem deffendentis versus dictos actores super suis pretensis debitis Et rationibus eorundem in contrarium ... Lata die lune xj februarii millesimo quingentesimo xxvj°." The monition was apparently issued and ignored, as Lheureux was excommunicated for 10£t on September 26, 1527 (ADSM 5273, Harfleur). On proof of obligations generally, see Lefebvre-Teillard, *Les officialités*, 229–235.

126 BN Latin 18371, 78: "Acta judicialis super cedullam papiream [template with date of 1506]: Constitutis personaliter in judicio coram nobis ... Petro N actore una et Johanne N reo altera ex partibus Super eo quod dictus actor citari et evocari fecerat coram nobis ad dictam diem dictem Johannem ad cognoscendum vel negandum quandam cedullam papiream signo manuali ipsius johannes ut dicebat idem petrus signata necnon super contentis in eadem ... Quiquidem johannes visa et inspecta eadem cedulla recognovit quod ipsa erat proprio suo signo manuali signata"; on the *agnitio cedule*: Lefebvre-Teillard, *Les officialités*, 234.

127 Guymier, *Pragmatica Sanctio*, 215v-218v: "Abusum etiam illum cultui divino manifeste derogantem: quo nonnulli ecclesiarum canonici contrahentes debita sic se creditoribus

instance. Still in the sixteenth century did priests borrow by pledging their sacerdotal capacity.

The excommunications or suspensions resulting from citations, monitions, and letters of *nisi* gave rise to mandates that were transmitted to parish priests.[128] At the officiality of Montivilliers during the fifteenth-century, excommunications *per placet*, that is, concerning subjects of another ecclesiastical judge, were recorded in the form of a brief mandate to the excommunicate's parish priest: "To the parish priest of Saint-Jouen in the jurisdiction of Rouen: Martin Prévôt was excommunicated on Monday after Corpus Christi 1433 at the request of Guillaume Perrin alias Le Mouillé for a debt of 45st."[129] Parish priests were to read out the names of excommunicates during the vernacular prayers and announcements known as the *prône* or the bidding of the bedes that took the place of the contemporary homily during the parish mass and, in some places, to post the names on a placard. Late-thirteenth-century statutes of the diocese of Coutances specified that "on pain of excommunication every priest should have a chart or placard on which he write the names of his excommunicated parishioners, and for which causes, and how many times, and at whose request, as well as by whose authority each is excommunicated, and he should thus denounce the excommunicates on several days, even should nobody request this."[130] We might pause to consider the impact of the only vernacular section of the mass when it took shape as a laundry list of monitions and excommunications. The proclamation of crimes entailing automatic excommunication (generally those against churchmen or church property) quarterly or on Holy Thursday (hence the Bull *in coena Domini*) may not have differed greatly from priests' announcements in ordinary parish masses. Was there was time left over after the publication of excommunications and monitions for the explanation of the Pater, the Ave, or the Apostles' Creed? There may

obligare: ut nisi statuto tempore satisfaciant a divinis cesset officio abolentes et obligationem huiusmodi etiam in iureiurando firmata fit irritam decernentes."

128 BN Latin 18371, f.66: "De excommunicacionibus: Officialis corbeiensis curato vel presbitero tali salutem Mandamus vobis quatinus sentenciam excommunicacionis a nobis latam in Petrum N pro debito occasione et ad instantiam Johannis N palam presencie et solemniter in plena ecclesia vestra immonetis aut immonari faciatis et de hoc nobis rescripbatis si opus sit Datum etc."

129 ADSM G 5270, 77: "Presbitero sancti jovinij jurisdictionis Rothomagensis martinus prepositi excommunicatus est pro judicato xlv s contra guillermum perrin alias le moullie lune post eucaristie xpi [1433]."

130 Guillaume Bessin (ed.), *Concilia Rotomagensis provinciae accedunt diocesanae synodi pontificium epistolae …* (Rouen: François Vaultier, 1717), *Concilia Constantienses*, 543–559, at 545: "XV. De excommunicatis … Jubemus, sub pena excommunicationis injungentes, ut quilibet Sacerdos schedulam habeat vel cartam ubi nomina excommunicatorum parochiae suae scribat, et ex quibus causis, et quot, et ad quorum instantiam, necnon cujus auctoritate singuli sunt excommunicati, et singulis diebus sic eos excommunicatos denuntiet, licet à nemine requisitus."

not always have been, as the curé of Varces in the Dauphiné complained to his bishop in 1446 that he spent most of his time at mass reading citations and sentences of excommunication.[131]

Cases moved quickly if the initial sanction proved ineffective. The late-fifteenth-century style of the officiality of Corbie provided that if the specified person failed to pay "within five days … we would excommunicate him and declare him to be such."[132] The formulary of roughly 1529 from the Saint-Brieuc prescribes that the cited debtor was to be automatically excommunicated in "minor" cases, presumably the cases under 10st that did not require written citation, after eight days; in major cases, after fifteen days. Ten days after the excommunication, if the excommunicate remained obdurate, his sentence was to be "aggravated." Ten days after that, his sentence was to be "reaggravated." Ten days after that, his family and tenants were to be interdicted or banned from the church.[133] In practice, the interval was often closer to a month, if not longer, between aggravations of a sentence of excommunication. After a year, obdurate excommunicates were liable to prosecution as presumptive heretics.[134] If this seems harsh, the admittedly late statutes of Saint-Brieuc did seek to mitigate the practice, forbidding excommunications for sums of less than 12dt and requiring that excommunicates be recorded and reported at diocesan synods.[135] Major cases of debt, greater than 32s 6dt, as well as those concerning exempt (i.e., clerical) persons, required more formal and careful procedures than debts concerning less than 10st, which could be judged verbally.[136] Generally, with the exception of documents sealed by the officiality, which were presumed authentic,[137] proof rested on a Christian's word – the word of the accuser, of the accused, or of witnesses.

131 Paravy, *De la chrétienté romaine*, 463–464.

132 BN Latin 18371, 55v.

133 BN Latin 1458, 121.

134 Elisabeth Vodola, *Excommunication in the Middle Ages* (Berkeley: University of California Press, 1986), 164–190. The *Établissements de Saint-Louis*, 1: 127 (Paul Viollet (ed.), *Les Etablissements de saint Louis accompagnés des textes primitifs et de textes dérivés, avec une introduction et des notes* (Paris: Librairie Renouard, 1881), II: 238–242), provided that secular courts could seize the property and persons of debtors excommunicated for a year and day, fining them 9£p upon their absolution (of which lay justice was to have 3£p); an edict of Charles V of 1371 provided for the seizure of excommunicates' property after a year: Isambert 5: 353–355. In England the writ of *significavit* provided for the arrest of excommunicates after a similar interval: F. Donald Logan, *Excommunication and the Secular Arm in Medieval England. A Study in Legal Procedure from the Thirteenth to the Sixteenth Century*, Pontifical Institute of Medieval Studies, Studies and Texts 15 (Toronto: PIMS, 1968).

135 BN Latin 1458, 127.

136 BN Latin 1458, 116r-v. The English do not always appear to have accepted the apparently common French practice of proceeding directly from verbal citation to automatic or verbal excommunication, challenging sentences *sine scriptis*: Helmholz, "Excommunication," 215.

137 e.g., BN Latin 1458, 119v.

Canonical procedure offered creditors a marvelous opportunity to recover or renegotiate their debts and to damage the credit of insolvent borrowers or capital enemies. Most cases seldom went further than the chain of citation or monition, automatic excommunication, and absolution. This was because all stages of canonical procedure cost money, the cost increasing with each stage toward trial. Citations were cheap. Monitions were cheap. The submission of libels detailing cases, the taking of testimony, and final or definitive judgments were less cheap. As today, most civil cases were settled or abandoned before final judgment. When someone excommunicated for debt was absolved, this could be recorded in court books with a marginal note specifying when and why he or she had been absolved or, more appropriately for a procedure that has left few written traces, simply by crossing out the relevant entry.[138]

The meaning of excommunication for debt

Excommunication for debt confirmed that credit was at once a moral, social, and economic quantity that reflected the state of one's soul, one's social status, and one's economic position. The fact that creditors could easily spend more than the value of the debt in question while seeking its recovery suggests that debt existed in a web of relations that were more than purely economic. Daniel Lord Smail has made a strong case that this displays the uncontrolled, subrational hatred common in late medieval society.[139] It is nevertheless possible that this testifies to rational but angry litigants seeking to ruin the credit and livelihood of delinquent borrowers, a reasoned if potentially expensive goal. Church courts made attaining this goal easier, as Edward Iacobucci has observed that "the reputational sanction that the wrongdoer bears from certain conduct will generally *depend* on the size of the legal penalty associated with that conduct."[140] Because one can scarcely imagine something more important to

[138] The same is true of a relaxation or temporary absolution, which could be accompanied with marginal reference to a "retrusion" into excommunication if the debtor failed to make a scheduled payment: e.g., AN Z[1o]17, 101v: "Relassacio. Officialis etc salutem in domino mandamus vos quatinus sententia excommunicacionis aggravacionis et reaggravacionis in talem pro contumacia seu pro re ad instanciam talis quas huic ad quasimodo de consensu et voluntate talis etc relaxamus et suspendimus relaxatum et suspensum dicto tempore durante a nos in ecclesiis vestris palam et publice nuncietis Dato termino domini etc Die etc."

[139] Smail, 17: "I would insist only that the pursuit of grudges, rather than a reasoned preference for rationality or a desire to achieve an outcome, was the chief motive for the investment [in lawsuits]"; a sentiment nuanced at 20: "This is why people in late medieval Marseille pursued grudges and vendettas: to protect their good names," which could well be an economically, socially, and politically rational pursuit.

[140] Edward Iacobucci, "On the Interaction between Legal and Reputational Sanctions," *Journal of Legal Studies* 43:1 (2014), 189–207, at 191.

believing Christians than salvation, excommunication was an outstanding means of damaging the credit and of wounding the honor of one's capital enemies. It mobilized the sanctions of the Church to repair the wounded credit of a lender, seller, or other aggrieved party. To take an example from late medieval Paris, Agnesot, wife of Jean de La Court, paid 4dp (5dt) in court costs on July 31, 1385 to have the cleric Jean Sassier sentenced to pay her 2 *francs* (2£ 8st) for calling her a whore in court. On August 19, now authorized to act independently in court by her husband, she paid 8dp (10dt) to have Sassier warned that he could be excommunicated for failing to pay his debt. On August 28, Sassier promised to pay. On September 2, Agnesot proposed to have Sassier excommunicated for nonpayment. The official convened them for further arguments, for which she and he each paid 8dp (10dt). On September 4, the official ordered him to pay within the week or be excommunicated. On September 26, Agnesot came to court to confirm that he had paid.[141] Sassier was not excommunicated. For 20dp (25dt), Agnesot repaired her credit and received 2fr (2£ 8st). This is reflected the fact that someone's credit was then a comprehensive, nonnumerical evaluation of his or her place within society. Because society was the Body of Christ, Christians were bound – and sought – not only to perform the duties requisite to salvation, minimally, annual confession and reception of the Eucharist, but to preserve the bonds of charity with their fellows. Charity could manifest itself as forgiveness, particularly of insults or quarrels, or as charitable, interest-free extensions of credit. Conversely, those who refused to satisfy creditors acted uncharitably, warranting their exclusion from the Body of Christ. Persistence in this uncharitable behavior resulted in the aggravations and reaggravations of excommunication that marked the growing gravity of their sin. Whereas citations, monitions, and simple suspensions or excommunications were delivered personally or announced during the main Sunday mass, aggravations and reaggravations could be accompanied by liturgical curses that deployed the incantatory power of magical words and actions.

Procedural handbooks or styles and collections of legal templates or formularies illustrate how the rituals marked the excommunicate's progressive exclusion from the religious and economic community. A simple excommunication passed without much ceremony. Having failed to respond to a canonical summons or to heed a monition, the delinquent was denounced as excommunicate at the Sunday parish mass and his name was entered into the list of excommunicates. If this failed to bring about the desired effect, the creditor or the official could

[141] Petit, *Registre des causes civiles*, 166, 177, 181–182, 184, 186, 194.

aggravate the sanction. Under its "rubric on excommunications," the 1474 Style of the officiality of the Abbey of Corbie provided an elaborate progression of ceremonial curses more elaborate than the progression of excommunication-aggravation-reaggravation. The first excommunication is a simple injunction to parish priests in a case explicitly of debt: "we command you to announce or to have announced the sentence of excommunication pronounced by us against Peter N for debt at the request of John N openly and solemnly in your church." The second enjoined the priest to repeat the sentence "as many times as you shall celebrate the divine office on Sundays, feasts, and weekdays," while ringing the churchbells and extinguishing candles. The third asked the priest to command that the obdurate excommunicate be shunned. The priest was to:

> forbid all your parishioners on pain of excommunication lest they should presume consciously to communicate with the excommunicate as long as he should remain under sentence of excommunication with respect to food, drink, the village oven, the mill, fire, water, socializing, chatting, working, selling, paying, sitting, walking, greeting him, entering his house, eating, drinking, selling or giving him bread, wine, meat, fish, or other of life's necessities, or any other act.

The fourth added that no work could be done for the excommunicate and that his family had to be shunned as well. The fifth – entitled "be they ruined (*confundantur*)" – provided that the "unrepentant (*animo indurato*)" man who "feared not the [power of the] keys (*non formidat claves*)" be denounced twice at vespers and thrice at mass with ringing bells, candles lit then extinguished, and the clergy prostrate. Tradesmen were commanded not to trade with him or his family.[142] A matter of debt, certainly a breach of the bonds of credit that bound individuals to each other, became a matter of "contempt of Holy Mother Church" and led to the exclusion of the excommunicate and his family from the community of those seeking salvation through Holy Mother Church, which was also the economic community within which the excommunicate subsisted.

The liturgical curses deployed against excommunicates were modeled after those once used to defend church property.[143] The forms survived into the sixteenth century, explicitly in matters of debt. The curse with candles trodden underfoot, described by Hostiensis as an episcopal prerogative, appears to have been practiced by archdeacons and abbots wielding the power of jurisdiction and by the priests of their territories.[144]

142 BN Latin 18371, 66–68.

143 Lester K. Little, *Benedictine Maledictions: Liturgical Cursing in Romanesque France* (Ithaca: Cornell University Press, 1993); Beaulande, *Le malheur*, 31–37.

144 Hostiensis, *Summa aurea*, ad X.5 De sent exc. v. Quot sunt species excommunicationis, 491v: "debent 12 sacerdotes episcopum circumstare et lucernas ardentes, id est,

These liturgical curses were designed to terrify, to shame, and to effect the death and damnation of the excommunicate. Two late medieval French liturgical handbooks make this interpretation of the extinguished candles irrefutable, both to historians and to anyone witnessing the ceremony: "as this light in my hands is extinguished, so be their eyes and lives extinguished."[145] The connection is explicit: the title of a "form of a letter of malediction" from Marseilles *c.*1490 recalls that the Middle-English verb *cursen* meant (as for the French *maudire*) "to excommunicate" into the sixteenth century, when one still spoke of the list of offenses resulting in automatic (*latae sententiae*) excommunication as the "Great Curse."[146]

That excommunicates were in contemporary parlance "accursed" or "*maudits*" emphasizes that summoners, ecclesiastical judges, and plaintiffs availed themselves of the Church's magical power to make spoken words and deeds efficacious. I speak of magic with respect to the terror of excommunication advisedly, for the word "ritual" does not do the conceptual work of the word "magic." The priest's announcement of an excommunication from the rood screen changed not just legal and sacramental reality but (as plaintiffs hoped and excommunicates feared) "real" reality, menacing the excommunicate with the death of his or her earthly body as well as his or her eternal soul. Excommunicates behaved as if they were terrified, either of being deprived of the sacraments or of the Church's curses (although this is not necessarily an either/or proposition ...): thus nearly 99 percent of the residents of the exemption of Montivilliers excommunicated between 1499 and 1530 are recorded as having been absolved. Moreover, doubts about using the term "magic" with reference to judicial and sacramental acts may dissimulate uncritical assumptions. From an anthropological, external, and analytical perspective, are not sacraments rituals that magically effect what are believed to be real changes through the performance of correct words and actions? Privileging sacraments or eucharistic transubstantiation as a

candelas in manibus tenere, quasi in conclusione anathematis, vel pro, id est, excommunicationis, q.d. excommunicatio erat ante hanc solennitatem, sed modo dici potest anathema proiicere debent in terram et conculcare pedibus 11 q.3 debent, et de hoc anathemate potest intelligi quod est mucro episcopalis 16 q.2 visis in fine. quia nullus potest excommunicare cum tali solennitate nisi episcopus sit." The liturgy of anathematization appears not to have been used for the first excommunication, which Hostiensis explained could be announced simply or solemnly, but for aggravations of the first excommunication.

145 Thirteenth-century theological collection of the Abbey of Cuissy: "et ainsint comme ceste chandoile est estainte de mes mains, ainsint soit estainte leur lumiere et leur vie"; late-thirteenth-century pontifical of Beauvais: "et sicut extinguntur he lucerne in oculis hominum, sic extinguatur lucerna eorum in perpetuum"; cited in Beaulande, *Le malheur*, 32.

146 Little, *Benedictine Maledictions*, 44.

type of magical transformation is to adopt an internal, Catholic perspective – a Counter-Reformation perspective, I might add, as Bob Scribner has shown.[147] Why should the priest's words of consecration be any more constitutive than a witch's curse, when the latter is believed to be effective? Why should they be any more constitutive than a judge's sentence, when the latter's words transform not just legal reality but reality, remaking the legal subject into a guilty object of punishment? Just as the sacraments were valid *ex opere operato*, so when all legal requirements were fulfilled did a tribunal's final judgment transform "Louis de Berquin, accused of heresy," into "Louis de Berquin, convicted heretic," resulting in his execution by fire.[148] Judicial formulas were close in form and in location to sacramental transformations: mandates of excommunication – *maledictions* in French and *curses* in English – were read out before the offertory at mass. The very terminology blurs magical and judicial formulas.

I concede that to speak of magic is to import the language of early modern scholarship into medieval territory. This is not unmerited, as recent scholarship suggests that we need not presume a spectacular break between "medieval" and "early modern" religious practice. Tom Brady has observed to me that the "present fashion among scholars of the Reformation is that the [Protestant] Reformation was a medieval event."[149] Heiko Oberman's medieval Luther, John Bossy's and William Christian's communal Christians, or my creditors and debtors inhabited a world in which there was a gradient of sacral or magical power, from sacerdotal and sacramental to illicit and this-worldly popular uses, from the Eucharist to blessed salt and even to the magic squares on scraps of paper that were fed to sick horses.[150] Along with holy water and blessed bread believers took

[147] Tyler Lange, "Revisiting the Legacy of Ernst Kantorowicz," *Sixteenth Century Journal* 42:4 (2011), 1003–1026, at 1024 n.82; Scribner, "Cosmic Order and Daily Life: Sacred and Secular in Pre-Industrial German Society" and "Ritual and Popular Religion in Catholic Germany at the Time of the Reformation," in R. W. Scribner (ed.), *Popular Culture and Popular Movements in Reformation Germany* (London: Hambledon Press, 1987), 1–16 and 17–47.

[148] AN U 419, 182r-185v, Arrêts and Sentences against Berquin, at 185v: "Consideratis considerandis maturaque inter nos deliberatione sepius habita et agitata CHRISTI nomine invocato per hanc nostram diffinitivam sententiam quam solum Deum pre oculis habentes in his scriptis fecimus NOS te Ludovicum berquin hereticum pertinacem et errorum iniquitatis filii Martini Lutheri eiusque sequacium defensorem judicioque seculari Relinquendum declaravimus et declaramus Et te judicio seculari potius legitimis contra hereticos pertinaces inditis et usitatis puniendum relinquimus."

[149] Personal communication, July 23, 2014.

[150] e.g., →S A T O R
A R E P O
T E N E T
O P E R A
R O T A S

home words and forms for their own use: after mass on the fourth Sunday of Lent 1583, Barbara Wilhalmin climbed onto the rood screen in the village of Hindelang in the Prince-Bishopric of Augsburg, and deployed the language of canonical malediction to refute an accusation of witchcraft when she called on her accusers to "give her their reply before God's tribunal in the Valley of Jehoshaphat, on the third or fourth day, or on some other day as it may please God, and for this they were summoned in the name of God the Father, the Son, and the Holy Spirit. Which order or summons she shouted once, twice, and a third time."[151] Barbara's appropriation of canonical procedure demonstrates a faith in the efficacy of the spoken word, which faith she shared with creditors who believed excommunications for debt to be effective and with the overwhelming majority of excommunicates who sought absolution. Pre-Reformation Christians did not misunderstand the priest who declared in the vernacular during a solemn excommunication: "just as this candle is extinguished by my hands, so may their light and their life be extinguished."[152]

The Provençal formulary provides that in cases of formal malediction or the aggravation of an initial excommunication the priest was to announce the excommunicate's pertinacity at mass. Then, "with acolyte, in surplice and stole, carrying a cross and holy water, he was go to the church door singing Psalm 108 to the end and throwing three stones from the church door in sign of the eternal curse that God placed on Dathan and Abiron, whom the earth swallowed alive."[153] According to the late-sixteenth-century statutes of the Norman diocese of Évreux, a coffin draped "as if there were a dead man to bury" surrounded by candles and a basin of holy water was placed before the rood screen. The excommunication was fulminated, the candles extinguished, the coffin asperged, and the congregation encouraged "to weep for the excommunicate as if he were truly dead."[154] This was a dry funeral, so to speak, seeking to utilize the same magical mechanism as those who inserted the names of their enemies into prayers for the dead. In the Southern French diocese of Périgueux, the instigator of the excommunication paid to bring a coffin to the church door. After Sunday's parish mass, the

[151] Wolfgang Behringer, *Shaman of Oberstdorf: Chonrad Stoeckhlin and the Phantoms of the Night*, H. C. Erik Midelfort (trans.) (Charlottesville, VA: University of Virginia Press, 1998), 89.

[152] See note 145.

[153] Aubenas, *Recueil de lettres des officialités de Marseille et d'Aix*, II: 57–58, which has *Deus laudem mean ne carceris* [recte *tacueris*] for the psalm.

[154] Jacques Éveillon, *Traité des excommunications et monitoires. Avec la maniere de publier, executer, et fulminer toutes sortes de Monitoire, et excommunications* (Paris: E. Couterot, 1672), 374–384.

priest came with two acolytes in liturgical garb to sing Psalm 108 while the church bells rang. They then burnt the coffin, each casting six stones at it. In the nearby dioceses of Vienne, Embrun, Grenoble, Avignon, and apparently those of Lyon and Augsburg, the ceremony similarly involved ringing church bells, extinguishing candles, overturning the processional cross, singing the response *Revelabunt celi* (based on Job 20–21), the antiphon *Media vita*, and Psalm 108, and throwing three stones from the church door.[155] *Revelabunt celi* cursed the sinner who rejected God based on Job 20:27–29: "The heavens shall disclose the iniquity of Judas [often rather 'of him (*eius*)' as in the passage from Job] and the earth shall rise up against him and his sin shall be manifest in the day of the Lord's wrath with those who said to the Lord God, 'Leave us, we do not wish knowledge of your ways.'"[156] In *Media Vita* the faithful appealed to God: "In the midst of life we are already in death,/From whom can we seek help except you, Lord,/Who on account of our sins is rightly angered?/Holy God, holy strong, holy and merciful Savior,/Deliver us not to bitter death."[157] In sum, at the paid request of a creditor or other offended party, the clergy launched curses designed to kill and to damn the debtor or other offender.

The chosen psalm, 108 in the Vulgate, 109 in modern editions, illuminates the whole ceremony. It is a counter-curse invoking Jehovah against an enemy:

> … Set thou a wicked man over him: and let Satan stand at his right hand.
> When he shall be judged, let him be condemned: and let his prayer become sin.
> Let his days be few; let another take his office.
> Let his children be fatherless, and his wife a widow.
> Let his children be continually vagabonds, and beg …
> Let the usurer (V *foenerator*, AV extortioner) catch all that he hath … (v. 6–11).

The debtor is to be identified with a "sinner" and "deceiver" (v. 2) to be cursed, while his creditor is to be identified with the "poor man with contrite heart" (v. 17), the "suffering poor man" with "anxiety in his breast" and "knees weakened from fasting" (v. 22–23). The creditor asks God to

155 Éveillon, *Traité des excommunications*, 378.

156 Cited from the University of Waterloo's Cantus database of Gregorian chant, where the text is found as early as 980 in a manuscript from Saint-Gall and as late as 1580 in an antiphonary from Augsburg, http://cantusdatabase.org/id/007543.

157 Little, *Benedictine Maledictions*, 237. This grouping of psalm, response, and antiphon appears in an early-sixteenth-century manuscript of liturgical music from Lyon: Fiona Shand, "A New Continental Source of a Fifteenth-Century English Mass," *Music & Letters* 88:3 (2007), 405–419, 406, n.3.

stand "at the right hand of the poor man, to save my soul from my persecutors" (v. 31). Use of this text puts the debtor in the place of persecutor, and his creditor in the place of the righteous, powerless poor man whom the Church was supposed to aid. No one could mistake who the victim was, for the Marseille formulary, like other formularies, announced that the object of the letter had been "excommunicated, aggravated, and reaggravated ... at the request of such a person from such a place."[158] With the invocation of Dathan and Abiron, swallowed alive into Hell for their revolt against Moses's priestly authority (Num. 16:25–30), the ceremony recalled the potential consequences of the Church's sanctions. These texts help us to make sense of a practice that is, to our sensibilities, a gross abuse. To wit, because "poor," powerless creditors had sought the Church's aid, excommunication punished a twofold insult to Christ's body: the debtor's perjury wounded another of Christ's members at the same time as his or her contumacy flouted the Church's authority.

The creditors who sought to exclude their debtors from Heaven were not usurers, neither in the record nor, it appears, in reality. Much of the debt disputed before church courts appears to have originated in the sales on credit that bridged the gaps of an economic year closely governed by the rhythms of the agricultural year. Plaintiffs were wounded parties, unpaid sellers or service-providers and defrauded purchasers rather than covert usurers. They were like the priest Mathieu de Oisy, who sought 46sp (55s 2dt) from Copin de Sarcelles for a gray horse sold on credit before the diocesan officiality of Paris in 1387, or the shepherd Thomas Berquignart, who sought 10sp (12s 6dt, of an initial 28sp or 35st) from Jean Aux Fèves of Drancy for keeping his ewes and wethers for two months before the archdiaconal officiality of Paris in 1494.[159]

Still, not everybody approved of excommunication in cases of debt. Each time that an excommunicate died unabsolved, thereby condemned to burial in unconsecrated ground and likely to eternal damnation, it could give rise to the impression that the Pre-Reformation Church was in effect selling its salvific magic to creditors. Yes, bishops (and creditors![160]) sometimes granted temporary absolutions so that excommunicates could make their Easter communion or so that their corpses could be buried in consecrated ground; yes, priests sometimes absolved excommunicates on their deathbeds.[161] Over the fifteenth century, however,

[158] Aubenas, *Recueil de lettres des officialités de Marseille et d'Aix*, II:58.
[159] Petit, *Registre des causes civiles*, 421; AN Z[1o]7, 201v.
[160] See the formula of providing for absolution until Quasimodo cited above, p. 68, n.138.
[161] Paravy, *De la chrétienté romaine*, 465, 483–484; e.g., BN Latin 10930, 12v–13: "Quo modo presbiter debet absoluere morientem in articulo mortis: Dominus noster episcopus X per suampiissimam misericordiam te absolvat Et ego auctoritate omnipotentis

more and more elite observers expressed their dislike of excommunication for debt. Jean Gerson (†1429) observed that when the power of excommunication founded on Matthew 18 was applied "to the defense of temporal property and authority, it introduces a great confusion into the Church, it leads to contempt and denigration of this most fearful evangelical censure, such that I have seen it to encourage not spiritual health but fatal snares for the souls of many."[162] Gerson's pastoral concern to discourage spiritual despair as well as contempt for the Church's sacraments reflects the difficult task of parish priests, who had to read out long lists of citations and excommunications during the only vernacular section of the mass, all the while repressing discord within their congregations and preventing excommunicates from falling away from the institutional Church. Pierrette Paravy's study of the late medieval Dauphiné illustrates both of these consequences: creditors accused debtors, whose curses they feared, of witchcraft, and in one case debtors accused a creditor of witchcraft; it further appears that frequent use of ecclesiastical sanctions in the Dauphiné encouraged a more aggressively separatist, anti-Catholic Waldensianism.[163] Even when the frequency of excommunications did not lead directly to heterodoxy, it could induce violent, bitter responses: at Pirton in the diocese of Lincoln around 1446, twelve men forced the summoner and his clerk to eat the writ of excommunication they were about to serve, for which most of them were appropriately excommunicated.[164] As such men likely still sought salvation, their attitude to the institutional Church must have been complex, to say the least. The sanctions designed to promote reverence for the Church's precepts and jurisdiction could as well fissure as unify the sacramental community.

dei et petri et pauli apostolorum eius et domini nostri pape Gregorii divini providentie pape xi in hac parte commissa ab omnibus peccatis tuis de quibus fuisti vos ore confessus et corde contritus eciam a sententia excommunicacionis si quam meministi steterit ut ignoranter et eadem auctorite et auctoritatibus quibus super do penam et culpam in quantum claves sancte matris ecclesie si extenduntur in nomine patris et filii et spiritus sancti amen.

Dispensatio ut corpus mortui excommunicati sepeliatur in terra sancta: Guido episcopus etc rectori etc si vobis constitit quod B tempore quo vivebat esset verus catholicus et quod dum in extremis laborabat signa penitencia apparuerit in eodem non obstante quod non recepit in extremis confessionem penitentie et eucaristie sacramentum super quibus tenore presencium nostre dispensamus corpus seu cadaver ipsius tradatur esse sepulture Datum etc."

162 Gerson, "De potestate ecclesiastica considerationes quattuor," in Louis-Elliès Dupin (ed.), *Opera omnia* (Antwerp: Sumptibus societatis, 1706), II: 232.

163 Paravy, *De la chrétienté romaine*, 824–825, 750–752.

164 Cited in A. Hamilton Thompson, *The English Clergy and their Organization in the Later Middle Ages* (Oxford: Oxford University Press, 1947), Appendix II, on p. 208.

Excommunication for debt was a corollary of the necessity of transactions on credit in the late medieval economy. It is not coincidental that the apparent peak of the practice toward 1500 was followed by the reorganization of the spheres of ecclesiastical and royal justice in France and England and then by the Protestant Reformation. Both were clearly reactions to the type of Church that could offer this sort of civil remedy. Excommunication for debt killed relations of trust between clergy and faithful and poisoned communal relations even as it filled a useful economic function. However easy it is to view the practice as an abuse, its frequency indicates that excommunication for debt manifested less the desire of the officials of ecclesiastical tribunals to profit from small-scale credit relations than the desire of Christians across the continent to use canonical procedures to remedy that which lay courts would not or could not cheaply or easily remedy.[165] From a pastoral perspective, excommunication for debt embodied the Church's real efforts to impose honest and charitable relations within the Body of Christ. From a practical perspective, it manifested a very real need for an institution to back verbal and private credit in an age of scarce, depreciating specie and limited financial instruments. These are not contradictions, as the Church exists in the world. Who could assert that sacraments and sacramentals were never used (and are not used) to both spiritual and worldly ends? We can easily grasp the economic rationale for excommunication for debt. Grasping the religious rationale for the practice is more challenging, perhaps because we have reversed the situation at the end of the Middle Ages. Then, morality shaped the economy. Now, the economy shapes morality, as we have ethicized the principles of the market.

[165] So Elsener, "Die Exkommunikation," 85: "Bei allen Klagen und Protesten, die aus den deutschen mittelalterlichen Geschichtsquellen über den Mißbrauch der Exkommunikation an unser Ohr dringen, sind die Klagen über die Anwendung der Exkommunikation im Schuldprozeß eher selten."

2 The supply of ecclesiastical justice

The phenomenon of excommunication for debt was largely demand-driven. This was characteristic of the development of ecclesiastical courts in general: demand for arbitration drove the development of late antique episcopal tribunals, demand for the ratification of contracts drove the institutionalization of officialities around 1200, and demand for the posterior ratification of verbal or privately recorded credit drove the expansion of procedural excommunications in the fifteenth century. Even so, supply-side factors briefly played a role during the fifteenth century. For a time, the late medieval crisis of landed incomes made judicial income an important component of the income of prelates possessing the power of jurisdiction.

Late medieval landed incomes

Prelates were landowners, judges, and pastors. Their income as landlords was tied directly to the output and price level of grain and other agricultural products on their estates. It was also tied to commercial activity for bishops who held rights to collect tolls, excises on marketed goods, or other levies on commerce. Their income as pastors was tied indirectly to agrarian output and price movements, since tithes were levied as a proportion of agricultural output. While these could be consumed on the spot, in the last centuries of the Middle Ages they were generally either marketed after collection or commuted into monetary payments. The collection of tithes was often leased to entrepreneurial tithe-farmers, who paid a variable but predetermined lease to the tithe-holder, pocketing what was ideally a surplus. This added another potential layer of fraud to that perpetrated by the peasants themselves, as it was in the interest of both peasants and tithe-farmers to minimize the reported agricultural yield.[1] Prelates also collected the income of vacant benefices in

[1] Marie-Thérèse Lorcin, "La fraude des décimables: mouvement court ou mouvement long?" in J. Goy and E. Le Roy Ladurie (eds.), *Prestations paysannes. Dîmes, rente foncière et mouvement de la production agricole à l'époque préindustrielle*, Cahiers d'études rurales

their gift, further tying their income to tithes and rents. Judicial income was tied to agricultural prices, though both civil and criminal litigation could slightly lag price movements.[2] For these reasons, prelates' incomes moved with that of the economy as a whole.

There has been much debate about whether there was a "crisis of feudalism" or simply an "agrarian crisis" in the late Middle Ages. Guy Bois initially proposed the former in unorthodox Marxian terms as a crisis of the feudal mode of production.[3] As rents dwindled in the late fourteenth and fifteenth centuries, Bois argues, Norman nobles turned to the State to extract more surplus from the peasantry forcibly. In his view, the exactions of lords differed little from those of the State; feudal extraction was equivalent to feudal state extraction. This standpoint reduces the importance of the emergence of Old Regime fiscality in the mid-fifteenth century, with the consolidation of the *taille royale* at the expense of the *taille seigneuriale* and the exemption of the privileged orders from this general, royal tax. Charles VII's achievement becomes simply the introduction of a new method of preserving feudal class relations, as William Beik has argued.[4] In contrast, *annaliste* and neoclassical economic historians favor the less ideologically freighted term of agrarian crisis. Their late medieval crisis is by no means opposed to the phenomenon identified by Bois. Indeed, one can trace a process similar to that identified by Bois in Normandy in the Paris basin, thanks to the work of Guy Fourquin.[5] Particularly in Northern France, but more widely, war compounded the demographic, epidemiological, and economic consequences of the fourteenth-century Great Famine and Black Death.

By 1400, lords took in considerably less than their ancestors had in 1300. The picture did not improve for much of the fifteenth century. As a result, forms of management shifted. In England and France, lords farmed out their demesnes, abandoning direct management.[6] They also began to press harder on income that did not derive from stagnant or declining ground rents. In some regions, where vestigial serfdom

4 (Paris: Éditions de l' École des Hautes Études en Sciences Sociales, 1982), 599–606, esp. 603–604 and the discussion at 782–783.

[2] Briggs, *Credit*, 179–193.

[3] Bois, *Crise*, translated as *The Crisis of Feudalism: Economy and Society in Eastern Normandy, c.1300–1550* (Cambridge: Cambridge University Press, 1984); see too R. J. Holton, *The Transition from Feudalism to Capitalism* (New York: St. Martin's Press, 1985).

[4] William Beik, *Absolutism and Society in Seventeenth-Century France State Power and Provincial Aristocracy in Languedoc* (Cambridge: Cambridge University Press, 1985), and "The Absolutism of Louis XIV as Social Collaboration," *Past & Present* 188 (2005), 195–224.

[5] Guy Fourquin, *Les campagnes de la région parisienne à la fin du Moyen Âge* (Paris: PUF, 1964).

[6] Fourquin; Christopher Dyer, *An Age of Transition? Economy and Society in the Later Middle Ages* (Oxford: Oxford University Press, 2005).

survived, lords could try to squeeze *chevage* or *taille* payments from serfs, force them to purchase their own freedom at the cost of heavier dues, or could try to revive defunct or near defunct dues.[7] They could also lean more heavily upon judicial fees or upon the revenues of banal mills, ovens, and forests, as did the barons of Pont-Saint-Pierre in Normandy.[8] At Pont-Saint-Pierre, we can see how market forces – in this case the demand for firewood – aided the enhanced extraction of surplus: during the difficult period at the end of the Middle Ages the source of the bulk of the barons' income shifted from rights of justice and lordship to domanial sources, principally the sale of firewood.[9] Indexed with respect to monetary value at 100 (or 1,149£t) for 1389–1390, Pont-Saint-Pierre's revenue slid to 36 (412£t) in 1454–1455, only climbing out of the forties to 93 (1,063£t) in 1506–1507. Once inflation had begun to compound the sixteenth-century price revolution, the index attained 262 (3,009£t) in 1558–1559 and 1099 (12,625£t) in 1571–1572, a peak not again seen till 1645–1645.[10] The revenue of this considerable lay lordship declined late in the fourteenth century to a mid-fifteenth century lowpoint, recovering swiftly – though less spectacularly than the figures suggest, given the inflation of grain prices in particular – in the sixteenth century. The pattern is not uncommon.

Although some "old" noble families foundered, some bourgeois became considerable landowners, and most Western European peasants escaped the vestiges of serfdom, there was no collapse of either the economic or the political system. This was not the collapse of feudalism. The composition of the landowning class was always fluid and there had been no single form of serfdom across the provinces of France, let alone across Western Europe, with local conditions and local history

[7] Anne-Marie Patault, *Hommes et femmes de corps en Champagne méridionale à la fin du Moyen Âge*, Annales de l'Est 58 (Nancy: Université de Nancy II, 1978); Christopher Dyer, *Lords and Peasants in a Changing Society: The Estates of the Bishop of Worcester, 680–1540* (Cambridge: Cambridge University Press, 1980); Jane Whittle, *The Development of Agrarian Capitalism: Land and Labour in Norfolk 1440–1580* (Oxford: Oxford University Press, 2000); Mark Bailey, *The Decline of Serfdom in Late Medieval England: From Bondage to Freedom* (Woodbridge: The Boydell Press, 2014).

[8] Jonathan Dewald, *Pont-St-Pierre 1398–1789: Lordship, Community, and Capitalism in Early Modern France* (Berkeley: University of California Press, 1987).

[9] Dewald, *Pont-St-Pierre*, 213–268, table at 218–219. The inflection points for this transition seem to occur around 1482–1483, when income from the sale of wood reached 20 percent of domanial income and domanial income attained 28 percent of total seigneurial income, and 1558–1559, when income from the sale of wood reached 58 percent of domanial income (peaking at 86 percent in 1571–1572!) and domanial income composed 72 percent of total income (90 percent in 1571–1572). This reflects the differential inflation of the sixteenth-century, in which wheat and wood prices inflated much faster and much more than other items of consumption.

[10] Dewald, *Pont-St-Pierre*, 235.

shaping the precise forms of servitude. There was, however, considerable reorganization of landholding at the end of the Middle Ages, whether through the consolidation of holdings, changes in cultivation patterns, or through the farming out of remaining directly cultivated demesnes, and therefore also considerable reorganization of the composition of noble incomes. Peasant living standards improved during the fifteenth century, when wages rose absolutely and with respect to prices, allowing laborers to purchase more meat and wine or good ale and to spend less on bread. This last phenomenon indicates how the incomes of landowners either stagnated or declined at the end of the fourteenth century. With labor scarce and agricultural prices often low, and personal serfdom rarer and rarer, landowners were less able to dictate favorable terms when negotiating leases. Although fixed rents in kind cushioned landowners to a degree, the real value of money rents declined as prices rose and as late medieval princes debased their currencies.[11] For the sixteenth century, Tom Scott, countering attempts by Peter Blickle and others to link the German Peasants' War of 1525 to a crisis of feudalism, has shown that the reality was exactly the opposite. The late medieval agrarian crisis had passed by 1525. The Peasants' War reflected a push for more resources by landowners who were doing increasingly well, often at the expense of peasants who had lived relatively well in the fifteenth century and who were incipient "agrarian [not *mercantile*] capitalists."[12] In France, that crisis had largely passed by 1500, at least for landowners. For France's artisans, the crisis had yet to come, as there remains an economic element to the draw both of Protestantism and of radical Catholicism.[13]

Arguing that the late medieval agrarian crisis was over by 1500 and that agrarian capitalism was incipient from the same period does not invalidate Bois's proposition that the fourteenth- and fifteenth-century decline of landed incomes drove French nobles to throw their cards in with the expanding royal state so as to secure a larger portion of the growing royal tax take. This would not have been irrational, as the State continued to grow in the late Middle Ages. By becoming royal officials, nobles confirmed their exemption and commoners could gain their exemption from

[11] The Parlement of Paris executed term contracts according to the nominal values rather than contemporary equivalents, even after debasements or reinforcements of the coinage: Timbal, *Les obligations contractuelles*, I: 335–390.

[12] Tom Scott, "The German Peasants' War and the 'Crisis of Feudalism.' Reflections on a Neglected Theme," *Journal of Early Modern History* 63 (2002), 265–295.

[13] Natalie Zemon Davis, *Society and Culture in Early Modern France* (Stanford, California: Stanford University Press, 1975); Emmanuel Le Roy Ladurie, *Carnival in Romans*, Mary Feeney (trans.) (New York: Georges Braziller, 1979); Bottin, *Seigneurs*; Robert Descimon, *Qui étaient les Seize? Mythes et réalités de la Ligue parisienne (1585–1594)*, Paris et Île-de-France Mémoires 34 (Paris: Klincksieck, 1983).

the principal land tax, the *taille*, in addition to wages and the opportunity for additional perquisites of office. The best of these fringe benefits was the ability to place relatives or clients within the royal administration and within the church, securing power and income for a whole family or clientele. With the adoption first of informal and then formal venality of office, officers effectively purchased pieces of the State, enjoyed the income therefrom, and treated them as pieces of heritable and rentable real property. This paralleled their investment from the 1520s in the perpetual annuities issued by the king on the revenues of the municipality of Paris that initially guaranteed a return of more than 8 percent. If venal officeholders or purchasers of State debt were individually vulnerable to royal pression, as a body – and venal officeholders were particularly capable of acting collectively, as they often owned much royal debt and as they operated uniquely powerful institutions such as the Parlement of Paris – venal officeholders owned the early modern state.

The financial needs of late medieval nobles thus gave monarchs an opportunity to consolidate their rule by recentering networks of patronage around themselves. Early modern monarchs availed themselves of the opportunities for outsourcing administrative costs long used by the papacy, gratifying clients and repaying loyal lenders with benefices and venal offices as well as pensions or salaries weighing directly on overburdened royal finances. Whether we call this "bastard feudalism" or simply patronage, from the later-fourteenth-century kings and magnates endowed nobles and commoners with money fiefs and pensions so as to gain their loyalty.[14] In 1519, for example, Francis I showered two-score individuals with pensions to amounts ranging from the fabulous 24,000£t accorded each to his mother, his sister, and the dowager duchess of Bourbon (Anne, daughter of Louis XI) to the 200£t paid to Claude d'Urfé or the retainer of 60£t given to the ceramicist Gerolamo della Robbia.[15] To some, this was much; to others, less so: Alain d'Albret, who received 500£t from Francis, possessed an overall income of 150,000£t, equivalent to 2,185,185 days of paid labor for a day-laborer earning 2s 3d per day.[16] In total, and acknowledging the foolhardiness of taking sixteenth-century accounts at face value, Francis I spent a considerable amount on pensions. Table 2.1 offers the figures in livres tournois given by Philippe Hamon from two different sources.[17]

[14] P. S. Lewis, "Decayed and Non-Feudalism in Later Medieval France" and "The Pensioners of Louis XI," in *Essays in Later Medieval French History* (London: The Hambledon Press, 1985), 43–68 and 91–104.

[15] Mikhael Harsgor, *Recherches sur le personnel du conseil du roi sous Charles VIII et Louis XII* (Paris: Honoré Champion, 1980), IV: 2586–2588.

[16] Harsgor, *Recherches sur le personnel*, IV: 2569, 2588.

[17] Hamon, *L'argent du roi*, 10.

Table 2.1. *Pensions paid by Francis I (in livres tournois)*

	1515	1516	1517	1518	1519	1520	1521	1522	1530	1531	1545	1546
BN fr 17329	568,301	341,833							229,732	362,242	350,045	817,979
BN fr 4523	555,921	321,447	697,149	968,729	324,647	586,287	19,612	507,651				

Source: Hamon, *L'argent du roi*, 10.

Within a global expenditure of 6,000,000 to 7,000,000£t, this figure that appears generally to have tended to lie just north of 500,000£t was not enormous, roughly eight percent of the lower figure. From another perspective, this was equivalent to a single *décime* levied on the French clergy (470,000£t) or twice the cost of the king's *maison militaire* in 1516 (211,000£t).[18] In the terms used by Mikhael Harsgor in his analysis of late-fifteenth-century pensions, the pensions of 1520 represented 5,211,440 days of work for a laborer at 2s 3dt per day. Alternately, they represented the value of a single day of labor from of roughly one-third of the king's sixteen or so million subjects, potentially from every adult male in France. With such large sums at stake, even after the economy had recovered from the late medieval depression and the sixteenth-century price revolution had made itself evident, nobles continued to seek and kings continued to distribute additional shares of the surplus of agricultural production through this welfare system for the privileged, creating not just a "robe nobility" of primarily judicial servants of the monarchy but a "sword nobility" of ostensibly military servants of the monarchy.[19] This sociogenesis appears to have begun in response to the late medieval agrarian crisis and facilitated the growth of the State on an ecclesial model at the end of the Middle Ages. While one cannot shake the notion that there was some crisis of lords' legitimacy, some kind of questioning by newly relatively advantaged peasants that caused lords to have recourse to the State to extract further surpluses, this is not our focus. What is important is that the transformation of lordship at the end of the Middle Ages lay in the direction of nobles' greater reliance upon the State.

Prelates' incomes: reform and revenue

Churchmen were not immune to the effects of the economic conjuncture of the fifteenth century. The economic transformation of lordship made ecclesiastical lords just as dependent as lay lords on the monarch for pensions, patronage, and offices. Within prelates' complicated bundles of revenues, the importance of judicial income increased in the early fifteenth century as their overall incomes declined. As lay lords turned to banal dues and farms, ecclesiastical lords turned to the dues

[18] Hamon, *L'argent du roi*, 5.

[19] Robert Descimon, "*Nobles* de lignage et *noblesse* de service. Sociogenèses comparées de l'épée et de la robe (XVe–XVIIIe siècle)," in R. Descimon and Élie Haddad (eds.), *Épreuves de noblesse: Les expériences nobiliaires de la haute robe parisienne (XVIe–XVIIIe siècle)* (Paris: Les Belles Lettres, 2010), 277–302; Joseph Morsel, "Inventing a Social Category: The Sociogenesis of the Nobility at the End of the Middle Ages," in Jussen, *Ordering*, 200–240.

that reflected their jurisdiction over their subjects. Excommunications for debt peaked in the middle of the fifteenth century and diminished rapidly thereafter. Demand and supply coincided to favor the practice, until sixteenth-century price increases and the actions of European governments reduced both the supply of and the demand for ecclesiastical civil justice. Economic changes encouraged legal developments, making ecclesiastical jurisdiction less important to prelates' financial security. Michèle Bordeaux has demonstrated that French ecclesiastical incomes peaked near 1300 and only reattained these levels toward 1500.[20] Bordeaux's survey, based on the records of ecclesiastical taxation, approximates the general movement of landed incomes in the later Middle Ages, including those from the barony of Pont-Saint-Pierre cited above and those from the archbishopric of Rouen to be discussed below. Like the incomes of the prelates studied by Bordeaux, the income of the barons of Pont-Saint-Pierre declined late in the fourteenth century to a mid-fifteenth-century lowpoint, but recovered, it seems, less rapidly than did the income of prelates in the sixteenth century.

It has been suggested that more aggressively collected tithe-income permitted ecclesiastical incomes to recover more swiftly than lay incomes.[21] Moreover, if religious institutions gained less from donations of land over the last three centuries of the Middle Ages, they invested the yield of previous gifts in purchases of new land.[22] Although this might suggest a cooling of the ardor of Christian belief, all indications are to the contrary. Indeed, Guy Fourquin reveals that the cathedral chapter of Paris invested considerable pious bequests *of cash* in purchases of land at the end of the Middle Ages.[23] We must have care as we interpret the religious significance of investment patterns. R. N. Swanson has remarked upon the difficulty of reckoning the place of indulgences and alms in ecclesiastical incomes. He nevertheless compares income from the plenary indulgence offered by the guild of Our Lady in the not particularly large English town of Boston in the 1520s (£1,600 sterling or 12,800£t) to the total income of the bishoprics of Exeter and Salisbury or to the yield of a clerical tenth from the entire province ofYork.[24] Both Swanson

[20] Michèle Bordeaux, *Aspects économiques de la vie de l'Église aux XIVe et XVe siècles* (Paris: R. Pichon et R. Durand-Auzias, 1969), esp. 339–362.

[21] Bottin, *Seigneurs*, 66–71, 177–185, 228–234.

[22] Bordeaux, *Aspects économiques*, 314–318.

[23] Fourquin, *Les campagnes*, 463–465.

[24] Swanson, *Indulgences*, 441. The pardon was a "Jubilee indulgence, for visitors to Boston church on the Marian feasts and within the following week who extended 'helping hands' and completed a threefold circuit of seven altars within the church … equivalent to the pardon obtained by visiting the *limina* of SS Peter and Paul in Rome and the rest of the seven principal basilicas in Rome" (54).

and Virginia Reinburg, who cites rubrics from French Books of Hours, convey the vibrancy of interest in devotional indulgences, that is, pardons for saying a particular prayer: for example, "Pope Sixtus, the fourth of that name, composed this prayer and gave to all who say it devoutly before the image of Our Lady of Loreto 11,000 years of indulgence."[25] Fewer gifts of real property – or waning recourse to excommunications in cases of debt – may signify not a cooling of Christian faith but the transformation of its expression.

We piece together the changing makeup of ecclesiastical incomes from the fragmentary accounts that survive. These suggest that prelates turned to judicial revenue when they saw their landed income decline. In other words, they expanded the supply of ecclesiastical justice, potentially by advertising that summoners – who (i) were often notaries, and (ii) whose witness was tantamount to a court judgment – would issue summary, verbal citations, and monitions. At Grenoble in 1361, early in the late medieval crisis, a notary purchased the farm of the officiality for 500 florins (666£ 13s 4dt) of entry fees and an annual payment of 300 fl (400£t) to the bishop. The officiality was clearly profitable at that date. It swiftly grew more so. The farmer's annual payment was doubled from 1381 and attained 1,400 fl (1,866£ 13s 4dt) by the mid-fifteenth century, when, together with the revenues of the officiality covering the territories of the duke of Savoy at Chambéry, farmed-out judicial revenue amounted to roughly 2,150 fl (2,866£ 13s 4 dt), or half of the bishop's income. By 1497, this had fallen to 1,650 fl (2,200£t) or 16 percent of the bishop's income of roughly 10,000 fl (13,333£ 13s 4dt).[26] At Grenoble, judicial income peaked both absolutely and as a proportion of episcopal revenue around 1450, at the worst economic conjuncture of the century. At its height, judicial income composed half of the Bishop of Grenoble's income. It was collected by a contractor and derived in part, as Pierrette Paravy has shown, from cases of debt. Just as in the case of demesnes across Europe, the officiality of Grenoble was farmed out, leased to one of a new class of semiproprietary manager. As has been observed of English farmers,[27] this can only have encouraged judicial contractors to look out for their bottom line, so as not to lose money. Luckily for litigants, it does not appear that officialities were commonly farmed out as a whole.[28] In Chartres, Paris, Montivilliers, and Rouen officials and auditors were officers of the relevant

25 Reinburg, *French Books of Hours*, 167.

26 Paravy, *De la chrétienté romaine*, 277–287.

27 Whittle, *Development*; Dyer, *An Age* and *A Country Merchant*.

28 Although individual offices may often have been, as the synodal statutes of Bourges forbade the farming out of the offices of sealer and receiver of fines, both of whom we shall learn to have been frequent excommunicators (1528): "Decernit quod emendae

archdeacon, abbess, or archbishop. It therefore all the more interesting then, that the fruits of justice appear everywhere to have peaked absolutely and proportionately in the second half of the fifteenth century.

The archbishopric of Rouen

Trends in the richly documented income of the Archbishop of Rouen approximate those of the Bishop of Grenoble. At Rouen, the accounts survive in a series complete enough to permit me not only to trace the outline of archiepiscopal revenue, as Bordeaux did on the basis of the records of *décimes* on the clergy, but to analyze its shifting composition over time. Every semester until sometime after 1407 and every year from some time prior to 1413 the archbishop's receiver drew up statements of total expenses and income, which were subsequently audited in the archbishop's *chambre de comptes*. The entries, broken down by category and time period, are transferred from similarly prepared, shorter if more detailed subsidiary accounts for each component of the archbishop's income, such as that from the sealer of the diocesan officiality or the receiver of fines, which survive in large numbers. The general accounts were drawn up neatly on parchment, likely in triplicate.[29] The paper workbooks in which the archbishop's receiver recorded daily transactions survive only exceptionally, but testify to receivers' extraordinary ability to balance income and expenditure with reasonable consistency in the absence of any system of double-entry bookkeeping.[30] The preserved full accounts begin in 1378 and proceed with some lacunae to 1549; few subsequent accounts survive, primarily from periods during which the see was vacant. To judge from an inventory composed for Archbishop Nicolas de Saulx-Tavannes (r.1734–1759) in 1747, very few records then in existence were lost during or after the French Revolution.[31] Of the 107

imposterum non dentur ad firmam, nec etiam jus sigilli dominorum praelatorum" (Mansi 32: 1144).

[29] According to Armand Jamme, in the Comtat Venaissin one copy of fourteenth-century accounts was retained by the treasurer, one went to the Apostolic Chamber, and one was archived at Carpentras. At Rouen, because some copies survive in duplicate, others are marked "pro camera" (e.g., G 43), and others retain parchment tags marking the year for easy retrieval (e.g., G 37), it is likely that the receiver retained one copy, sent another to the chamber for auditing, and sent the last copy to the archbishop.

[30] e.g., ADSM G 99, Michaelmas 1518 to Michaelmas 1519, when the receiver, Sire Pierre Roussel, took in 20,982£t and spent only 16,443£t. Sixteenth-century receivers consistently managed a profit for the archbishop, as the economic situation made this easier, even in spite of the expenses for completing the cathedral and for satisfying an increasingly demanding fisc (and in the absence of any apparent recourse to double-entry bookkeeping).

[31] ADSM G 1, 6–7.

mentioned, nine are missing from the series currently in the departmental archives in Rouen, including that for 1360, the earliest by eighteen years. Twenty-five registers were subsequently added, presumably from other archival deposits, of which only one, for the vacancy of the see following Saulx-Tavannes' death in 1759, is posterior to his inventory.

The elaborate charge-discharge system of accounting based on audited subsidiary accounts used at Rouen weighed charges against the bailiff or receiver (income) against discharges (expenses including late or unpaid rents), to ascertain whether or not he owed money or goods and, if so, how much.[32] This magnificent technique of management and of remote surveillance would have established the liability of the archbishop's receiver and that of every subordinate official. The Rouen accounts seem novel, although we know little of the accounting practices of nonroyal late medieval French aristocrats, apart from the princes of the South (Savoie, the Dauphiné, the Comtat Venaissin, or Provence).[33] They are certainly more elaborate than those that survive for other Northern prelates.[34] The Rouen accounts may testify to the adoption of the practices developed at the pontifical court in Avignon to manage the papacy's vast fiscal apparatus and landed possessions.[35] The date of 1360 assigned to the earliest account in the inventory of 1747 would place the origins of this system during the episcopate of Philippe d'Alençon (r.1359–1375), the nephew of Philip VI perhaps acquainted with forms of accounting used by the Capetians and their Valois successors.[36] The series of accounts could just as well have commenced under Jean de Marigny (r.1347–1351), who would have been familiar with royal accounts from his activity as *lieutenant du roi* in Languedoc in the 1340s, or Guillaume (II) de Flavacourt

[32] Mark Bailey, "Manorial Accounts," in *The English Manor c.1200-c.1500* (Manchester: Manchester University Press, 2002), 97–116, esp. 102–103.

[33] See the activity and publications of members of the Agence Nationale de la Recherche's program on the *Genèse médiévale d'une méthode administrative* (GEMMA). *Formes et pratiques des comptabilités princières (Savoie, Dauphiné, Provence, Venaissin) entre XIIIe et XVIe siècle*: e.g., Armand Jamme, "Du journal de caisse au monument comptable. L'évolution de l'enregistrement dans le Patrimoine de Saint-Pierre (fin XIIIe – XIVe siècle)," in *La comptabilité pontificale*, Mélanges de l'Ecole française de Rome, Moyen Âge 118:2 (2006), 247–268, or the accounts of Savoyard castellanies posted by Jean-Louis Gaulin and Christian Guilleré at www.castellanie.net.

[34] Accounts of the Bishop of Paris's *temporel* are simpler and much shorter: those for 1344–1345 and 1407–1409 are published by Fourquin (280–281) on the basis of AN LL 13 and 14; those for 1545 and 1596 (albeit an "abrégé") are at AN L 432 n°s 70, 72; those for 1665–1682 are at AN LL 385 C.

[35] We await the forthcoming work of Amandine Le Roux on the accounting of papal collectors.

[36] This system of accounting would then complement Philippe's cartulary, ADSM G 7, in the same way that Pierre de la Jugie's *Livre vert* would have complemented general accounts at Narbonne (see note 38).

(1357–1359), who was chancellor of Charles, comte de la Marche (later Charles IV of France), in the 1310s and likewise *lieutenant du roi* in Languedoc in the 1340s.[37] Yet, because the earliest account surviving today dates from 1378, the system could be ascribed either to Pierre de la Jugie (r.1375), papal courtier and former Archbishop of Narbonne familiar with the administration of a diocese from which he was mainly or entirely absent,[38] or Guillaume de Lestranges (r.1375–1389), another curialist often absent on papal business and former Bishop of Carpentras. This system of accounting was apparently maintained until the arrival of the princely dynasts (the Bourbon, Joyeuse, Harlay, and so on) in the middle of the sixteenth century.

The data drawn from these accounts run from 1378 to 1550 with few gaps. To 1407, the years are combinations of the semesters from Christmas to the Nativity of John the Baptist, June 24, and from then until the following Christmas. From 1413, the years run from Michaelmas, September 29. I have not regularized them to align with calendar years, so that the year marked 1456 runs from Michaelmas 1455 to Michaelmas 1456. I have expanded incomplete years, for example those ending early on account of the death of an archbishop, proportionally to cover the full accounting year and divided accounts such as ADSM G 9, which covers forty months, into accounting years. This may not the best solution, but was the best available to me.[39]

These figures show that in 1378, 55 percent (10,730 of 19,463£t) of the archbishop's income came from his spiritual justice; in 1400, 56 percent (6,216 of 11,105£t); in 1451, 41 percent (1,175 of an abnormally and abysmally low 2,876£t); in 1501, 37 percent (5,601 of 15,327£t); in 1545, 21 percent (6,641 of 31,277£t); and an ever-diminishing percentage thereafter. Percentages are not the entire story, as the absolute amount of important components of judicial income declined even as other sources of income grew: the Register of Excommunicates brought in 468£t in 1378, 329£t in 1400, 13£ 10st in 1451, 44£ 18st in 1501,

37 On these and succeeding archbishops, see Vincent Tabbagh (ed.), *Fasti ecclesiae gallicanae. Répertoire prosopographique des évêques, dignitaires et chanoines de France de 1200 à 1500, t. II: diocèse de Rouen* (Turnhout: Brepols, 1998), 102–114.

38 The Rouen accounts bear some resemblance to a catalogue of rights composed for Pierre de la Jugie at Narbonne as reconstructed by Marie-Laure Jalabert, *Le Livre Vert de Pierre de la Jugie. Une image de la fortune des archevêques de Narbonne au XIVe siècle* (Perpignan: Presses universitaires de Perpignan, 2009). The *Livre Vert* was not an annual account but could have served as a basis for annual accounting.

39 Economic historians frequently compute decennial averages to work with fragmentary data. See Thomas Piketty's justification of the practice: "Technical appendix of the book 'Capital in the twenty-first century' Appendix to chapter 10. Inequality of Capital Ownership Addendum: Response to FT," http://piketty.pse.ens.fr/files/capital21c/en/Piketty2014TechnicalAppendixResponsetoFT.pdf.

Figure 2.1 Income from the Register of Excommunicates at Rouen (in livres tournois).
Note: Logarithmic scale; trendline is five-year moving average.
Source: ADSM G 8-G 137.

11£ 2st in 1545, and 15s 4dt in 1591, before disappearing entirely from the accounts.[40] If we assume parity of citations or monitions and absolutions and that these cost 4dt and 5st,[41] the figures imply 1,404 citations or monitions and absolutions in 1378, 987 in 1400, 40.5 in 1451, 134.7 in 1501, 33.3 in 1545, and 2.31 in 1591. The initial precipitous decline may be particular to Rouen, reflecting an early abandonment of recourse to ecclesiastical sanctions for some transactions. Thereafter, however, after a short rise interrupted by the hostilities of the late Hundred Years War, income from excommunications rose before beginning a terminal decline *c.*1510, as shown by the logarithmic scale (displayed with a five-year moving average) in Figure 2.1.

The decline indicates waning demand for excommunication and the impact of royal legislation. In 1539, the Edict of Villers-Cotterêts restricted the competence of ecclesiastical tribunals over layfolk.

[40] All figures are drawn from a spreadsheet based on ADSM, G 8-G 137. I used 1451 rather than 1450, because there was no income from the register in the accounting year 1450, which began on September 29, 1449. The French retook Rouen on October 29, 1449.

[41] As before the contemporary officiality of Corbie: BN Latin 18371, 172–178. The real number of sanctions and absolutions would have of course diverged, as temporary absolutions or relaxations cost 2s 6dt and the sealer sometimes reduced fees for the desperately poor.

Thereafter, excommunications no longer would have sanctioned the debts of layfolk but, for instance, a minor cleric who failed to appear in court for the appointment of his curator.[42] In the sixteenth century, demand for the enforcement of minor debts was increasingly satisfied by more elaborately recorded instruments of credit, by settling debts before jurisdictions such as the *plaids à mace* of the bailliwick of Rouen, the records of which survive from 1483, or by summary judgment of debts by merchants in the consular jurisdiction created at Rouen in 1556.

The subheadings of the general account and the accounts of subordinate officials allow us to discern the annual and the long-term rhythms of judicial revenue. Let us take the fiscal year running from Michaelmas 1460 to Michaelmas 1461 as an example.[43] The first item in the general account is "income from the seal of the court christian of Rouen from notarial services." This referred to the cost of drafting contracts, dispensations, and absolutions. It is divided into monthly entries, the first clearly covering the month between Michaelmas and November 2: "[on] Sunday November 2 the parchment used by the notaries cost 51£ 1s 4dt." In November it cost 38£ 10s 1dt, in December 34£ 6s 6dt, in January 37£ 3s 10dt, in February 30£ 17s 8dt, in March 47£ 2s 7dt, in April 37£ 13s 3dt, in May 34£ 19s 8dt, in June 36£ 15s 3dt, in July 39£ 12s 11dt, and in August and September together 49£ 11dt. This yielded, relatively consistently with exceptions of a peak in Lent (March) and of low receipts during the harvest in August and September, 438£ 4st. The next entry concerns sealing fees ("*lesmolument du scel de la court*"), which earlier accounts separate into that "for the seal (*pro sigillo*)" and that "for graces" or "absolutions (*pro graciis* or *des absoutes*)."[44] Subsidiary accounts reveal these to have included dispensation from the requisite number of wedding bans or from pronouncing them in the place of origin, for letters of *purificetis* permitting women to be churched, and for letters of *admittetis* commanding that priests be instituted with certain benefices.[45] For 1460–1461, Master Gilles Deschamps, the sealer, paid 617£ 5st in three installments, of which unfortunately only one is dated. The next judicial subheading concerns the fees for the "approval

[42] From a formulary of *c.*1520: ADSM G 5255, n.p.: "Citacio in plena parrochia contra minorem ... Excommunicatio super hoc ..."

[43] ADSM G 58.

[44] For consistency I have transferred the latter to the heading for the Register of Excommunicates, inflating that figure if these *absoutes* reflected the absolution of reserved cases by the archbishop's penitencer.

[45] ADSM G 274. See the sealer's account for 1433 for the distinction "pro sigillo" and "pro graciis" and the more detailed paper draft of 1435 for the distinction "pro dispensacione bannorum," "pro littera purificationis," and "pro littera de admissetis." The first cost 10st per bann omitted and the last two 5st.

of testaments (*approbacions des testamens*)," the probate jurisdiction covering pious bequests and movables not devolving by local custom. On January 20, Master Jacques Fouques, *maître des intestats*, paid 32£ 5s, at an unspecified date 300£ "for the testament of My Lord [Bishop] of Bayeux (*pour le testament monseigneur de bayeulx*)," on April 22 30£ 11s 6d, and on September 29 56£ 9s for a total of 419£ 5s 6dt. As metropolitan of Bayeux, the Archbishop of Rouen received 300£t to approve the bequests of his suffragan's testament, a considerable sum in comparison to the 5st or 10st often paid for proving ordinary testaments.[46] The next subheading was that of the clerk of the *vicairerie*, who paid 300£t on December 24, 220£t on March 19, 300£t on June 2, 300£ on August 9, and 245£ 1s 3dt on September 28, for a total of 1,365£ 1s 3dt. The accounts of the vicariate reveal this to have concerned the fees deriving from the collation and possession of curacies, the approval of confraternities and chaplains, the legimitation of bastards, permissions for tonsures and ordinations, approvals of the nonresidency of parish priests, licenses for selling of indulgences within the diocese, and, importantly to the context of late medieval credit, dispensations from oaths. These dispensations last manifested the archbishop's power to dissolve or to relax solemn oaths made, as noted earlier, implicitly or explicitly before God. Most of these dispensations did not dissolve contracts outright but extended the term of payment by one year – making them equivalent not to royal *lettres de rescision* annulling the terms of contracts but to royal *lettres de répit* delaying the pursuit of creditors. In 1465–1466, the clerk of the vicariate issued such dispensations to 127 individuals at a cost of 10s each for a total of 63£ 10st.[47] One, the very first, granted respite to a grand personnage indeed, "the Lord John, Duke of Bourbon and of the Auvergne, Lieutenant of the Lord Charles, Duke of Normandy!" The archbishop's spiritual justice extended into private law and into contracts when his official chose whether to command the observance of a promise or to dispense if temporarily from its observance. In either case, his choice confirmed that contracts were also a religious matter. From a creditor's perspective, however, ostensibly secular contracts were not safe from the archbishop's clerks.

For the Register of Excommunicates Messires Jehan le Normant and Jehan Avis, *gardes des registres des excommuniés*, paid 13£ 10s on an unspecified date and 105s on September 28. What these numbers signify is an interesting question. If the cost of absolutions were counted under

[46] For cost, see the accounts of the *Magister testatorum et intestatorum* for Michaelmas 1505–1506: ADSM G 278.

[47] ADSM G 147.

the headings for sealing fees at this time, and assuming that these cost 4d each, this implies that an improbable 1125 citations or monitions were issued. The real number is doubtless lower, as general monitions or *monitoires* cost much more than simple monitions or citations, and I have counted absolutions under this heading (even in years where the receiver placed this income elsewhere). If we turn to subsidiary accounts,[48] we can learn something of the rhythm of excommunications, a subject to which I shall return in the following chapters. The following chart is derived from Table 2A.1 (see the Appendix to this chapter) tracking fees from the registers of excommunications for four years. The table is centered on the movable feasts for 1460–1461, the account for which begins the Sunday after Michaelmas 1460. The latest series is slightly off, as the accounting day appears to have shifted from Sunday to Thursday. Easter came on April 12 in 1433, on April 5 in 1461, on April 20 in 1511, and on March 27 in 1524. If one were to ask what a world that lived by liturgical time looked like, it would be this one, in which some payments were due on Michaelmas, Lady Day, March 25, or some other fixed day, and in which creditors could choose to exert the maximum amount of force against delinquent debtors during a season of which the place in the calendar year varied considerably. Had I aligned the tables and charts below according to the calendar year, the Lenten lumps would not line up and would make little immediate sense. Scanning the amounts received by week in the Appendix to this chapter reveals a spike in excommunications during Lent, an increase represented in Figure 2.2. In 1460–1461, this rise begins between the week following the first Sunday of Lent or *Invocavit* Sunday (8s 6dt) and that following the second Sunday of Lent or *Reminiscere* Sunday (18s 4dt) and ends with a precipitous fall from Holy Week (23s 6dt) to the week following the Sunday after Easter or *Quasimodo* Sunday (2st). The pattern is nearly identical for subsequent years, though the amounts are greater and the "hangover" of increased excommunications continues later past Easter in the latter two years. Conforming to the general pattern of incomes and grain prices, the income from this register doubles between 1460–1461 and 1510–1511 but diverges from sixteenth-century price movements, declining by a fifth between 1510–1511 and 1523–1524. We shall revisit that decline. In general, a considerable minority of revenue was received during Lent. In 1433 (NS), 44 percent of the revenue came in during Lent, 46 percent if we include the entry that combines the weeks of Palm

[48] ADSM G 276. The folded parchment accounts in this series are not individually numbered, and the eighteenth-century dates in Arabic numerals on their covers can be wrong by many years.

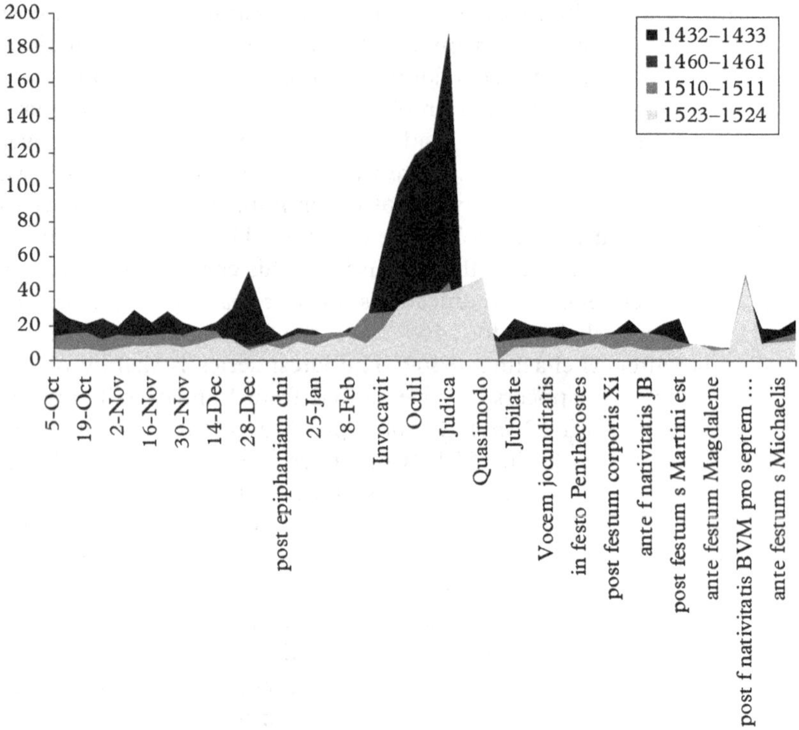

Figure 2.2 Income from the Register of Excommunicates at Rouen, aligned on the Paschal cycle for 1461 (in livres tournois).
Source: ADSM G 276.

Sunday and Easter. In 1461, 38 percent came during Lent, 39 percent if we include the week before *Quasimodo*. In 1511, 25 percent came during Lent, 27 percent if include the week before *Quasimodo*. This rose to 35 percent, 43 percent if we include Easter week, during Lent 1524.

Even if its magnitude decreased over time, why do we find a spike in excommunications during Lent? The other apparent peak is only that, since it represents the inclusion of all seven weeks of the traditional Harvest-Tide under the same entry. Divide by seven and it disappears. The high number of excommunications during Lent reflects the calculated use of canonical procedure by creditors, that is to say, the deployment of spiritual sanctions to economic (to recover a debt) and social ends (to humiliate a borrower and to ruin his or her credit). Again, as Edward Iacobucci has observed: "the reputational sanction that the wrongdoer bears from certain conduct will generally *depend* on the size

Table 2.2 *Judicial income, Archdiocese of Rouen, 1461*

Notaries' fees	437£ 4st
Seal of the officiality	617£ 5st
Probate	419£ 5s 6dt
Clerk of the vicariate	1,365£ 1s 3dt
Registers of excommunicates	18£ 15st
Court fees	80£ 5s 2dt
Fines and reconsecration of churches	1,034£ 1s 10½dt
Vicariate of Pontoise	171£ 8s 6½dt
Total Judicial Revenue	4,143£ 6s 4dt

Source: ADSM G 58.

of the legal penalty associated with that conduct."[49] Since the twenty-first canon of the Fourth Lateran Council *Omnius utriusque sexus* (1215, X.5.38.12) required annual reception of the Eucharist by the faithful, generally on Palm Sunday, Holy Thursday, or Easter Sunday,[50] Lent was an effective period during which to exert spiritual pressure upon debtors. Excommunication in December was potentially less grave, unless the debtor were on his or her deathbed. Excommunication during Lent was graver, as it threatened to bar the believer from the yearly reception of the Eucharist that marked him or her as a creditable, orthodox member of the community, and guaranteed a chance at Heaven.

Returning to the general account, the fees of litigation and of putting forth the articles of one's case in writing ("*du taux et des posicions de la court*") was 80£ 5s 2d in 1460–1461. For "fines and the reconciliation of churches (*amendes et reconciliations desglises*)," polluted by blood, semen, or the body of an excommunicate, Master Geoffroy Charles, *promoteur d'office*, paid 212£ 2st on December 16, 346£ 12s 6dt on April 3, 192£ 17s 3dt on June 3, 264£ 19s 3dt on September 29, and an additional 17£ 10s 10dt "to close his account (*par la fin de son compte*)." Master Jehan Volet, vicar of the archbishop at Pontoise, an enclaved territory near Paris, paid 171£ 8s 6½dt. The fees for 1461 are represented in Table 2.2.

Looking at the microcosm of a single year, we can see how the a posteriori jurisdiction of the archbishop over contracts (18£ 15st) remained minor from a financial perspective in comparison to the use of his seal for written contracts and dispensations (437£ 4s + 617£ 5s = 1,055£ 9st). Fines swamped the meager return of court fees. The two vicariates,

[49] Iacobucci, "On the Interaction," 191.

[50] Toussaert, *Le sentiment*, 168–180, indicates a very few, doubtless very pious communicants at Christmas, Candlemas, Assumption, and All Saints.

issuing other types of dispensations and managing the diocese's clergy, together brought the archbishop 1,536£ 9s 9½d. It is also worth noting that the last entry of the section concerning the archbishop's spiritual revenue is that of the "prisoners' bread (*pain des prisonniers*)," confirming that the officiality of Rouen still imprisoned a considerable number of individuals at the end of the Middle Ages.[51] The receiver ought to have taken in 72£ 13s 9dt for eighty-three individuals. Most of these individuals consumed between one and three dozen loaves, valued at 3st the dozen, suggesting that their stays were relatively short. If they consumed three loaves per day, most only stayed between four and twelve days. In the unlikely event that they consumed only one loaf per day, the implausibly long range of detention would then lie between twelve days and four weeks. Still, some prisoners consumed thirty dozen loaves each, implying stays of at least three months. Most prisoners did not pay, as a corresponding expense in the discharge section of the account marked most of these charges as "irrecoverable and worthless (*inutilles et de nulle valleur*)." Overall, the archbishop's jurisdiction over contracts brought in far less income than, for instance, dispenses from the banns of marriage. Even at the worst economic conjuncture of the fifteenth-century, demand must have predominated in generating excommunications for debt.

Turning from the microcosm to the secular trend, the following charts of the revenues of the Archbishop of Rouen from 1378 to 1550, provides the context for preceding figures. The first (Figure 2.3) demonstrates the movement of landed income during the late Middle Ages and the sixteenth-century price revolution as well as the importance of judicial income in the fifteenth century for one of the two richest dioceses in France.[52]

The light area represents judicial income, the darker area is added to represent total income. The solid line is a twenty-year moving average of total income and the dotted line one of judicial income. What is clear is that revenue fell precipitously to its mid-fifteenth-century nadir before beginning an astonishing rise at the end of the century. The low point was reached in 1447, when commerce in Normandy had virtually ground to a

[51] The *Registre des écrous* of the archbishop's prisons survives for 1531–1550: ADSM G 4900. At Montivilliers, we find ADSM 5273, Saint-Sauveur, 1525: "Johannes totee excommunicatus pro rebellione et infractione carceris contra dominum promotorem de die martis xix[a] septembris / absolutus die feste pasche." On imprisonment, see Nicole Castan, "La préhistoire de la prison. Le temps médiéval," in J.-G. Petit et al., *Histoire des galères, bagnes et prisons, XIIIe-XXe siècles. Introduction à l'histoire pénale de la France* (Toulouse: Privat, 1991), 19–44; De Carbonnières, *La procédure*, 240–254; Claustre, *Dans les geôles*, 313–419.

[52] The other is Narbonne; Pierre de la Jugie held each diocese successively!

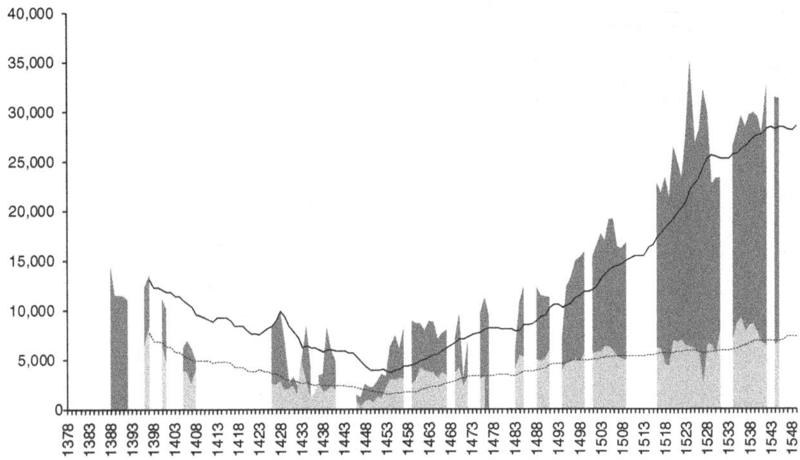

Figure 2.3 Revenues of the Archbishop of Rouen, 1378–1549 (in livres tournois): judicial and total income.
Source: ADSM G 8-G 137.

halt as the last conflicts of the Hundred Years War and the taxes required to pay for them ravaged the region.[53] After the French retook Upper Normandy in the late autumn of 1449, agricultural prices and maritime commerce rebounded, drawing the revenues of justice along with them, though more slowly than the archbishop's income as a whole. Judicial revenue was proportionately more important in the fifteenth century, particularly in the 1450s and 1460s when judicial business rebounded more swiftly than commerce or agriculture (here the moving average is not helpful, as it obscures year-to-year movements). The second chart (Figure 2.4) contrasts income (solid line) and expenses (gray line), giving the balance (dotted line).

By the second decade of the sixteenth century the archbishops of Rouen were turning a fine profit, even with the considerable expenses of cathedral-building and increasingly frequent royal taxation weighing upon them.

Like other prelates, the archbishops of Rouen benefitted from the sixteenth-century recovery of prices through direct seigneurial income on land and commerce (the "temporalities"), tithes, annuities secured on their properties, other types of lending, and the revenue from vacant benefices, all of which were inflated by rising agricultural prices. At

[53] Michel Mollat, *Le commerce maritime normand à la fin du Moyen Âge* (Paris: Plon, 1952), 1–116, is incomparable on the slow pace of recovery to 1475.

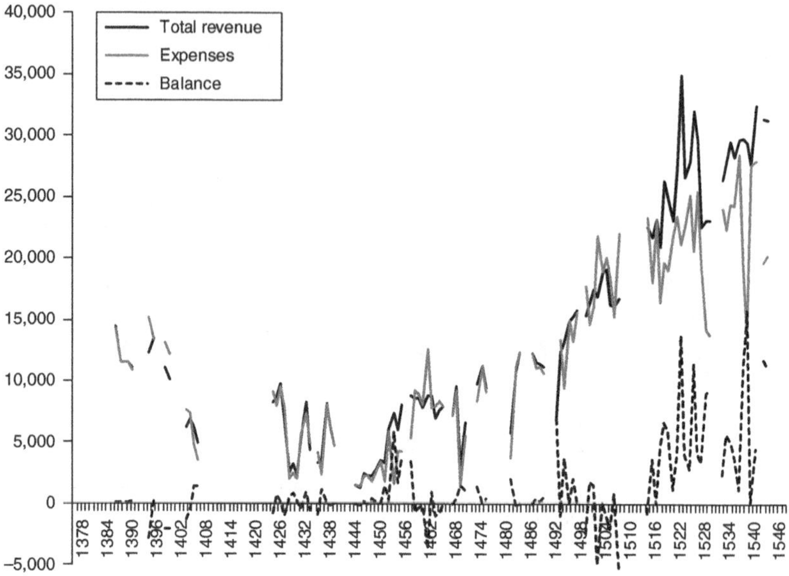

Figure 2.4 Revenues of the Archbishop of Rouen, 1378–1549 (in livres tournois): revenue, expenses, and balance.
Source: ADSM G 8-G 137.

Paris, the price of a setier (1.561hL) of wheat in 1431 was 2.76 sous in 1450 .75s, in 1500 1.09s, in 1520 1.69s, in 1550 4.15s, and in 1600 a considerable 8.65s.[54] In other words, taking 1431 as a probably inflated index of 100, the price of wheat per setier was 27 in 1450, 39 in 1500, 61 in 1520, 150 in 1550, and 313 in 1600. The less complete records given by Mollat for Rouen reveal prices of 10, 13, and 14£t per muid (18.73hL or 1 muid 4 setiers of Paris) of grain in 1406, 8£ 5st in 1445–1446, 12£t in 1476–77, 36£lt in 1500, 32£ 6st and 38£ 8st in 1516, 48 and 72£t in 1524 (the latter for grain purchased in Brittany), and 216£t in 1575.[55] We can see the immensity of the sixteenth-century price revolution, in which the price of this most important commodity increased at least 500 percent between 1450 and 1550. Figure 2.5 compares the archbishop's total revenues (in £t) as a proxy for grain

[54] Richard Bonney's European State Finance Database after M. Baulant, "Les prix des grains à Paris de 1431 à 1788," *Annales ESC* 23 (1968), 538–539.

[55] Mollat, 376–377. On the metrology of Paris and of Rouen, see Guy Bois, "Comptabilité et histoire des prix: le prix du froment à Rouen au XVe siècle," *Annales ESC* 6 (1968), 1262–1282, at 1267–1269.

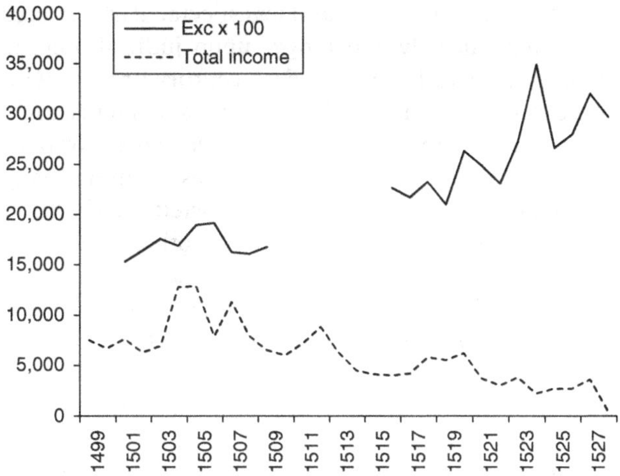

Figure 2.5 Total revenue of the Archbishop of Rouen (in livres tournois) against excommunications at Montivilliers, 1499–1530 (× 100). *Sources:* ADSM G 8-G 137, G 5273.

prices in Upper Normandy to the number of excommunications at Montivilliers times one hundred: the decline of excommunication in the face of rising grain prices is clear.

The relationship is not causal. Nevertheless, after 1500 judicial income had become insignificant within the archbishop's enormous income and within those of other prelates. Whereas lay lords such as the barons of Pont-Saint-Pierre relied heavily upon the sale of domanial firewood or banal dues and all lords began to consolidate and farm out their holdings in this period, ecclesiastical lords had additional means of benefitting from rising grain prices.[56] Tithes and the income from vacant parishes permitted their incomes to increase more swiftly than those of lay lords lacking the suppletive value of royal pensions.

The supply of ecclesiastical justice withers

The recovery was swift and spectacular at Rouen, for Normandy suffered exceptionally during the later Hundred Years War. In dioceses where bishops were poorer in land or had no access to the profits of maritime

[56] The Archbishop of Rouen's ability to skim profits from Atlantic commerce through levies at the ports of Rouen and of Dieppe was exceptional. The records of these levies are one of Mollat's principal sources.

commerce, revenues recovered more slowly and less spectacularly. Poorer bishops probably relied more heavily and longer upon judicial income than did the Archbishop of Rouen. In the sixteenth century prelates who lived of judicial income resisted increasingly frequent and increasingly successful attempts to deprive them of competence over matters of debt if not over civil matters of any kind. Lucien Febvre has examined why the Archbishop of Besançon in the Franche-Comté resisted the abolition of excommunication for debt six years longer than the other prelates of the Spanish Netherlands (1565–1571): he feared losing a crucial source of income. Aside from judicial business, the diocese of Besançon yielded only 3,000 comtois francs (4,500£t) annually. The 4,000 or 5,000fr (6,000–7,500£t) of income from citations and sealing fees for absolutions would certainly have been welcome to the archbishop. An inquest launched by Philip II of Spain to investigate the practice estimated that the legal fees deriving from debt cases before the officiality of Besançon drained the province of 40,000 to 80,000fr (60,000–120,000£t) annually in the 1560s.[57] Even accounting for the wages of practitioners and the officiality's operating costs, the bishop's share of this was doubtless considerable in comparison to his minuscule landed income.[58]

What was the effect of this on the ground? Philip II's inquest offers some eloquent examples. The regions' parish priests testified to 85 excommunicates, to more than 200 excommunicates, even to 580 excommunicates within certain large parishes.[59] They had been excommunicated for "loans, purchase orders for animals, payment for meals in taverns, sureties for others' debts, slander and assault, payment for merchandise sold on credit, and other similar cases,"[60] Given the proliferation of relations of credit, such sentences piled up against the spendthrift, unlucky, or impoverished: in a register of 1570, Febvre counted, within one quarter of a vast parish, "98 parishioners ... excommunicated in consequence of one citation; 18 by 2; 10 by 3; 3 by 4; 7 by 5; 6 by 6; 1 by 8." In another quarter, 70 were excommunicated as the result of one citation, "25 by 2, 7 by 3, 4 by 4, 7 by 5, 2 by 9, 1 by 12, and 3 by 13." At Longechaux, Michel Goussot was excommunicated twenty-two times and his two sons twice each; Pierrot Regnier was excommunicated twenty-eight times, Claude Regnier thirty-two times![61] Even if Archbishop Claude de la Baume was personally unscrupulous, Febvre observes that Besançon was a one-industry town for which the chief

[57] Febvre II, 15, 29. [58] Febvre II, 28.
[59] Febvre II, 13–14. [60] Febvre II, 2.
[61] Febvre II, 15. The present-day population of Longechaux is 55.

industry was the excommunication of debtors. Of course, the archbishop and his officials would not have been able to profit from a booming business of citation, excommunication, and absolution in civil matters had not a considerable web of debt tied his flock together.

As Febvre's figures from the Franche-Comté illustrate, it required a considerable number of excommunications to make real money.[62] In 1494, each absolution brought the Archdeacon of Paris twelve times as much (4sp/5st) as each citation (4dp/5dt). In the early sixteenth century at the metropolitan officiality of the Archbishop of Sens, each citation cost 4dt and each sentence 4s 6dt. A general monition cost 2st and an absolution 5st. Each temporary absolution for testifying in court or pursuing a case cost 4s 4dt, each absolution with the consent of the creditor cost 3s 10dt, and each single-day absolution was taxed at 12dt for the first day and 5dt for each subsequent day, with an additional 20d for the seal of the officiality and a further 20dt for the official's signet.[63] By 1583, however, demand had apparently dropped, for even with considerable inflation, a general monition from the officiality of the Bishop of Auxerre cost only 15dt.[64] By then, as the example of Rouen demonstrates, prelates had little need for judicial income. Such fees for citations and absolutions were essentially equivalent to rounding error on episcopal incomes and only existed in response to demand for a new use of the power of the keys in matters of property and violent crime. Believers nevertheless continued to seek salvation within the Church in spite of these fees. With no better choice, they were trapped between economic and religious imperatives. If the case of Besançon represents a late and exceptional metastasis of excommunication for debt, the evidence from Chartres, Paris, and Montivilliers to be examined in the following chapter confirms the ubiquity of recourse to ecclesiastical justice in disputes concerning minor, unwritten credit relations.

Demand for excommunication in cases of debt was great, yet the case of Besançon demonstrates the potential profit of such practices to unscrupulous prelates and to probably still more unscrupulous legal practitioners. We cannot entirely ignore supply-side factors in explaining the phenomenon of excommunication for debt. Although the procedure reflected a very real need for the enforcement of parol contracts and deeply held beliefs about the meaning of relations of credit within the Christian community, the peak of excommunications for debt coincided

[62] At Corbie debt cases yielded half as much as matrimonial, assault, or criminal cases: BN Latin 18371, 178: "ITEM notandum est quod in causis matrimonialibus iniuriarum et criminalibus tam pro sigillo quod aliis dupliciter et duplicatur salarium."

[63] BN Latin 4812, 74v, 76v.

[64] BN Latin 4812, 54.

with the nadir of ecclesiastical incomes. Not surprisingly, this conjuncture stimulated a variety of movements to control or to end excommunication for debt across Europe. In England, from the 1490s royal courts began to hear the types of debt cases that church courts once heard. In France, church courts had been threatened at least as long. In terms of statutes, the Ordinance of Villers-Cotterêts of 1539 ought to have abolished – and did, it appears – the retroactive jurisdiction of ecclesiastical tribunals over the contracts of layfolk. The Council of Trent further encouraged the decline of excommunication for debt elsewhere by restricting the use of spiritual sanctions and by stripping deans and archdeacons of much of the jurisdiction they had formerly enjoyed. Inflation and economic growth made judicial income increasingly unimportant to sixteenth-century prelates. Thus, as the conviction that the competence of church courts in matters of debt was abusive grew and as European princes moved to strip this competence from church courts, prelates had little reason to struggle against the loss of what was then less lucrative capacity. Moreover, enforcing contracts through church courts rather than through the confessional did not accord with Tridentine visions of the proper role of the episcopate within the reformed Catholic Church.[65]

Appendix: income from the Register of Excommunicates in the Archdiocese of Rouen by week, aligned on the Paschal cycle for 1461

Table 2A.1 *Income from the Register of Excommunicates in the Archdiocese of Rouen by week, aligned on the Paschal cycle for 1461*

Sunday	1432–1433	1460–1461	1510–1511	1523–1524
Oct. 5	30s	3s 6d	13s	5s 8d
12	23s 4d	4s 6d	15s 3d	5s 2d
19	20s	3s 8d	15s 7d	5s 6d
26	23s 4d	6s	12s	4s
Nov. 2	18s 5d	5s	14s	6s 2d
9	28s 4d	5s 8d	13s	7s 2d
16	20s 10d	4s 6d	14s	7s 4d

[65] See the classic article of Hubert Jedin, "Das Bischofsideal der katholischen Reformation. Eine Studie über die Bischofsspiegel vornehmlich des 16. Jahrhunderts," in *Kirche des Glaubens. Kirche der Geschichte. Ausgewählte Aufsätze und Vorträge*, 2 vols. (Freiburg: Herder, 1966), II: 75–117.

Sunday	1432–1433	1460–1461	1510–1511	1523–1524
23	27s 6d	5s 2d	15s	8s 2d
30	20s 9d	6s 4d	13s 9d	6s 4d
Dec. 7	17s 6d	6s 6d	17s	9s 2d
14	21s	7s 2d	16s 6d	12s 6d
in festo sancti thome	28s 9d	8s	5s 3d	11s 2d
28	50s 6d	8s 6d	7s	5s
post circoncisionem dni	20s	2s 4d	9s 6d	8s 4d
post epiphaniam dni	13s 4d	4s 6d	11s 7d	6s 2d
Jan. 18	18s	5s 6d	15s	9s 8d
25	15s 10d	6s 2d	14s 6d	7s 6d
Feb. 1	11s 9d	6s 8d	16s	11s 4d
8	17s 6d	7s	15s 9d	13s 4d
15	20s	7s 4d	26s 6d	9s 4d
Invocavit	63s 9d	8s 6d	27s 9d	18s 2d
Reminiscere	100s	18s 4d	28s 3d	31s 6d
Oculi	118s 4d	35s	30s 6d	36s 6d
Letare	126s 3d	35s 4d	36s	38s 2d
Judica	188s 4d	25s 2d	45s	39s 6d
in Ramis palmarum		23s 6d	7s 6d	43s 6d
Quasimodo	20s 10d	2s	13s 6d	48s 1d
in Misericordia dni	12s 3d	5s 4d	10s	[illegible]
Jubilate	23s 4d	3s 8d	11s 6d	7s...
Cantate	19s	6s	12s 6d	7s...
Vocem jocunditatis	17s 6d	5s 2d	13s	7s...
post Ascensionem dni	18s 4d	5s 4d	11s 6d	8s...
in festo Penthecostes	15s	8s 2d	14s	7s...
in festo sancti Trinitatis	14s	4s	15s	9s...
post festum corporis Xi	15s	4s 6d	15s	5s 6d
post festum s Barnabe	22s 6d	5s 6d	15s 6d	7s 4d
ante f nativitatis JB	14s	4s 8d	16s	5s 2d
ante f ss Petri et Pauli	20s 6d	5s 4d	14s	5s 4d
post festum s Martini est	23s 4d	4s 2d	10s	5s 8d
Jul. 12		5s	8s 6d	9s 4d
ante festum Magdalene		6s 4d	7s 6d	5s

Sunday	1432–1433	1460–1461	1510–1511	1523–1524
in festo beate Anne		7s	6s	6s 2d
post f nativitatis BVM pro septem ebdomadarum tempore messium durante	42s 6d	18s	6s 6d, 7s, 6s 6d, 5s, 7s 6d, 10s, 7s 6d	5s 6d, 5s, 5s 2d, 5s 6d, 5s 8d, 9s 4d, 11s 2d
ante festum s Mathei	17s 10d	5s	9d	9s 4d
ante festum s Michaelis	17s	6s 4d	12s 6d	9s 6d
Oct. 4	22s 6d	4s 8d	16s	10s 4d
Total	66£ 1s 5dt	18£ 15st	36£ 16s 2dt	29£ 15s 6dt

Note: Easter came on April 12 in 1433, on April 5 in 1461, on April 20 in 1511, and on March 27 in 1524. The figures imply that there were roughly 264 excommunications and absolutions in 1433, 75 in 1461, 147 in 1511, and 119 in 1521, in line with trends outlined in the preceding chapter.

Source: ADSM G 276.

3 Case studies: demand for ecclesiastical justice

The following case studies of excommunications by officialities at Chartres, Paris, and Montivilliers allow us to explore the economic and social dimensions of excommunications for debt. Examined line-by-line, surviving registers of excommunications reveal a flexible procedure, well-adapted to the flexible, common, and often unwritten or unauthenticated forms of credit on which late medieval daily commerce and administration functioned. As with the civil business of lay courts, it was demand that drove the operation of ecclesiastical tribunals, and only secondarily the desires of judges, auditors, and other court officials. As the prelates of France told Philip VI at the Assembly of Vincennes (1329):

> The Gallican church is accustomed to judge layfolk in personal actions … a custom evidently introduced through the choice and will of the people, who prefer to seek remedies from an ecclesiastical judge than a secular judge … Many more choose to obligate [themselves] in church courts than in secular courts, and would prefer to cease making the contracts without which they cannot live rather than to submit themselves to a secular court.[1]

As the Clerk of the late-fourteenth century *Songe du Vergier* put it: "it is beneficial to the entire commonwealth that Christians have many judges before whom they might oblige themselves."[2] This chapter will take a broad perspective on 11,031 cases to show why demand for excommunication for debt remained strong into the sixteenth century. It will suggest one way in which late medieval Christians understood charity by examining sanctions against those felt to have violated the spirit of equitable exchange and faithful obligation that bound Christ's faithful to each other. Here are four examples of the chapter's source base.

First case: in the parish of Saint-Laurent in Paris "on Holy Saturday 1434 (OS) Guillaume Vye alias Pontaux was excommunicated at the request of Jacques Vigneron by Jacques Vigneron," one of the

[1] *Libellus domini Bertrandi adversus Magistrum Petrum de Cugneriis*, cited in Esmein, "Débiteurs," 235 n.2.

[2] Cited in Bourlet and Claustre, "Le marché," 70 n.89.

summoners of the archidiaconal officiality.[3] Vye clearly had troubles with the Archdeacon of Paris's officiality. Whether the initial excommunication reflected a personal debt to Vigneron or unpaid services such as a citation or monition served on credit, Vye was absolved with a promise to pay 8sp (10st) within a month. Next year, however, he was again excommunicated, this time by the sealer, probably for an unpaid sealing fee, by the summoner Guillaume Gautard, probably again for a citation or monition, and by the court's prosecutor for contempt of court. This time, however, Vye was not absolved, as he died in the interim.[4] If he had failed to secure an absolution on his deathbed and his heirs had failed to secure posthumous permission to bury his body in consecrated ground, he would have died without the sacraments, been buried in profane ground, and, according to contemporary ideals of the "good death," probably gone straight to hell.[5]

Second case: in 1513, in the parish of Saint-Sauveur at Montivilliers in Upper Normandy, the cleric Jacques Brisebois was excommunicated five times, once each for sums of 2s 5dt, 7s 6dt, and 5st, and twice for contumacy.[6] These small sums would not indicate a semibankruptcy, except that excommunication for such small sums suggests that Brisebois had exhausted his credit: no one could trust him to pay even 5st without the threat of damnation.

Third case: on July 20, 1514, again at Montivilliers, the priest Sire Jean Gaffe was suspended from performance of spiritual functions at the request of Jean Regnard for a sum of 50st. On September 29, Sire Jean was excommunicated, on October 19 aggravated, and on November 24 reaggravated.[7] The first interval was long, but succeeding intervals were swift, with sanctions growing graver each month.

Fourth case: on July 30, 1518, at Montivilliers, Sire Nicolas Gabriel, priest, was suspended from performance of spiritual functions at the request of Philippe Paris for a sum of 6s 10dt. On August 3, Sire Nicolas

[3] AN Z[1o]17, Saint-Laurent, 1434 (OS): "Excommunicatus est guillermus vye alias pontaux ad instantiam jacobi viticole die sabbati sancti viticole / Absolutus est viij s p infra mensem."

[4] AN Z[1o]17, Saint-Laurent, 1436: ""Excommunicatus est guillermus ponthault alias vye pro contumacia ad instantiam sigilliferi curie / mortuus est / gautardi // Excommunicatus est idem ad instantiam guillermi gautardi // Item idem ad instantiam guillermi gautardi // Item idem ad instantiam promotoris curie super contentu curie viticole."

[5] Roger Chartier, "Les arts de mourir, 1450–1600," *Annales ESC* 31 (1976), 51–75.

[6] ADSM G 5273, Saint-Sauveur: May 23, June, November 13, January 28 (OS), February 8, 17, and 24 (OS).

[7] ADSM G 5273, Saint-Sauveur. The record transposes his excommunication and aggravation, probably an error of transcription from draft records.

had Jean Le Vavasseur excommunicated for the same amount.[8] Because Sire Nicolas was a priest, and was therefore suspended from divine service rather than excommunicated in first instance, he was able to use the spiritual sanctions of the officiality of Montivilliers to recover a debt so as to pay the debt for which he himself had been suspended from divine service by the same court.

Citations and monitions commonly cost 4 or 5dt. The four canonical summonses were often collapsed into one citation or monition and sentences of excommunication were generally aggravated every four weeks, sometimes only every two. Excommunication for debt imperiled a debtor's soul swiftly and cheaply. Few cases like the first one were necessary to remind living excommunicates of the extreme perils of their situation. Demand thus fed swollen late medieval registers of excommunicates. Yet who excommunicated? who was excommunicated? when? why? for which amounts? whose excommunication was aggravated? who was absolved? when?

What are the records of such practices? Although recourse to *lettres de chrétienté* declined over the thirteenth century, lay demand for the enforcement of unwritten contracts apparently composed a considerable proportion of the activity of church courts from the late thirteenth century. Synodal statutes from the diocese of Coutances prior to 1294 suggest that procedural excommunications had become quite common, more so than would be the case for ordinary ecclesiastical offenses. They specify that parish priests were not to absolve anybody excommunicated by the bishop, an archdeacon, or a rural dean, "even if shall have satisfied the plaintiff … until the priest shall have clear proof of his absolution." Further, the priest was to keep a "table or sheet on which he shall write the names of the excommunicates of his parish, and for which causes, and how many times, and at whose request, and by whose authority." These provisions tie the priest's capacity to summarily judge matters of debt to his capacity to excommunicate those thieves or malefactors denounced in confession: "we forbid any [priest] to excommunicate for a debt … unless the parishioner confess the debt publicly to the priest … for the priest may indubitably do justice when he encounters [the criminal] and is certain of his guilt."[9] By 1300, then, it appears that priests

[8] ADSM G 5273, Saint-Sauveur. Sire Nicolas was suspended once in 1515 for 8st, and nine times in 1518 for an uncertain cause, for contumacy, and for the 6s 10dt mentioned above, 4£ 12st, 8s 1dt, 6st, 43st, 10st, excommunicated for 10s 10dt to the same man a month later. He was suspended in 1519 for 30st, 10s 6dt, 5st, and 10st, and twice for 15st. In 1520, he was suspended for 10st.

[9] Bessin (ed.), *Concilia Rotomagensis*, 545, c. 15: "Nullus excommunicatus à Superiore, pro absoluto habeatur, nisi constet de ipsius speciali mandato. Praecipimus ut nullus

were summarily excommunicating debtors in procedures for which no written trace would exist unless one of these *schedulae* or *cartae* should have survived. By 1300 it also appears that bishops, archdeacons, and rural deans were formally excommunicating debtors in procedures that did leave written traces. Matters of debt are present in a formulary of the officiality of the Bishop of Tréguier in Brittany dating from *c.*1312–1315.[10] The diocesan officiality of Chartres appears to have kept lists of excommunicates on large parchment folios from the early 1340s at the latest that bear some resemblance to the "table or sheet" requested in the diocese of Coutances.[11] The cause was not always specified in these early sheets, although amounts were often enough to indicate that some excommunications were in matters of debt: for example, "on Tuesday after *Laetare* Sunday 1342 (NS) Guillaume Breton was excommunicated at the request of Guillaume de la Noue for a debt of 17s 6d."[12] At Chartres, these details are included in the earliest complete surviving register of excommunications and fines, which begins forty years later.

By the middle of the fourteenth century at the latest, then, officialities across Northern France had begun to keep registers that specified when, at the request of whom, for what cause, often for what amount a believer had been excommunicated, and, ideally, when or whether he had been absolved. This must reflect a bureaucratic development in response to considerable use of this type of sanction in response to lay demand, as excommunication for debt was more a by-product of canonical procedure than a goal, at least from the clerical, judicial perspective. To put it another way, if ecclesiastical judges fretted about adultery or priests in concubinage, layfolk were concerned with credit, both in a monetary sense and in a moral or figurative sense, as frequent cases concerning

Presbyter excommunicatos à Nobis, vel Archidiacono, vel Decano, pro absolutis habeat, vel in Ecclesia recipiat, etiamsi de se conquerenti satisfecerit, et ei constiterit, donec à Nobis, vel ejus excommunicatore, de ejus absolutione ei constiterit evidenter … Jubemus, sub poena excommunicationis injungentes, ut quilibet Sacerdos schedulam habeat vel cartam ubi nomina excommunicatorum parochiae suae scribat, et ex quibus causis, et quot, et ad quorum instantiam, necnon cujus auctoritate singuli sint excommunicati, et singulis diebus sic eos excommunicatos denuntiet, licet à nemine requisitus … Similiter inhibemus ne aliquis pro debito eorum, coram eis recognito, excommunicare audeat, nec pro debitis suis, nisi in generali pro jure suo, nisi parochianus jus Presbytero debitum publicè fateatur. Licet enim de malefactore vel raptore Sacerdoti constiterit per confessionem, et conquerens justitiam ecclesiasticam postulet exhiberi; Presbyter indubitanter justitiam exerceat, licet in conspectu suo eum videat, et certus sit de ejus reatu: quia quae per confessionem novit, nescit ut homo, sed ut Deus."

[10] BN NAL 426.

[11] ADEL G 813, Register of the officiality of Chartres, is bound in a folium of the Register of Excommunicates from the 1340s.

[12] Binding of ADEL G 813, 1341 (OS): "Guillermus breton pro eidem guillermo de noa xvij s vj d martis [post letare]."

debt and defamation illustrate. We underestimate the place of matters of debt in the business of ecclesiastical tribunals for two reasons: first, debt cases only rarely proceeded beyond a citation or a monition and the resulting excommunication for contumacy to the litigation proper that appears in audience registers or in final judgments; second, the underlying debts were not always recorded and, if they were, the record seldom survives. Whereas the archdiocese of York kept registers of obligations confessed in court in the fourteenth century, French courts appear not to have kept such records: there are only the few obligations jotted down on the last folios of a fifteenth-century register from the officiality of Montivilliers and scattered recognizances of debt in the civil registers of the archidiaconal officiality of Paris that survive from the 1470s. This means that the underlying obligations were either verbal or privately recorded, in which case they were probably destroyed. Registers of excommunicates are therefore indispensable to the history of the practice, a practice conducted, not necessarily off the books, but off the books that historians ordinarily examine. We must carefully examine surviving registers of excommunications to grasp the commonness of the practice in late medieval France.

Why have I chosen the register of excommunications of the officiality of the Sub-Dean of Chartres from 1380 to 1436, that of officiality of the Archdeacon of Paris from 1426 to 1439, and those of the officiality of the Abbess of Montivilliers from 1433 to 1461 and again from 1499 to 1530? In first place, they survive and as a group traverse the last three centuries of the Middle Ages. In second place, Véronique Beaulande did not examine them in her recent study of excommunication in the ecclesiastical province of Reims. Finally, I believe these sources to be indicative, if not perfectly representative, of the potential functioning of ecclesiastical tribunals elsewhere in France and in Europe.

The sub-decanal officiality of Chartres, 1380–1436

The sub-dean of the cathedral chapter of Chartres was archdeacon of the town and suburbs (*ville et banlieue*) of Chartres with jurisdiction over eighteen parishes in the fourteenth century and nineteen in the eighteenth century.[13] The register G 817 of the departmental archives of the

[13] *Pouillé du Diocèse de Chartres* (Chartres: Nicolas Doublet, 1738), 1, 4. The Augustinian Abbey of Saint-Jean en Vallée remained in the former parish of La Madeleine, just as the Benedictine priory of Saint-Martin au Val remained in the parish of Saint-Brice. Between 1436 and the eighteenth century, then, Barjouville had been deducted and the hospital of Saint-Julien des Aveugles and the parish of Saint-Ladre des Lèves in the banlieue had been added to the sub-dean's jurisdiction.

Eure-et-Loire is organized roughly alphabetically by parish: Saint-André (*Andreas*), Saint-Aignan (*Anianus*), Saint-Barthélemy (*Bertholomeus*), Saint-Jacques de Barjouville (*Beriovilla*), Saint-Chéron (*Caraunus*), Saint-Denis de Champhol (*Campus Folius*), Sainte-Foi (*Sancta Fides*), Saint-Hilaire (*Hillarius*), Saint-Jean en Vallée (*Johannes in Valleya*), Saint-Julien du Coudray (*Jullianus de Coudreyo*), Saint-Pantaléon de Lucey (*Leuge*), Saint-Laumer de Luisant (*Launomarus*), Saint-Martin-le-Viandier (*Martinus Vitandarius*), Saint-Michel (*Michael*), Saint-Martin au Val (*Martinus in Valle*), Saint-Hilaire de Mainvilliers (*Manuvillare*), Saint-Maurice (*Mauricius*), and Saint-Saturnin or -Cernin (*Saturninus*). The register lists first the excommunications within a given parish and then the fines in a following section by year. It is missing the first folios and is recorded in hands of declining clarity on paper. Even though Charles Donahue's guide to the records of church courts proposes that the register may be incomplete, this does not appear to be the case.[14] The register begins with excommunications and fines for the parish of Saint-André (*Andreas*) in 1393 and proceeds in the order given above to those for Saint-Saturnin (*Saturninus*). Since other parishes begin in 1380 or 1381, the register may lack only one folio. Continuing until 1436 for some parishes, it covers nearly sixty years, the longest of any single register consulted. As previously noted, there does appear to have been a previous tradition of recording excommunications at Chartres, as a bifolium from a register covering the 1340s survives as the binding of the register of civil litigation beginning in December 1380. Compared to the register from the 1340s, which specified only the year, the excommunicate, the excommunicator, absolution (indicated by crossing out the entry), and only rarely the cause or the amount if a monetary debt, the register beginning in the 1380s also gives the day, the cause, and the summoner, the last probably to facilitate the administrative review of verbal citations.

Around Chartres, the difficult period between 1380 and 1436 was marked by the economic, social, and political disruptions of war and the accompanying food scarcity and epidemics. Like Paris and other French towns, Chartres and the surrounding plain of the Beauce passed back and forth. Though Charles VII recovered the town in 1432, Claudine Billot has shown that recovery from the depopulation of the region and the economic dislocation of what contemporaries remembered to be sixty years of war – nearly corresponding to the years covered by the register examined – did not really begin until after 1450.[15] The *pays chartrain*

[14] Charles Donahue Jr., *The Records of the Medieval Ecclesiastical Courts, Part I: The Continent*, Comparative Studies in Continental and Anglo-American Legal History 6 (Berlin: Duncker und Humblot, 1989), 105, states that it ends at M.

[15] Claudine Billot, *Chartres à la fin du Moyen Âge* (Paris: Éditions de l'EHESS, 1987).

entered the period of the register having already had a difficult fourteenth century. Afflicted by the famines of 1315–1322, the Black Death of 1348, and war from 1357 onward, the region was impoverished. In 1369–1370, many parish priests of the northern portion of the diocese of Chartres could not pay their papal taxes.[16] More seriously, and perhaps signifying the region's real difficulties, the cathedral chapter confronted what amounted to a rebellion in its villages in two waves between 1386 and 1396. The villagers refused both to perform the labor services of haying on the chapter's demesne and to carry dues of hay to the chapter's barns. Though the chapter sued the villagers before the Parlement of Paris, it ultimately ceded, preserving the minimal *cens* recognizing its lordship but reducing the heavier *taille* by half.[17] There was some economic recovery in the 1380s and 1390s, when refugees from the Hundred Years War in Guyenne migrated and purchased or leased lands in the area.[18] Difficulties returned during the struggle between Armagnacs and Burgundians allied with the English in the years following the assassination of the Duke of Orléans in 1407. After the Burgundian faction took the town in 1417, they expelled partisans of the Armagnacs and gave their property to loyal supporters.[19] Prudent families had members in both camps.[20] A concentration of hoards buried during the years of English occupation suggests that these were years of considerable pillage that suppressed normal economic activity.[21] Furthermore, trade was displaced from French-held Orléans to Paris through 1432.[22] Figure 3.1 distinguishes the proportion of excommunications for debt (*pro judicato*) and for all other causes for each year covered by the register.

Though considerable fluctuations undermine any hope to determine a "typical" year, it is evident that judicial business was rising until the disturbance of war interrupted this trend in 1415. It may be that the increasing frequency of sanctions in the 1390s is tied to the expulsion of France's Jews, in that Christian creditors may have stepped into the place of Jewish lenders and availed themselves of ecclesiastical sanctions against defaulters. As the absolute number of excommunications shrank after 1415, the predominance of debt in motivating them grew. Demand for the excommunication of debitors diminished, it is true, but less than demand for excommunication in other cases. Furthermore, it is not improbable that the official and some of the auditors fled Chartres after 1417, as did many of the cathedral canons.[23] The depressed judicial

[16] Billot, *Chartres*, 33. [17] Billot, *Chartres*, 39–42.
[18] Billot, *Chartres*, 42. [19] Billot, *Chartres*, 43–45.
[20] Billot, *Chartres*, 44. [21] Billot, *Chartres*, 51.
[22] Billot, *Chartres*, 49–50. [23] Billot, *Chartres*, 57–58.

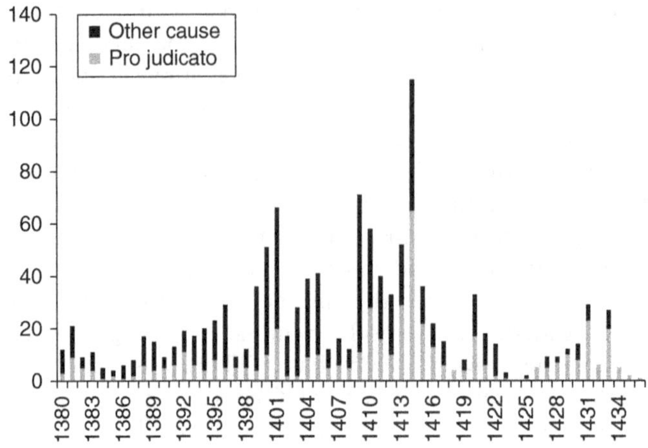

Figure 3.1 Excommunications by the Sub-Dean of Chartres, 1380–1436, by year and cause (stacked chart).
Source: ADEL G 817.

activity evident after 1415 continued to mid-century, as economic depression followed upon political instability. The amount of wheat and oats distributed to holders of capitular prebends declined even after 1432 and remained negligible until through the 1460s.[24] The pattern at Chartres is similar to the pattern at Rouen, in that the difficult economic and political situation in the middle of the fifteenth century caused it to diverge from the trends evident in other officialities, where recourse to excommunication appears to have peaked around 1450.

At Chartres, as elsewhere, jurisdictions proliferated: the bishop had his officiality, the grand archdeacon his, the dean and chapter theirs, and the sub-dean his, which was separate from that of the dean and chapter. In and around the cathedral close there were five scaffolds or gallows, although three of them may have belonged to the secular jurisdiction of the bishop, the chapter, and the hospital.[25] These symbols of jurisdiction advertised opportunities for forum-shopping. Proliferating jurisdictions in a town of 5,000 to 6,000 could nourish numerous personnel. Although court officials often cumulated multiple functions, they were decently remunerated: on May 4, 1413, the Dean

[24] Billot, *Chartres*, 59.

[25] Billot, *Chartres*, 127. Lucien Merlet counted twenty-four officialities within the late medieval diocese of Chartres, assuming that rural deans had them and that the cathedral dean and chapter did not share an official: "Registres des officialités de Chartres," *Bibliothèque de l'École des Chartes* 17:2 (1856), 574–594, at 575.

and Chapter of Chartres agreed that each was to pay their official 20£t annually, for a total salary of 40£t.[26] All these church courts provided a quick, cheap, and efficacious means of pression upon delinquent debtors and capital enemies. A scrap of paper containing a citation from the diocesan officiality of Chartres pinned inside the cover of the Register of Fines from 1400 onward suggests that a reasonable interval was offered to those cited: Jean Bardet and Jean Petit were summoned for the Thursday after the Feast of St. Bartholomew 1403 on the preceding Friday, giving them a full week to respond.[27] Even if cited parties had heard of their summons, they could choose not to respond, either because they had no means to satisfy their creditors short of making a *cessio bonorum* or because they calculated that they would be able to secure absolution by Easter, perhaps on more favorable terms from their creditors.

The form of the sub-dean's register indicates its twofold function. First, like the charge-discharge accounts of the previous chapter, it illustrated for which sums the official or sealer of the officiality was responsible, namely, only those for fines that had been paid and for excommunications or absolutions that had been issued. Second, the register showed which believers were obliged to the official, either because they had been fined or because they had been excommunicated. The fines listed were most often given as punishments in the moral cases that were the mainstay of litigation before ecclesiastical tribunals: adultery, concubinage, assault, defamation, and failure to perform one's Easter duty. For example, in 1415 in the parish of Saint-André Alain Caradou was fined 5st for failing to communicate at Easter on the Monday after *Quasimodo*. He was excommunicated on an unspecified day for nonpayment, but then paid and was absolved. John de la Scenserie was fined 7s 6d for assaulting Jean Gardemont, a layman, on Tuesday after the Feast of St. Barnabas. He did not pay. Pierre Germain, cleric, was fined 40s for assaulting Gilotte Doguet, a laywoman, with a sword and drawing blood

[26] ADEL G 815, 113r-v.

[27] ADEL G 813, one of four citations pinned to the inside of the cover: "Offic[ialis] carn[otensis] pr[esbiter]is o[mn]ibus nob[is] subd[itis] sal[ute]m in d[omi]no Cit[etis] pen[dente] c[aus]a cor[am] nob[is] ad diem ~~lune post fest[um] pos[t]~~ Jovis post fest[um] b[eat]i bertholomei ap[osto]li inter Joh[ann]em bardet Joh[annem] petit q[uod] just[um] fu[er]it Ins[uper] datum Anno d[omi]ni mill[esim]o cccc^{mo} tercio die ven[er]is preced[enti]." I have left the brackets and strikethrough in to convey how abbreviated – and therefore illegible even to those literate in Latin but unfamiliar with legal matters – such citations were. The register of fines may be that of the Grand Archdeacon's official or that of the bishop's.

on the Thursday after the octave of St. Martin.[28] He did not pay. Drouet Manette confessed to committing adultery repeatedly with Jeanne, wife of Olivier Le Clerc. He was fined 20s on the Thursday after the Feast of the Circumcision. Jeanne was not fined on account of her poverty; Drouet paid up; neither was excommunicated. Excommunication followed failure to pay a fine relatively swiftly. Since the Church had little physical force, it quickly turned to exclusion from the sacraments. In 1416, again in the parish of Saint-André, Jean de Gays, layman, was fined 10s for assaulting Renaud du Tours, cleric, on the Tuesday after the Translation of St. Stephen (August 8, since the Feast is August 2 and Easter came on April 19 in 1416). For failing to pay this fine, Jean (here called Pierre de Gays, though there was no Pierre mentioned among those fined at this time) was excommunicated at the request of the official by the summoner Guiguenay, ostensibly for knocking out the eye of the cleric Jean Belin on the Wednesday after the Feast of St. Bartholomew (August 31, since the Feast is August 24). Perhaps there had been a brawl with many participants, or perhaps the clerk was in error about the name of Jean/Pierre de Gays and about the precise details of his crime. In addition to displaying the fluidity of medieval names, potentially imprecise record-keeping, and likely the willful inaccessibility of those accused of crimes before their judges, this case illustrates that those fined as punishment may have been given roughly three weeks to pay before they were excommunicated. Since Jean/Pierre de Gays is not recorded as having paid his fine or as having been absolved, perhaps he was a vagabond cleric or layman posing as a cleric who simply departed Chartres and changed his name. Excommunication was more effective against members of the community, who could be named with confidence and shamed. Within a town such as Chartres, where ties of descent, patronage, spiritual kinship, commercial relations, and other elective affinities bound the residents to each other, the impact of excommunication must have been great.

This would have been all the more the case for excommunications for debt, which proclaimed to the community that one of its own had failed to honor a debt when it was called in and potentially that the debtor was insolvent or that a state of enmity now existed between the creditor and the debtor. Daniel Smail has made the case that civil suits in late medieval Marseille were components of calculated strategies that displayed enmity through emotional and legal actions both inside and outside the courtroom.[29] Cost/benefit analysis goes beyond the monetary

[28] The *festum sancti Martini estivale* on July 4, not Martinmas, the *festum hyemale*, on November 11.

[29] Smail, *Consumption*.

cost of litigation to comprehend the extremely valuable and satisfying diminution of an enemy's honor or credit. No less than lay tribunals, church courts were sites and mechanisms of retribution and conflict over resources as much as of social control by the Church.

Thus, in 1415 in the parish of Saint-André, for instance, in addition to the André Caradou mentioned earlier, Étienne Baudet was excommunicated, apparently twice, on the Friday after *Laetare* for debts of 56st and 19st to Thomas Le Joly. He paid, as these two entries are struck through. On the Friday after *Judica*, Jean de Péronne was excommunicated for a debt of 3s 4dt to Raoul Fonteneau. He too paid. In 1416 in addition to Jean/Pierre de Gays mentioned earlier, Jeanne called "*Joue de brebis*" was cited and excommunicated on the Friday after the octave of the Translation of St. Benedict at the official's request by Guiguenay. She was not absolved. On Monday after the Feast of St. Hilary, Jean Roger was excommunicated for a debt of 10s 10dt to Blanot Triquet. He was not recorded as having been absolved. However, Jean Gombaust, excommunicated for a debt of 2s 11d to Jean Chartier on Wednesday after *Invocavit* or the *Dimanche des Brandons* (first Sunday of Lent), and Jean Montureau, excommunicated for a debt of 3s 1dt to Jean Belher on Friday after *Laetare* (fourth Sunday of Lent), were absolved. Lent was, as noted earlier, a popular time to excommunicate. Two of three excommunications, the two for debt, in 1415 and two of five, of three for private debts, came during Lent. Creditors knew that unabsolved excommunicates would be barred from performing their Easter duty, menacing their souls and risking additional ecclesiastical punishment. They consequently chose to exert maximum pression upon borrowers during Lent. At Chartres, 119 entries lack a legible date. Of the rest, 259 excommunications came during Lent and a further 113 in the five weeks following the Sunday after Easter. This amounted to 23.5 percent of excommunications for which a date was specified (21.2 percent of all excommunications) during Lent and 33.8 percent (30.5 percent) if the period immediately following Easter is included. Roughly a third of excommunications therefore came during a fifth of the year. If we look only at the 492 excommunications *pro judicato*, 167 or 34 percent came during Lent. Including December (29), January (17), and February (18), we get 231 or 47 percent. A third of excommunications for debt occurred during Lent. Nearly half of excommunications for debt occurred between Advent and Lent, the period preceding Easter when each Christian conventionally prepared for the annual reception of the Eucharist mandated in 1215 by *Omnis utriusque sexus* (X.5.38.12). The type of excommunication most likely to result from the (ill) wishes of another Christian was employed in a coldly – or hotly, as Smail reminds us – calculated manner. Whether the goal was the recovery or renegotiation of an outstanding debt or the diminution of a capital enemy's credit and honor, creditors knew when it was best to manipulate the procedures of ecclesiastical tribunals.

Let us return to the causes and distribution of excommunication at Chartres. Of 1,220 entries in the database, derived from the list of excommunicates, 430 or roughly a third specified no cause; 492, roughly another third, were for debts (*pro judicato*), roughly 40 percent; 90 were for the assignation of a court date or perhaps a payment deadline (*pro assignacione* [*terminis*]); 57 were for contumacy; 49 were for assault; 48 for failure to communicate at Easter, of which many were issued in the week after *Quasimodo*, the Sunday after Easter, indicating that parish priests were quick to denounce parishioners who failed to perform their Easter duty; 17 excommunications were for adultery; 10 for concubinage; 8 concerned fines; 4 were for work on feast days; 2 for contempt of court; 2 for blasphemy; 2 "for many causes" (*in pluribus locis*); and only 1 for defamation. Of those for debt, the average amount was 25st, a little more than 2£t. The median was only 10st, five to ten days' wages for a male laborer. The maximum amount was 32£ 7st. The minimum a bare 6dt, probably reflecting a creditor's spite or injury, given that he or she probably only stood to regain 2d paying for the monition. As to when, between 1380 and 1436, an average of almost twenty-two persons per year were excommunicated in the town and suburbs of Chartres. This average dissimulates extreme variations from year to year, however, from a high of 115 to minima of 1 to 3. Yet 22 and even 115 excommunications per year are not overwhelming frequencies in a town of 5,000 to 6,000. If we assume (as I have for Paris) households of four, this would mean that a member at most of 8 percent, on average of 1.6 percent, and minimally of 0.1 percent of households was excommunicated by the sub-dean each year. Of these excommunicates, 727 or 60 percent were marked as having been absolved in the register, 493 or 40 percent were not.

That 40 percent of excommunicates were not recorded as having been absolved is something of a puzzle. Jacques Toussaert believed that the existence of many multiple and long-term excommunicates indicated tepid religiosity among late medieval Flemings.[30] Should we then assume that late medieval Chartrains were indifferent to the sanctions of Holy Mother Church, that the guardians of the Virgin's veil were Jean Delumeau's veritable pagans, or that they were proto-Protestants? That would be to go too far with respect to residents of this pilgrimage destination. I envision

[30] Toussaert, *Le sentiment*.

five causes for this large minority of the unabsolved. First, perhaps some of the unabsolved were transients, whose names were not securely known and who simply departed Chartres after being denounced as excommunicate. Excommunication might be a creditor's only recourse against this type of believer, who probably lacked any real property or even much movable property. Indeed, this was one justification for excommunicating debtors, as will be noted in the following chapter with respect to the custom of Brittany. Second, some of the unabsolved may have been the truly poor, those lacking any means to satisfy their creditors. However, because canon law specified that "satisfaction is whatever the creditor wills"[31] and because it is commonly noted that an excommunicate has been absolved "through the plaintiff's consent (*parte consentiente*)," creditors who refused to let paupers off the hook could have been judged particularly stubborn and un-Christian. Their confessors may well have withheld absolution until they forgave their debtors. Third, as remarked earlier, for all but the most pious laity late medieval sacramental practice entailed reception of the Eucharist once per year. Being barred from the sacraments kept believers from the church during services but otherwise may not have greatly impacted their lives, unless they wished to access another sacrament, such as marriage or extreme unction. The stakes were then, of course, higher. Neither could excommunicates marry nor, if they died unabsolved, could they be buried in consecrated ground. In the last case, however, some formularies and some merciful ordinaries provided for the absolution of excommunicates on their deathbeds or for the transfer of their bodies into consecrated ground.[32] One case from Chartres does undermine the assertion that excommunication did not ordinarily trouble daily life: on Tuesday after the octave of Martinmas 1409 in the parish of Saint-Cernin Jean Goulet was excommunicated at

[31] Guillaume Durand, *Speculum judiciale* (Basel: apud Frobenos fratres, 1574), IV:III, 361 n.8: "Quid si contra te est lata sententia executionis, nisi michi solveris decem usque ad pascha, ut extra de app. [X.2.28] postea ego reputo mihi satisfactum esse, licet in veritate non solveris infra termino? Dic, quod non est excommunicatus. satisfacere enim est, sicut voluerit creditor, ff de pig. not. actio, l. si rem § omnis [Dig. 13.7.9.3], arg. extra. de usu. consuluit [X.5.19.10]." Dig.13.7.9.3: "Satisfactum autem accepimus, quemadmodum voluit creditor, licet non sit solutum."

[32] Paravy, *De la chrétienté romaine*, 465. They did the latter perhaps as commonly as prelates commanded the disinterment of the corpses of excommunicated debtors, though the evidence for excommunications in articulo mortis is spectacular only from a pastoral perspective. One might contrast the formula for the disinterment of a contumacious excommunicate given by Esmein, "Débiteurs," 239–240 (from Durand, *Speculum*, l.IV, pt.III, De sepulturis, no.8) with the mercy evident in the formulary of the officiality of Le Mans (*c.*1429), BN Latin 10930, which contains templates "how a priest should absolve a dying person on his deathbed" and "dispensation so that the body of an excommunicate might be buried in consecrated ground" at 12v–13.

the request of the official "for having contracted with the excommunicate Jean Rousseau (*pro pactione habita cum johanne rousseau excommunicato*)." This is, however, the only time that anyone was excommunicated for doing business – and not for socializing – with an excommunicate. What type of contract is not specified, but apparently it was one that his neighbors thought could not be concluded with an excommunicate, since someone must have denounced Goulet to the officiality. Interestingly, Rousseau may have been excommunicated by another jurisdiction: while his servant John (*Johannem famulum johannis rousseau bolengarii*) had been excommunicated on Monday after Michaelmas by Jean Trouin, the master himself appears in the register only when requesting the excommunication of Jeanne la Volette in the parish of Saint-Hilaire for a debt of 5st, as we might expect of a baker, who would have sold most often on credit.[33] Aside from this unclear case, no one appears to have been punished for commerce with an excommunicate during the fifty-seven years covered by the register. By mid-century, indeed, the Council of Basel issued a decree "that excommunicates are not to be shunned (*De excommunicatis non vitandis*)," confirming that the Fathers at Basel were aware of just how common excommunications – and excommunications for debt – were.

The fourth means of explaining why 40 percent of excommunicates are not recorded as having been absolved is indifference. Pierrette Paravy has proposed that the abuse of excommunication for debt encouraged the growth of a stridently separatist Waldensianism in the fifteenth-century Dauphiné.[34] Others have suggested a connection between the practice and the persistence of Lollardy in England, and with later support for the reforms of the Reformation Parliament.[35] Because the evidence from France demonstrates that plenty of French subjects were excommunicated for debts, does this mean that the French were more tolerant of the errancy of this human institution? That is unlikely, given the clear hopes for reform of Church and society among French clergy and laity in the fifteenth century.[36] More likely, it was such practices that pushed French men

[33] There may have been another Jean Rousseau, a painter, in Chartres at the time: Billot, *Chartres*, 135.

[34] Paravy, *De la chrétienté romaine*, 750–751.

[35] Richard Wunderli, *London Church Courts and Society of the Eve of the Reformation*, Speculum Anniversary Monographs 7 (Cambridge, MA: Medieval Academy of America, 1981).

[36] Inter alia, Noël Valois, *Histoire de la Pragmatique Sanction de Bourges sous Charles VII* (Paris: Alphonse Picard et fils, 1906); Brian Patrick McGuire, *Jean Gerson and the Last Medieval Reformation* (University Park, PA: Pennsylvania State University Press, 2005); Daniel Hobbins, *Authorship and Publicity Before Print: Jean Gerson and the Transformation of Late Medieval Learning* (Philadelphia: University of Pennsylvania Press, 2009);

and women, even as they availed themselves of spiritual sanctions in matters of debt, to support the efforts of the king of France and his officers to reform ecclesiastical justice by limiting its scope to its "proper" boundaries. Charitably, we can interpret demand for spiritual sanctions against debtors not as hypocrisy but as the typically human tendency to hold simultaneously to incompatible truths. Growing distaste for excommunication for debt in the sixteenth century signals not "secularization" in the sense of a less religious society but hopes to spiritualize ecclesiastical institutions by "secularizing" certain of their functions in handing them over to lay authorities. That layfolk increasingly sought secular remedies for matters of debt is a sign of the importance they placed on new ideas about what a "reformed" Church should do. As R. N. Swanson has observed, "[t]he relationship between secular and spiritual courts was actually determined not by the supreme authorities in either field, but by those who sought justice."[37] Whether this means that Christians grew more pious the more they "voted with their feet" to limit the judicial capacity of the earthly Church, as early modern and contemporary Protestants might argue, or that they had begun to cordon "religion" off as a separate, pure, irrational, limited realm best experienced on Sundays, I leave up to the reader.[38] In the end, that 40 percent of Chartrain excommunicates are not recorded as having been unabsolved probably indicates not widespread detachment from the institutional Church but the fifth possible explanation: imperfect record-keeping.

Who excommunicated and who was excommunicated? How many times? As one might expect in a patriarchal society,[39] men predominated as excommunicators and as excommunicates. One thousand and eighty of 1,220 excommunicates or 88.5 percent were lay males or clerics in minor orders, 40 were unmarried women (or women not specified as married), 32 were widows, 26 were married women, 13 were couples (the economic unit was excommunicated, as at Paris and at Montivilliers), 10 were priests, two each were two men and a layman and a priest conjointly,

Jean-Marie Le Gall, *Les moines au temps des réformes: Frances, 1480–1560* (Seyssel: Champ Vallon, 2001).

37 Swanson, *Church and Society*, 185.

38 Swanson, *Church and Society*, 190.

39 Barbara A. Hanawalt, *The Wealth of Wives: Women, Law, and Economy in Late Medieval London* (Oxford: Oxford University Press, 2007); Martha C. Howell, *The Marriage Exchange: Property, Social Place, and Gender in Cities of the Low Countries, 1300–1550* (Chicago: University of Chicago Press, 1998); Barbara Diefendorf, *Paris City Councillors in the Sixteenth Century: The Politics of Patrimony* (Princeton: Princeton University Press, 1983); Sarah Hanley, "Engendering the State: Family Formation and State Building in Early Modern France," *French Historical Studies* 16:1 (1989), 4–27; Julie Hardwick, *The Practice of Patriarchy: Gender and the Politics of Household Authority in Early Modern France* (College Station, PA: Pennsylvania State University Press, 1998).

and one each was an executor, a group of churchwardens, a man and his concubine, and a man and an unmarried woman conjointly. Seven hundred and fifty-eight of 1,220 excommunicators or 62 percent were laymen or clerics in minor orders, 359 officers of the court (rising to 368 if we count the nine instances in which Gillot Morély, the *promotor*, may have acted as a private individual), 26 were widows, 23 were priests, 16 were unmarried women, 13 were convents, 4 were groups of churchwardens, 3 each were confraternities and two men, and one each was a knight, an executor, a married couple, an officer and a widow conjointly, and a married woman alone. Thirty percent of excommunicators were officers of the court, a greater proportion than at Paris or at Montivilliers. Yet it could alternately be argued that this is a rather low figure for the weight of the Church's social control as exercised by the sub-dean's officiality, since private initiative therefore lay at the root of 70 percent of excommunications. As the figures given are limited to excommunications, rather than fines, which mostly concerned moral cases or assault in this period, it does not wholly transform our view of church courts. It does remind us that ecclesiastical tribunals were not only instruments of an oppressive Church but also, as Smail has shown for civil courts in late medieval Marseille, tools for insulting enemies. Here, church courts had an advantage: the *viguier* of Marseille could condemn someone to death, but the Sub-Dean of Chartres could consign him to Hell.

As to the frequency of excommunication, Table 3.1 analyzes those who either excommunicated or were excommunicated over the period covered, demonstrating that most excommunications were one-time events for both parties.

The outlier, who excommunicated 314 times, is not unexpected: "pro nobis," which is to say, "at the request of the promotor or auditor." Not unconnected to these ex officio excommunications were the fourteen excommunications by Georges Amyot, a summoner who may also have acted as an auditor of the officiality, the thirteen by Jean Poneau, the official, the nine by the sealer of the court, and the five by "the proctor of my lord the Sub-Dean," who must have acted as a sort of solicitor-general. Of the multiple excommunicates, Pierre Grenet was excommunicated a total of twenty-three times. Eighteen of these appear to have occurred between January and the end of Lent 1405 (NS) with a further two in June and July 1405. That twenty of these excommunications at the request of different individuals occurred during the first six months of 1405 (in our dating) suggests that Pierre Grenet encountered a crisis of credit amounting to a bankruptcy early in that year. Similarly, Pierre Fromentin was excommunicated thirteen times in total, once in 1400, once in 1401, once in 1408, and ten times in 1403. He was

Table 3.1 *Frequency of sanctions at Chartres, 1380–1436*

Number of sanctions	Persons sanctioned	Persons requesting sanctions
0	641	394
1	532	878
2	127	77
3	45	27
4	20	6
5	13	3
6	5	0
7	5	3
8	2	3
9	1	0
10	1	0
13	1	1
14	0	1
23	1	0
314	0	1

Source: ADEL G 817.

excommunicated thrice for the *promotor*, thrice for Etienne Aliot, and four times for Sire Renaud Fornigaust. That the 1403 excommunications came during the winter points to an acute crisis at that time, but in the context of perennial problems with Fromentin's credit. Other potential bankrupts appear in the register: for instance, Pierre *de Busto* was excommunicated for debts of 15st, 10st, 20st, 50st, and 56s 8dt to five different individuals between December 1413 and Lent 1414 NS).[40] If frequent excommunicators were likely court personnel, frequent excommunicates were likely bankrupts. The late medieval equivalent of the early modern insult "bankrupt (*banqueroutier*)" was "excommunicate (*excommunié*)." The latter emphasized the moral status of the debtor, though moral issues were not irrelevant to the former, especially because early modern French law would distinguish culpable *banqueroutiers* from unfortunate *faillis*, as I shall discuss in Chapter 4. Since 641 individuals of the 1,394 mentioned in the Chartres register were never excommunicated, while only 394 never excommunicated, more individuals experienced excommunication, potentially for debt, than requested it. That the vast majority of excommunications for debt came between private individuals (446 of

[40] ADEL G 817, Saint-Saturnin. The first excommunication came on Wednesday after the Feast of St. Lucy, the next two on Saturday after Epiphany, and the last two on Thursday after Ash Wednesday.

487 excommunications for debt for which the requester was legible[41]) is consonant with the proposition that the spiritual sanctions of the Sub-Dean of Chartres were most often deployed in matters of private debt at the end of the Middle Ages.

The archidiaconal officiality of Paris, 1426–1439

My second database is constructed on the basis of the register of excommunications of the archidiaconal officiality of Paris from 1426 to 1439. There were three archdeaconries in the diocese of Paris: Paris, Josas, and Brie. The Archdeacon of Paris or Grand Archdeacon had jurisdiction over the *archiprêtré* of the Madeleine (or of Paris containing the parishes of the *cité* and the Right Bank), and the rural deaneries of Chelles and Montmorency. As at Chartres, his was not the only nearby officiality: the bishop, the cathedral chapter, the abbots of Saint-Germain and Saint-Denis, and the archdeacons of Josas and Brie had theirs, and not far away the Archbishop of Rouen had a vicar exercising his spiritual jurisdiction at Pontoise. All these excommunicated for debt. Unfortunately only the records of the archdeaconry of Paris survive in any quantity, in fragmentary series from the late fifteenth to the early sixteenth century. While previous registers exist, as do posterior registers, there are no audience registers of the same date range as the surviving register of excommunicates. I will nevertheless draw on examples from the most proximate years, 1384–1387 and the 1470s, 1480s, and 1490s, to illuminate excommunications from 1426 to 1439.

In the French national archives, $Z^{1o}25$ is the earliest surviving register of a Parisian officiality, containing the fines assigned by the archidiaconal officiality from October 24, 1355 to the Saturday after *Laetare* Sunday 1367 (OS). Containing fines for concubinage and assault that could give rise to excommunications at the request of the receiver of fines, it confirms that careful records were kept of the considerable amount of the business before the officiality in the middle of the fourteenth century. In contrast to Chartres, where fines and excommunications were recorded in the same volume, there must have existed at Paris a separate register of excommunications and of absolutions. This parallel register may have been lost already by 1500, when it would have been of little use to retain century-old lists of fines or excommunications, if not after

[41] Four were illegible. Of the remaining forty-one requesters, twenty-seven were officers of the court such as the sealer, the promotor, the proctor of the sub-dean, and the summoners, two were confraternities, nine were convents, and three were churchwardens.

1789Dor in 1871. The register of civil audiences of the diocesan officiality for 1384–1387, published by Joseph Petit in 1919, is more relevant. It is full of recognizances of debts and disputes over them, as a glance at the index under the headings "debts (*debita*)," "obligation (*obligatio*)," or "cash (*pecunia*)" confirms. The register mentions fifty-one debts of one sort or another deriving from condemnations and obligations confirmed by letters of *nisi* or issuing from failure to comply with the terms of monitions. Excommunications for simple contumacy, for failure to respond to a citation, do not appear. Eleven of the debts included in the 1384–1387 register originate in cash loans or extensions of verbal credit (*mutua*), the other obligations arose from judicial fines, rents, services, or purchases of bread, wine, cloth, iron, and so on. The cash loans are not enormous by lordly standards, but would have been quite large to ordinary people, justifying their enrollment by the officiality: 6 *francs* 8s 6dp, 2fr, 2fr, 12fr, 34fr, 19fr less 2sp, 6fr, 6fr 4sp, 15fr of an initial 30fr, 3½fr, 5fr, on average (though driven up by a few large amounts) about 12£t.[42] Each of the instances in which these debts appear in the register cost at least 8dp and often 12dp, in addition to the notarial and sealing fees for drawing up the letters of *nisi* that frequently resulted, and were notably larger than the relatively small debts that appear to have been at the basis of many excommunications for debt – which, as we have seen, could potentially be recovered for 4dp. Although only part of the Archdeacon of Paris's civil competence is evident in the audience register, the evidence from Chartres and from Paris together illustrate that the sanctions of Northern French officialities were frequently used in the negotiation of debt at the end of the fourteenth century.

The register AN Z^{1o}17 of excommunications from 1426 to 1439 suggests that this competence over debt was mainly exercised with respect to parol contracts or private obligations, which had to be proven in court. It is organized by parish, though not alphabetically. The clerk began with the parishes of the Right Bank, proceeded to those of the *cité*, and finally to those of the countryside. It is headed: "This paper or register is the paper or register of excommunicates of the court of the Lord Archdeacon of Paris, when the most circumspect and conscientious Master Nicolas Fraillon, professor of both laws, was Archdeacon of Paris, and the venerable and circumspect Master Jean Hubert, doctor of canon law, conservator of the privileges of the University of Paris, was official of the said court, begun by me Yves Krahan, clerc of the diocese of Saint-Pol-de-Léon, auditor and keeper of the said register of excommunicates, in the

[42] In *livres tournois*: 7£ 14s 7½dt, 2£ 8st, 2£ 8st, 14£ 8st, 40£ 16st, 22£ 13s 6dt, 7£ 4st, 7£ 9st, 16£ 12st, 4£ 4st, 6£t.

year 1426 (OS), in the fifth indiction, in the tenth year of the pontificate of the lord Pope Martin V, on the Monday after the Purification of the Blessed Virgin Mary in the month of February." Nicolas Fraillon, who may have helped to negotiate the Treaty of Arras in 1435, diligently cultivated the rights and income of the Archdeacon of Paris. He is credited as the first archdeacon to claim the inheritance of subject parish priests. When the curé of Fontenay died in 1433, Fraillon claimed his bed and its coverings, surplice, and amice, or their monetary equivalent. When the curé's heirs appealed to the *Requêtes du Palais*, Fraillon was awarded 60sp (72st). Subsequent archdeacons claimed more: in 1480 François Hallé gained in addition the breviary, silver belt, and pillow of the curé of Belloy. In 1623, the Archdeacon of Paris claimed a curé's robe, bonnet, and mulet. In 1644 Antoine de Verthamon claimed a curé's horse, golden belt, soutane, and movable possessions![43] Jean Hubert, for his part, may have had some role in the foundation of the Collège de Sainte-Barbe, but was surely more influential as regent of the Faculty of Canon Law, in which capacity he first appears in the fall of 1424.[44] Yves Krahan was, to judge from the register, at once *apparitor* or summoner, auditor or judge (*audienciarius*), guardian of the register of excommunicates, and perhaps ecclesiastical notary. This Breton summoner diligently delivered ninety-five citations over the period covered by the register. Others summoned far more often, however: of 3,069 excommunicates, Jacques Vigneron cited 734 or nearly one quarter, Jean Gaillard 477, Guillaume Gautard 440, Raoul Tasse 238, Raoul Fuillet 123, Guillaume de Menehy 104, Robert Cuignet 103, Master Jean Barret 67, Simon Bacot 65, Master Guillaume Marchand 59, *Evenus* Bloescaut 51, Master Jean Louchard 46, Hugues de Beaumont 32, [Pierre?] Dusseau 29, and others only once or a handful of times. Occasionally, the archdeacon's prosecutor, the promotor of justice, summoned in person: Master Jean Louchard summoned forty-six times; Master Jean Laurent summoned alone four times and once in conjunction with the summoner de Beaumont; Master Henri Camus summoned twice; Master Guillaume du Bois never summoned. Thus, aside from Louchard, promotors seldom summoned. Roles were relatively clearly demarcated within the organization of the Archdeacon of Paris.

[43] Jean-François de la Croix, *Dictionnaire historique des cultes religieux, établis dans le monde depuis son origine jusqu'à présent* (Paris: Vincent, 1770) v° "archidiacre," I: 130–132. Much of the story is summarized in the *arrêt* of the Parlement of Paris for the Archdeacon of Josas against the curés of his archdeaconry in 1684: AN L 419 n° 240.

[44] Victor Chauvin, *Histoire des lycées et collèges de Paris* (Paris: Librairie L. Hachette, 1866), 138. On his career, see volume 1 of Fournier and Dorez's *La Faculté de décret de l'université de Paris au quinzième siècle* (Paris: Imprimerie nationale, 1895). In 1425, he noted that a manuscript of Bernardus Compostellanus's *Causae decretalium* (Sorbonne MS 793) was his (224v).

Much of the register Z[1o]17 concerns the big parishes of the Right Bank, where the bulk of the archdeacon's jurisdiction was located, along with a few parishes of the City and of the suburbs. The frequency of sanctions corresponds to the intensity of commerce and density of population, as Map 3.1 illustrates.

Two thousand eight hundred fifty or 93 percent of 3,069 sanctions were issued in these thirteen parishes. The first eleven are most important and are all large parishes of the commercial Right Bank. The last two are on two of the main roads into Paris, the former in the *bourg* of the Abbey of Saint-Denis, itself a commercial center. The remaining rural or tiny urban parishes are mentioned only a handful of times, sometimes with only one or two sanctions recorded in each. The register nevertheless mentions sixty of the approximately 194 parishes subject to the jurisdiction of the Archdeacon of Paris, to judge by the *pouillé* drawn up for Archbishop Christophe de Beaumont in the eighteenth century.

The register covers the economically and politically disturbed years between the bloodletting following the violent Burgundian entry into Paris in 1418, the deaths of Henry V and Charles VI in 1422, and the crisis years of the late 1420s and early 1430s, when Charles VII struggled against the Regent Bedford before retaking the city in 1436. In the archdeaconry of Paris between 1426 and 1439, excommunication touched 6.5 to 24 percent of households over the period covered, assuming households of four persons,[45] at a relatively consistent pace, as Figure 3.2 illustrates.

The rhythm of excommunications per Paschal year varies greatly. In addition, the figures for 1427 and 1428 would rise significantly, nearly to the level of 1429, if the excommunications recorded indifferently for 1427/8 were included. These are unmarked entries before those for 1429, in parishes for which the beginning of entries for 1428 is not indicated. The steep decline in 1439 probably reflects not a drastic decline in their frequency but the beginning of a new and lost register of excommunications. Guy Fourquin's economic study of the Parisian basin at the end of the Middle Ages suggests the causes of the uneven frequency of

[45] This range is based on the database constructed from AN Z[1o]17. It assumes households of four persons and that the central right-bank parishes of the city were densely populated in the fifteenth century, as much of the expansion in population from 100,000 in *c.*1430 to 600,000 residents in *c.*1730 occurred in outlying districts. I, therefore, reduce the population figures given in the 1767 *pouillé* by a generous two-thirds. Dividing instead by 6 doubles the percentages to give a range of from 13 to 48 percent households touched by excommunication. I have taken 100,000 as the population of Paris in this period as it facilitates computation and sits midway between Jean Favier's low estimate of 50,800 residents and high estimate of 146,000 residents: *Les contribuables parisiens à la fin de la Guerre de Cent Ans. Les rôles d'impôt de 1421, 1423 et 1438* (Geneva/Paris: Librairie Droz, 1970), 10.

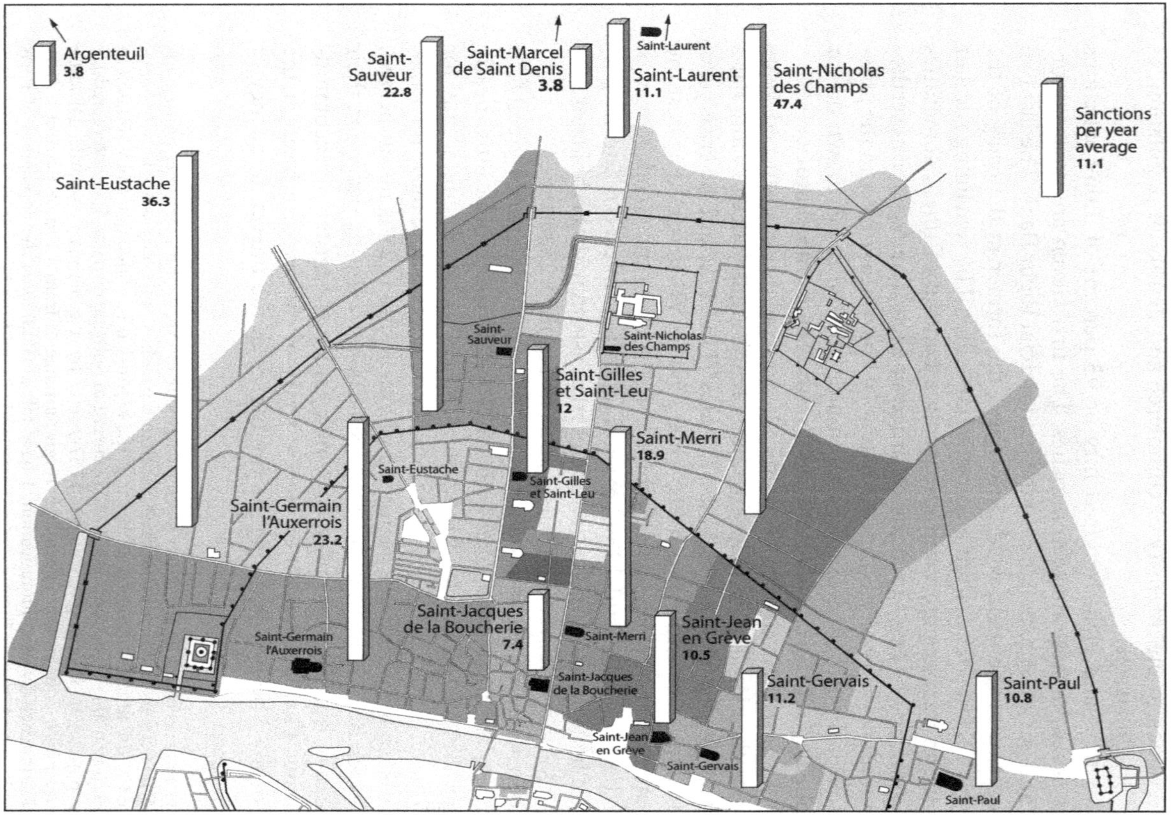

Map 3.1 Sanctions by the Archdeacon of Paris, 1426–1439, by year and parish (thirteen largest parishes). *Source:* AN Z[1o]17.

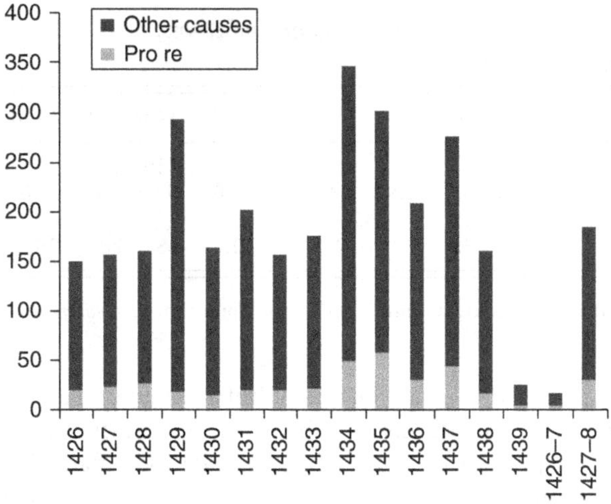

Figure 3.2 Excommunications by the Archdeacon of Paris, 1426–1439, by year and cause (stacked chart).
Source: AN Z[1o]17.

excommunications. Fourquin enumerates the *malheurs* of these years of woe: flooding in the summer of 1426; disease and deflation in 1427, with flooding in June; frost in June 1428; scarcity of grain late in 1429 – accompanied quite clearly by an increase in excommunications; famine and scarcity in 1430, with frost at Easter; scarcity early and late in 1432, with epidemics from September to November and flooding in April; harsh, long winters in 1433–1434, 1434–1435, and 1437–1438; and scarcity in the winter of 1435–1436.[46] Recalling that the years given in my table are in Paschal dating (Old Style), and that the year 1429 continued until Easter 1430, the increase in 1429 may reflect the doubling of grain prices to 40s per setier late in the calendar year 1429. In times of economic and commercial difficulties, it seems, excommunications nearly doubled.

Table 3.2 compares the numbers of excommunicates with wheat prices in livres per setier (156 L or 4.4 bushels), suggesting the effect of price movements on excommunication. I include also Guy Fourquin's index based on the income received by the Almoner of Saint-Denis from property transfers (including *rentes*) unfortunately only between 1410 and 1433 (1410 = 100) and his figures for the revenue of the lease for the port of Neuilly in *livres parisis* to illustrate the commercial difficulties of this period.[47]

[46] Fourquin, *Les campagnes*, 333.

[47] Unfortunately, the price series begins in 1431 and the register ends in 1439. For prices, I used Richard and Margaret Bonney's now unavailable European State Finance Database, itself based on Micheline Baulant, "Le prix de grains à Paris de 1431 à 1788," *Annales ESC* (1968), 538–539. For the rest: Fourquin, *Les campagnes*, table XIV, 385, and table I, following 352.

Table 3.2 *Excommunications per year and economic indicators, Archdeaconry of Paris, 1428–1440*

Year	1428	1429	1430	1431	1432	1433	1434	1435	1436	1437	1438	1439	1440
Exc	160	292	163	201	157	175	345	300	208	275	159	26	
Grain				2.76	2.25	5.50	1.89	1.37	1.68	4.06	5.95	4.18	1.17
Index	16	?	>5	7	>13	11							
Neuilly	42	42	42	32	32	32	32	32		28	28	28	28

Sources: AN Z/1o/17; Baulant, "Prix de Grains," 538–539; Fourquin, *Les campagnes*, 352, 385.

Prices have been regularized to calendar years, but I have left excommunications in Paschal years, as defaults on subsistence or cash-flow borrowing would have lagged periods of high grain prices. Periodic flambées of excommunications would then signify the breakdown of overstressed credit networks, as creditors and vendors called in outstanding debts to pay their own accounts. That the 1673 Code of Commerce restricted debts to "bakers, *pâtissiers*, butchers, cooks, etc." to a term of six months and debts to wholesale or retail merchants and building contractors to one year implies that bakers and other sellers on credit previously had to extend rather longer-term debts, perhaps even the delays in payment of two years or more that would make the spike in excommunications of 1434–1435 a delayed after-effect of the spike in grain prices in 1433.[48] Overall, although the years between 1426 and 1439 were certainly atypical, comprehending the political, social, and economic dislocations of war, the records of excommunication do not suggest that daily life ground to a halt. Indeed, how could it? Inhabitants of this metropolis of more than 100,000 needed to provision themselves. They may indeed have had more frequent recourse to credit to do so, given the evident and precipitous decline in economic indicators. Rents and commerce declined consistently and steeply: from 1424 to 1427 the lease of the port of Neuilly had yielded 48£p per year; by 1437 it could only be let for 28£p. Excommunications and grain prices fluctuated far more from

48 Isambert 19:92–107, at 94: Tit.1: "Art. 7. Les marchands en gros ou en détail, et les maçons charpentiers, couvreurs, serruriers, vitriers, plombiers, paveurs, et autres de pareille qualité, seront tenus de demander payement dans l'an après la délivrance. Art. 8. L'action sera intentée dans six mois pour marchandises et denrées vendues en détails par boulangers, pâtissiers, bouchers, rôtisseurs, cuisiniers, couturiers, passementiers, selliers, bourreliers et autres semblables." Even more remarkable is Art. 9: "Voulons le contenu ès deux articles ci dessus avoir lieu, encore qu'il y eût eu continuation de fourniture ou ouvrage; si ce n'est qu'avant l'année ou les six mois, il y eût eu compte arrêté, sommation, ou interpellation judiciaire, cédule, obligation ou contrat."

year to year, implying that the debt that gave rise to excommunications was incurred for the costs of daily sustenance and trade. The volatility of the declining economic situation during the 1420s and 1430s may explain why the Paris records are studded with tradesmen, women including female merchants, as well as high-level bankers and merchants. If those at the bottom of society were most at risk, all needed to mobilize credit in order to survive in this period of famine and of bullion famine.

What do changing levels of excommunication tell us about Parisians at the end of the Middle Ages? Jean Favier has described the fifteenth century as the period when Paris shifted from being predominantly a center of commerce to being predominantly a center of government, as the expansion and deepening of royal control over the kingdom increased the preponderance of the royal administration within the capital. During the first half of the century, "the least daring men took as few risks as possible in small-scale, relatively unprofitable commerce, the more astute entered royal service."[49] The uncertain and variable returns of commercial ventures paled in comparison to the surer return of royal service. Capital fled toward land, toward loans to the king, and toward the growing royal administration as families invested in the royal offices, the "soap for serfs (*savonnette à vilain*)" that guaranteed the privileges of nobility to a new social category, the robe nobility. This is not to say that Paris ceased to be a commercial center, for royal officials and their households had to eat and be heated, royal business required parchment, paper, and sealing wax, and the immense ceremonial apparatus of the king, the church, and the town required rich cloth, candles, precious metals, and other ornaments. Commerce served the nascent State and commerce required much credit to function, both short-term, informal credit and long-term, formal credit. Old Regime elites lived not of commercial banking but of the relatively sure profits of State finance.[50]

The register of excommunications for the archdeaconry of Paris tells us about the short-term, informal, unwritten credit given by bakers or wine merchants to customers, by purveyors of cloth or leather to tailors or shoemakers, by "friends" (in the medieval sense including one's "carnal friends" or family members) to other "friends" to pay a pressing debt such as a fine, a tax, a ransom, rent, or the accrued costs of food or wood or for survival. Because these sorts of things generally concerned amounts too minor to merit being drawn up formally by a notary, were

[49] Jean Favier, "Une ville entre deux vocations: la place d'affaires de Paris au XVe siècle," *Annales ESC* 28:5 (1973), 1245–1279, at 1253.

[50] Beik, *Absolutism*; Daniel Dessert, *Argent, pouvoir et société au Grand Siècle* (Paris: Fayard, 1984), and *L'argent du sel. Le sel de l'argent* (Paris: Fayard, 2012).

that even desirable,[51] they only passed into the historical record when they resulted in an excommunication – that is, when a creditor chose to deploy spiritual sanctions against a borrower – or when a probate inventory included a list of verbal debts. The latter, however, only survive in Paris from the late fifteenth century. For instance, the inventory drawn up for Marion, widow of Richard Le Sage, in 1503 concludes with the widow noting that her husband had lent Jean Bonneau 6£t at the same time as her husband owed Bonneau 14£t for two years of a lease due on the next Saint-Rémy; neither transaction appears to have been written or formalized, at least in authentic form.[52] The humbler inventory drawn up in 1530 for Marion Herault, widow of Jean Le Rat, concludes with notices that she had 12£t in cash belonging to her and her children, that "*noble homme*" Gallois Mydoigt owed her husband 20sp back wages for cultivating Mydoigt's vineyard, and that Guillaume Benoist called "*Dez bousté*" owed her husband back wages of 4£t; the latter two debts are not recorded as being written.[53] Evidently the widows, like their deceased husbands, lacked written proof of such debts. Yet still they included them in the inventories, because the underlying contracts were enforceable through the threat of spiritual sanctions.

Lamentably, the register of 3,069 entries primarily concerning the commercial heart of Paris does not always specify the amount at the base of a given excommunication, because many were the outcome of a failed citation rather than a monition to pay a confessed or adjudged sum, that is, for contumacy rather than for debt. Of 3,069 sanctions, 487 lack a specified cause; 1,949 or 63.5 percent, were for simple contumacy (*pro contumacia*) and 478 or 15.6 percent for an amount (*pro re*) probably originating in monitions or in unwritten obligations formalized as condemnations or recognizances of debt before the officiality or the Châtelet. Some of these reflected unpaid judicial fines, as at Chartres,

[51] Daniel Vickers explains that accounting for certain items loosely rather than precisely rendered obligations incalculable and flexible: "Errors Expected: The Culture of Credit in Rural New England, 1750–1800," *Economic History Review* 63:4 (2010), 1032–1057.

[52] AN MC XIX 67: "Item declaira ladicte vefve que ledict deffunct durant son vivant avoit preste audict jehan bonneau cy dessus nomme la somme de six livres tournois/ Item declaira aultrement ladicte vefve que au sainct remy prouchain venant seront deues deux annees audict bonneau a cause du louage ou ledict deffunct estoit demoure ouquel tenoit tenoit a louage dudict bonneau aupres de vij lt par an."

[53] AN MC XIX 67: "Plus a declaire ladicte vefve avoir en deniers contens appartenans a elle et a sesdits enffans la somme de douze livres tournois. Item plus estre deu a ladite successeure par noble homme galloys mydoigt la somme de xx sp de reste des labours faitz par ledit deffunct pour ledit mydoigt/ Item estre deu a ladite successeurs par guillaume benoist dit dez bouste iiij lt aussi pour labours de vigne faitz pour luy par ledit deffunt."

which immediately led to excommunication upon default, though this was also the case for condemnations and recognizances of debt, as noted in the previous chapter. Forty-two or 1.4 percent came as the result of both contumacy and a debt; 29 or 1 percent were for court costs; and 116 or 4 percent were for court costs and contumacy together. Because many excommunications for debt came as the result of failure to respond to a summons, the rubric of contumacy likely contains many cases of debt, though we cannot securely know how many.

The distribution of sanctions by year varied, though not so much as at Chartres. From 1426 to 1438 inclusively, an average of 211 excommunications per year were registered in the archdeaconry of Paris. Excluding peak years of 1429 (292 excommunications), 1434 (345), 1435 (300), and 1437 (275), the average is 170. However, there remain 184 excommunications for which it is unclear whether they were issued in 1427 or 1428.[54] Depending on the distribution, including these would raise the overall average and push those two years into the range of the peak years previously mentioned. This is a considerable number. As noted earlier, over the slightly more than thirteen years covered by the register, one member of between perhaps a quarter of the households of the big right-bank parishes had been excommunicated. It is true that a few of these were for moral cases and that a small minority of these excommunications were incurred by "repeat offenders." Ecclesiastical justice played a considerable and evident role in minor credit in late medieval Paris.

Ecclesiastical justice also reveals that recourse to minor credit extended from the top to the bottom of the social hierarchy. Perhaps because Paris was a richer town, larger than Chartres by a factor of twenty (5,000 versus 100,000 inhabitants), more widows, women, and priests were involved in credit.[55] Parisian widows, women, and priests were more numerous and wealthier than their Chartrain analogues, whose hometown was already declining. Paris, in contrast, was dynamic and cosmopolitan. Laymen of course predominated as at Chartres. Two thousand four hundred twenty-five excommunicators were laymen acting alone, as were 1,498 of excommunicates. In addition, one knight, one *damoiseau*, and one squire were excommunicated. Two squires, one *damoiseau*, and one knight excommunicated. Other laymen were excommunicated in economic or legal units: five with an unmarried woman (in one of which her name was

[54] There are also twenty-six excommunications for 1439, obviously an incomplete listing, and thirty for which the date is wholly uncertain.

[55] As Philip T. Hoffman, Gilles Postel-Vinay, and Jean-Laurent Rosenthal, *Priceless Markets: The Political Economy of Credit in Paris, 1660–1870* (Chicago: University of Chicago Press, 2001) have shown for a later period.

given first), forty times with their concubines, three times with another man, seven times with a son, seventeen times as minors with their guardian, fifty-six times with their wives. In these last cases, the names are given in two forms: either as, for instance, "Marion La Gravansonne and her husband are excommunicated" or "the wife of Jean Langlois and her husband are excommunicated" or as "Jean Ludonnier and Jeannette his wife are excommunicated."[56] That the woman's name was given first in one of the excommunications of a male-and-unmarried-female pair and in twenty-six of the husband-and-wife pairs suggest that these excommunications reflected debts incurred by the wife, with the husband's name included so as to put the whole household economic unit's resources at risk. The first formulation could reflect debts contracted by the wife and the latter debts contracted by the husband. Here we glimpse the economic role of women, who would necessarily have been involved in market relations, even their employment was mainly in the "hidden" employment of tasks within the home or home workshop. Only a few women were independent merchants in their own right (*marchandes publiques*), with many more active in peddling, piecework, or informal salaried labor. Upper-class women helped to manage commercial enterprises or to managed property, particularly the wives of royal officials whose duties kept them from their lands, to be sure, but women's wage-labor was broadest at the bottom of the social scale, where survival depended on each additional penny and on the wife's credit with the baker, butcher, and innkeeper.[57] Women not mentioned as married were excommunicated alone 361 times, with a guardian 7 times, 4 times as *marchandes publiques* who could trade independently, and 52 times as wives authorized to trade and to litigate independently of their husbands. Nineteen widows were excommunicated. In the other direction, women requested far more excommunications than at Chartres: 190 ostensibly single women requested excommunications, 11 widows, 4

[56] e.g., AN Z[1o]17, f.1 (1426, Saint-Germain): "Excommunicatus est johannes ludonier et johanneta eius uxor pro johanne beauvies pro contumacia," "Excommunicata est mariona la gravansonne et eius maritus pro magistro petro fabri pro contumacia per tasse"; f.44, (1438, Saint-Paul): "Excommunicati sunt uxor Johannis anglici et eius maritus ad instantiam guilloti cruel [pro] contumacia/ absoluti mediante cessionis [sic; sc bonorum]." To be absolved of some kind of debt, Jean Langlois and his wife ceded all their property to the beautifully named Guyot Cruel.

[57] On the struggles of poor Parisians, one might project Sharon Farmer's *Surviving Poverty in Medieval Paris: Gender, Ideology, and the Daily Lives of the Poor* (Ithaca: Cornell University Press, 2002), retroject Hufton's *The Poor of Eighteenth-Century France*, and translate Dyer's *An Age of Transition?* in light of Bronislaw Geremek, *The Margins of Society in Late Medieval Paris* (Cambridge: Cambridge University Press, 1987), and Cohen, *Peaceable Domain*.

married women, and 8 *marchandes publiques*. In total, almost 7 percent of excommunicators were women and 14.4 percent of excommunicates were women. It may be that wealthier female creditors more often used royal courts because those with illiquid dowry property sold authenticated or notarized *rentes* and those with investable capital purchased *rentes*. It may be that female-headed households relied more upon credit to provision their households or to secure the materials for crafts.[58] That twice as many women were excommunicated as solicited excommunications is indicative of a famine of ready cash among women. Because credit was vital to navigating daily life, and because its moral dimension remained so important for women, women defended their good name, often through litigation over defaming words.[59]

Groups of churchwardens were excommunicated once and excommunicated others four times. Officers of two confraternities excommunicated once each. As at Montivilliers, and as Julie Claustre has shown concerning royal officials at the Châtelet, churchwardens and the officers of confraternities probably sanctioned in the course of official business or at the closing of accounts when new officers entered into functions. The Abbey of Saint-Victor excommunicated the same man in 1437 and again in 1438. Priests excommunicated individually twenty-nine times and in a pair twice. They were excommunicated individually forty-seven times, once in a pair with the priest's concubine in a moral case and at least four times explicitly suspended from the capacity to perform the sacraments. This may reflect a particularity either of practice or of record-keeping, as elsewhere priests were first suspended from sacramental functions before being excommunicated as a secondary sanction. There are not many priests mentioned in the Paris register, where the sanctions of church courts were directed mainly at layfolk. Court officials, however, played a large role, as only two of them were excommunicated against 1,202 sanctions – more than one-third – issued at their instigation. In one-fifth of all sanctions the requestor was the promotor of justice, the archdeacon's prosecutor, but for the rest it was not infrequently a summoner. The prominence of summoners as excommunicators suggests either that they were minor lenders who pursued private debts through ecclesiastical sanctions from a privileged position as officers of the court or, as the fact that the summoner and the plaintiff are sometimes the same suggests,

[58] 14.4 percent approximates the percentage (13.8 percent) of females among heads of household assessed in the Parisian subsidies of 1297–1300: Sharon Farmer, "Merchant Women and the Administrative Glass Ceiling in Thirteenth-Century Paris," in Theresa Earenfight (ed.), *Women and Wealth in Late Medieval Europe* (Basingstoke: Palgrave Macmillan, 2010), 89–108, at 92.

[59] e.g., Wunderli, *London Church Courts*, 63–80.

that they summoned on credit and then excommunicated delinquents. It is also likely that, like summoners elsewhere, Parisian summoners (listed as "*clerici officii*" at the end of the register) acted as ecclesiastical notaries and ratified debts contracted in their presence with warnings to pay on pain of excommunication.

The amount at issue was seldom indicated, because excommunications at Paris came predominantly for contumacy. Excommunications *pro re* appear to have been confined to unpaid judicial fines and to the relatively few debts recorded in letters of *nisi* or as recognizances in the registers of court sessions. The amount was not legally important, rather the broken promise that established the church's jurisdiction in the matter and the disobedience of court orders that gave rise to the excommunication. Of only sixty-two amounts specified, the greatest was 40sp and the least 8dp. The average was 5.9sp (7.5st) and the median 4sp (5st). The debts at the root of excommunications for contumacy may have been larger, though we cannot know, as a fee of 4dp to summon a delinquent debtor was an economical means of recovering a debt of a few *sous* or even one of 8dp. Judging by the amounts recorded, the archidiaconal officiality of Paris was truly the smallest small-claims court examined here, but the data may be skewed by the small sample size. The officials of the Sub-Dean of Chartres and the Abbess of Montivilliers dealt with greater amounts on average, but none of these amounts approaches the hundreds of livres disputed before royal bailliwicks or seneschalsies and parlements. Even the officialities of Chartres and Montivilliers dealt with amounts that were on average nearer to the 50s or 60s boundary that distinguished lords who held rights to low justice, whose courts tried amounts up to that threshold, from lords who held rights to middle justice, whose courts tried amounts above that threshold, than was the case at Paris. It may be that studying excommunication for debt at Paris brings us as close as the historical record permits us to get to the day-to-day small extensions of credit on which premodern society functioned. Those who pursued a debt of 5st – a laborer's weekly wages – may be the humblest civil litigants, we find as plaintiffs in late medieval courts. At the Châtelet, in contrast, debts often amounted instead to a few weeks of a laborer's wages![60] In these excommunications for contumacy and for small sums, we can hear the echoes of the small commerce, of the small loans, of the small purchase and sales credits extended every day by vendors and service-providers as the price of doing business and, from another perspective, as the price of living in Christian society.

[60] Claustre, *Dans les geôles*, 430.

We can also look at these data in terms of networks. We can map the frequency of the connections between formed between individuals or economic units revealed through ecclesiastical sanctions. Frequent excommunicators are major small-time lenders, whether merchants, artisans such as bakers, as well as the few possible usurers whose usury is nevertheless invisible in the records of procedures presuming "amicable, interest-free cash loans" (*ex amicabili mutuo*). Of repeat excommunicators, nine of the eleven most frequent are officers of the court, likely seeking to recover court costs and their salaries. Although church courts did assign a very few excommunications as punishments,[61] most of sanctions requested by the archdeacon's prosecutor (*promotor justitiae*) concerned contumacy and debts reflecting court costs (*pro suo salario*). Of the 130 sanctions issued at the receiver of fines's request, though no cause is given for 33, 87 or 67 percent (90 percent of those with specified cause) are for debts. That 18.2 percent of all excommunications for debt came in response to the Receiver's request confirms that only debts confessed in court, formalized in authentic instruments, or owed to officers of the court (as was the case before the Châtelet for debts to court officers[62]) gave rise immediately to excommunication without prior citation. The band of potential usurers extends from the five who excommunicated ten times to the two who excommunicated sixteen times. Of repeat excommunicates, no one was excommunicated more than thirty-eight times, with the next most excommunicated two individuals being sanctioned twenty-one times each (Table 3.3).

Recalling that we see only breaks in credit relations that led to ecclesiastical sanctions here, the predominance of one-time excommunications, as 1,252 or 41 percent of excommunicators sanctioned once and as 993 and 32 percent of excommunicates were sanctioned once, conveys the magnitude of minor credit in late medieval Paris. The floating mass of credit on which society functioned is otherwise invisible except when it appears exceptionally in probate inventories or other scattered documents. One might object that only 1,289 individuals were responsible for all 3,069 excommunications and that 1,722 individuals made up the totality of excommunicates (of those whose names are legible). This means that at least 1,632 individuals never excommunicated anyone and that at least 1,199 individuals mentioned in the register were never excommunicated. However, because 1,200 or 39 percent of sanctions were issued at the instigation of court officials, the balance is closer

[61] Beaulande, *Le malheur*, 77–154.
[62] Claustre, *Dans les geôles*, 164–165. These amounted to 15 percent of all *écrous* requested in 1488–1489.

Table 3.3 *Frequency of sanctions at Paris, 1426–1439*

Number of sanctions	Persons sanctioned	Persons requesting sanctions
0	1199	1632
1	1252	993
2	224	174
3	98	48
4	43	27
5	34	10
6	15	9
7	17	3
8	13	1
9	3	5
10	5	1, Jean Courtin
11	1	0
12	3	1, Robin Massard
13	2	3, Thomas Morelli; Pierre Dovier; Jean Després
14	3	1, Renaud Marchandon
15	0	0
16	1, Me Jean de la Poterne	2, *Robert Cuignet, Summoner*; Richard Foullon
17	1, Vincent Gaultier	0
18	2, Etienne Rose; Jean Hollant	0
19	0	0
20	1, Michel Roujault	0
21	2, Jacques Odot; Henri Maricle	1, *Guillaume de Menehy, Summoner*
22	0	1, Guillaume Guynot
26	0	1, *Jean Galland, Summoner*
38	1, Robin Gorget	1, *Sealer of the Court*
50	0	1, *Raoul Tasse, Summoner*
64	0	1, Jean Le Queux
65	0	1, *Jean Gaillard, Summoner*
85	0	1, *Jacques Vigneron, Summoner*
91	0	1, *Guillaume Gautard, Summoner*
130	0	1, *Receiver of Fines*
599	0	1, *Promotor of Justice*

Note: Names of court officers in italics.
Source: AN Z/1o/17.

to even among excommunicates and excommunicated. With sanctions by court officials subtracted, the average number of excommunicates per excommunicator falls from 2.38 to 1.39. Much excommunication was unconnected to other canonical litigation and simply concerned debt between private individuals.

Many Parisians were probably creditors and debtors at the same time. Even the great were tied up in webs of credit for small amounts. It is a shame that we know little of the Robin or Robert Gorget who was excommunicated thirty-eight times,[63] more than anyone else in the register, or of the six individuals excommunicated between 17 and 21 times. We know something more than is provided in the register of two individuals: Master Jean de La Poterne and Jean Le Queux. The former, goldsmith, moneychanger, and alderman (*échevin*) of Paris in 1422–1428 and 1433–1436, was excommunicated sixteen times, including twice by the promotor and once by the receiver of fines. Particularly vulnerable to the demands of clients and the changing constellations of those in political power in virtue of his elevated social position, Master Jean probably stood at the center of a considerable network of lending and borrowing. Furthermore, the line between public and private finance was blurred, if it existed at all. Officials covered personal shortfalls with public funds and, conversely, covered official shortfalls with loans of their own money. In the 1420s and 1430s, Master Jean therefore faced the extraordinary financial demands both of his two periods in office as *échevin* and of his professional status as a moneychanger. Because he apparently often could not pay immediately when others called in his debts, he appears to have been constrained by his position to stretch his probably considerable "credit" farther than it could bear. Indeed, although he paid a great deal to the king immediately prior to and immediately following this period, he was excommunicated throughout the years covered by the register. It is consequently remarkable that such an individual's soul was imperiled sixteen times in the intervening period for only 4dp paid to the archdeacon's receiver: in the subsidies on the *bourgeois* of Paris that bracket the period of the register, Master Jean paid 25 *francs* (30£t) in 1423 and 20sp (25st) in 1438. In 1423, only 49 of 502 individuals taxed paid more than him; in 1438, 252 of 578 did.[64] This confirms that he was very wealthy. Of perhaps 25,000 Parisian households (again taking a "middle" estimate of 100,000 for the city's population), only between 500 and 600 or 2 to 2.4 percent of heads of household paid anything. Though the truly powerful and privileged bargained their assessment

[63] Gorget was excommunicated five times by the sealer, perhaps for absolutions or for obligations authenticated by the officiality, seven times by the summoner Guillaume Gautard, four times by the summoner Jacques Vigneron, and three times by the promotor (one of those conjointly with his wife). Other than one-time excommunications, he was sanctioned twice by Jean Imbert and three times by Thomas Morelli or Morély. There is no indication that any of these were moral cases. Gorget excommunicated only Louise, widow of Guillaume Le Maire, once in 1435 and once in 1436, perhaps because he was so often excommunicated as to preclude access to ecclesiastical sanctions against his own debtors for much of the period covered by the register.

[64] Favier, *Les contribuables*, 54, 252, 269, 330.

down and nobles and clergy were exempt, Master Jean's household was wealthier than either 99.8 percent, to judge from the amount taxed in 1423, or 99 percent, to judge from that taxed in 1438, of Parisian commoner households. He slid an income percentile within the commons which would have *begun* at $612,000 (rounding down to the 99.5 percentile) in terms of United States incomes in 2012 to one which would have begun at $394,000 between 1423 and 1438.[65] We cannot know if Master Jean was excommunicated by any of the other Parisian officialities, or prosecuted at the Châtelet, as their records do not survive for this period.

Excommunication provided the less-great with a valuable recourse against debtors great and small. Since the other multiple excommunicates do not appear in the contemporary tax assessments, they were probably not so grand as Jean de La Poterne. Frequent excommunicators do not appear in the tax rolls, with one potential exception. Jean Le Queux excommunicated an astonishing sixty-four times over the course of fourteen years, in a range that ranks him with the officers of the officiality. He probably issued numerous small loans. If this Jean Le Queux can be securely identified with the homonym who paid two ounces of silver in the subsidy of 1421, then he was a baker whose annual income was ostensibly 25£t, as those with 100£t in annual income were supposed to have paid one mark in this subsidy.[66] This baker might then have been drawn into petty money-lending in consequence of selling on credit, as many bakers did. In 1421, Le Queux was taxed in the quarter of the Temple, which is consistent with the fact that the parishes of those whom he excommunicated were mainly those of the Right Bank: Saint-Gilles and Saint-Leu, Saint-Pierre des Arcis (in the City), Saint-Laurent, Saint-Jacques de la Boucherie, Saint-Nicolas des Champs, Saint-Paul, Saint-Sauveur, Saints-Innocents, Saint-Eustache, Saint-Germain l'Auxerrois, Saint-Gervais, and in the *banlieue* Pantin, La Chapelle, and Saint-Marcel in the *bourg* of Saint-Denis. The few amounts mentioned are consistent with repeated sales on credit or small loans: 12sp, 21s 4dp, 2s 8dp, 4s 8dp, 4sp, and 8dp. Such lending would have been a precarious business in the 1420s and 1430s, when war gravely disturbed commerce in the Paris basin. Since Le Queux was in the lowest class of the 1421 subsidies (aside from 24 who paid only one ounce according to its second

[65] Emmnauel Saez and Thomas Piketty, "Income Inequality in the United States, 1913–1998," *Quarterly Journal of Economics* 118:1 (2003), 1–39, Excel table updated to 2012 posted at http://elsa.berkeley.edu/~saez/. These percentiles include only realized capital gains in the income figure, because they derive from income-tax data.

[66] Favier, *Les contribuables*, 9, 19–21, 54, 196.

repartition), and since only around 500 Parisian heads of household were taxed in 1423 and in 1438 as opposed to more than 1,300 taxed in 1421, it is not surprising that he does not appear in the rolls of later subsidies. Even though the difficulties of Parisians during the economic conjuncture of the 1420s and 1430s were exceptional, recourse to ecclesiastical sanctions in cases of minor debt was anything but exceptional in late medieval Northern France. Jean Le Queux, apparently a baker who emitted much minor credit, is exactly the type of person whom one would expect to have had frequent recourse to ecclesiastical sanctions.

The mid-fifteenth-century register of the archdeaconry of Paris probably testifies to the practice near its peak. Because it covers only thirteen years in the first half of the century, the sixteenth-century transformation of ecclesiastical justice is invisible. The average of 211 excommunications per year between 1426 and 1439 is a considerable figure. By the end of the century, when, it is true, peace had returned to the region, excommunication for debt persisted: visitation records for the archdeaconry of Paris in 1468–1470 indicate that 2 of 60 parishioners (probably heads of household) at Saint-Pierre in Gonesse were excommunicated for debt, 1 of 24 at Saint-Nicolas in Gonesse, 1 of 8 at Saint-Nicolas in Frépillon, and 1 of 50 at Saint-Leu-la-Forêt. Two of 36 at Notre-Dame in Stains did not make their Easter communion, probably for the same reason, as did 1 of 50 at Aubervilliers, 1 of 40 at Notre-Dame in Saint-Denis, 1 at Saint-Sulpice in Le Pin, and 1 at Saint-Sulpice in Aulnay-sous-Bois.[67] The number of sanctions issued appears nevertheless to have declined considerably.

By the 1490s, the accounts of the archdeaconry from March 1, 1494 (NS) to February 28, 1495 (NS) show that the overall number of excommunications had declined by 70 to 80 percent from the mid-century level.[68] Out of a total income of 481£ 10s 5dp, citations brought in 19s 11½dp, general monitions 1£ 14s 10½dp, and absolutions 9£ 5s 9 ½dp. These were not enormous sums in comparison to the two largest items in the archdeacon's income, fines of 74£ 1s 8dp (15.3 percent) and payments on the occasion of visitations of 206£p (42.8 percent), but did help to provide 187£ 3s 5½dp of profit to the archdeacon after

67 Pierre-Clément Timbal and Bernadette Auzary, "Visites décanales faites dans l'Archidiaconé de Paris en 1468–1470," *Revue historique de l'Eglise de France* 62:169 (1976), 361–374, at 368.

68 AN L 517 n° 74. Exceptionally among the Parisian sources, we can compare this register to the contemporary civil register, AN Z[1o]7, where we find no overlap, because L 517 n° 74 recorded the income (hence liabilities) of the archdeacon's sealer and receiver and Z[1o]7 recorded the business and income of the official and greffier. The sealer and receiver must have recorded citations, monitions, fines, etc. initially in now lost notebooks before compiling the neat, final account that survives.

the deduction of operating expenses. Without the visitation income, the archdeacon would have lost money, as one would expect if we view the activity of courts as driven by demand rather than by supply. Demand for ecclesiastical sanctions was waning. If we assume that a citation cost 4dp, as is likely and as it apparently cost in the late fourteenth century, at most sixty citations were issued. Thirteen general monitions were issued at a cost of 1s each. Forty-two absolutions were sealed for 4sp each, as were ten relaxations for 2sp each. The official's profit from excommunication obviously came primarily from the fees for sealing absolutions, which yielded less than 10£p. As we have seen at Chartres and at Rouen, the rhythm of citations and excommunications corresponded to the liturgical calendar, with a considerable spike during Lent. During Lent 1495 (NS), over a quarter of the income from citations (5s 6½dp of 19s 11½dp) came during March (Easter 1495 came on March 30), nearly half of the year's income from citations (8s 9dp) came during Lent and the three weeks following *Quasimodo* Sunday. Roughly a third of income from absolutions and relaxations came during March as well (50sp of 9£ 5s 9½dp). However, while the rhythm remained similar to previous years, the overall frequency of citations, excommunications, and absolutions was falling. In comparison to the mid-century, when the officiality would have taken in between 34 and 60£p from between 170 and 300 absolutions, the archdeacon received 9£p from a maximum number of 52 absolutions or relaxations in 1494.

Most of the financial benefit of the procedure accrued not to the archdeacon, however, but to the lender or seller who requested the excommunication, doubtless deploying this judicial sanction in an extrajudicial conflict. Indeed, as citations cost only 4dp at Paris, they offered creditors a particularly cheap means of recovering small debts. This was all the more the case because the royal court of first instance at Paris, the Châtelet, was expensive and required more extensive proof than existed for debts of a few sous, and rarely more than a few pounds. It was particularly reluctant in the fifteenth century to credit obligations with anything but an "authentic" seal, that is, the seal of a royal court or tabellion. Because customary France so long doubted the value of even notaries' signatures (*seings manuels*), litigants lacking an authenticated document were at a disadvantage in lay courts. Many in the fifteenth century appear to have turned instead to church courts for a swift, cheap remedy. As Jean Favier has pointed out, in 1419 the Parlement rejected a notarized letter of change because the signature was insufficiently known and asserted that the letter of change created no obligation of the drawer (*tireur*) to the acceptor (*donneur*). In Favier's words, "the most minor transactions suffered from legal costs: when an artisan wished to give a quittance to another artisan in 1425, they had to use two notaries of the officiality."[69] The debt must have been large or the trust between these two artisans minimal for them to have recourse to so formal a mechanism. Because of its evidentiary standards and the cost of its procedures, royal justice focused on larger, authenticated obligations or on the debts that royal officials issued in the context of official business that were *ipso facto* authentic. Julie Claustre has accordingly found that 80 percent of imprisonments for debt at the Châtelet of Paris in 1488–1489 were in consequence of debts sealed by the prévôté of Paris; three quarters of the remaining 20 percent were in consequence of debts pursued by royal officers in the course of their offices.[70] According to the figures given by Pierre-Clément Timbal, the cost of written obligations amounted to at least 5 percent of the amount concerned and at worst a full third.[71] According to Claustre, in 1425 the *brevet* of a notarial instrument would have cost up to 16dp (20dt), while the *grosse* or full form would have cost up to a considerable 2s 8dp (3s 4dt).[72] Even then, securing its execution could be costly. Imprisoning a debtor for two nights, a common strategy, cost 2s 8dp on average, surpassing the daily wage of a Parisian construction laborer in 1500–1505 (2s 6dt).[73] The debts pursued at the Châtelet were consequently relatively large, with 71 percent for amounts greater than 50sp, 47 percent for amounts greater than 100s or 5£p, and 4 percent for amounts greater than 1,000s or 50£p.[74] Forty-three percent therefore were for amounts between 5 and 50£p, that is, for more than twice a laborer's annual wages. If creditors chose to pursue their debts before church courts, the fees were lighter, the procedure quicker, and proof based on sworn testimony. In late-fifteenth-century Paris, to summon a borrower cost 4dp (5dt), whereas to enregister an obligation on pain of excommunication cost 2sp (2s 6dt); at Auxerre in the late sixteenth century, a summons still cost only 4dt.[75]

The next evidence for the civil business of the Archdeacon of Paris's court, in addition to the condemnations and obligations of debt scattered

[69] Favier, "Une ville entre deux vocations," 1252.
[70] Claustre, *Dans les geôles*, 164–165.
[71] Timbal, *Les obligations*, I: 40 n.112.
[72] Claustre, *Dans les geôles*, 186–187.
[73] Claustre, *Dans les geôles*, 351; Baulant, "Prix et salaires," 981.
[74] Claustre, *Dans les geôles*, 213.
[75] AN L 517 n° 74; AN Z[1o]6: "veneris xx[a] junii [1483] Condempnatus est dominus michael belin de suo consensu in somma novem franchorum xix dp erga johannem picquet mercatorum draperium parisiensem causis contentis in cedula debitoris vidz pro vendicione et liberacione panni in somma predicta comprehensis tribus solidis pro expositis in prosecucione continentis in dicta cedula ad solvendum dictam sommam quatuor terminis consuetis equis porcionibus ... Et fuit monitus primo 2o 3o et quarto etc ... [in margin] ii s per creditorem"; BN Latin 4812, 76v.

in the civil audience registers, is the sealer's account for the year beginning on Easter 1550 (April 6). It comes from the tenure of Archdeacon Eustache du Bellay, subsequently Bishop of Paris from 1551 to 1563 and nephew of the Louis du Bellay (†1523) who was archdeacon in 1494. Until his death on August 12, Master Jean Demoretz was the official. That very same day, du Bellay appointed another licentiate in canon law, Master Martial d'Auvergne, in his place. Table 3.4 shows that the court's activity had decreased from the level of 1494 and still more from that of 1426–1439.

Between 1494 and 1550, receipts of the seal had not quite doubled, mainly in consequence of 510£t of income from contested or vacant benefices, as opposed to the less than 60£p received from that same source in 1494. Without this sum, itself reflecting the sixteenth-century inflation of grain prices and landed incomes, income from the seal would have fallen by an absolute 30 percent and by still more if we were to account for inflation between 1494 and 1550.[76] In real terms, the receipts of the seal had fallen 74 percent from the equivalent of 873 *setiers* (1332hL) of wheat to the equivalent of 227 *setiers* (346hL) of wheat. Of course, the effective fall was not so great, as the price of grain inflated more rapidly than the price of other consumer goods. With respect to the business of citations and absolutions, in 1550 the category of citations was absent. The yield of what had been fifty citations or so at 4dp/5dt each in 1494 was not worth counting in 1550. General monitions, however, were more important, illustrating the development of what would become a common recourse during the Old Regime in cases of property crime.[77] In terms of the number absolved, in comparison to 1426–1439, when the Archdeacon of Paris would have received 34 to 60£p (42£ 10st to 75£t) from between 170 and 300 required absolutions, in 1494 he received only 9£p (11£ 5st) from a maximum number of 52 absolutions or relaxations, and in 1550 only 7£t from thirty-one. Fewer absolutions signifies fewer excommunications, since the omission of the category of citations from the later account indicates that there probably were not large numbers of unabsolved excommunicates in mid-sixteenth-century Paris. There may have been a number of Protestants, but by this point their trials were a matter not for ecclesiastical tribunals but for the Parlement of

[76] Baulant, "Prix de grains," 537–538, gives values of .69£t the setier for 1494 and 4.15£t for 1550.

[77] Pierre Dupont, *Les monitoires à fin de révélations dans la procédure séculière* (Paris: Librairie Arthur Rousseau, 1930); Éric Wenzel, "La pratique du monitoire à fin de révélation sous l'Ancien Régime, à travers l'exemple du diocèse d'Autun (1670–1790)," *Mémoires de la Société pour l'histoire du droit et des institutions des anciens pays bourguignons, comtois et romands* 57 (2000), 283–300.

Table 3.4 *Revenue of the Sealer of the Archdeacon of Paris, 1494 and 1550 (former figures converted from livres parisis into livres tournois)*

Headings	1494 (AN L 517 n°74)	1550 (AN Z1o18)
Arrears	3£ 17s 8dt[1]	Not included
Citations	1£ 11dt	Not included
General monitions	2£ 3s 7dt	12£ 3st
Dispensations from banns and nonresidence	90£ 10s 7dt[2]	91£ 4st
Dispensations for burials	4£ 6s 7dt	2£ 6st
Synodal dues	300£ 16s 7dt[3]	23£ 7st
Absolutions	11£ 12s 3dt	7£ 7s 6dt
Fines	92£ 12s 1dt	65£ 18s 6dt
Receipts from vacant benefices	0	350£t
Receipts from disputed benefices	74£ 10st	160£t
Receipts from installation fees	9£ 12s 6dt	28£ 15st
Fees for tonsuring and ordination	22s 6dt	Not included
Mortuary dues of curés	9£ 10st	Not included
Total	602£ 4s 3dt	941£ 1st

[1] Figures for 1494 converted from livres parisis into tournois and rounded to the nearest whole penny.

[2] Accounted separately: dispensations from banns only and letters of purification for women to be churched: 7£ 5sp; dispensations for nonresidents of the diocese: 65£ 3s 5½dp.

[3] Accounted separately: fees from visitations: 206£p; synodal dues: 32£ 1s 3dp; fees from churchwardens and midwives on visitation: 2£ 12sp.

Sources: AN L 517 no.74, Z/1o/18.

Paris. The decline from a few hundred excommunications in the middle of the fifteenth century to about fifty at its end and thereafter to roughly thirty by the middle of the sixteenth century rather reflects the restriction of ecclesiastical competence to the debts of clerics. Church courts' competence with respect to the debts of layfolk had waned long before the Ordinance of Villers-Cotterêts killed it in 1539. As in England, ecclesiastical civil jurisdiction had begun to recede well before any Protestant attacks on the old Church.

Let us return to the 1550 account. At 1st each, 243 general monitions brought in 12£ 3st:[78] 113 of these were issued by the sealer, Master Judas Gontier;[79] 130 were issued by his clerk, Master Jacques Plantin, in his absence. The rhythm is hard to determine, because the clerk deposited

[78] AN Z1o18, 5-9v.

[79] Master Judas is unnamed in the account except as a witness to the oath of Martial d'Auvergne as official on August 12 (AN Z1o18, 39v), together with Guillaume Grisieu, Loup Proffit, Jean Petot, Denis Costurier, Nicolas Proffit, a certain Raffelin, "*aliis promotoribus assistentibus.*"

Table 3.5 *Monitions per month issued by the Sealer of the Archdeacon of Paris, 1550 (OS)*

Apr. 1550	May	Jun.	Jul.	Aug.	Sept.	Oct.	Nov.	Dec.	Jan. 1551	Feb.	Mar.
9	15	17	8	8	7	7	8	9	7	9	10

Source: AN Z/1o/18.

the 6£ 10st from the monitions that he had issued in one lump sum on May 17.[80] The rhythm of monitions issued by the sealer, which are listed by date, is discernable in Table 3.5.

Since the register covers dates from Easter 1550 (April 6) to Easter 1551 (March 29), we can see that general monitions were not issued according to a rhythm corresponding to the liturgical year, though the rise in May and June could correspond to a rise in thefts during the hungry period of the agricultural year before the harvest. The absence of a liturgical rhythm makes sense, since general monitions were intended to aid the recovery of stolen property or the disclosure of the details of a crime rather than the recovery of a private debt. In contrast, Table 3.6 shows the rhythm to be clear with respect to absolutions.[81]

Of twenty-eight absolutions and three relaxations (temporary absolutions, particularly for priests who had been suspended from the ability to perform the sacraments), none came in the three months following Easter 1550, while eleven, one-third of the total, came at the end of Lent 1551: one each on March 11, 12, 14, 20, 21, and 24, two on March 26, and three on March 28, the day before Easter! The overall number was quite low, compared to 1494, and was composed mostly of clerics (six clerics and fourteen priests). By 1550 the Archdeacon of Paris's civil jurisdiction primarily concerned the debts of clerics, as prescribed by the Ordinance of Villers-Cotterêts (1539).[82] In the absence of other records, we cannot say whether the layfolk had been sanctioned in matters concerning tithes or other debatably ecclesiastical matters. Of the

[80] AN Z[1o]18, 6: "Die eadem a magistro jacobo plantin scriba archidiaconatus pro summis dispensationum absolutionum monitionum generalium emendarum aliorumque actorum per eum sigillatorum et expeditum absente sigillifero recepta summa sex librarum decem solidorum." If these 130 monitions had all been issued in the accounting year prior to May 17, and we add them to the 24 issued by the sealer during those months, then 63.67 percent of monitions were issued in April and May. Of course, it is probable, although the length of the sealer's absence is unknowable.

[81] AN Z[1o]18, 24–26.

[82] Isambert, 12: 600–640.

Table 3.6 *Absolutions per month by the Sealer of the Archdeacon of Paris, 1550 (OS)*

Apr. 1550	May	Jun.	Jul.	Aug.	Sept.	Oct.	Nov.	Dec.	Jan. 1551	Feb.	Mar.
0	0	0	2	3	5	2	1	4	3	0	11

Source: AN Z/1o/18.

excommunications or suspensions giving rise to the absolutions recorded in 1550, four had no cause, four were for debt (*pro re*), two derived from obligations recognized in court, and twenty-one were for contumacy.[83] At least half of the financial cases concerned clerics. From these absolutions (5st for an absolution, 2s 6dt for a relaxation), the archdeacon took in a minimal 7£ 7s 6dt. By 1550, ecclesiastical jurisdiction could not be the mainstay of any prelate's income. The Archdeacon of Paris, like the Archbishop of Rouen, was then more concerned to secure the revenues of vacant benefices. Because the fees appear to have stayed the same since the fifteenth century, and because the differential inflation of the sixteenth century increased the prices of wheat and wood in particular and inflated wages, "consumers" of justice either chose not to use or were being diverted from an increasingly favorably priced ecclesiastical justice.

By the appearance of the next surviving Parisian record, the journal of court sessions (*plumitif d'audience*) for the archidiaconal officiality of 1571 (AN Z^{1o}28), there is much civil business, concerning inheritances and loans, but the parties are clerics. Unfortunately, all we have here are the records of litigation for large amounts: for example, a cleric against a priest in a matter of 50£t on January 5. The small sums at the root of most excommunications for debt would not appear in such records. In criminal matters, layfolk still appear in 1571, but in matrimonial or moral cases, not in cases of debt except as plaintiffs against clerics. Ecclesiastical tribunals now essentially lay within the limits that would bind them until the Revolution.[84] By this point we might presume that the excommunication of layfolk for debts had disappeared from the Paris basin. The following chapters will explore the economic and political causes of this disappearance, a disappearance that reflects how

[83] It may be that the sanctions *pro re* reflect punishments and that, as Cosme Guymier reasoned in the passage cited in Chapter 1, all excommunications for debt were effectively excommunications for contumacy.

[84] D'Alteroche, *L'officialité*. We await a study of Parisian officialities during the period between Lefebvre-Teillard's and d'Alteroche's.

"Tridentine" notions of the proper place and functioning of ecclesiastical justice as well as the actions of the monarchy and the Parlement of Paris reshaped the competence of ecclesiastical tribunals over the sixteenth century. To conclude, I will cite a citation that encapsulates the transformation of ecclesiastical justice over the sixteenth century: on April 11, 1625, the (now[85]) archiepiscopal official of Paris cited the parish priest of Le Mesnil at the request of the promotor for disobedience of the synodal statutes "and other scandals."[86] This was an entirely clerical affair: one priest summoned another priest at the request of a priest acting as the archbishop's prosecutor for contravention of regulations pertaining only to diocesan clergy. As applied here, canon law governed not so much the moral conduct of lay Christians as the behavior of clerics.[87] The clericalization of canon law was a general trend across the Catholic world. A graver, more particular if belated consequence of the Council of Trent for the archidiaconal officiality of Paris was its disappearance between 1571 and 1614.[88] At some intervening point, the Archdeacon of Paris decided that it was no longer financially viable to hold court. This happened even before the Parlement of Paris decided in 1619 that the archdeacons of Paris, Josas, and Brie had only what Charles Fevret summarized as "a minor and temporary power of correction during the course of the visitation."[89] At Paris

[85] The diocese of Paris was raised to an archdiocese in 1622.

[86] Insert in AN Z^{1o}41: "OFFICIALIS PARISIENSIS Omnibus presbyteris notariis et apparitoribus nobis subditis salutem in domino Vobis mandamus quatenus ad instantium et requestam venerabilis promotoris causarum officii curiae nostrae Archiepiscopalis eo nomine pro publico et justitiae interesse actoris Citetis peremptorie et personaliter Coram nobis ad diem primam juridicam nisi etc alioquin etc Magistrum Johannem Turgault presbyterum rectorem curatum ecclesie parochialis de mesnillo S. dyonisii in diocesi parisiensi et habituatum in ecclesia sancti Benedicti bene verbi in hac urbe Super contraventione statutorum Illustrissimi et Reverendissimi Archiepiscopi parisiensis atque nonnullis scandalis per eum commissis et alijs obiectionibus dicti promotoris responsurum ulteriusque processurum prout juris et rationis erit locum Inthimacione assueta Datum Parisijs Anno domini millesimo sexcentesimo vigesimo quinto die undecima mensis Aprilis. [Signed] ROUSSEAU." The underlined lines draw attention to the target and requestor of the citation, apparently retained as a template. Signifying the progress of record-keeping, the mandate was subscribed: "Praesens mandatum executum fuit per me presbyterum subsignatum juxta suum tenorem alloquendo Jacobum du ruel scholasticum domesticum dicti Turgault in suo domicilio repertum in Collegio thesaurariorum cui copiam dedi praesentibus magistris Bertrando pasturel Radulpho le vennier presbyteris et jacobo des masures cum multis alijs testibus anno et die supradictis. [Signed] Herault."

[87] Prodi, *Una storia*, ch.6.

[88] As one can see from the register of the officiality of Paris for 1614: AN Z^{1o}29. According to AN Z^{1o}41, in 1624 Sire Denis Le Blanc, Archdeacon of Brie and Canon of Paris, was official of Paris. He did not hold a separate archidiaconal tribunal. Perhaps the loss of jurisdiction explains why Parisian archdeacons so zealously pursued the property of dead curés in this century.

[89] Fevret, *Traité de l'abus*, 2nd ed. (Lyon, 1667), I: 508–509: "une legère et momentanée correction … in transitu visitationis."

the late adoption of the Council of Trent's circumscription of the competence of archidiaconal jurisdiction formalized a prior development. By the early seventeenth century, there was only enough demand for ecclesiastical justice around Paris to support one officiality: the bishop's. Abundant litigation over debts then filled the dockets not of ecclesiastical but of secular courts.

The abbatial officiality of Montivilliers, 1433–1463 and 1499–1530

The final case study is constructed on the basis of two registers of excommunications of the abbatial officiality of Montivilliers in Normandy. The first register covers the economically difficult years between 1433 and 1463 at the end of the Hundred Years War, when the French retook Normandy and when the region began its slow recovery from the disturbances of war. The second register is the latest in my study, running from 1499 to 1530 and testifying to the decline of ecclesiastical tribunals during the sixteenth century. The officiality of Montivilliers is unusual in two ways, both as a jurisdiction and in its economic and social environment.

I shall begin with the first particularity. The Abbey of Montivillers was an exempt spiritual jurisdiction. For this reason, its abbess was not just secular lord of the abbey's fiefs but effectively archdeacon of the fourteen parishes that composed its exemption. The exemption of Montivilliers is one of the great success stories of the political achievement of religious women in the later Middle Ages, for the abbesses of Montivilliers were *naturales dominae* in virtue of their office rather than, as for female heiresses, in virtue of their birth.[90] The Abbess of Montivilliers was more powerful even than the prince-abbesses of the Holy Roman Empire in that she also held the power of spiritual jurisdiction. The Abbey of Montivilliers was old, Merovingian foundation, originally dependent on the Abbey of Fécamp.[91] When the abbey was refounded during the reconstruction following the Viking invasions, the Benedictine nuns of Montivilliers were richly endowed

[90] Serena Ferente, "*Naturales dominae*: Female political authority in the Late Middle Ages," in G. Calvi (ed.), *Women Rulers in Europe: Agency, Practice and the Representation of Political Powers (XII–XVIII)*, European University Institute Working Paper 2008-2, 45–61.

[91] Paul Le Cacheux, "Le fonds de l'officialité de Montivilliers," in *Travaux de la semaine d'histoire du droit normand tenue à Guernesey du 26 au 30 mai 1927* (Caen: Imprimerie A. Olivier et M. Caron, 1928), 275–305; Jean-François Lemarignier, *Étude sur les privilèges d'exemption et de juridiction ecclésiastique des abbayes normandes depuis les origines jusqu'en 1140*, Archives de la France Monastique 44 (Paris: A. Picard, 1937); Marc Venard, "Les visites pastorales de l'exemption de Montivilliers du XVIe au XVIIIe siècle," in *L'Abbaye de Montivilliers à travers les âges (Colloque de 1986)*, *Recueil de l'Association des Amis du Vieux Havre 46* (1988), 85–106; Dom Gaston Lecroq, *L'Abbaye de Montivilliers* (Fécamp: L. Durand et fils, 1936).

by the dukes of Normandy. In 1035, Duke Robert of Normandy freed the lands of Montivilliers from any secular or ecclesiastical imposition or tax (*consuetudo*), as Richard II had done for the Abbey of Fécamp in 1006 and as he had done for the Abbey of Cerisy, and had this donation confirmed by the Archbishop of Rouen.[92] Such exemptions had not initially been grants of ecclesiastical jurisdiction but what Jean-François Lemarignier has called "the Cluniac formula of exemption" that freed monasteries from fiscal and judicial subjection to lay magnates.[93] Grants of immunity did not at first entail freedom from episcopal jurisdiction. Over the eleventh century, however, favored monasteries received gifts of, to quote from the grant to Saint-Julien of Tours in 1053, "tithes, *primitias* [an augmentation of the tithe], burial rights, synodal dues, visitation dues, and all the forfeitures from those guilty of sacrilige, theft, or violation of a cemetery, together with all those dues received by episcopal agents."[94] Although the ducal privileges freeing the abbeys of Cerisy (in 1032) and Montivilliers (in 1035) from the dues that signified the jurisdiction of the duke (*consuetudo terrena*) and of the Archbishop of Rouen (*consuetudo ecclesiastica*) were issued with the consent of the Archbishop of Rouen, they were not confirmed by pope.[95] As subjection defined in terms of fiscal exactions gave way over the twelfth century to subjection defined in terms of jurisdiction, the scope of these exemptions grew. Their validity and exact nature nevertheless remained uncertain.

The religious of Montivilliers did not cease to amplify their exemption. In a pancarte issued by William the Conqueror between 1068 and 1076 further lands were added, along with the phrase "possessing the same rights in every holding that the church [sc. the monastery] of Fécamp possesses in its holdings (*in omni tenetura, sicut tenet Fiscannensis ecclesia*)" following the freedom from *omni episcopali consuetudine*.[96] The list of proprietary churches foretells the exemption of the later Middle Ages with the exception of one loss and four additions.[97] Already during the

[92] Le Cacheux, "Le fonds," 278; Lemarignier, *Étude*, 61, and, for an edition of Montivillier's foundation charter, 235–246.

[93] Lemarignier, *Étude*, 42.

[94] Lemarignier, *Étude*, 73 n.38.

[95] Lemarignier, *Étude*, 44.

[96] Paul Le Cacheux believed (278–279) that the phrase to have been inserted at the beginning of the fourteenth century into the copy of Montivilliers's foundation charter confirmed by the Chancery of Philip the Fair in 1305. cf Lemarignier, *Étude*, 236 n.4, 242 n.23.

[97] Vasouy near Honfleur was lost. The church of Petit-Tanville, within the commune of Le Fontenay, was replaced by that of Le Fontenay proper. The parishes of Gournay, Saint-Barthélemy, Saint-Martin-du-Manoir, and Saint-Sauveur, created toward 1200 out of the north aisle of the abbey church, were added. On the identification of *Petitonvilla*, see J. Adigard des Gautries, "Les noms de lieux de la Seine maritime attestées entre 911 et 1066," *Annales de Normandie* 8:3 (1958), 299–322, at 317–318; for that of *Washuic*, idem, "Les noms de lieux du Calvados attestés entre 911 et 1066," *Annales de Normandie* 3:2 (1953), 135–148, at 145–146.

reign of Innocent III (r.1198–1216), the Abbess of Montivilliers or her dean held an ecclesiastical tribunal ("*placita christianitatis*"), although the pope ruled that she was to exercise this jurisdiction conjointly with the Archdeacon of the Greater Caux.[98] In spite of this, from 1284 the abbess conferred benefices without the archdeacon's concurrence. In the person of her dean and official, often the same person, the abbess visited the parishes of her exemption, held synods of its clergy, administered ecclesiastical justice, and chose the prelate who would consecrate those whom she approved for holy orders.[99] Still, because Montivilliers enjoyed no explicit grant of immediate subjection to the Holy See, because the abbess appointed no penitentiary to approve sins reserved to episcopal absolution, because appeals went to Rouen, and because the archbishops of Rouen sought to extend his right to visit the convent to the entire exemption, the extent of the monastery's jurisdiction remained uncertain. Though the abbesses and nuns resisted these visitations, into the fourteenth century the abbess's jurisdiction was in theory exercised conjointly with the Archdeacon of the Greater Caux, who received 40£t from the fruits of the abbess's justice.[100] This situation lasted until the Great Western Schism, when rival popes sought supporters across Christendom, and particularly in regions such as Normandy, which lay on the border between the English, who adhered to the Roman pope, and the French, who adhered to the Avignon pope. Abbess Marguérite de la Rivière seized this opportunity to escape the Archbishop of Rouen's supervision. On July 1, 1384 the Avignon pope Clement VII confirmed Montivilliers' exemption. On July 9, he expanded the abbey's exemption, freeing the abbess, the nuns, her official and his court officers, and all parishes and priories dependent upon the monastery from the jurisdiction of the Archbishop of Rouen. This bull was published by an apostolic notary in the cathedral of Rouen on September 24, 1384.[101] The privilege was consonant with canon law, and in the context of the schism magnified Clement VII's papal authority: Hostiensis had advised that "women are prohibited [from being arbiters or judges] ... unless the pope gives them the authority to judge ... otherwise they can neither judge, nor excommunicate, nor assign penance."[102] By papal authority,

[98] ADSM 54 H 3, Bull of Innocent III (1215).

[99] Lemarignier, *Étude*, 227–228. The last competence was withdrawn in 1634.

[100] Le Cacheux, "Le fonds," 286–290. The six archdeacons of the archdiocese of Rouen were the Grand Archdeacon, and those of the Greater Caux, of the Lesser Caux, of Eu, of the French Vexin, and of the Norman Vexin.

[101] Le Cacheux, "Le fonds," 290; eighteenth-century copies of the bulls are in ADSM 54 H 36.

[102] Hostiensis, *Summa aurea* (Venice: heredes Melchior Sessae, 1570), ad X.1.43, De Arbitris, v^{is} Quis possit esse arbiter, f.111, n.3: "Item fœmina prohibetur. C. cod. l. ul.

then, women could judge ecclesiastical crimes, issue excommunications, and assign penance, exactly as the Abbess of Montivilliers did through her dean or her official.

The exemption of Montivilliers survived the Middle Ages, even though the Council of Constance and the Pragmatic Sanction of Bourges had revoked all privileges conceded after the papacy of Gregory XI. The privilege even survived the eighteenth century, when Nicolas de Saulx-Tavannes, Archbishop of Rouen, asked, à propos of his attempt to deprive the Abbess of Montivilliers of her tribunal: "is there anything more monstrous or more indecent in the ecclesiastical hierarchy than to see a girl presiding over synods and assemblies of parish priests?"[103] Saulx-Tavannes was evidently less successful at depriving the Abbess of Montivilliers of her exempt jurisdiction than the Official of Paris who successfully deprived his diocese's archdeacons of their right to independent jurisdictions in 1619. Until the Revolution, the abbesses of Montivilliers wielded their crozier: they or their vicars appointed and instituted parish priests, authorized preachers, confessors, and pardoners, issued marital dispensations, held synods, judged through their officials, and received the income of their nearly episcopal or archidiaconal function.[104] Within the exemption of Montivilliers, a woman wielded the power of the keys. Her officiality derived its authority from a woman.

The jurisdiction of Montivilliers was particular for a second reason: it covered a zone of estimable commercial activity. It was nevertheless not the only tribunal covering this area. The dense judicial network of the region included the officialities of the archbishop and the exempt officialities of Montivilliers and Fécamp. In addition to these *plés de chrétienté*, the network included also the network of royal, formerly ducal courts. Vicomtes and baillis held *plés* or *plaids à héritage* for real property, *plés à meuble* for movables, and criminal assizes. Local lords also held their own *plés*. All of these also sealed contracts, initially through their *sceaux aux contrats* or *aux obligations* and then through their tabellions. Litigants could therefore choose to bring extrajudicial disputes before the officiality of Montivilliers, which is not to say that it did not offer advantages in speed, in cost, and in efficacity when compared to secular courts. The

ff de regu. iur. l.2 33.q.5 mulierem 3.q.7 § tria. nisi Papa hoc fecerit, id est, auctoritatem iudicandi tribuerit, quod facere potest. 8.q.1 verior 33.q.4 si quas 22.q.2 cum devotissimam 2.q.5 Mennam. et accedit. supra, de of. dele. cum vigesimum. Alias non potest iudicare, nec excommunicare, nec pœnitentias dare, ut probant iura superius allegata, et infra, de pœnitentiis, nona. Nisi consuetudo terræ repugnet quando potest iudicare et arbitrix esse."

103 Le Cacheux, "Le fonds," 282.

104 Le Cacheux, "Le fonds," 280–281.

abbess's jurisdiction was not of course limited to her officiality, as, like most European prelates, she also possessed secular jurisdiction as a lord.

The abbey's secular jurisdiction came at first by grant of the dukes of Normandy. Its foundation charter granted the first abbess, the duke's own aunt, in addition to a number of particular properties, "the entire faubourg of Montivilliers with the toll and all exactions, and the port of Harfleur with toll and beaching rights for ships, with blood justice and license for one ship."[105] In the fourteenth and fifteenth centuries, these tolls gave the abbesses of Montivilliers access to the tolls and excise dues of an important manufacturing and trading center. Until it silted up at the end of the fifteenth century, Harfleur, only 4 km or so downstream from Montivilliers, was a busy port. Into the sixteenth century, Montivilliers itself was a major produce of expensive, high-quality woolen cloth on a par with the best broadcloth from the Low Countries. In 1396, the king's procureur told the Parlement of Paris that the "best and finer cloths of higher price have been and are those of Brussels and Montivilliers" in comparison to the "inferior and coarser cloths of lower price such as those of Bernay and others from Lower Normandy."[106] At the 1428 Geneva fair, the dukes of Savoy purchased *écarlate* of Montivilliers at 5£ 10st per *aune* (118.84cm by the early-sixteenth-century measure of Paris, current in fifteenth-century Upper Normandy), broadcloths of Rouen at from 31 to 49£t each, of Montivilliers at 42 to 46£t each, and of Louviers from 19 to 24£t each.[107] From 1280 to 1429, the *écarlate* of Montivilliers was considered best in quality at the fair of Chalon-sur-Saône, that of Rouen second, and that of Harfleur third.[108] *Écarlate* was the most expensive, finest broadcloth dyed scarlet with kermes.[109] Sold by the *aune*, it was extremely expensive, particularly as broadcloths were quite long, those, for example, of Louviers were set at 19½ *aunes* of Paris in 1409.[110] Assuming a similar length, the price paid per *aune* suggests that each *écarlate* of Montivilliers was worth about 110£t in 1428. In the early sixteenth century, the best

[105] Lemarignier, *Étude*, 242–243; according to n.24, *licencia de navi* signifies license for one ship to trade within the Seine estuary and other Norman rivers free of tolls.

[106] Henri Dubois, "Drapiers normands aux foires de Bourgogne à la fin du Moyen Âge," *Annales de Normandie, Hors-Série: Recueil d'études offert en hommage au doyen Michel de Boüard* 1:1 (1982), 229–242, at 233 n.18 bis.

[107] Dubois, "Drapiers normands," 239.

[108] Dubois, "Drapiers normands," 240.

[109] John Munro, "The Rise, Expansion, and Decline of the Italian Wool-Based Textile Industries, ca. 1100–1730: A Study in International Competition, Transaction Costs, and Comparative Advantage," University of Toronto, Department of Economics, Working Paper no. 440 (2011), 1–137, at 12 and the studies there cited in n.48, www.economics.utoronto.ca/index.php/index/research/workingPaperDetails/440.

[110] Mathieu Arnoux and Jacques Bottin, "Autour de Rouen et Paris: Modalités d'integration d'un espace drapier (XIIIe-XVIe siècles)," *Revue d'histoire moderne et contemporaine* 48:2 (2001), 162–191, at 178.

broadcloths, not of *écarlate* but of ordinary colors, cost roughly 100£t each. Montivilliers and Harfleur were therefore sites of trade in the salt of the coast, the wheat of the plateau of the Caux, the high-value textiles of the region, and products such as Burgundian wine brought down the Seine or English wool brought across the Channel.

Even if the cloth industry of Montivilliers stagnated after 1450, when the gradual but inexorable decline of Harfleur began to cut the Caux region off from international commerce,[111] the Abbess of Montivilliers's income – and the business of her spiritual justice – still benefitted from the region's cloth industry and commerce, directly through tolls and excises on fairs and markets and indirectly through the leases of houses and tenures in the region the value of which was nourished by commerce, particularly during the recovery of commerce that Michel Mollat has identified from 1475. Although the importance of Harfleur declined after 1500, the foundation of Le Havre in 1517 more than made up for the decline of Harfleur in terms of commerce at the mouth of the Seine: the lease of tolls there rose from 22£ 10st in 1518–1519 to 30£t in 1519–1520 to 200£t in 1522 and to 400£t in 1531.[112] Even if such developments were less than ideal for the abbess, who would have seen the leases and tolls that fed her income decrease in a Harfleur putatively depopulated by two-thirds already in 1496,[113] we may not be able to assume economic decline within the exemption of Montivilliers. The frequency of excommunications for debt and the fact that men such as the illustrious Dieppois merchant Jean Ango, equipper of voyages to the New World, had leased the farm of the abbess's mills in 1506–1507, suggest that lucrative opportunities in commerce and in administration remained.[114] This lease was part of a diversified portfolio of investments, as the younger Ango also leased the farm of the Viscounty of Dieppe between 1512 and 1540, equipped numerous expensive, and profitable ships either alone or in partnership, and, somewhat later, suffered losses amounting to 650,000 *écus* (1,300,000£t) between 1522 and 1537 when corsairs captured seven ships returning from Brazil and Guinea, among other destinations, without going bankrupt.[115] When we recall that the Abbess of Montivilliers took in somewhat more than 2,530£ 9s 11 1/4dt in 1522–1523 (this sum only concerns income that passed by her

[111] Arnoux and Bottin, "Autour de Rouen et de Paris," 173.

[112] Mollat, *Le commerce*, 370.

[113] Mollat, *Le commerce*, 360.

[114] ADSM G 5273, Saint-Sauveur, 1506 (OS). As the elder Jean Ango died toward the end of the reign of Louis XII, it is probably the younger, more famous Ango who excommunicates in this entry.

[115] Mollat, *Le commerce*, 499, 503.

receiver), the appearance of fabulously wealthy entrepreneurs suggests that we had best not imagine Montivilliers to be an agricultural backwater, in spite of its relatively small population, which oscillated between 3,000 and 4,000 during the Old Regime.[116] As Arnold Esch has observed, "the pattern of documentary survival makes the Middle Ages seem more agrarian than it otherwise would seem to have been."[117] Even agriculture was big business, as the tithe-farmers we shall encounter below illustrate. The documentary preponderance of long-distance trade in comparison to largely undocumented local trade often causes the historian to "give a gram of pepper greater weight than a ton of salt."[118]

Excommunications at Montivilliers, 1433–1463

The register of excommunications at the officiality of Montivilliers covering the middle third of the fifteenth century survives only in part, and almost escaped my notice, as it was divided into at least four fragments for subsequent reuse prior to the summer of 1478.[119] The sections covering the parishes of Saint-Sauveur, the main parish for Montivilliers housed in the expanded nave of the abbey church, and of Saint-Germain in the suburbs of Montivilliers are missing, which is a shame because both parishes had a large number of excommunicates in the sixteenth century. Excommunications for the parish of Sainte-Croix in the suburbs of Montivilliers are found in one piece of the register, those for Harfleur from 1433 to 1438 in another, and those for Harfleur from 1438 to 1463 and for the remaining parishes of the exemption in still another.[120] 1,493 sanctions are listed by parish in what remains of this register, with an additional section for the abbess's extraterritorial jurisdiction (*extranea jurisdictio*) over nonresidents of the exemption. If we estimate the number of sanctions from the two missing parishes according to the proportions of the sixteenth-century register, the whole register for 1433–1463 would have contained something like 2,550 sanctions in total. This works out to roughly eighty-two sanctions per year, half the rate in 1499–1530, probably on account of the disturbances of the

[116] ADSM 54 H 163, 62v; Ernest Dumont and Alphonse Martin, *Histoire de la ville de Montivilliers* (Fécamp: L. Durand et fils, 1886), I: 7. Bottin, *Seigneurs*, 218, gives the following figures for the abbey's revenues: 4,511£t (1557–1558), 3,997£t (1570–1571), 7,637£t (1591), 7,712£t (1605).

[117] Esch, "Überlieferungs-Chance," 536.

[118] Esch, "Überlieferungs-Chance," 563.

[119] Entries in the reused portions of the register begin in the summer of 1478.

[120] ADSM G 5280, G 5271, and G 5270, respectively.

last two decades of the Hundred Years War. The 1430s and 1440s were years of considerable conflict along the lower Seine. Mollat has collated descriptions of the desolation of the Caux region between the failed rebellion of 1435 and the 1450s: peasants who had fled, unrecognizable villages, fields and roads covered with brush and trees, wolves and eagles proliferating, rent rolls filled with entries specifying that tenures were "completely ruined," "of no value," "of little value," "houses in ruins," or "no income."[121] Still in 1484 did Jean Masselin not unreasonably complain to the Estates General that Normandy remained depopulated and impoverished, as there were only 5,976 souls in the 221 parishes of the diocese of Rouen where there had been 14,992 by his reckoning in the thirteenth century.[122] In 1440, for instance, it is reported that cloth merchants of Montivilliers had fled to Abbeville for safety.[123] It would therefore be unwise to underestimate the disturbances of war to daily commerce in Upper Normandy during the middle third of the fifteenth century.

The 1,493 sanctions in the surviving portions of the register of excommunicates is surely a frequency depressed by war. Of these, 767 or 51 percent were issued for debt (*pro judicato* [*summe*]) and 633 or 42 percent for contumacy. Letters of *nisi* are mentioned thirty-four times, again indicating that most excommunications for debt reflected not acts sealed by the court but private or unwritten acts that came under its jurisdiction through monitions, summary judgments, or final judgments. Figure 3.3 gives the number of excommunications each year, with the proportion of excommunications for debt shown in lighter gray.

The data clearly convey the degree of the economic and social dislocation in Upper Normandy in the 1440s and early 1450s: the number of sanctions issued fell continuously to a very low level in the last two years of English occupation: 1448 and 1449. This decline signals a depressed frequency of commercial contracts and a steep decline in litigation as residents of the area fled or left off commerce as too dangerous. There may well be another cause in that the official may have fled Montivilliers for all or part of the year 1441, when no sanctions were issued. That drapers of Montivilliers had fled to Abbeville in 1440, as mentioned earlier, implies that this period may have been even more difficult for the abbess's subjects than 1449, when the French retook the region. Excluding the

[121] Mollat, *Le commerce*, 1–88, cited passages at 66, where Mollat observes that the revenues of the castellany of Tancarville fell from 3,700£t to 1,000£t, a decline comparable to the mid-century decline of the revenues of the Archbishop of Rouen.

[122] Mollat, *Le commerce*, 67.

[123] Jean-Louis Roch, "Entre draperie rural et draperie urbaine? La draperie foraine de Rouen à la fin du Moyen Âge," *Annales de Normandie* 48:3 (1998), 211–230, at 223.

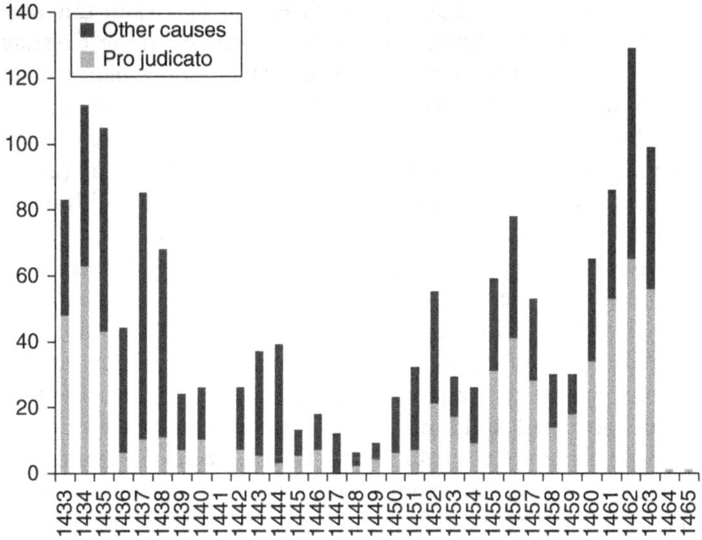

Figure 3.3 Excommunications by the Abbess of Montivilliers, 1433–1463, by year and cause (stacked chart).
Sources: ADSM G 5280, 5271, and 5270.

entries for 1464 and 1465, which surely failed to make it into a succeeding register, the recovery was swift if not complete by 1462 and 1463, when 99 and 129 sanctions were issued, respectively. That more than half of these were explicitly for debt implies that commerce, contracts, and litigation concerning contracts were growing. Still, the recovery had far to go, as the officiality issued around 200 sanctions in the first decade of the sixteenth century, when Upper Normandy's economic recovery was finally completed and the stage set for sixteenth-century expansion.

The amounts at issue suggest both that excommunications for debt reflected local, humble, relatively minor trade and credit and that mid-century disturbances artificially raised the value of debts negotiated through excommunication. Of the 511 amounts specified as the basis of a sanction, the largest amount was 179 *saluts d'or* (358£t at the official, below-market conversion rate) in 1455, the smallest 2st. The average was 132st or 6£ 12st, the median only 40st or 2£t. A number of large amounts skewed the sample upward, as the median was far closer in value, for instance, to twenty days' work for a laborer at Rouen (more in the countryside, where wages were 20 to 25 percent lower) or to about 4 *mines* (380L) of wheat purchased at Rouen, perhaps enough to feed one individual for between 150 and 300 days.[124] Because entries in this register were dated according to liturgical time, for example, on the Tuesday after the octave of St. Martin, on the Friday after Corpus Christi, and so on, we can easily see on which days the court most often granted excommunications. The officiality of Montivilliers and its officers were most active on Monday (220 sanctions), Thursday (285), and Saturday (269). The court sometimes sat on Tuesday (151) and Friday (134), seldom on Wednesday (87) and almost never on Sunday (a bare 5 sanctions).

Individual cases allow us to imagine the types of debts at the root of excommunication when we look at the few that specify debts in kind. On the Friday after the Purification of the Virgin 1433 (OS), Guillaume Beusse or Beauce, cleric, of Harfleur was excommunicated for an obligation of 100 lbs of wax at the request of Colin Raoul in virtue of letters of *nisi*.[125] He was absolved, fulfilling what was probably a sale on credit. On the Thursday after Epiphany 1458 (OS), Colin Labbé of Turretot (10 km north of Montivilliers) was excommunicated for a judgment of thirty cartloads of wood at the request of Jean Aubourg. He was absolved, so here we may presume a sale on credit of a valuable commodity.[126] On the Wednesday after the Conception of Virgin 1461, Gauffroy Goudain was excommunicated for a debt of 81 *boisseaux* (12.8hL or 36.4bu) of barley at the request of Richard Enguerrand alias Coynet.[127] This "foreigner" or nonresident of the exemption is not recorded as having being absolved. Although the entry is near the end of the register, Goudain may never have delivered. Optimistically for his soul, perhaps he was absolved in his home jurisdiction and failed to communicate this to the officiality of Montivilliers. These debts in kind could be relatively large, like one of 72 *boisseaux* (11.4hL or 32.4bu) of 1433,[128] if not on the scale of Rouennais grain merchants. We find also debts in kind of plaster: on the Tuesday before the Feast of St. Austrebertha 1461 (OS), Jean Dubois was excommunicated at the request of Robert Dejean for a debt of five *mines* of

[124] Bois, *Crise*, 102, 77. Bois ("Prix du froment," 1268) estimates the mine of Rouen to have been between 90 and 100 L in the fifteenth century. The last figure is a back-of-the-envelope calculation based on applying the midpoint of Bois's metrological range to Philip Slavin, *Bread and Ale for the Brethren: The Provisioning of Norwich Cathedral Priory, 1260–1536*, Studies in Regional and Local History 11 (Hatfield: University of Hertfordshire Press, 2012), 18, 149. It depends on whether one projects from the amount of bread alotted to the monks at Norwich, 2,830 kCal per day, or the amount probably consumed, 1,915 kCal per day. The latter figure is more likely here.

[125] ADSM G 5280, Harfleur.

[126] ADSM G 5271, Extranea jurisdictio.

[127] ADSM G 5271, Extranea jurisdictio.

[128] ADSM G 5271, Octeville: Nicolas Millet excommunicated at the request of Gaufroy ... for contumacy on the Monday after the Purification of the Virgin.

plaster (worth 12s 6dt[129]). He was aggravated on the Saturday before Laetare. He then must have secured temporary absolution, as he was again excommunicated on May 16 before securing absolution at some subsequent point.[130] We can also imagine the types of person involved in excommunications for debt. On the Thursday after Jubilate 1462, Master Jean Le Sauvage, priest, was suspended from divine service at the request of Thomas Le Roux for a debt of 10 *écus* (15£t). On June 4, however, Master Jean was temporarily absolved for twenty days, pledging six ells or *aunes* of white cloth.[131] It does not appear that Master Jean relapsed into excommunication on account of default. This priest (in fact, these priests, as Le Roux is called Sire Thomas in the marginal note) may well have been involved in trade, although six ells is not a particularly large amount of nevertheless probably expensive cloth. Judging by the mean and average debts, such small credits bulked large in the business of the court. We also find those we might expect, such as Jean Frontault the Elder, who in 1463 was excommunicated by the churchwardens of Rolleville for a debt of 23st owing at the closing of his confraternity's annual accounts.[132] None of these amounts are particularly large.

The frequency of excommunications also suggests that the officiality of Montivilliers dealt mainly in the minor credit of daily life. The region's wealth rested on a multitude of small transactions, on the proliferation of minor credit. Almost half of all sanctions were requested by an individual once over the period covered and were received by an individual once over the period covered, as Table 3.7 demonstrates.

Court officials, as expected, excommunicated relatively frequently, with 225 sanctions coming *pro officio* or *per nos*, for example, by the Official, and 41 additionally at the request of the promotor of justice. Together almost 18 percent of sanctions were requested by these officers, a figure that rises to 8.6 percent if we include excommunications at the request of the abbess and convent as a (financial, since these appear to have targeted tithe-farmers) unit. That the churchwardens of Rolleville excommunicated twenty parishioners of Rolleville at one stroke in 1434 suggests that there was a serious dispute within the parish about a levy, perhaps to pay for the repair of the church or presbytery. It is somewhat less likely, though not impossible, that the debts (all twenty had been

[129] Bois, *Crise*, 80–83. If the mine of plaster even approached the mine of wheat at around 95L, this was a considerable volume of plaster: 4.75hL.

[130] ADSM G 5271, Harfleur.

[131] ADSM G 5271, Extranea jurisdictio: "absolutus per retrusionem usque ad xx dies consentiente domino thoma tradidit in pignore sex ulnas panni albi die iiij[ta] junij."

[132] ADSM G 5271, Rolleville.

Table 3.7 *Frequency of sanctions at Montivilliers, 1433–1463*

Number of sanctions	Persons sanctioned	Persons requesting sanctions
1	610	711
2	113	92
3	49	39, *Magister testatorum*
4	15	14
5	17	6
6	10	3
7	7	6
8	3	0
9	4	0
10	0	1, Pierre Remon
11	0	1, Sire Pierre Seney
12	1, Jean Ogier	0
13	3, Philippe Mustel, Jean Perier, Colin Chapelain alias Loriaulx	0
14	0	2, Sire Guillaume de La Haye, Abbess and Convent of Montivilliers
15	0	0
16	0	0
17	0	0
18	0	0
19	1, Jean Le Noir alias de Marseilles	0
20	1, Guillaume Beusse, clerc	1, Churchwardens of Rolleville
22	1, Pierre Morel	0
23	1, Ami La Mouque	0
27	1, Guillaume Gobart	0
34	1, Bertrand Castille	0
41	0	1, *Promotor of Justice*
225	0	1, *Official*

Note: Names of court officials in italics.
Sources: ADSM G 5280, 5271, 5270.

excommunicated *pro judicato*) at issue concerned a tax which the churchwardens had been charged to collect. Rolleville may also have been an unusually restive parish, as seven parishioners were excommunicated in 1463 by the churchwardens, again for debt, and with only one entry specifying that the amount originated in the annual auditing of a confraternity's accounts.[133] Another anomaly, Guillaume de La Haye, who

[133] ADSM G 5271. The amounts in 1463 were 100st, 23st (Jean Frontault *senior* "*pro residuo compotorum suorum confratrie pro thesauro ecclesie de rollevilla*"), 9st, 9st, 6st, 4st, 3st, 2st.

requested sanctions fourteen times, might also be counted among the officers of the court, as he is sometimes mentioned as a summoner. The amounts concerned in sanctions requested by de La Haye suggest that he may also have been a lender, in addition to acting as a summoner and a tax collector: 3 *écus* (82s 6dt) and 20st in 1435, 80 *saluts d'or* (90£t) as tax collector (*receptor cuiusdam subsidii*) in 1437 (OS), 30st in 1452, 16s 9dt in 1456 (OS), 7s 6dt *per nisi* with another in 1459 (OS), 20st in 1460 (OS), and 4st in 1461 (OS).[134] That five of eight were requested between January and Easter suggests that Sire Guillaume also sought to use excommunication when it would be most efficacious. In any case, Sire Guillaume's exemplary *cumul des fonctions*, in which he appeared over the course of thirty years as summoner, royal tax collector, and possibly as lender, explains his frequent mention in the register. For most others, however, requesting and receiving sanctions was an infrequent, largely one-off occurrence. Extending credit and taking credit must, however, have been quite common.

Overall, of those excommunicated, 112 were not recorded as having been absolved, 7.5 percent of the total. With respect to the abbess's extraterritorial jurisdiction over the subjects of other prelates, 52 of 208 or 25 percent of those sanctioned under this category not surprising failed to be absolved. Of the residents of the exemption of Montivilliers only 60 of 1,285 or 4.7 percent failed to be recorded as absolved, even in this difficult period. In comparison to the early sixteenth century, when 16.3 percent of sanctions were issued via the abbess's extraterritorial jurisdiction, between 1433 and 1463 only 13.9 percent of surviving records – and probably 8.2 percent if we expand the overall number of citations proportionally to include the two missing parishes – were issued against nonresidents of the exemption. Depressed commerce must have lowered demand for and recourse to this particular capacity. What is interesting, however, is that the fifteenth-century register is far clearer about which excommunications of the abbess's subjects reflected sanctions issued by other prelates. Such excommunications *per placet* are noted seventy-one times. They originated in conflicts passed within another jurisdiction or ratified by another officiality and communicated to the priests of the exemption of Montivilliers.[135] The format

[134] The last, smallest amount probably originated in a citation on credit as the target, Renaud Philippe, merchant of Harfleur, was excommunicated at de La Haye's request on the Saturday after *Judica* Sunday, after having another resident of Harfleur summoned on the Wednesday after St. Valentine's Day 1461 (OS) "*ad prestandum juramentum*," presumably the oath of calumny, (G 5271). Philippe otherwise appears six more times requesting sanctions in ADSM G 5270 and G 5271.

[135] ADSM G 5271: Harfleur, 1459 (OS): "racione contractus habiti Rothomagensis"; Harfleur, 1460: "per registrum domini officialis Rothomagensis."

must have been similar to that recorded for Montivilliers itself in that excommunications were sent to the nonresident individual's home parish: for example, when on the Thursday after the Feast of Sts. Peter and Paul in 1433 Mathieu Gournies had Vincent Haurs excommunicated for debt, the mandate was sent "to the parish priest of Fontaine-la-Mallet in the jurisdiction of Rouen."[136] These excommunications *per placet* were issued fifty-six times by the official of Rouen, six times by the official of Lisieux, five times by the official of Bayeux, once each by the officials of Fécamp, Évreux, and the Dean of Lisieux, and once without specified origin, illustrating a range of contracts that ranged up and down the Norman coast.

International trade appears obliquely, as when Guillaume Benselin, bourgeois of Rouen, had Pierre Morel excommunicated by the diocesan Official of Rouen for one wey of English wool (half a woolsack) on the Thursday after Pentecost 1459.[137] It is fortunate that Morel was absolved, because, although the entry did not specify the value of this wool, this may have been a relatively large debt in monetary terms. Given that a sack (364 lb or 165 kg) of the best English wool cost between £2½ and £13 sterling (20£t to 104£t at a rough exchange rate of 8£t to the pound sterling),[138] and given the quality of Montivilliers broadcloth, we can assume that the value of this debt was near the top of the range, 50£t or more. It is not hard to imagine why Morel was excommunicated twenty-two times (twenty of these were *pro judicato*, as was one collective excommunication with another party) between 1451 and 1463. If he were a merchant who put out wool to be spun, woven, fulled, sheared, and dyed into the expensive broadcloth of Montivilliers, he had little choice but to purchase wool on credit. In the depressed 1450s, when international trade remained disrupted – and when Spanish merino was not yet really of sufficient quality, Morel's supply would have been expensive and uncertain and his sales equally unnerving. The business would have often seemed and would have often been near to failing. Its continuation depended on the goodwill of his creditors, whose patience he apparently exhausted a score of times. Morel's creditors are often enough merchants of Rouen. Witness the slow liquidation of his debt

136 ADSM G 5271, Extranea jurisdictio.

137 ADSM G 5270: "Petrus morel excommunicatus pro judicato unius ponderis lane de anglia contra guillermum benselin civem rothomagensem auctoritate domini officialis rothomagensis de die jovis post festum penthecostes domini." *Pondus* conventionally translates wey; there are two weys to a woolsack.

138 Munro, "Italian Wool-Based Textile Industries," 4, according to a Parliamentary ordinance of 1454. Munro suggests that the actual price range was narrower: in 1499 the best Leominster wool cost £25.807 and cheaper, mid-range Rutland wook cost £6.548 per sack. Each sack made 4.33 broadcloths by his reckoning, although this would vary a small amount from each French cloth-making center to another on account of different statutory lengths.

to Thomas Raoul or his repeated excommunication by Guillaume Benselin, who supplied him wool at least once. Witness too his excommunications of Bertrand Castille, who was himself excommunicated thirty-two additional times by others. Castille appears to have been a merchant of Harfleur like Morel, who contracted with merchants of Paris and Rouen, and was frequently excommunicated for debt between 1451 and 1461. Morel's appearance in the register may also reflect calculated foot dragging for business reasons, as he was absolved in every instance, even when a debt was transferred (as apparently in 1452 from Raoul Ferry to Guillaume Valeren) or when he had to agree to a payment plan (as when in 1463 he was absolved upon payment of 50st and promises to pay 100st on Quasimodo Sunday and 100st on the Feast of St. John the Baptist to Jean Deslaney.[139] We know that in the sixteenth century, merchants of Beauvais and Rouen bought wool on credit from Spanish merchants and that by 1,600 Netherlandish merchants at Rouen treated these bills as negotiable.[140] Here we catch a glimpse of a prior situation, when church courts facilitated the purchase and sale of wool and cloth on credit before French secular courts began to enforce endorsed bills.[141] Morel's economic activities are implicit in Table 3.8, which contains of sanctions involving him.

Morel in fact had recourse to international bankers for his credit needs, as he was excommunicated on the Saturday after the Assumption of the Virgin 1463 for a debt of 12 *écus* (18£t) *per nisi* by a certain Girard Isbarre.[142] If this Isbarre, who also appears as Girard Hysbarc in 1455,[143] is of the family of Parisian moneyers and bankers of Italian origin,[144] then we have an outstanding example of how the lower Seine from Paris to the sea constituted what Mathieu Arnoux and Jacques Bottin have called a

139 ADSM G 5271, Harfleur: "Absolutus per retrusionem solvendo in plus l s C s ad quasimodo et C s ad festum beati johannis baptiste."

140 Arnoux and Bottin, "Autour de Rouen et de Paris," 188–189.

141 Legal remedies concerning the transfer of bills obligatory to third parties appear in London in 1436, in Lübeck in 1499, in Antwerp in 1507, in Bruges in 1527, and were confirmed for the Low Countries in legislation of the States General in 1537 and 1541: John Munro, "The Medieval Origins of the Financial Revolution: Usury, Rentes, and Negotiability," *The International History Review* 25:3 (2003), 505–562, at 551–554. In France, these would have been enforceable before the consular jurisdictions established in major cities from the 1550s onward: Alexandre Lefas, "De l'origine des juridictions consulaires des marchands de France," *Revue historique de droit français et étranger*, 4ème série, III (1924), 83–120. Munro (556) does note that only in 1704 did an Act of Parlement make endorsed bills obligatory as legally binding as endorsed bills of exchange in England.

142 ADSM G 5271, Harfleur.

143 ADSM G 5270, Harfleur, when a Sire Pierre de Hell … excommunicated him for a debt of 4£ 5st. He was absolved.

144 Favier, "Une ville," 1268 and n.83; Léon Mirot, "Études lucquoises II. Les Isbarre, monnayeurs royaux, Augustin Isbarre," *Bibliothèque de l'École des Chartes* 88 (1927), 275–314.

Table 3.8 *Excommunications of and by Pierre Morel (bold if he is requesting against someone else)*

Year	Requestor (bold if PM is requesting)	Cause	Amount	Date
1437	**Toustain Hany**	Judicato	8£t	Sabbati post f. s. Anne
1451	Robert Le Pant…	Judicato	110st	Martis post misericordia
1451	Thomas Raoul, bourgeois de Rouen	Judicato per placet	11£ 15st	Martis ante f. concepcionis beate Marie
1451	Thomas Raoul, bourgeois de Rouen	Judicato per placet	100st	Lune post reminiscere
1452	Pierre Remon	Contumacia ad confitendum		Martis post quasimodo
1452	Thomas Raoul, bourgeois de Rouen	Judicato per placet	26st	Mercurii post f. translacionis s. Martini
1452	Raoul Ferry, bourgeois de Rouen	Judicato per placet/ Aggravatus	14£ 10st	Martis ante f. Symonis et Jude
1452	Guillaume Valeren	Judicato per placet	14£t	Mercurii post f. hyemale s. Martini
1452	Guillaume Benselin	Contumacia		Veneris post f. epiphanie Dni
1452	Guillaume Valeren	Judicato per placet	12£t	Mercurii post brandones
1453	Pierre Cusquel, bourgeois de Rouen	Judicato per placet	55st	Lune post f. epiphanie Dni
1453	**Bertrand Castille**	Judicato	30st	Jovis post oculi
1454	**Bertrand Castille**	Judicato	6st	Lune ante f. beate Marie Magdalene
1456	Laurent Herbert	Judicato per placet	4 *écus*/6£t	Absolved on August 5
1457	Jean Robellot, bourgeois de Rouen	Judicato per placet	37s 4dt	
1457	**Jean Le Page of Gravenchon**	Contumacia (in Extranea Jurisdictio)		Jovis post f. omnium ss.
1458	Guillaume Benselin	Judicato per placet	*unius ponderis lane de anglia*	Jovis post penthecosten Dni
1459	**Bertrand Castille**	Judicato	26st	Sabbati post cineres
1460	Guillaume Benselin	Judicato per placet	21st	Jovis post cantate
1462	Jean Courtois	Judicato	57s 10½dt	May 4

Year	Requestor (bold if PM is requesting)	Cause	Amount	Date
1462	Robert Dejean, also exc. Guil. Morel	Judicato (pro termino festi penthecostes)	12£ 10st	Jul. 9
1462	Jean Le Sesne, bourgeois de Rouen	Aggravatus per placet		Oct. 16
1462	**Jean Ogier**	Contumacia		Lune post f. s. Dionisii
1462	Germain Canu	Judicato	9 *écus*/13£ 10st	Sabbati post f. s. Martini hyemale
1462	Pierrre Prudhomme	Judicato	10st	Veneris post f. s. Romani
1462	**Hamin Martel alias de Caux**	Judicato	30st	Sabbati post f. ss. Petri et Pauli
1463	Girard Isbarre	Judicato de nisi	12 *écus*/18£t	Sabbati post assumpcionem beate Marie
1463	Jean Deslaney	Judicato	15£t	Jan. 4
1463	Jean Davy	Judicato	15st	Veneris post invocavit
1463	Procureurs de la confraternité de Saint-Michel	Judicato	40st	Jovis post oculi

Sources: ADSM G 5280, 5271, 5270.

single "textile-producing region (*espace drapier*)."[145] We also have an insight into the network linking international bankers, regional merchants, and the local manufacturers who transformed Morel's English wool into *drap de Montivilliers*. Just as they probably bought their bread with credit, so at a far higher level Morel bought his business's "bread" on credit. Even for Morel the credit by which he lived may have been informal or even verbal, as letters of *nisi* are mentioned with respect to Morel only in the Isbarre entry.

The important role of church courts in securing the private credit necessary to commerce is also evident with respect to one of the frequent excommunicates: Table 3.9 shows that Guillaume Beusse, cleric, was excommunicated twenty times between 1433 and 1456 (his homonym, Guillaume Beusse, alias Aux Oiseaux, was excommunicated nine times individually and once with his wife over the same period[146]). What is interesting about Beusse's excommunications is that they come in two

145 Arnoux and Bottin, "Autour de Rouen et de Paris."

146 Beusse the cleric resided in the parish of Sainte-Croix at Montivilliers, Beusse aux Oiseaux in the village of Rouelles.

Table 3.9 *Excommunications of Guillaume Beusse, cleric*

Year	Requestor	Cause	Amount	Date
1433	Colin Raoul	Judicato de nisi	100 lbs wax	Veneris ante purificationem
1433	Guillaume Poulain	Judicato	9£t	Sabbati post reminiscere
1433	Pierre...	Judicato	36s 3dt	
1434	Guillaume Restout	Contumacia		Lune ante nativitatem s. Johannis Baptiste
1434	Robinet Martin	Contumacia		Mercurii ante f. s. Martini hyemale
1434	Sire Jean Guillos	Judicato (twice, probably with intervening absolution)	12£t	
1435	Raoul Hachart	Judicato	55st	Veneris post ascensionem Dni
1435	Sire Jean Guillos	Judicato	12£t	Sabbati post f. ss. Petri et Pauli
1437	Adam Féron and Pierre Sergent	Judicato	35st	Jovis post...
1456	Jean Dubost	Judicato	10£t	Martis post f. b. Lucie virginis
1456	Jean Le Cauchois	Judicato de nisi	4£ 12s 6dt	Sabbati post f. nativitatis Dni
1456	Raoul de Seusebec	Judicato	30st	Sabbati post reminiscere
1456	Guillaume Sanson	Judicato	46st	Sabbati post quasimodo
1456	Richard Galopin	Judicato	17s 6dt	Jovis post letare
1456	Jean Dubois de Rolleville	Judicato	8£ 10st	Martis post f. ss. Jacobi et Christophori
1456	Guillaume des Mons	Judicato	79s 6dt	Lune post f. s. Michaelis in monte gargano
1456	Robert de la Ville de Saint-Romain	Judicato	100st	Sabbati post f. s. Austreberthe
1456	Denis Portefer	Judicato	6£t	Jun. 13
1456	Raoul Le Tendre	Judicato	50st	Jovis post f. s. Mathei apostoli

Source: ADSM G 5280.

bursts, in 1434–1435 and again more seriously in 1456–1457, suggesting that Beusse's enterprises, whatever they were, brought him to bankruptcy twice in the middle of the fifteenth century. Beusse's credit dried up in two main periods. These were probably not debts deriving from court fines, as 18 of 20 were for debt and only one creditor requested sanctions against Beusse more than once.

Guillaume Beusse the cleric does not appear to have excommunicated anyone. This cleric of diminished credit appears to have secured absolution only at considerable cost. For instance, in early 1457 (NS) he had to pay Jean Le Cachois 60st on a debt of 4£ 12s 6dt to secure his creditor's consent to his absolution.[147] For Beusse it was apparently a struggle to keep up with frustrated creditors: in the register his two excommunications in December 1456 and further excommunication in Lent 1457 (NS, on Reminiscere Sunday) are crossed out in one stroke with the marginal note that one of the summoners "certified that he was absolved for all these cases on the Saturday after Judica Sunday."[148] Beusse was promptly excommunicated by another creditor on the Saturday after Quasimodo Sunday. At some point, an excommunication of Laetare Sunday was inserted after the Quasimodo one, and was struck out together with it when Beusse satisfied those two creditors. Reminiscere was the second Sunday of Lent, Laetare the fourth, Judica the fifth, Quasimodo the Sunday after Easter. Because Lent was a good time to put pressure on debtors, Beusse's credit may have evaporated earlier in 1456. His creditors only began to press him through this channel in December of 1456, though we cannot, unfortunately, know how long-standing the debts at issue were, only that excommunication was followed swiftly by satisfaction, certainly in the run-up to Easter.

One means of satisfaction that ratified the transfer of debts was the *cessio bonorum* by which insolvent debtors relinquished their property, including debts owed to them, to their creditors. Yet our sources do not permit us to say whether credits were ceded to creditors singly or in bulk in a *cessio bonorum*. For example, at some date prior to 1460 Jean Le Vavasseur alias Cannet of Harfleur ceded a debt of 60st to Master Jean Fabri, who in that year suspended Sire Jean Langlois, the debtor and a nonresident of the exemption.[149] The debt prompting this cession

[147] ADSM G 5280, Sainte-Croix, 1456: "dicitur quod soluit lx s debet residuum."

[148] ADSM G 5280, Sainte-Croix, 1456: "Michael Cacherat constituit [quod] absolutus [est] pro omnibus scriptis de die sabbati post judica."

[149] ADSM G 5271, Extranea jurisdictio: "Dominus johannes langlois presbyter suspensus a divinis [pro judicato] lx[ta] solidorum contra magistrum johannem fabri habentem jus cessionis a johanne cannet."

may have been commercial, as Cannet excommunicated others twice in 1459 and 1462 (OS) and was himself excommunicated six times between 1452 and 1461: three times for contumacy in 1452 (at the request of the same individual), once for a debt of 9£t in 1457, once for contumacy with respect to "affirming or denying a certain item in a paper bill or account book (*pro contumacia ad confitendum vel differendum quoddam factum contentum in quadam cedulla papirei*)," and once for a debt of 22 *écus* (33£t) in 1462.[150] The debt at issue may also have originated in Fabri's duties as an officer of lay or ecclesiastical courts: Fabri was a summoner and he or his homonym was "commissioner at the pleas of Rouelles in 1434."[151] Summoners and judges often absolved on credit, when the creditor had been satisfied: at Harfleur Guillaume Gobart was "absolved by Fabri and owes 20dt for sealing his absolution" on the Saturday after Pentecost 1463 and later in separate cases was "absolved by Fabri and must pay sealing fees before Easter" on the Saturday before the Feast of St Michael's apparition on Monte Gargano (May 8) and was "absolved by Fabri and owes sealing fees etc." on the Thursday before Christmas.[152] In any case, Langlois was not absolved, so that, if Fabri found Cannet's attempt at satisfaction unsatisfactory, he nevertheless failed to excommunicate him again before the register ends. Credit extended the purchase of wool sacks as well as the payment of court costs.

The importance of commercial credit is evident in the three mentions of partners or *consortes* in the register. On the Tuesday after Martinmas 1452 Pierre Venard had Pierre Roger and Guillaume d'Aoust, *consortes*, excommunicated for a debt of 26 *écus* (39£t). They were absolved provisionally until the Saturday before Christmas and are not recorded as having relapsed into excommunication. On the Thursday after Corpus Christi 1454 Jean Noël and Richard Quesnel, *consortes*, had Bertrand Castille, a frequent excommunicate (thirty-four times!), excommunicated for contumacy. Finally, on the Saturday after Quasimodo 1460 Girard Farin and Jean Marel, *consortes*, had Jean Alès excommunicated for contumacy through the abbess's extraterritorial jurisdiction. Alès is

[150] ADSM G 5270, Harfleur, for 1452; G 5271, Harfleur, for the rest.

[151] ADSM G 5271, Rolleville: Guillaume Enguerrand was twice excomunicated during Lent for contumacy "quia non comparuit coram domino johanne fabri commissario in placitis de roueulla ... et hoc laturus testamentum veritatis in quadam causa civili mota et pendenti coram dicto seneschale"; the register records Fabri as absolving fifteen times.

[152] ADSM G 5271, Harfleur, 1463: "absolutus per fabri et debet xx d pro sigillo absolutionis," "absolutus per fabri et debet sigillum solvere ante pascha," "absolutus per fabri et debet sigillum etc."

not recorded as having been absolved.[153] What type of partnership bound these three pairs? Had they equipped ships for trade? We cannot know, but these men of different surnames clearly acted in at least one instance as an economic unit. They also were in two cases residents of a busy port and in the other a nonresident of the exemption. All these things suggest that these were commercial partnerships, as does the large size of the debt mentioned, 26 *écus*, and the fact that the debt was denominated in gold coins.

This is significant. The fact that debts are either recorded in gold or in silver money of account, never in actual silver or billon coins, offers an interesting insight into how the monetary situation in mid-fifteenth-century Upper Normandy impacted credit relations. Bimetallic accounting reflects both a monetary problem and a cultural convention. The monetary problem was that the legal exchange rate of gold coins varied between French and English territory and that the official value of gold coins differed considerably from their value in trade. During the English occupation, the English-minted *salut d'or* had a legal value of 22s 6dt and the French *écu d'or* a legal value of 27s 6dt. After the French took back Upper Normandy in 1449, the former traded at 30st at Dieppe and 30s 9dt at Rouen and the latter at 29s 3dt at Dieppe and 30st at Rouen.[154] How to reckon that in an official record? Better, as the receivers of the archbishops of Rouen did occasionally, to keep accounts of payments in gold separately from payments in silver (just as payments in kind were counted separately). Better too to conceal the valuation of gold coins above the official rate. As to cultural conventions, Rémy Ambühl has observed of ransoms in this period that gold coins:

> were the main unit of payment for the whole ransom business, even at the lower echelons of the social hierarchy. This is noticeable in the counter-rolls of English-held Norman garrisons where … ransoms were paid in gold coins (*saluts d'or*) but where the expenses of custody were paid in silver marks even when the sums did not exceed 10 *saluts d'or*. The conversion of billon and silver coins into gold coins was not a straightforward transaction and was further complicated by the different currencies in circulation in the kingdoms of France and England, by the politics of debasement in the early fifteenth century and, finally, by the general shortage of bullion which marked the end of the Middle Ages.[155]

[153] ADSM G 5270, Harfleur, for the first two, and G 5271, Extranea jurisdictio, for the last. Farin also excommunicated Alès once for contumacy on his own.

[154] Mollat, *Le commerce*, 380. The disparity was not much better for higher value silver or "white" coins: the *grand blanc* was traded at 11dt instead of its official value of 10dt and the *gros* at 2s 9dt instead of 2s 6dt.

[155] Rémy Ambühl, *Prisoners of War in the Hundred Years War: Ransom Culture in the Late Middle Ages* (Cambridge: Cambridge University Press, 2013), 162. He further notes that "each type of coin had a specific function. For most people, silver coins were the

High-value and bulk trade also appears to have been structured by prices calculated and negotiated in the values of gold coins. This is not to say, however, that such transactions were only regulated in gold, simply that gold – whether *saluts* or *écus* – served as a suppletive money of account.

Three examples from Mollat's study of Norman commerce demonstrate just how complicated the satisfaction of a debt could be, even when it was specified in money of account. Paying up immediately was clearly difficult, and required debtors to draw on their own credit, on their reserves of cash (of many different types), and on their stock of goods. Thus, on November 18 at Rouen 1472 the sum of 55£t was paid in the form of 10 *écus* valued at 28s 1½dt each (14£ 1s 3dt), 10 *saluts* at 30s 3dt (15£ 1s 6dt), 17 ducats at 30s 3dt (25£ 14s 3dt), and 2st in "white" or fine silver money (with 1st of the total apparently rebated). On September 13, 1473 at Harfleur the sum of 400£t was paid as 57 *écus* (81£ 4s 6dt), 1 English *gros* (18£t), 3 Breton *targes* (24£t), 2,400 *blancs* valued at 10dt each (100£t), 160£t in English pence valued at 7 1/4dt each, a noble of Henry [VI?] (3£ 2st), a noble of Edward [IV] (3£ 12st), a Flemish "*riddre*" (1£ 11st), 7 Rhenish *mailles* (8£ 3s 4dt), and finally 7s 2dt in white money.[156] A verbal balance transfer or one noted in a merchant's daybook or recorded in a private bill would have required far less calculation. The periodic prohibition of all or some foreign coins would made payment in coinage difficult, difficulties compounded when payment was made in part also in kind. Letters of change, attested in Normandy from the early fifteenth century concerning the sale of fish from Dieppe to Paris, could facilitate the process, but only partly: in 1522 Guillaume Lefèvre settled a large debt of 1,328£ 10s 11dt to the Parisian merchant François Daubret in the following manner: Daubret, debtor of the Italian bankers Bonvisi, drew a letter of change on Lefèvre for them. Lefèvre then had his factor in England credit Daubret with £15 sterling through the Bonvisi brothers' agent in London. Lefèvre also drew a letter of change on the Bonvisi for Daubret concerning the 500 *écus à la couronne* that they owed him. Lefèvre completed the payment by transferring to Daubret a debt of 120£t that another resident of Rouen owed him and by delivering a barrel (*tonneau*) of combs and 180 reams of paper worth 250£t.[157] This example is late and large, but conveys the head-spinning complexity not only of international but of regional trade on credit. We cannot forget that until 1449 in Upper Normandy, regional trade was international trade. When during the middle third of the fifteenth century the

most important. They were used for the major payments of everyday life: wages, rents, taxes. The billon, whose silver content was almost negligible, was mainly used in towns and cities for small day-to-day purchases. Gold coins, on the other hand, were used in international banking and in large payments between princes."

156 Mollat, *Le commerce*, 381–382.

157 Mollat, *Le commerce*, 390.

officiality of Montivilliers executed debts in kind, in money of account (*livres tournois*), in French gold coins (*écus*), and in English gold coins (*saluts*), it functioned as an international merchants' tribunal. Whether one traded for English or for Spanish wool in cloth-making did not change this. In fact the acceleration of international trade in the second half of the fifteenth century only exacerbated the problem. Just as Pierre Morel had in 1458 bought English wool through a Rouen merchant – who could have had to navigate the treacherous waters of international payment – so in 1460 it is possible that the Basque-sounding Martin Dyureguy of Boulougne was excommunicated for a debt of 26 *écus* 15st (39£ 15st) incurred while reloading a ship that had brought Spanish merino wool or iron from the Basque country to Harfleur.[158] In the sixteenth century the merchants of Upper Normandy would trade from Africa to America.

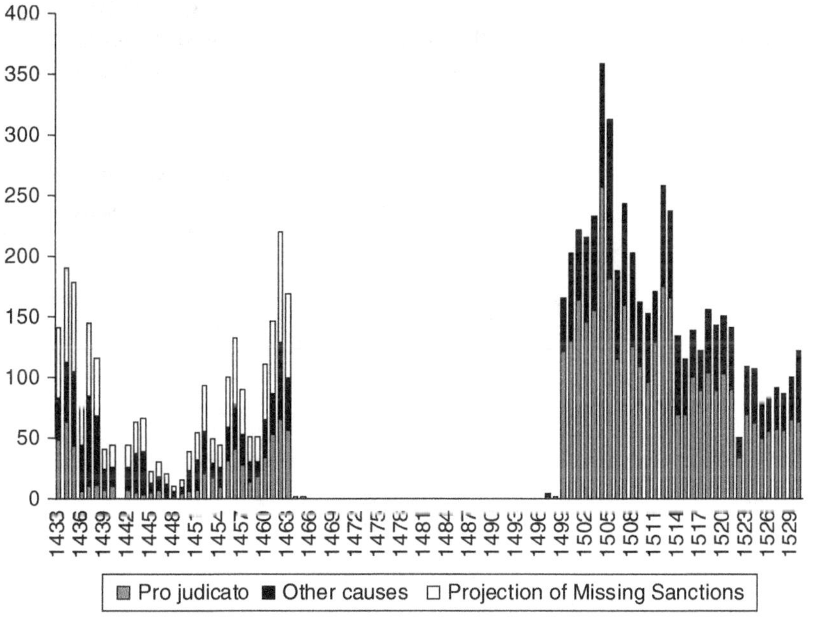

Figure 3.4 Excommunications by the Abbess of Montivilliers, 1433–1463 and 1499–1530.
Sources: ADSM G 5280, 5271, 5270, and 5273.

158 ADSM G 5271, Harfleur: "Martinus dyureguy commorans in villa bononie in picardia morimensis diocesis qui alias elegit domicilium suum in villa harefloti in domo nicola baudier armigeri excommunicatus pro judicato xxvj scutorum xv solidorum contra reginaldum phelipe de die xvij^{a} mensis aprilis iiij^{C}lx post pascha." Dyureguy was not absolved.

Because the register covering the years 1464 to 1498 is lost, two charts bridge the gap between the dismembered register of 1433 to 1463 and that of 1499 to 1530. The first (Figure 3.4) places excommunications in both periods on the same scale. It includes a projection for sanctions in the two parishes for which fifteenth-century records are lost based on proportions in the sixteenth-century register.

The second (Figure 3.5) projects the long-term trends in landed income, cost of living, and excommunication for debt. The sources are Guy Bois's index of the cost of food (1464 = 100) and decennial averages (or as near as can be computed, given lacunae) of the number of excommunications at Montivilliers (these should be, but are not in chart, raised by thirty-five excommunications per year to make up for the two missing parishes) and of the revenue of the Archbishop of Rouen divided by one hundred.[159]

Though we lack data for excommunications at Montivilliers between 1464 and 1498, it would appear that the frequency of spiritual sanctions increased even faster that the cost of living or the archbishop's revenue until 1500.[160] Thereafter, the divergence was notable, though

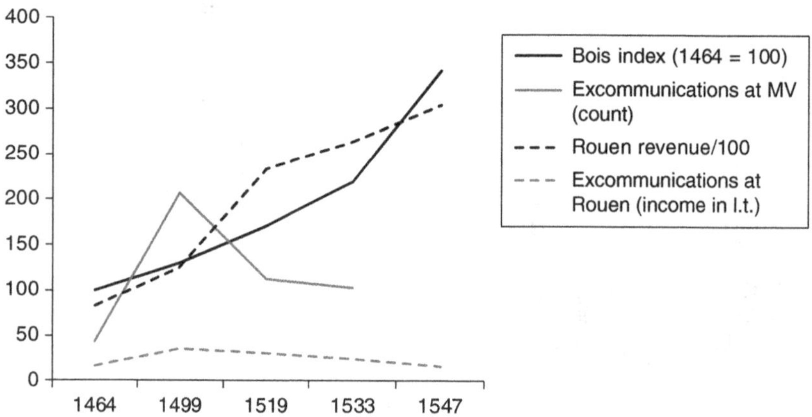

Figure 3.5 Trends in excommunications and income at Montivilliers and Rouen, 1464–1547.
Sources: ADSM G 8-G237, 5280, 5271, 5270, 5273; Bois, *Crise*, 101.

159 Bois, *Crise*, 101; the rest from the spreadsheet constructed for Rouen on the basis of ADSM G 8-G 137 and from the databases constructed for Montivilliers on the basis of ADSM G 5270, 5271, 5273, and 5280.

160 Absolutions at the officiality of Châlons display a similar pattern: after a sharp uptick in the 1460s and 1470s, there is a sharp decline around 1500 and then stability until another sharp decline in the 1530s: Beaulande, *Le malheur*, 169.

here again we lose data on excommunications at Montivilliers after 1530. The following section explores this early-sixteenth-century divergence.

Excommunications at Montivilliers, 1499–1530

The register ADSM G 5273 begins abruptly: "The Register of Excommunicates of the Spiritual Court of Montivilliers in the Parish of Saint-Sauveur in the Year of Our Lord 1499." It continues year-by-year and parish-by-parish over the parishes subject to the Abbess of Montivilliers, along with a considerable section for her "Extraterritorial Jurisdiction" (*extranea jurisdictio*), each section marked by protruding, labeled leather thumb tabs. The entries for each parish are mostly broken into two groups, as in the late 1520s the scribe overran the space allotted for each parish in 1499 and began to fill in blank sections where they occurred. There are 5,249 cells sanctioned, which, as noted earlier, sometimes contain more than one person, because excommunication in cases of debt was directed less at an individual than at an economic unit. The cause was illegible for only 165 sanctions, generally those on the initial, damaged pages; 3,440 or 65.5 percent of excommunications were "for a judgment of a certain amount" (*pro judicato summe*, often just recorded as *pro judicato*). The creditor's name and the amount accompany the overwhelming majority of entries in the register. Of these, 1,518 or 30 percent were for contumacy, though some of these were also for contumacy in cases of debt. Indeed, of the 143 cases, mainly under the rubric for the abbess's extraterritorial jurisdiction, of excommunications for a violated contract (*racione contractus*), 70 were for contumacy and 73 *pro judicato*. As discussed in Chapter 1, excommunications for contumacy in cases of debt would have resulted from failure to respond citations to appear in court. Excommunications for an adjudged sum would have resulted from failure to comply with verbal or written monitions to pay on pain of excommunication. Still in the sixteenth century the officiality of Montivilliers sealed a number of contracts, for there are eleven references to excommunications on account of letters or clauses of *nisi* (*per litteram* or *clausulam de nisi*). Two of these mention debts of grain, one of cloth, and one of a thousand tiles, suggesting that large payment orders may still have been guaranteed by letters of *nisi* as late as February 1520 (NS), the date of the latest excommunication explicitly in consequence of letters of *nisi* recorded in the register.

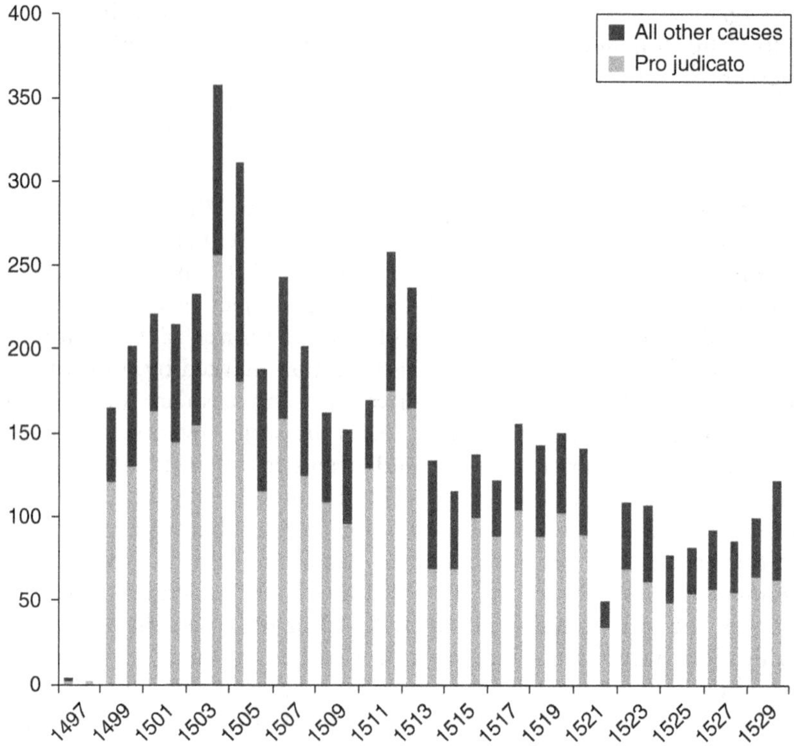

Figure 3.6 Excommunications by the Abbess of Montivilliers, 1499–1530, by year and cause (stacked chart).
Source: ADSM G 5273.

The average number of excommunications per year at Montivilliers was 164 per year, fewer, it is true, than the 211 excommunications per year at the mid-fifteenth-century archidiaconal officiality of Paris. The average is misleading, as the stacked bar chart in Figure 3.6 reveals a clear secular decline, not during a period of acute crisis as at Paris a century before but during one of economic growth.

The six excommunications recorded for 1497 and 1498 are exceptional, almost certainly transcribed tardily from wandering scraps of paper or parchment in a register that actually begins in 1499. The long-term trend needs no explanation.

Even when the long-term movement of the number of excommunications per year is broken down by parish, the pattern is similar, with the

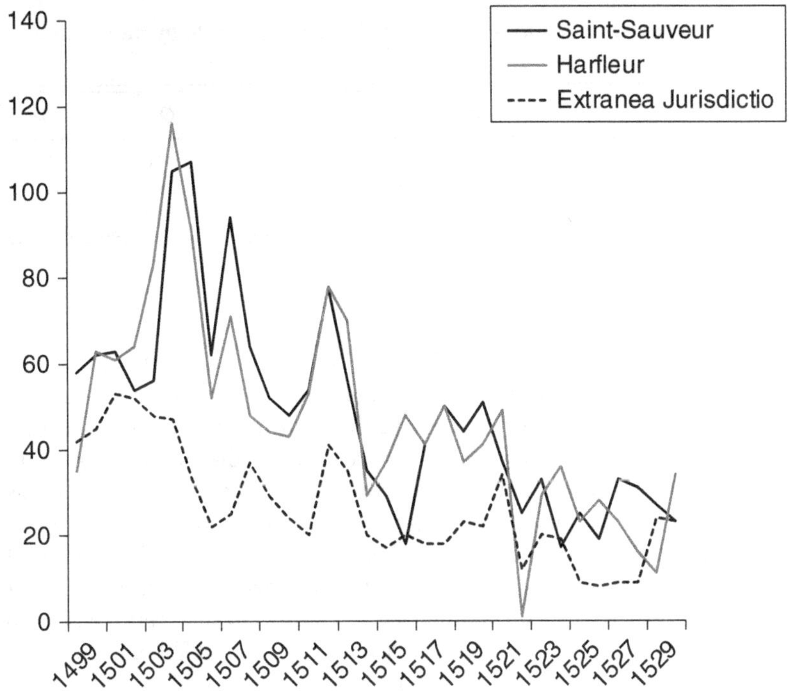

Figure 3.7 Excommunications at Montivilliers, 1499–1530, in the three largest "parishes."
Source: ADSM G 5273.

exception of tiny villages that saw only a handful of sanctions each year. Figure 3.7 displays the year-by-year figures for the three largest "parishes" of the exemption, counting the abbess's extraterritorial jurisdiction as a fictive parish.

As at Paris, where most excommunications by the archidiaconal officiality occurred in the big, commercial parishes of the Right Bank, the geographical distribution of sanctions by the officiality of Montivilliers corresponds to their populousness and to the importance of regional commerce for the abbess's subjects in Harfleur and Montivilliers. Saint-Sauveur, adjoining the abbey in the center of Montivilliers, and Harfleur were large commercial parishes. The remaining rural parishes saw little activity, rarely more than ten sanctions each per year. The trends on the two preceding charts are clear: the frequency of sanctions declined swiftly over the first third of the sixteenth century, at a rate

Table 3.10 *Excommuncations at Montivilliers, 1499–1530, by month and by cause*

Month	*Jan.*	*Feb.*	*Mar.*	*Apr.*	*May*	*June*	*July*	*Aug.*	*Sept.*	*Oct.*	*Nov.*	*Dec.*
Count	401	405	647	435	413	461	447	164	425	410	362	372
Pro j.	240	255	473	297	247	306	307	117	244	266	226	270
Other	161	150	174	138	166	155	140	47	181	144	136	102

Source: ADSM G 5273.

of about two fewer sanctions each year. The unevenness of this decline must reflect the different rhythms of excommunication in debt cases and in other moral cases: recourse to excommunication in moral cases would vary according to their frequency or according to the officiality's desire to exert social control; recourse to excommunication for debt would, as elsewhere, probably vary according to economic conditions, the political situation, and litigants' choices. Until 1500 or so the frequency of excommunication tracked or even exceeded economic indicators. It thereafter diverged as creditors increasingly chose to seek remedies from other jurisdictions. By the time that the Ordinance of Villers-Cotterêts deprived officialities of this capacity in 1539, there would have been few excommunications in cases of debt.

In terms of the annual rhythm, here again we find a clear preference for excommunications during Lent. The dates in ADSM G 5273 are given according to day and month rather than by liturgical indicators, as in the fifteenth-century register. Two months stand out over the course of the register, as Table 3.10 illustrates: March and August.

Lent most often coincided with the month of March, when excommunications jumped sharply by 160 percent over the February total, which was close to the average for the rest of the year. As Véronique Beaulande has noted,[161] creditors recognized that Lent was the best time to put effective sacramental pressure on debtors. There is an equally sharp drop during the harvest in August, when excommunications fell to 36 percent of their July level, a drop also evident at Rouen. This reluctance to pursue debts during the harvest suggests that the type of debt pursued through ecclesiastical sanctions was closely tied to the rhythms of the agricultural year. In September, as leases came due and as borrowers could be assumed to have the means to pay their debts, excommunications rebounded to around 400 before subsiding

[161] Beaulande, *Le malheur*, 246–248.

somewhat toward the end of the year. The rhythm of excommunications *for debt* becomes still clearer if we filter out excommunications for other causes, as in Figure 3.8.

In March, 73 percent of excommunications were for debt. In contrast, in September, only 57 percent were for debt. Excommunications for other causes were nearly flat throughout the year, excepting the drop during the harvest. Excommunications for debt but not, as Figure 3.8 illustrates, excommunications for other causes nearly doubled during Lent.

To speak of excommunications alone is not to tell the whole story. Excommunication was the primary sanction recorded in these register, as noted earlier, but priests were in first instance suspended from the capacity to perform the sacraments (*suspensus a divinis*) before being excommunicated. Whereas this appears to have been imperfectly recorded at Chartres and at Paris, perhaps being assumed by the record-keepers, systematic use of this sanction is recorded at Montivilliers. For priests, excommunication came as a secondary, more serious sanction in cases of manifest disobedience and pertinacity. Thus, on July 20, 1514, Sire Jean Gaffe was suspended at the request of Jean Regnart for a debt of 50st. When Sire Jean did not pay in the following two months, Regnart had him excommunicated on September 29.[162] Then on October 19, potentially consecrating a bitter enmity, Regnart had the priest's excommunication aggravated. On November 24, he had it reaggravated. Though Sire Jean was eventually absolved, this sequence illustrates in exemplary form the progression of sanctions, here apparently after Regnart lost patience with Sire Jean. Plaintiffs seem to have requested new sanctions roughly every month that a debt remained uncollected, considerably longer than the short intervals prescribed by the regulations of ecclesiastical courts.[163] With respect to simple suspensions, the Montivilliers register records 572 suspensions from divine service against priests, 11 percent

[162] The register records Sire Jean as having been excommunicated on October 19 and aggravated on September 29, which must be a transposition, since the last three sanctions are entered in close order in the register, probably copied from a journal or other provisional record, perhaps from a notebook or from aides-mémoire like those interleaved in the registers from Chartres and Paris.

[163] At the officiality of the Abbey of Corbie in the late fifteenth century a monition led to excommunication within five days: BN Latin 18371, 55v. At the diocesan officiality of Saint-Brieuc in 1529 a citation led to excommunication within eight days in cases under 10st and after fifteen days in larger cases; after ten days, the sentence could be aggravated, after another ten days reaggravated, and after a further ten days could be expanded to bar the excommunicate's family and tenants from entering churches: BN Latin 1458, 121. Excommunicates could be prosecuted as presumptive heretics after a year: Vodola, *Excommunication*, 164–190.

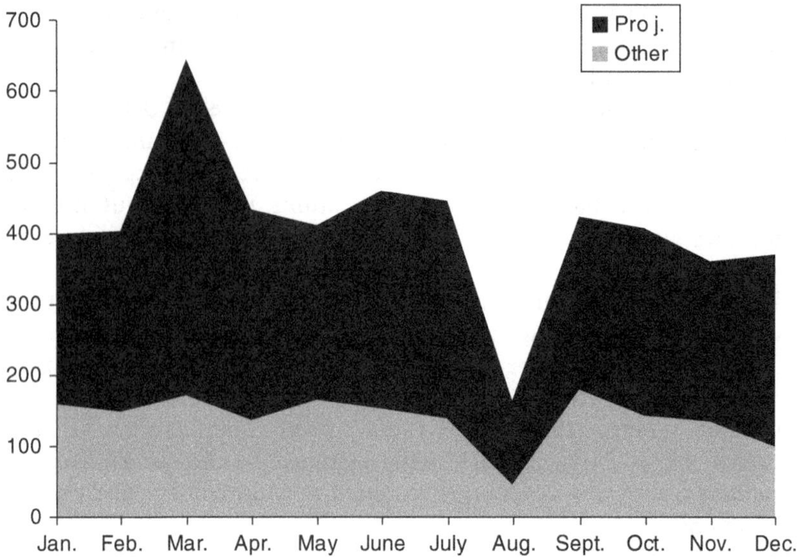

Figure 3.8 Excommunications at Montivilliers, 1499–1530, by month and cause.
Source: ADSM G 5273.

of all sanctions. The absolute number remained relatively constant over the years covered. Thus, as the overall use of excommunication declined, the involvement of priests loomed ever larger. Figure 3.9 demonstrates that, if we add those named as clerics, who had been excommunicated rather than suspended, to the number of suspended priests and compare this figure to the total number of sanctions, we see that the court's spiritual weapons were increasingly directed against the clergy the farther we move into the sixteenth century.

Whereas in 1500 priests and clerics had made up about 10 percent of those sanctioned through excommunication or suspension (though this seems to be a bit low, as the scribe may have neglected to record who was a simple cleric, since those in minor orders were excommunicated just like layfolk), by 1530 the clergy made up around 60 percent of those sanctioned. Declining demand for excommunications at the officiality of Montivilliers resulted in the practice's clericalization over a period of only thirty years.

Excommunication and suspension were not the only sanctions, as we have seen. There was also retrusion, the relapse into excommunication that followed a temporary or provisional relaxation of an excommunication,

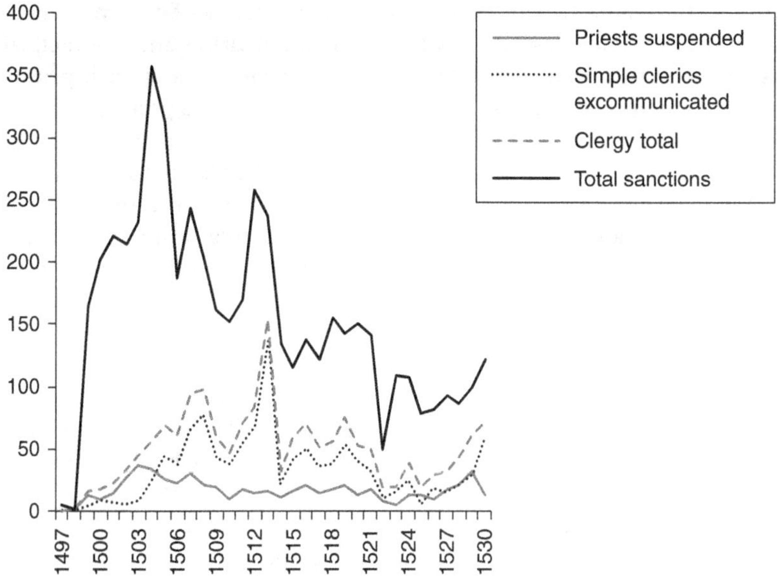

Figure 3.9 Excommunications at Montivilliers, 1499–1530, by clerical status.
Source: ADSM G 5273.

which I have counted as identical to excommunication. Relaxations were cheaper than full absolutions, costing half as much as a full absolution, 2s 6dt as against 5st in fifteenth-century Paris. Beyond simple suspension or excommunication, there were also the aggravation and the reaggravation of an excommunication. At Montivilliers, there were 335 aggravations between 1499 and 1530, but only 12 reaggravations. This means, on average, ten aggravations per year and one reaggravation every third year. These more serious sanctions, especially the most serious, reaggravation, were used sparingly. Why? Because we do not have the formulary of the officiality of Montivilliers, we have only slight evidence for the elaborate liturgical curses – the dramatically extinguished candles, the bells, the cursing psalms and antiphons, the dry funerals, the burning coffins – attested elsewhere for these truly exceptional sanctions. We do know that in 1386 the abbess's dean ordered the parish priests of the exemption to announce certain excommunicates "publicly in your churches on multiple Sundays and Feast Days, having lit and extinguished candles and having rung the church bells," just as in the more elaborate cursing liturgies attested elsewhere.[164] Although the frequency of excommunication in the surviving register would have made it tiring and impractical to stage such theatrical excommunications for each case, parish priests may have been required to perform the full rites for aggravations and reaggravations. It may then be that plaintiffs were reluctant to request these graver sanctions on account of a sense that these dramatic rituals more gravely and more effectively imperiled debtors' salvation – and, in popular understanding, well-being in this life – than a simple excommunication proclaimed from the chancel. The targets of such sanctions were recalcitrant debtors, thus also recalcitrant sinners and probably plaintiffs' capital enemies.

Cases that led to the aggravation or to the reaggravation of an excommunication did not concern larger amounts, implying either creditors' desperation or their malice and either debtors' obstinacy or their abject poverty. Of those sanctions listed as reaggravated, in which all but two were *pro judicato*, the debts at issue were of 42s 6dt, 50st, 9s 6dt, 10s 4dt, and 58s 6dt, together with a fine of 4£t. What unites the cases is the obduracy or the effective bankruptcy of the excommunicate. Obduracy is invisible, but piecemeal bankruptcies are not. As there was as yet in French law neither criminal bankruptcy (*banqueroute*) nor insolvency (*faillite*), only the *cessio bonorum* that expunged a debtor's obligations until "he should come to a more prosperous situation,"[165] our register repeatedly records cascades of excommunications and sometimes the cessions by which insolvent excommunicates satisfied their creditors. For instance, Richard Fourmilly effectively went bankrupt in 1520: he was excommunicated ten times for different causes in 1520–1521, aggravated once, and reaggravated twice at the request of ten different groups of private individuals for relatively small debts.[166] Fourmilly, six times listed as a cleric, was absolved in these cases, so he must have somehow repaired his credit in 1521. However, he was again excommunicated for

[164] ADSM G 5321: "publice in ecclesiis vestris, singulis diebus dominicis et festivis candelis accensis et extinctis, campanisque pulsatis." The mandate has tails for the seals of the exemption's curates.

[165] I discuss the distinction between culpable and capital bankruptcy (*banqueroute*) and simple insolvency (*faillite*), created in this period, in the following chapter.

[166] By Adam Legier for 10st on March 23; by Guillaume Grant and Jean Quevin for 13st and by Robert Becquet for 36s 5dt on March 27; by Master Jacques Benest, priest, for 12l 7s 6d on June 25, 1520; by Mathieu Becquet for 30st on July 11; by Guillaume Gaubert, Jean Quevin, and Colin Nouvel for 13st on an unspecified date; by François Marcis for 9s 6dt on October 12, aggravated on November 18, and reaggravated on December 15; reaggravated by Colin Tison for 10s 4dt on December 16; by Jean Le Tellier for 6s 6dt on October 19, 1521; by Richard de Escaill ... for 5s 4dt on January 23; and by Colin Tison for 5s 4dt again on February 16. It is likely that the two groups of men seeking to recover 13st were the churchwardens of Saint-Sauveur.

2s 6dt in 1527 and again for 2s 10dt on March 3, 1528. In the later of these instances, the small amount illustrating the exiguity of his credit by that point, he is not recorded as having been absolved. By then, Fourmilly could not be trusted to pay back 2s 10dt without the threat of damnation! Perhaps he escaped Montivilliers, perhaps his absolution was recorded in the subsequent, lost register of excommunicates, or perhaps a merciful priest absolved this inveterate debtor on his deathbed. Given that his family, or at least individuals sharing his surname, figures prominently in the register, it is more likely that his absolution was recorded in a subsequent register. In a case contrasting with that of the bankrupt cleric, as the result of a canonical monition issued on the basis of a contract recorded in an account book (*racione contractus et comperte*), Jean d'Escrepintot the Younger excommunicated Gauffroy Guy, proctor of Saint-Michel de Vaucelles in the diocese of Bayeux, on January 24, 1508 (OS) for a debt deriving from stonework delivered to Saint-Michel and again, probably after a temporary absolution, on March 17.[167] Evidently at his wits' end concerning this long-standing debt, d'Escrepintot had Guy's excommunication aggravated on August 20, 1509, and again on August 26, 1510. He had him reaggravated on November 22, 1510, this time only referring to the contract between the two men ("*racione contractus*," like most other excommunications *pro judicato* under the heading of *Extranea jurisdictio*). Guy then had himself "relaxed" or temporarily absolved, because d'Escrepintot had to have him "retruded" into an aggravated and reaggravated excommunication ("*aggravatus et reaggravatus per retrusionem*") on August 4, 1511. Since Guy was recorded as absolved, we may assume that after two and half years of spiritual sanctions, Guy paid up or at least came to a satisfactory agreement with d'Escrepintot.

Not all excommunicates so obdurately resisted the power of the keys. The vast majority of excommunicates were absolved. Of 5,249 sanctions, 5,011 or 95.4 percent were recorded as having been absolved. 233 or

[167] ADSM G 5273, Extranea jurisdictio, 1508: "Gauffridus guy dyocesis baiocensis monitus et excommunicatus pro judicato unius tumbe petre de ranville septem pedum a toise concepte et trium pedum unius poyet de brese concepte bone et legantis [sc legalis] necnon quinque tonnellorum alterius petre de gre ranvilla similiter bone et legalis prout in literis continetur contra Johannem descrepintot juniorem racione maiore liberationis premissis super habulum de harefloto racione contractus et comperte de die mercurii xxiiij januarij." Conversely, Julie Mayade-Claustre relates how the Archdeacon of Bayeux had a carver of tombstones imprisoned in the Châtelet for two days for failing to deliver within the time specified by his contract, and this after fining him 10 *écus*: "Le corps lié de l'ouvrier. Le travail et la dette à Paris au XVe siècle," *Annales HSS* 60:2 (2005), 383–408, at 392 and there too n.34.

4.4 percent were not recorded as ever having been absolved. The difference between the two figures represents four economic cells within which only certain members were absolved. It comes as no surprise that "foreigners," inhabitants of other dioceses or exceptions excommunicated at the request of the abbess's subjects were far less frequently absolved than were her subjects. Of 858 of excommunicated "foreigners," 178 or 20.7 percent were never absolved (only certain members of three additional cells were absolved). Subtracting these "foreigners" who could more easily escape the real impact of the abbess's sanctions through the ignorance of their parish priests or the connivance of their ecclesiastical judges, only 55 of 4,391, a bare 1.25 percent of excommunicates inhabiting the parishes of her territory, were not recorded as having been absolved over the thirty years covered in ADSM G 5273. In sixteenth-century Upper Normandy, almost all of the spiritual subjects of the Abbess of Montivilliers were eager to return to the embrace of Holy Mother Church. Because there were few real bars to business with excommunicates in this period, the high percentage of absolutions signals widespread desire to have access to the sacraments and to be a member of the sacramental community in good standing – and thereby to repair one's damaged credit, something intimately connected to one's moral and sacramental standing. Even if no one was barred from doing business with excommunicates, excommunicates may have had more difficulty in accessing credit, as the sanction signified their impaired moral, social, and economic reputation. Individuals therefore overwhelmingly sought to repair marks against their credit, even though the debts in question were most often rather modest. The single largest debt was one of 603£ 5s 8dt (I shall return to this debt below), the smallest one of only 12dt. The average amount was 71.5st or about 3½£t, twenty days' wages for a mason and roughly 32 days' wages for a laborer. The median was, however, 30st or 1½£t, confirming that the bulk of excommunications were for small amounts, for only six days' wages for a mason and not much more than thirteen days' wages for a laborer.[168] Excommunication for debt was mainly used for the minor, verbal extensions of credit on which day-to-day, small-scale commerce and provisioning functioned.

When we turn to who excommunicated whom, we discover further aspects of this practice. Four thousand five hundred fourteen economic cells were involved in 5,249 sanctions,. Because economic cells

[168] Bois, *Crise*, 91–110. Bois gives 5st as the daily wage of a mason and 2s 3dt as that of a laborer at Rouen in the first half of the sixteenth century. In the county of Tancarville, wages were lower, 4st for a mason and 2st for a laborer. Women's wages were generally half those of men.

sanctioned or were sanctioned, an individual could appear, for instance, three times: once as an individual, once as proctor of a confraternity, and once as an economic cell with a wife. Table 3.11 illustrates the frequency of sanctions at Montivilliers between 1499 and 1530. The first column shows the number of individuals who were sanctioned by the number of times that they were sanctioned, and the second column shows the number of individuals who requested sanctions by the number of times that they requested sanctions.

Sanctions were mainly one-time or two-time events, aside from the exceptional cases examined below: 1,690 or 32.2 percent of sanctions were one-time events for the individual sanctioned;[169] 644 or 12.3 percent of sanctions were directed twice against the same individual. For an individual to be excommunicated more than eleven times was exceedingly rare. In terms of those who requested, 1,778 or 33.9 percent of sanctions were one-time events for the requestor.[170] An additional 702 or 13.4 percent of sanctions were requested twice by the same person. An individual seldom requested sanctions against the same person more than nine times. The data therefore overwhelmingly reveal creditors deploying sanctions once or twice against debtors and, conversely, debtors being sanctioned only once or twice. The populations excommunicated and excommunicating were fairly distinct: 2,180 cells never excommunicated anyone; 2,124 cells were never excommunicated. The 203 or 4.5 percent of cells that both excommunicated and were excommunicated received only 599 or 11.4 percent of sanctions and issued only 575 or 11.0 percent of sanctions. This means that 2,073 or 45.9 percent of cells requested 4,672 or 89.0 percent of sanctions and that 2,091 or 46.3 percent of cells received 87.7 percent of sanctions. With 203 exceptions, excommunicators and excommunicates appear to have been different types of person, perhaps because the very poor would have been least able to extend credit of any sort. Whereas the daily wages of Norman urban laborers in Rouen, Tancarville, and perhaps Montivilliers reached over 2st and those of masons over 4st, those of rural laborers on the Cistercian grange of Valasse were paid only 1st per day in 1518 and 1539.[171] Although the laborers of Valasse were also fed, a not inconsiderable benefit in a period of inflated grain prices, their wages were very low. Such men – and certainly their wives, likely paid a miserable 6dt per diem – were unlikely to

[169] Subtracting 58 entries for which the name of the sanctioned is illegible gives 1,632 or 31.1 percent.

[170] Subtracting 177 entries for which the name of the sanctioner is illegible gives 1,601 or 30.5 percent.

[171] Bois, *Crise*, 107.

Table 3.11 *Frequency of sanctions at Montivilliers, 1499–1530*

Number of sanctions	Persons sanctioned	Persons requesting sanctions
1	1690	1778
2	323	351
3	151	139
4	89	84
5	47	43
6	25	29
7	31	17
8	11	18
9	13	12
10	13	9
11	9	5
12	5	1
13	7	4, Robert Regnart, Jean…, Jean de la Fontaine, Jacques Portier
14	3	2, Romain le Sage, Jean Regnart
15	3, Thomas Bacon, Robert Avisse clerc, Etienne Asse clerc	2, Richard Noël, Cardin Agnès
16	3, Sire Jacques Durant, Sire Etienne le Comte, Pierre Lescolier clerc	1, Sire Jean Castellion
17	0	3, Robert le Gendre, Jean Reaulté, Guillaume Regnault
18	4, Sire Laurent le Merchier, Pierre Taffournel, Michel Tanquerel l'aîné clerc, Etienne de la Noe clerc armiger	2, Me Guillaume Mesegnel prêtre, Jacques Regnart
19	1, Roger Tanquerel	1, Pierre Hemery
20	3, Robert Morice, Richard Gosselin clerc, Philippe Sieurin clerc	0
21	1, Sire Raoul Broyart	0
22	3, Nicolas le Comte[1], Nicolas de Brys clerc, Jean d'Escures clerc	0
23	2, Pierre le Valois clerc, Henry Davy	1, Raoul le Comte
24	0	0
25	1, Jean Desert clerc	1, Philippe Paris
26	3, Thomas Mahaut clerc, Guillaume le Tellier[2], Guillaume Guillart	1, Richard Apris
27	2, Martin de Pimont clerc, Jean Savary[3]	0
28	0	1, Robert Avisse
29	0	0
30	0	0
32	1, Me Denis Taffournel	0
35	0	1, Jacques Quevin
36	0	1, *Sealer of the Court*
37	2, Sire Pierre Frontault, Nicolas Deslaney clerc	0

Number of sanctions	Persons sanctioned	Persons requesting sanctions
39	0	1, Richard Gaultier
40	0	1, *Master of Testaments*
43	1, Bertrand Prudhomme clerc	0
55	1, Nicolas Geoffroy clerc	0
67	1, Éliot Passilly clerc	0
70	1, Guillaume Reboursel clerc	0
87	0	*Promotor of Justice*
103	0	*Official of Montivilliers*
425	0	*Receiver of Fines*

Note: Names of court officials in italics.

[1] To be identified with Nicolas Le Comte, clerc, excommunicated ten times, thus thirty-two times in total? with Sire Nicolas Le Comte, priest, excommunicated four times, thus thirty-six times in total?

[2] In 1511, *procurator domine.* To be identified with Guillaume Le Tellier, clerc, excommunicated seven times, thus thirty-three in total? with Sire Guillaume Le Tellier, priest, excommunicated eleven times, and therefore forty-four in total? with Guillaume Le Tellier the Younger? the Older?

[3] In 1506, *notarius curie nostre.* To be identified with Jean Savary, clerc, excommunicated seven times, thus thirty-four in total? with Sire Jean Savary, priest, excommunicated nine times, thus forty-two in total? with Jean Mogres alias Savary, who sanctioned once and was sanctioned once?

Source: ADSM G 5273.

accumulate the debts that would put them in the position to excommunicate. They were far more likely to buy on credit or to solicit small loans or prolongations of dues that amounted to loans from lords, farmers, or others with economic power.

Let us turn therefore to the identity of sanctioner and sanctioned, before considering frequent excommunicates and frequent excommunicators individually. Nobles rarely appear, explicitly in fewer than 2 percent of sanctions at Montivilliers, perhaps reflecting their absence from mid-level commerce but certainly reflecting the prevalence of what Bruce Campbell has referred to as tenant-on-tenant exploitation.[172] Nobles were less likely to excommunicate for "a green bench and two footstools" or "15st and a cow,"[173] as lords could easily press

[172] Campbell, "The Agrarian Problem in the Early Fourteenth Century," *Past & Present* 188 (2005), 3–70, at 69–70 on "rent-seeking" tenants. Nobles may be undercounted, as their status was not legally important.

[173] ADSM G 5273, Saint-Sauveur, 1503: "Nicolaus du gardin excommunicatus pro judicato unius virge [viridei?] scamni et duorum scabellorum contra dominum petrum gascoing presbiterum de x[a] julij"; Saint-Sauveur, 1504: "… excommunicatus pro judicato xv s et lx s vel una vacca contra margarinum … de xx[a] junij."

indebted subjects or tenants through threats of demanding rents often years in arrears and ultimately of dispossession.[174] Clerics played a large role and are probably undercounted, as it was important judicially only to note whether the target of a sanction was a priest, who would then be suspended from the ability to celebrate divine service in the first instance rather than being excommunicated like simple clerics or layfolk. Still less was it necessary to note the status of the requestor of the sanction, as this made no difference in capacity to excommunicate. That said, after having consistently marked as clerics those only occasionally noted as such to correct for presumed underreporting, 1,308 sanctions were directed against single clerics, with clerics appearing in a handful of additional mixed cells. Six hundred twenty-eight sanctions were directed against individual priests, who appeared in a further handful of mixed cells. This means that 1,936 or 36.9 percent of sanctions were directed at the clergy. As one doubts that one-third of the population of Upper Normandy consisted of male clerics, this overrepresentation indicates that the clergy were involved in commerce and lending and suggests that excommunication or suspension for debt gave layfolk a weapon against delinquent clerical debtors, who would otherwise have invoked their clerical immunity to escape lay justice. In the other direction, only sixty-three sanctions were requested by clerics and only 560 by priests. These 623 clerical requests constituted only 11.9 percent of sanctions. In terms of clerical status, then, ecclesiastical sanctions were deployed asymmetrically by layfolk against clerics. Excommunication was a cheap and effective remedy against clerics who flouted lay justice. The impunity of clerical lawbreakers who invoked their clerical exemption from lay justice was a common late medieval complaint: as Jean Le Lièvre, *avocat du roi* in the Parlement of Paris, claimed in 1516: "most often ecclesiastical judges, as soon as a cleric is transferred to them, fine him and set him free. Crimes thereby remain unpunished, which is an abuse."[175] Requestors of spiritual sanctions could savor their effectiveness and their cheapness, as well as the fact that these sanctions were deployed by the Church against its own. What the vicomte of Montivilliers could not do against clerical debtors by distraining their

[174] Julien Demade, "La fonction de l'endettement et de la justice dans le rapport seigneurial, ou la grâce comme contrainte (Franconie, XVe siècle)," in Claustre, *La dette*, 69–119.

[175] AN X^{2a}71, 246r. "le plus souvent les Juges deglise incontinent que on leur a rendu ung clerc ilz les pugnissent emenda pecuniaria et leur donnent conge et parce moyen demeurent les cas impugniz et non corrigez qui est ung abuz." On clerical immunity, see Génestal, *Le* privilegium fori.

persons or property, the official of Montivilliers could by distraining, so to speak, their sources of income and their souls.

The Abbess of Montivilliers's officials requested a great many spiritual sanctions. Never sanctioned as such, the five officials of her court were the five most frequent excommunicators. The receiver of fines requested 425 sanctions, the official or auditor standing in for him 103 sanctions, the promotor of justice 87 sanctions, the master of wills 40 sanctions, and the sealer of the court 36 sanctions. These 691 sanctions were, however, only 13.2 percent of the total issued, so at Montivilliers it appears that most of the business of the court was private, as the abbess's personal receiver and proctor seldom appear. Churchwardens and the officers of confraternities appear in the records, often in disputes between the current and the outgoing officers, doubtless over their accounting. Groups of churchwardens were excommunicated sixteen times and officers of confraternities eleven times as a group. Conversely, churchwardens requested eighty-one sanctions, while only one confraternity requested sanctions, probably on the occasion of its annual closing of accounts, when one set of administrators or *échevins* replaced another.

Women figure in the records: fifty-three excommunications were deployed against widows, thirteen explicitly in their capacity as their husbands' executors. twenty-eight sanctions were deployed against wives, eighteen against wives and husbands conjointly, sixteen against women and men not specified as their husbands, and fifty-five against women not mentioned as married. Five female merchants (*marchandes publiques* or *mercatrices publicae*) appear. Ginesse Camarguy was excommunicated for a debt of 7s 6dt to Henri Perrier on July 13, 1510. Germaine Fourmilly excommunicated Pierre Taffournel for three and a half barrels of "light, good, sellable" beer (*trium barricolorum seu cadorum arves* [?] *cum dimidio cervesie albe bone et mercabilis*) on April 2, 1508 (OS). Taffournel was relaxed at some point and then retruded into excommunication on May 12, 1509 for a debt of half a barrel of beer, having in the intervening period delivered the other three barrels. In addition to this, between 1500 and 1515 Taffournel was excommunicated twenty times and requested sanctions three times. This Germaine Fourmilly, wife of the Guillaume Fourmilly or Fremilly himself present in the register, also had Pierre Viart, cleric, excommunicated for a debt of 4st on June 5, 1512 and aggravated on July 15; she had Jean Desmons excommunicated for contumacy, once in March 1513 and again on April 19, 1513. The third *marchande publique* listed, Annette, the wife of Raoulin Passilly, was excommunicated on October 4, 1514 for contumacy at the request of Jeanne Lauret and on March 3, 1529 for contumacy by the Prior and Convent of the Virgin of Les Villettes, the last time in her capacity as executrix of the late Master Nicolas Basin. Her husband Raoul or Raoulin requested excommunication once and was himself excommunicated five times, once in conjunction with his relative Éliot Passilly. Fourth was Jacqueline, wife of Jean Noël, who had Master Renaud Renbours, clerc, excommunicated for contumacy on February 18, 1528 (NS). Finally, Jeanne, wife of Pierre Tirel, had the same Éliot Passilly, cleric, excommunicated for a debt of 33st on August 3, 1530. Pierre Tirel had himself been excommunicated three times in January–February 1513 (OS), perhaps during credit difficulties. As "public merchants," these women traded and litigated in their own name and without the supervision of their husbands. Overall, women figured in 170 or 3.2 percent of sanctions received. Women requested 249 or 4.7 percent of sanctions. Of these, women not specified as married requested 126 sanctions, men with their wives 15 sanctions, widows 76 sanctions (6 times as executors), and wives alone 32 sanctions. Vastly underrepresented, "covered" in legal terms by their husbands and the networks of male relatives who guarded a family's patrimony, women more often sanctioned than they were sanctioned. One suspects that women who litigated over credit were those who had the most of it and who acted as executors for husbands or close male relatives.

Two important categories of debt appear in the register, tavern expenses and tithes, illustrating the range of potential uses of spiritual sanctions. Innkeepers appear explicitly twenty-one times in the register, six times soliciting and fifteen times receiving sanctions, though the same individuals, not noted as innkeepers, appear more frequently. Jean Le Vavasseur, cleric and innkeeper, was excommunicated on December 23, 1506 for a debt of 16st by Perronet de la Fontaine. Raoulin Maré, innkeeper, was excommunicated by the official on March 26, 1511 "for manifest offenses and rebellion before us in court (*pro manifesta offensa et rebellione coram nobis judicialiter*)." Jean Viart, innkeeper, was excommunicated eleven times and aggravated twice in 1523 by eight different individuals for contumacy and for debts ranging from 12s 6dt to 8£t. These occurred in a cluster from April 17 to November 16, 1523. Because Viart was absolved of all of these excommunications, though only at length for at least two of them, which were aggravated, one may assume that he suffered an acute credit crisis in early 1523 and had been unable to pay his suppliers. As plaintiffs, innkeepers were also active. Richard Apris, innkeeper, had Jean Auffray the Younger, squire, excommunicated on March 2, 1519 for contumacy. Apris also requested twenty-six sanctions against others. As only six of these were for contumacy, and even though Apris was not explicitly noted as an innkeeper in these cases, it is likely that these sanctions concerned unpaid tavern expenses, some of which mounted to more than 11st.

Like bakers, innkeepers were probably constrained to extend small credits to customers – credits that could eventually attain considerable size.[176] Jeannetonne, wife of Raoulin de Scribe, innkeeper, had the vagabond priest Sire Pierre Gascoing suspended once in 1520 and once in 1521. Raoulin de Servile, innkeeper, had Thomas Hyebleron excommunicated on April 11, 1521 for contumacy. Colin Agnel, innkeeper, had Jacques du Buc, cleric, excommunicated for a debt of 11s 4dt on November 16, 1526. It appears that Agnel had little need to call in his debts, as he only excommunicated one other person, in 1510 for contumacy. Colin Agnel's relative Guillaume Agnel, also called Barat or Baratte, appears in the register as a tithe-farmer. This would suggest that excommunication was the weapon of the weak and poor, who had little credit to protect, were it not that Richard Apris's relative Sire Jean Apris, also appears in the register as a tithe-farmer. Richard himself is occasionally referred to as "the honorable (*honorabilis*)" as well! Rather than absolute poverty, frequent excommunication may still reflect a lack of credit relative to the demands placed on it by self and others, as the examples from Paris illustrate and as seems to be the case for a spendthrift young clerk of Montivilliers: on October 26, 1520 Nicolas Lescolier, "was excommunicated for a debt to Jean des Prés of 12st for tavern expenses."[177]

Tithe-farmers (who leased tithing-rights) appear explicitly only a handful of times, although one gets the impression that such entrepreneurs were common enough. They used excommunication to coerce recalcitrant tithe-payers into recognizing their property rights. For instance, in 1517 (OS) Sire Jean Compéry, vicar and tithe-farmer of Rouelles had Jean Desert, cleric, excommunicated on March 2 and aggravated on March 13 for contumacy for failing to pay the gross tithes (*grossas decimas*) on grain and minor or "green" tithes (*minutas et virides decimas*) on animals and other crops.[178] Such cases could concern relatively

[176] John Munro notes that Antwerp and Lier forbade innkeepers to sell on credit in 1442 and 1457: "Deflation and the Petty Coinage Problem in the Late-Medieval Economy: The Case of Flanders, 1334–1484," *Explorations in Economic History* 25:4 (1988), 387–423, at 415.

[177] ADSM G 5273, 34v: "Nicolaus lescolier nepos magistri nicolay excommunicatus pro judicato somme xij[im] solidorum turonensium pro expensis taberne contra Johannem des preez in domo eiusdem facto de die xxvj[a] mensis octobris." Lescolier was excommunicated as well for 3st on August 3, 14st on September 21, 48st on October 4, and 7s 6dt on January 19 (1521, NS).

[178] ADSM G 5273, [125]: "Johannes Desert excommunicatus pro contumacia in assignatione ad dandum decimas omnium et singulorum agniculorum ovilium vaccarum vitulorum prociculorum jumentorum equorum poullains gallice lanarum linrum et aliarum rerum que decimari solent et computari inter minutas et virides decimas in dicta parochia contra dominum johannem comperi vicarium dicte parrochie de rouella necnon contra eundem comperi tanquam firmarium grossarum decimarum dicte ecclesie sub honestis dominabus et religiosis abbatissa et conventu montisvillaris ad dandum

large sums, as when on December 18, 1523 Master Jean Prudhomme and Master Raoul Regnard, priests and tithe-farmers of Saint-Sauveur excommunicated Colin Franchois and Jacques Le Croq of the jurisdiction of Rouen for 10£t, presumably the tithes on property that Franchois and Le Croq held within the parish of Saint-Sauveur. Tithe-farmers also litigated even when this did not lead to excommunication: on December 9, 1507, the official ordered Jean Ardenne to pay Sire Louis Morin, curé of Fontenay, his tithes of wool, lambs, and calves; on the same day, the official ordered Éliot Passilly and Jean Herault to pay Sire Guillaume Le Flament, vicar and farmer of Gournay, their tithe of wood; on August 7, 1521, the official ordered Pierre Hermen to pay to Sire Pierre Ardenne, vicar of Épouville, 30st for the tithe on the house he had sold for 15£t.[179] The first case concerns a debt arising from a parishioner's simple refusal to pay his tithes. The second is more interesting, as Passilly and Herault had clearly leased woods near Gournay. The official decided that these entrepreneurs had to pay the tithe of wood "commonly called the *bois du boulle* [sc. *boulaie*]" to another entrepreneur. Repeated excommunications for scores of cartloads of wood indicate the rising profitability of wood in the sixteenth century – and the concomitant attractiveness of leathing cutting or tithing-rights to it. The last case could conceal either the real sale of a house or the sale of a *rente* with a capital of 15£t (Norman annuities yielded the tenth penny). Tithe-farmers stood at the intersection of many different levels of commerce and credit. For tithe-farmers, excommunication secured their property rights, foreshadowing its early modern deployment against occult theft and property damage. Like other farmers, these agrarian capitalists showed the way forward, by using church courts to further their pursuit of profitable opportunities.

Frequent excommunicates were more likely to be clerics than frequent excommunicators, aside from officers of the court. The most frequently excommunicated individuals were five clerics and a priest: Guillaume Reboursel, excommunicated seventy times individually and twice with others (excommunicating four times); Éliot Passilly, excommunicated sixty-seven times individually and four times with others (excommunicating four times); Nicolas Geoffroy, excommunicated fifty-five times (excommunicating twice); Bertrand Prudhomme, excommunicated forty-three times individually and once with another (excommunicating

declarationem gerbarum bladi ordei avene et aliorum granorum computari solitorum inter grossas decimas et ext … unt super quadam … juxta declarationem dicti comperi dicto desert traditam de die martis secunda mensis martii anni domini mille quing^{mi} xvii^{i}."

[179] ADSM G 5274, 4, 4v, 27.

once); Sire Pierre Frontault, vicar of Verquetot, suspended thirty-five times and excommunicated twice (excommunicating four times); and Nicolas Deslaney, excommunicated thirty-seven times. Together these six men accounted as individuals for 309 or 5.9 percent of sanctions recorded in the register.[180] We will now examine Reboursel's and Passilly's appearances in the register.

Guillaume Reboursel's record spans the entire period from 1499 to 1530. He was cited almost exclusively in the parish of Harfleur, presumably his home and that of his family, as a Robert Reboursel from Harfleur studied theology at Paris in the 1490s.[181] Although Guillaume Reboursel was in minor orders, the fact that he was sanctioned 64 out of 70 times for debts in a notably commercial town suggests that he was involved in trade of some kind. He appears first on February 20, 1499, when Malon Jolys had him excommunicated for a debt of 4£ 6s 4dt. Jolys had this aggravated on March 3, including also a debt of 200 bundles of hay. Reboursel may have been shirking a purveyor of horse feed. The two weeks between the initial sanction and its aggravation suggest a pressing debt, of which Reboursel was ultimately absolved. In 1500, he was excommunicated twice, once in a group of four, perhaps partners in a commercial venture, and once for 4£ 6s 6dt. The similarity of the latter sum causes one two speculate that Jolys had used Reboursel's debt to him to pay Jean Roussel, who requested this excommunication, though no cession is recorded. It could also be that Reboursel borrowed from Roussel to pay Jolys. Reboursel was excommunicated twice in 1501, once for 7£ 10st and once for 6£ 17st. In 1502 he was excommunicated and then aggravated for a debt of 16s 6dt to Sire Guillaume Sav[ary?]. In 1503 he was excommunicated for debts of 37s 6dt to someone named du Val, 14st to Guillaume Guillart, and of 7s 8dt to Pierre de Saint-Aubin of the diocese of Rouen. The last had him aggravated, though Reboursel was again ultimately absolved. In 1504, he was excommunicated once by the receiver of fines for 2s 6dt and excommunicated and then aggravated by the master of wills for contumacy as executor of his apparent relative Blanchet Reboursel. Jean de Brumare had him excommunicated and

[180] If all the homonyms of Nicolas Le Comte, Jean Savary, and Guillaume Le Tellier, all three listed variously as laymen, clerics, and priests, can be securely identified, they would enter onto this list, as Le Comte would then have been excommunicated 36 times, Savary 42 times, and Le Tellier 44 times. It is, however, better to be cautious concerning families filled with homonyms (as with the contemporary brothers Jean du Tillet the elder and the younger or Jean de Selve the elder and the younger).

[181] James K. Farge, *Orthodoxy and Reform in Early Renaissance France: The Faculty of Theology of Paris, 1500–1543* (Leiden: Brill, 1985), 32. No Reboursels of Harfleur (or from anywhere else in the exemption) appear in the mid-fifteenth-century register discussed earlier.

then aggravated for 30st, Clément Noël had him excommunicated for 4s 6dt, and Jean Bonnard of the jurisdiction of Rouen had him excommunicated and aggravated for 16s 6dt. In 1505 Reboursel was excommunicated and aggravated by Guillaume Blancbaston alias Houssette for 22s 6dt, excommunicated by Raoul Guibelet for 55s 6dt, again by Blancbaston for a presumably residual 9st, and finally by Jean Perdu for 18st. In 1506 Reboursel was excommunicated by Jean Boucher for 35st, excommunicated and aggravated by the master of wills for contumacy, excommunicated by Jean Le Chau for 35st, and excommunicated by Bernard Cornet of the diocese of Rouen for contumacy. In 1508 he was excommunicated by Jean Syletage, proctor of the confraternity of Saint-Côme for 9st, and by Jean Tiberge for 8st. Conversely, he excommunicated Jean Savary once on March 22 and again on March 27 for 4£ 5st, presumably after Savary had been temporarily absolved. In 1510 Reboursel was excommunicated by Sire Denis Davis, curate of Rouville for 31s 6dt. In 1511 he was twice excommunicated by Sire Jean Apris, tithe-farmer of the parish of Saint-Germain, presumably where Reboursel owed tithes on land, first for 4£ 10st and then a month later for 38st. Jean le Bailly excommunicated him for 6£t on March 8 and Roger Philippe for the same on the next day, implying either a transferred debt or an equally shared commercial debt. Etienne du Port excommunicated him for 20st. Up to 1512, we can see Reboursel's excommunications as the price of doing business on credit and potentially as a strategic indifference to ecclesiastical sanctions so as to delay settlements.

In 1512 Reboursel's uncertain credit took a turn for the worse; he was excommunicated thirteen times for debts ranging from 6s 6dt to 60st, including once for 27st by Éliot Passilly – indicating that these two maximally excommunicated individuals had business with each other. In 1513 he was excommunicated twice, once by Éliot Passilly for 8s 6dt and once by Jean le Bailly, who had excommunicated him for 50st on January 14 of the previous year and then for 30st on March 18, for 30st, this time on April 30. Reboursel did, however, have Robert le Bailly, noble of Pierrefitte, excommunicated for contumacy in 1513. In 1514 Reboursel was excommunicated for a debt of 4£t and eighty pounds of "Jewish silk or says (*quatuor viginti librarum saginis de juif*)" by Zacharias Petit, whom we shall encounter again. Did Reboursel trade in cloth? In 1515 he was excommunicated for 60st by Guillaume Pallefrey, in 1516 by Jean Real for an unspecified amount and by Jean Compery for 75st, in 1518 for 47st by Guillaume Pierre and for 31st by Guillaume Prudhomme, in 1519 by Jean Le Bouteiller, squire (*scutifer*), for 39st. In 1520 he excommunicated Pierre des Champs, cleric, for contumacy and was excommunicated by Jean Malassigne for 3£ 15st. In 1521 he was excommunicated and aggravated by Pierre Danten for 25£t on June 6 and on August 18 and again by Jean Boudin for 185 pounds of "summer butter (*sagiminis estivalis*)" on January 9 and February 18. Did Reboursel then trade in butter as well? 185 lbs is certainly a large barrel. Perhaps Parisians already valued Norman butter as much they valued the fish of Dieppe? It is tempting to see here traces of the supply network for Les Halles, Paris's provisions market, though the butter could have been destined for Rouen or for a ship traveling to the New World. In 1524 Reboursel was excommunicated for contumacy by Sire Jean du Val, proctor of the confraternity of Saint-Laurent. In 1527 he was excommunicated by Pierre Danten for 14£ 7s 6dt on December 7 and aggravated on December 19 for the same amount. Danten excommunicated Reboursel again on February 26, 1528 for 8£t and on June 5, 1530 for 23s, though in the last case the Pierre Danten excommunicating was the son and heir of the prior excommunicator. What was the Dantens' relationship to Reboursel? Why did the elder Danten show himself so impatient? We do not know. What is clear is that Reboursel's debts were exceptional for two reasons, both in their relatively large amount and in that they so frequently imperiled his salvation. Was Reboursel a proto-Protestant, a tepid believer, or a convinced Catholic condemned to repeated excommunication by the nature of his business? The first possibility is not implausible, as Harfleur was later a center of Cauchois Protestantism.[182] The last is enticing, however. The exceptional frequency of Reboursel's excommunications suggests both the range and magnitude of his trade as well as his potential indifference to ecclesiastical sanctions during commercial difficulties. Was it better to drag one's feet in paying up when one's annual communion remained distant, stretching one's tenuous credit in the interests of profit?

The second major excommunicate, Éliot Passilly, cleric, appears in the register from 1502 to 1530. Excommunicated exclusively in Harfleur, he must have been like Reboursel a cleric in commerce. He was, however, excommunicated individually twenty times for contumacy and forty-seven times for debt. He was excommunicated five times with others and excommunicated others six times (see Table 3.12).

Passilly appears to be yet another Norman entrepreneur, trading at least in part in wood. On December 9, 1507 the official had sentenced him and Jean Herault to pay their tithe of wood to Sire Guillaume Le Flament, who was vicar and tithe-farmer of Gournay.[183] That Sire

182 On the problematic relations of the Abbey of Montivilliers, its tithe-farmers, its parish priests, and its parishioners in this period, see Bottin, *Seigneurs*, 116–131.

183 ADSM G 5274, 4v: "in causa decimali ... inter dominum guillermum le flament presbiterum vicarium et firmarium ecclesie parrochialis beate marie de gourneyo actorem ex una et heliotum passilly ac johannem herault correos sive deffendentes ex altera

Table 3.12 *Excommunications of Éliot Passilly (in bold if he is excommunicating someone else)*

Year (OS)	Month	Day	Requestor (bold if EP is requesting)	Cause
1502	5	19	Jean Bourderée	65st
1502	6	3	**Sire Robert de Hatentot prêtre, suspensus**	*Contumacy*
1502	6	8	Guy Morel	9s 5dt
1502	9	19	Guillaume Grambert	*Contumacy*
1502	9	26	Guillaume Grambert	*Contumacy*
1502	10	21	Jeanne Champion	40£t
1502	10	25	Robert le Carpentier	30£t
1502	11		Robert le Carpentier, aggravatus	30£t
1502	11	25	Jeanne Champion, aggravata	40£t
1502	2	23	Guillaume Reauté	*Contumacy*
1503	9	22	damoiselle Isabelle…	*Contumacy*
1503	11	16	Guillaume Amaury	*Contumacy*
1503	12	7	Guillaume Amaury, aggravatus	*Contumacy*
1504	6	21	Jean Sanisart	39st
1504	12	11	Guillaume Grambert	11£
1505	5	24	Thomas le Mercier	37£ 6st
1505	2	3	Jacques Portier	10s 3dt
1506	11	8	Jean Sanisart	6£ 9st
1506	3	15	Guillaume Grambert	*Contumacy*
1507	6	12	Guillaume Grambert	27£ 9st
1507	6	29	Robert de Reu	35st
1507	7	6	Nicolas de Saint-Aubin	7£t
1507	10	8	Roger Potier alias Philippe procureur de la charité de la Madeleine de la Coudray	*Contumacy*
1507	11	7	Jean Sanisart	53s 6dt
1507	3	30	Me Jean de Freville prêtre	6£t
1508	7	20	Robert de la Pierre	15£t
1508	12	2	Me Jean de Freville prêtre	25£t
1508	12	7	Sire Simon Cacheret prêtre	*Contumacy*
1508	1	19	Jean Sanisart	4£t
1508	3	9	Pierre de la Fontaine	118£t
1508	4	5	Jean le Sauvage	4£ 2s 6dt
1509	6	21	Roger Potier alias Philippe procureur de la charité de la Madeleine de la Coudray	
1509	7	6	Me Guillaume B…y	7£ 9st
1509	1	17	Jean Pelletier	4£ 2st
1510	7	19	Sire Denis Davy prêtre curé de Rouville jurisdictionis Rothomagensis	45£t
1510	10	26	Roger Potier alias Philippe procureur de la charité de la Madeleine de la Coudray	12£t
1510	11	14	**Pierrette Regnault**	*Contumacy*
1510	3	5	Raoul Auberée	60s 6dt
1511	10	3	Guillaume Foucher	4£t
1511	10	22	**Sire Raoul Broyart prêtre, suspensus**	35£t
1512	1	27	**Guillaume Reboursel clerc**	27£t
1512	3		Jean Canal	*Contumacy*

Year (OS)	Month	Day	Requestor (bold if EP is requesting)	Cause
1513	5		**Guillaume Reboursel clerc**	8£ 6st
1513	10	6	Guy Daniel	20st and a silver signet ring
1513	10	22	Jean Mallon	
1513	10	22	Raoul Auberée	4£ 5s 6dt
1513	11	21	Me Jean Bourgeois prêtre	*Contumacy*
1513	12	1	**Pierre Persac**	*Contumacy*
1513	2	4	Jean Pélerin jurisdictionis Rothomagensis	11£t
1513	3	18	Pierre Chambellan	*Contumacy*
1513	4	1	Éliot Passilly clerc	*Contumacy*
1514	5	18	Guillaume Mogres alias Savary	*Contumacy*
1515	10	17	Jacques Portier, also against Pierre de la Fontaine the Younger	62£ 13s 4dt
1515	10	29	Jacques Portier, also against La Fontaine, aggravati	62£ 13s 4dt
1516	7	9	Guillaume Tout...es	14£ 15s 9dt
1516	9	23	Jean Mogres alias Savary	55£t
1516	10	4	Guillaume Courmères paroisse de Briaulté	12£ 5st
1516	1	27	Jean Perrin	60£ 3st
1516	3	19	Colin de D...	*Contumacy*
1516	3	29	Sire Guillaume Le Flament prêtre, also against Jean Herault	7£ 2st
1517	5	26	Jean Oursel	*Contumacy*
1517	5	28	Guillaume Canely	21£ 8st
1517	6	22	Jean Oursel, aggravatus	*Contumacy*
1517	8	20	Me Jean Chevalier prêtre, reaggravatus	
1517	1	11	Jean Auber	
1517	1	14	Sire Guillaume Le Flament prêtre vicaire de Gournay, also against Jean Herault	36£t
1517	2	6	Jean Auber	
1517	3	2	Jean Maillart jurisdictionis Rothomagensis	25£t
1518	6	15	Jean Auber	
1523	6	12	Henri Bisset, also against Raoulin Passilly	*Contumacy*
1524	6	27	Guillaume d'Aboville alias le Gay	*Contumacy*
1524	3	9	Jean Milley	*Contumacy*
1524	3	17	Guillaume d'Aboville alias le Gay, aggravatus	*Contumacy*
1525	3	10	Jean Canal	15£ 78st
1526	5	19	Jean Canal	15£ 78st
1526	8	29	Jean Canal, retrusus	15£ 78st
1528	2	27	Jacqueline veuve feu Jean Millon	5£17st[1]
1530	6	21	Guillaume de Bris	8£t
1530	8	3	Jeanne femme Pierre Tirel marchande publique	33£t

[1] I have converted the sum "trium aureorum solis" not at the official rate, 40st per écu, but at that specified in 1525 at Harfleur: "Heliotus passily excommunicatus pro judicato xv£t ex uno et duorum scutorum auri valoris pro petia xxxix st in alio partibus contra johannem canal de die 3a mensis octobris."

Source: ADSM G 5273.

Guillaume had the pair excommunicated in 1516 (OS) and 1517 (OS) illustrates that Herault and Passilly together leased woods in the parish of Gournay for more than a decade. Furthermore, Passilly's debts to Jean Auber originated in 450 bundles of firewood (*quattuor centum cum dimidio fasciculorum bonorum et regalium* [recte *legalium*]) and to Jean Mallon in a thousand plus one box or *carton* (*unius milliaris cum uno quarterono buche*). Auber began pursuit in 1517 and was still pursuing Passilly in 1526, when he relapsed into excommunication for the last time on August 29 and subsequently absolved. Mallon only acted once, though he may have given up hope of payment. Passilly's credit network must have been as broad as Reboursel's, as no one excommunicated him more than the five times that Guillaume Grambert had between 1502 and 1507. For instance, the Pierre Le Fontaine the Younger with whom he was excommunicated three times also appears on October 21, 1508 in the officiality's register of sentences, when Le Fontaine and Pierre Beuger secured a judgment in a *causa pecuniaria* against Nicolas Trougnart for 64st and the court costs of Richard Apris.[184] That Apris, an innkeeper who requested sanctions twenty-six times and a relative of a tithe-farmer, was involved in the case illustrates the multiple relations of credit that bound together the residents of the exemption of Montivilliers. Their credit disputes came before the officiality for three reasons. Some merchants, like Passilly and Reboursel, had been tonsured and could invoke their clerical exemption from lay justice. Secondly, some excommunicates may have lacked substantial landed property on which to secure debt. Finally, the officiality of Montivilliers enforced commercial contracts in Harfleur and its hinterland in a manner analogous to that of the consular tribunals on a Netherlandish and Spanish model that spread across from France from the 1550s.[185]

Commercial debt, as we have seen for the fifteenth century, often involved the cloth industry of Upper Normandy. The cloth trade surfaces explicitly in the case of the largest debt in the register: on May 18, 1524 Guillaume Foucher was excommunicated at Harfleur for a debt of 603£

partibus ... Visis per nos peticione sive libello dicti actoris ... et contumacia dictorum deffendentium ... dictos correos esse condampnandos prout condampnamus ad solvendum tradendum et munerandum eidem actori decimam bos[c]i vulgariter nuncupati le boys du boulle."

184 ADSM G 5274, 13.

185 Lefas, "De l'origine"; Mollat, *Le commerce*, 448–450, surveys attempts to secure similar courts in Upper Normandy prior to the erection of a consular jurisdiction in 1556. See too Amalia Kessler, *A Revolution in Commerce: The Parisian Merchant Court and the Rise of Commercial Society in Eighteenth-Century France* (New Haven: Yale University Press, 2007).

5s 8dt to Master Nicholas Trougnart, Thibaud Braudy, and Jean Vimont. A prior entry puts us one step closer to the cloth industry: at some point after April 19, Jacques Foucher had been excommunicated for resisting the commissioners inventorying the movable property of Colette Petit: Master Nicolas Trougnart, Jean Vimont, and Thibaud Boudry.[186] Who was Colette Petit? Who were Guillaume and Jacques Foucher? In the register of sentences, we learn that Colette was still living on June 17, 1522 and that on February 4, 1523, "Jean Vimont, son of the late Colette," secured a judgment against his coexecutors that "each and every debt of the said deceased up to two months prior to her death pertained [to him] with the exception of what Boudin owed."[187] On July 29, 1523, Jacques Foucher had been excommunicated for impeding Master Raoul Regnart, *avocat* at the officiality, and Richard Becquet, notary, both priests, from performing their duty.[188] Why? Among the few surviving draft final judgments for the officiality, we find that on August 20, 1523 Jean Vimont and Thibaud Boudin, executors of the testament of the late Colette, widow of Zacharias Petit, secured a judgment against "Jacques and Guillaume called Foucher, calling themselves co-heirs of the said deceased," on the report of the commissioners, Regnart and Becquet, inventorying her movable property. For "transporting or bearing away six bundles of the best broadcloth (*sex bottas late de bonis*) of the said deceased from her house ... against our inhibitions," the Foucher brothers were sentenced to return the six broadcloths and to pay a fine of 60st.[189] But on July 24, 1524 the official, at the request of Guillaume Foucher, required Trougnart, Vimont, and Boudin to deduct 11£ 15s 4dt from his debt of 603£ 5s 8dt.[190] The Fouchers do not reappear in the register, so presumably they somehow settled this still enormous debt of 591£ 10s 4dt. Whether they did this through a complicated combination

[186] ADSM G 5273, Harfleur, 1524: "Jacobus foucher excommunicatus pro rebellione et impedimento facto commissariis procedentibus ad inventarium bonorum mobilium deffuncte collette petit contra magistrum nicolaum trougnart johannem vimont et theobaldum boudry ... Guillelmus foucher excommunicatus pro judicato vj[cc]iij # v s viij d contra magistrum nicolaum frougmart theobaldum braudy et johannem vimont de die xviija maij." This may be the son of another Guillaume Foucher, who was excommunicated and his widow after his death numerous times, though never for more than what appear to be fines of 30st. One notes – and despairs of the implications of – the orthography of Braudy's/Boudry's/Boudin's name shifting in each document.

[187] ADSM G 5274, 31, for Colette's last recorded appearance, and 38, for the sentence against Boudin and Trougnart.

[188] ADSM G 5273, Harfleur: "Jacobus fouchier excommunicatus quia impedit ma[ndatum?] ne adimpleretur per magistrum radulphum regnart nostre curie advocatum et ricardum becquet notarium presbiteros de die jovis penultima julij."

[189] ADSM G 5317, n.p. Broadcloth was referred to as *pannus latus* and as *tela lata*; hence *lata* here.

[190] ADSM G 5274, 40v.

of goods, coins of different types, and transferred credit, as in the payments cited by Mollat and included at the end of the previous section, we do not know. We do know, however, that Colette Petit had six very fine broadcloths in her house at her death, valued at more than 100£t each when the Fouchers attempted to assert their rights as putative heirs. Zacharias Petit's involvement in the cloth trade, and his widow's after his death after March 1519 (NS) is likely, given that Petit excommunicated six times between 1513 and 1519: on January 24, 1513 (NS) he excommunicated Jacques de Rouffosse of the diocese of Lisieux for contumacy on behalf of his wife Colette, heiress of the late Jean Vimont (perhaps a previous husband, as her son was called Jean Vimont). In 1513, on July 21 Petit excommunicated Nicolas Geoffroy, cleric, for a debt of 6£t and on December 13 Jaspard Le Larde (an Englishman named Jasper Bacon?) for a debt of 27s 5dt. On December 22, 1514, he excommunicated, as we have seen, Guillaume Reboursel for a debt of silk and 4£t and on April 11, 1515 (NS) Jean Fergant the Younger for 70st. On March 26, 1519 (NS) he excommunicated Richard Artus, cleric, for contumacy.[191] That his wife died with what was probably the very expensive, high-quality broadcloth produced at Montivilliers in her house, that Petit excommunicated for a quantity of silk, that Petit excommunicated Geoffroy, who himself excommunicated twice and was excommunicated fifty-five times, that Petit excommunicated Fergant, likely a tailor (he had been excommunicated in 1517 for undelivered items of clothing), and that Petit's wife contested the inheritance of Jean Vimont executed by a resident of Honfleur,[192] strongly suggest that Zacharias and Colette Petit traded in the cloth of Montivilliers and were enmeshed in a commercial network by ties of inheritance and debt – and of inherited debt. Because cloth was so expensive, it was probably sold on credit to tailors and to other retailers by those who organized its production and import. Merchants of Harfleur and Montivilliers were probably not so different from English merchants, up to 60 percent of the value of whose estates could consist of debts owing. On average, 19.8 percent of the assets of members' of the London merchant companies in 1535 were in goods and 48.4 percent in debts.[193]

[191] ADSM G 5273, in order: Extranea jurisdictio, Saint-Sauveur for two, Harfleur, Sanvic, Harfleur. The 80 lbs "saginis de juif" is almost certainly silk, not says or serge, as Jean Fergant was excommunicated at the request of Jean du Val on April 12, 1517 in Sanvic for a debt of "unius tunice nove panni violleti ad usus uxoris ac unam sargeam rubandam sarge vermeille."

[192] Jacques de Rouffosse is "de Honeflictu" in ADSM G 5273, Extranea Jurisdictio, 1503 and 1507. For Fergant, see the previous note.

[193] John Oldland, "The Allocation of Merchant Capital in Early Tudor London," *Economic History Review* 63:4 (2010), 1058–1080, esp. 1060–1061 concerning valuations for the subsidy of 1535–1536, and 1074 for the averages.

Zacharias and Colette Petit are, like my other examples, exceptional but indicative. A single one of the broadcloths left by Colette Petit at her death was worth about as much as a laborer at Rouen could hope to earn in six and a half years of labor, assuming 150 working days per year and a daily salary of 2st. We do well to remember that nearly half of sanctions were one- or two-time events and that these extreme multiplications of sanctions against one economic cell were rare. Frequent excommunicators were very rare. To excommunicate more than ten times over thirty years was extraordinarily unusual. The receiver of fines sanctioned 425 times, an average of 14 times per year for unrecovered fines. The official excommunicated 103 times, something more than 3 times per year, the promotor of justice 87 times, the master of wills 40 times, and the sealer 36 times for unpaid sealing fees. Aside from these, Richard Gaultier sanctioned 39 times, Jacques Quevin 35 times, Robert Avisse 28 times, Richard Apris 26 times, Philippe Paris 25 times, and Raoul Le Comte 23 times. Twenty-one further individuals each requested sanctions more than ten times. Who were Gaultier, Quevin, Avisse, Apris, Paris, and Le Comte?

Richard Gaultier is present in the register from 1499 to 1524. He does not appear to have been a resident of Harfleur. All but six of thirty-nine sanctions were for debt. In 1499 Gaultier excommunicated and aggravated Jean des Hayes of Criquetot for 105st, in 1500 he excommunicated Raoul Viart for 61s 3dt, in 1501 suspended Sire Jean Thoroude of Fontaine-la-Mallet, in 1502 excommunicated Guillaume Mogres alias Savary once for 7£ 11st and once for 41st and aggravated (without a prior excommunication being noted in the record!) Pierre de Grouchy for 12st. In 1504 Gaultier excommunicated Guillaume de Bonneville of Augerville for contumacy and twice suspended Sire Etienne le Comte for 14s 4dt. In 1506 he suspended Me Pierre, priest of Manéglise for 33st and Sire Jean Le Mouche Petit alias le Moulle for 8s 6dt, excommunicated a certain Nicolas and Robert de La Fontaine for contumacy and Thomas Mernil for 2 *écus*, officially worth 3£ 12s 6dt. In 1507 he twice suspended Sire Laurent Le Merchier, on November 15 for 27s 9dt and on December 29 for 38s 9dt. The difference in value here could represent an annualized interest rate of 300 percent! Perhaps the priest paid the interest, as Gaultier had suspended a Sire Jean Le Merchier (probably the clerk's error) for 27s 9dt on February 2. He excommunicated Raoulin Picot three times, for 64st at an unspecified date, for 31st on October 5, and for 2s 6dt on November 29, and Raoul le Maistre for contumacy. In 1509 Gaultier excommunicated Louis Varnier for 53 *écus*, officially 96£ 3s 3dt, and Guillaume Herouart, clerc, for 14st, and suspended Sire Etienne Le Comte for 9s 2dt. In 1512 he suspended Sire Robert Reaulté for 51st, Sire Laurent Le Merchier for 31st, Sire Jacques du Mont for 21s 7dt, an illegible name for 5st, Eustache Guerentes, noble, for contumacy, Guillaume Gascoing for contumacy in the matter of a broken contract ("*racione contractus*"), and Nicolas de la Vallée of Etainches for 119st. In 1516 he suspended Sire Mathieu Angomare for 29s 4dt and in 1520 excommunicated Denis Aubourg for 30lt, and in 1524 twice excommunicated and twice aggravated Denis Coste, cleric: on November 11 for 14s 2dt, a sanction aggravated on January 6, and on March 20 for 19st, a sanction aggravated on April 9. As elsewhere, it is unclear whether the increased sum represents interest or simply the extension of further credit. Fittingly, the last person excommunicated by Gaultier, Jean Frémont on March 6, 1524 for 60st, was absolved after bankrupting himself to secure absolution on the day before Easter ("*cessat bonis die sabbati pasche*"). Frémont's experience may not have been uncommon, as Martin de Pimont, cleric, was absolved of an excommunication for a debt of 14£t to Martin Michel only by making cession of goods on Holy Saturday 1530 (OS) ("*absolutus mediante cessione bonorum de die sabbati ante pascha domini v^c xxx*"). Such debtors, abandoning their property to their creditors on the day before Easter so as to preserve a chance at salvation and perhaps to avoid prosecution for failing to perform their "Easter duty," illustrate perfectly how astute creditors such as Richard Gaultier could manipulate the procedure of ecclesiastical courts. Appropriately, Gaultier was himself sanctioned once – and then not for debt – by the promotor, on October 23, 1517 "for violently assaulting Jean Estienne, cleric (*pro violenta manuum iniectione in personam johannis estienne clerici*)." Interestingly, in comparison with other frequent excommunicators, Gaultier excommunicated for relatively minor sums, closer to the mean of median of 30st for Montivilliers. Was he a rural loan-shark? Perhaps, as he excommunicated in many different parishes. He may have been a merchant who sold on credit.

Jacques Quevin, who requested sanctions thirty-three times and did so for far larger sums, was once mentioned as a merchant (*pro jacobo quevin mercatore*) in the register, when on June 8, 1522, he excommunicated Jean Quevin the Younger, cleric, for contumacy! He did not, however, only excommunicate relatives, though he did excommunicate and aggravate Raoul Quevin, cleric, for debt in 1530. Jacques Quevin excommunicated priests, more as the years went along, and everyone for amounts from as little as 15st to more than 60£t, but generally for debts of around 10£t, far more than was the case for Richard Gaultier (Table 3.13).

The first excommunication in Table 3.13, that of Pierre Viart, represents a debt transferred to Quevin by Nicolas Durant, Viart's original creditor (Quevin "*jus cessionis habente a nicolao durant*"). Guillaume Yngou owed Quevin 26 boisseaux of fine oats, Master Guillaume Herault owed 62£ 10st and 6 boisseaux of wheat, and 16 boisseaux of *méteil* or maslin, and Jean le Bailly owed 13 boisseaux of wheat, 27 boisseaux of barley,

Table 3.13 *Excommunications requested by Jacques Quevin*

Year (OS)	M	D	Sanction	Excommunicate	Cause
1516	4	3		Pierre Viart	15st
1518	3	15	Susp.	Sire Nicolas Gabriel prêtre	43st
1519	5	16		Philippe Sieurin clerc	7£ 10st
1519	10	17		Nicolas Lanchart jurisdictionis Rothomagensis	60st
1519	3	23		Pierre Martin	70st
1520	4	21		Noël Sates	20st
1520	7	31		Jean Paen alias Paris	26st
1521	9	3		Nicolas Blanchart	60st
1521	9	23		Jean du Jardin jurisdictionis Rothomagensis	*Contumacy*
1521	11	9		Guillaume Gascoing	11£t
1521	1	21	Susp.	Sire Gilles Fouquez prêtre	11£t 16st
1522	6	8		Jean Quevin le jeune clerc	*Contumacy*
1522	7	20	Susp.	Sire Robert Magnet prêtre	100st
1522	3	5		Philippe Fremorin	14£ 7s 6dt
1522	3	16		Philippe Sieurin clerc	14£ 17st
1523	10	18		Philippe Sieurin clerc	8£ 14s 6dt
1523	11	9		Philippe Goudin	6£ 15st
1523	12	4		Etienne Viard	56s 4dt
1523	1	27	Aggr.	Philippe Sieurin clerc	8£ 14s 6dt
1523	3	14		Me Guillaume de Fourmentin sousdiacre	10£ 12s 11dt
1524	6	16		Guillaume Yngou clerc	*Grain*
1524	3	9		Pierre Houel de Fontibus la Mallet	12£ 11st
1526	9	30		Jean Quevin janitor porte frangipoplicis	30st
1526			Susp.	Me Etienne de la Vallee prêtre jurisdictionis Rothomagensis	*Contumacy*
1527	11	19		Nicolas Lescolier	40st
1528	6	18	Susp.	Me Jean de Beauvais prêtre cure de Salmonvilla	18£t
1528	10	3	Susp.	Me Jean de Beauvais prêtre cure de Salmonvilla	18£t
1529	4	22	Susp.	Me Guillaume Herault prêtre	62£ 10st, *Grain*
1529	6	26	Susp.	Me Etienne de la Vallee prêtre jurisdictionis Rothomagensis	113st
1529	9	27	Susp.	Me Jean de Beauvais prêtre cure de Salmonvilla	18£t
1529	10	25		Jean le Bailly clerc jurisdictionis Rothomagensis	*Grain*
1529	12	29		Me Jean de Beauvais prêtre cure de Salmonvilla	18£t
1530	8	11		Raoul Quevin clerc	
1530	9	24	Aggr.	Raoul Quevin clerc	
1530	10	22		Jean Roussel clerc	110st

Source: ADSM G 5273.

and 25 boisseaux of oats.[194] Quevin traded in grain, either selling grain on credit to small consumers or purchasing it on credit from small producers. He may have purchased and sold grain through parol contracts, just as Neapolitan grain merchants used *contratti alla voce* into the nineteenth century.[195] Quevin also acted as a wool middleman or brogger, as Jean Roussel owed him 110st and "the wool he had collected in the current year from his sheep (*lane quam habuit et collegit in anno presenti ex suis ovibus*)." Quevin bears comparison to his English contemporary John Heritage, the wool brogger born around 1470 whose accounts provide the major source of Christopher Dyer's *A Country Merchant, 1495–1520*.[196] Like Heritage, Quevin traded in different kinds of merchandise. Just as Heritage traded between the Cotswolds and London, so Quevin connected the hinterland of Montivilliers to Rouen. Unfortunately, whereas Heritage's accounts have survived among the muniments of the Dean and Chapter of Westminster, we have only references to Quevin's records: in 1530 he excommunicated Raoul Quevin, cleric, on August 11 "for failure to return to the honorable Jacques Quevin a great many accounts, notes, and obligations made and recognized as well as for failure to render the proceeds thereof to Jacques Quevin."[197] Quevin aggravated his apparent relative on September 24 "for failure to return an obligation, viz, that of Nicolas Matherat for 4£ 8st, as well as for [failure to render] the remaining 3£ 4st of receipts according to the account and calculation."[198] Raoul Quevin must have acted as something like a collections agent or factor for his relative – an uncle? an older cousin? –, dunning debtors for their outstanding balances and making deals in the principal's absence. Jacques Quevin showed himself to hav been as merciless with this relative as with other debtors. In the end, he got satisfaction, as Raoul Quevin's name was struck out upon his absolution.

[194] Bois estimates the mine of Rouen to have been 90-100 L in this period. However, though there were six boisseaux to the mine, I will not venture conversion of these amounts, as the measures for maslin, barley, and oats were generally larger than the measures for wheat.

[195] Fontaine, *L'Économie morale*, 75.

[196] Dyer, *Country Merchant*. One wishes to know more of ecclesiastical justice in the Cotswolds between 1495 and 1520, when Heritage was active, and whether it played any role in enforcing unwritten credit issued and taken by Heritage. English record-keeping practices appear not to have included the separate ledgers of excommunicates used in contemporary France.

[197] ADSM G 5273, [193]: "ob deffectum tradendi et restituendi honnesto viro jacobo quevin quam plurimas schedulas scripturas et obligationes factis et recognitis et ob defectum non solvendi eiusmodi recepta contra jacobo quevin."

[198] ADSM G 5273: "ob deffectum tradendi et restituendi unam obligationem vz nicolai matherat ascend[entem] ad sommam iiii# viijst ac etiam pro somma xxx# iiijs vidt rest[ante] de receptis per dictum radulphum juxta compotum et calculum."

The question of mercy is not inappropriate. Indeed it is crucial, as it appears that the debts at the origin of the excommunications and suspensions recorded in the register yielded interest, sometimes at exorbitant rates, and were negotiable, passing from creditor to creditor as payment for other debts. Unfortunately I have access only to the judicial record, not to the conferences of excommunicators with their confessors concerning the restitution of excessive interest or cruelly pursued debts. I earlier suggested that Richard Gaultier may have charged Sire Laurent Le Merchier what would have amounted to 317 percent annualized interest, as his debt grew from 27s 9dt to 38s 9dt between November 15 and December 29, 1507. This possibility appears elsewhere in the register, though nowhere is it confirmed, as such a rate of interest on a simple cash loan would be difficult to reconcile with the prohibition of usury. It is therefore occluded, or at least unmentioned in the register. Thus, when Tassin Ruffin was excommunicated by Guiffard Bisset on May 3, 1505 for 60st and aggravated on May 12 for 61s 8dt, no interest is recorded. Yet in nine days, the sum had grown by 1s 8dt or 2.8 percent. Annualized (but not compounded!) this would be about 113 percent. Since Ruffin was a parishioner of Harfleur, this may not implausibly indicate the comparatively lower but still high range of rates of interest charged on small, short-term loans. For the same sum, 60st, François le Ture, cleric of Rambertot, was excommunicated by Pierre Gaultier on February 3, 1504. He was aggravated two days later for 62st. Here the sum had grown by 3.3 percent in two days, annualized to more than 700 percent. One hopes that this indicates the upper range of rates of interest on small, short-term loans. As he was not the abbess's spiritual subject, Le Ture's debt came under the abbess's extraterritorial jurisdiction, illustrating how her sanctions enabled creditors to pursue defaulters even outside of her territory proper. I shall return to this point shortly.

Mercy or the lack thereof also enters into consideration with respect to the negotiability of debt. The history of banking has focused on the endorsing of letters of change and other instruments of high finance, but the officiality of Montivilliers enforced transferred debts, which may well have been as negotiable within the commercial zone defined by her jurisdiction as bearer bonds at the later sixteenth-century Antwerp Bourse. It is not certain that these "rights of cession (*jura cessionis*)" always originated in quasi-bankruptcies (*cessiones bonorum*). They figure in the records of thirty-two sanctions in seven different parishes between 1500 and 1530. In all but one of the cases, the person who ceded the debt is named. The debts are relatively large, so the cessions listed in Table 3.14 may have allowed individuals to settle outstanding balances with their creditors.

It is a shame that we know neither the dates of transfer nor the dates of issue of the original debt. That would permit us to say more about how these debts circulated. It is nevertheless clear that they did.

This circulation of debt clarifies the murky world of daily credit at the end of the Middle Ages. Social and economic historians have often suggested that 'there must have existed' forms of unwritten obligation that supplemented the written credit that constitutes the historical record. Here we can skim the surface of the deep mass of credit implied but otherwise invisible in our sources. Verbal and privately recorded credit was negotiable, could be subject to interest, and functioned in varied situations between a range of types of creditor and debtor. At Montivilliers, debts in kind were noted sometimes without a monetary valuation as "forty-five cartons or carts of firewood (*quadraginta quinque cararum ligni combustibilis*)" and sometimes with a monetary valuation as "26 *boisseaux* of barley valued at 2st the *boisseau* and 26 of maslin valued at 3st the *boisseau* (*xxvi bucellorum ordei qualiter bucello valore iis vid et xxvi bucellorum bladi mescellonis qualiter bucello valore iiis*)."[199] The latter debt may well have originated in a payment of 6£ 10st in coin (perhaps less, in a common ploy to conceal interest), but could just as well reflect the delivery of other goods or the performance of some service. It could even, reversing the procedure of payment with diverse instruments of credit, goods, and coins seen in the examples from Mollat cited earlier, reflect outstanding balances from different sources consolidated into a single large debt of grain in which the price reference denoted the quality of grain required. Conversely, did not Colette Petit's six broadcloths appear in the register of excommunications simply as 603£ 5s 8dt? Could that debt not have been settled with a quantity of grain, cloth, and perhaps some specie, or even a ceded debt?

This may be economically significant. The relation between the nominal quantity of money (M), the velocity of money or the speed at which a unit changes hands (V), the price level (P), and a deflated Net National Income (Y) is described as MV = PY, to use John Munro's updated version of Irving Fisher's equation. Munro treats M as being equivalent to the quantity of specie in circulation – that is, the limited amount of "high-powered money" or M1 – prior to the establishment of effective secondary markets for government debt in the sixteenth century. The secondary market for public debt resulted from the introduction of the enforceable negotiability of bills of exchange assigned to third parties

[199] The examples are from ADSM G 5273: June 21, 1516, Rolleville, Noël le Franchois excommunicates Robert Gongnel, cleric; June 30, 1504, Rolleville, Jean Thibaud suspends Master Denis Taffournel, priest.

Table 3.14 *Ceded debts at Montivilliers*

Year (OS)	M	D	Excommunicate	At the request of	Jus cessionis from	Cause
1500	12	18	Robert Hardy	Jean Chirier	Nicolas Le Pêcheur	28st
1500	12	24	Robert Hardy	Pierre Tirant	Nicolas Le Pêcheur	27st
1502	10	5	Robert Auffray, noble	Jean Bonvesin	Jean de Guetteville	33£ 10st
1504	4	18	Me Jean le Normant prêtre	Raoul Le Moine	Guillaume Tirel	35st
1504	4	28	Jean Savary	Cardin Couel, of the diocese of Lisieux	Guillaume Gry	6£t
1504	5	14	Pierre Boivin	Richard Regnault	Jean Le Long	8£ 10st
1504	9	29	Pierre Boivin	Richard Regnault	Jean Le Long	8£ 10 st
1507	10	13	Guillaume Hébert, cleric, tuteur des enfants du feu Jean Hébert	Jacques Regnart	Robert Regnart	8£ 10 st
1507	1	21	Martin Frontault	Robert Vimart	Jean Perier	77st
1509	7	12	Jacuqes Bourguel, cleric	Raoul le Comte	Renaud du Node	7£t
1511	4	28	Jean Riche	Mathieu le Tellier	Nicolas Tirel	60st
1511	5	12	Jean Riche	Mathieu le Tellier	Nicolas Tirel	60st
1512	10	12	Richard Gosselin, cleric	Nicolas Tirel	Jean Becquet	*Contumacia*
1512	1	24	Nicolas Geoffroy, cleric	Robert Godillon	[unknown]	15st
1512	1	24	Henri Davy	Guillaume Potier	Mathieu Langevin, but ceded to Potier's wife	30st
1513	3		Jean le Viandier	Jean Angleby	Guillaume de…	6st
1513	10	8	Michel Tanquerel l'aîné, cleric	Jean Machecoeur	Mathieu Le Post	19 carts of wood
1513	4	8	Michel Tanquerel l'aîné, clerc	Jean Machecoeur	Mathieu Le Post	19 carts of wood
1515	10	21	Sire Jean du Bois	Richard Vimart	Vigor Capitaine	6£ 12st
1515	3	14	Michel Tanquerel, cleric	Charles Vimart	Jean Le Vavasseur	32st
1516	4	3	Pierre Viart	Jacques Quevin	Nicolas Durant	15st

Year (OS)	M	D	Excommunicate	At the request of	Jus cessionis from	Cause
1518	9	2	Nicolas Geoffroy, cleric	Richard Prudhomme le Jeune	Jean Lesbahy	24£t
1518			Pierre du Moustier	Colin Richard	Guillaume Le Post	39st
1521	2	1	Me Jacques Piedecoq prêtre	Cardin Agnes	Jean de Vermailles	4£t
1522	5	19	Thomas Cavalier, fils de Martin Cavalier	Me Guillaume de Bapaulmes prêtre	Robin Marssis	50st
1522	4	1	Philippe Sieurin, avocat en court laie	Guillaume Tirel, lieutenant particulier du vicomte de Montivilliers	Me Pierre des Champs, écuyer	7£ 6st
1522	6	1	Sire Nicolas Champaigne	Michel Hallé	Raoul Pate, then Collenet Hardouin	8£ 17st
1524	6	23	Nicolas Raulin, écuyer	Jacques Basin	Jean Daniel	40£t
1524	9	17	Nicolas Raulin, écuyer	Jacques Basin	Jean Daniel	40£t
1529	7	5	Sire Jacques Durant	Sire Pierre Ardenne	Michel le Comte	7£ 10st
1529	3	25	Me Jean de Beauvais curé de Salmonville	Robert Chapelain	Pierre Tasson	7£t
1530	12	15	Me Jean de Beauvais curé de Salmonville	Robert Chapelain	Pierre Tasson	7£t

Source: ADSM G 5273.

in decisions of the London Merchant's Court in 1436, of Antwerp's Merchant's Court in 1507, and of Bruges's Merchant's Court of 1536, decisions confirmed by the Netherlandish States-General in 1537 and 1541 but not by statute in England until the reign of Anne.[200] In

[200] Munro, "Money, Wages, and Real Incomes in the Age of Erasmus: The Purchasing Power of Coins and of Building Craftsmen's Wages in England and the Low Countries, 1500–1540." University of Toronto Working Paper No.1 for 2001, www.economics.utoronto.ca/public/workingPapers/UT-ECIPA-MUNRO-01-01.pdf, 14.

contrast, privately issued annuities or *rentes* were legitimate but imperfectly negotiable. In Paris, for instance, transfer was complicated and payment could be demanded from the property holder, even if ownership had been transferred in the interim, because a transferred annuity was still tied to a piece of real property.[201] Pamela Nightingale allows a role for private credit in temporarily swelling a declining money supply that nevertheless ultimately shrinks to reflect the underlying famine of specie.[202] In either case, the supply of specie or of specie and negotiable public debt ultimately constrains the supply of credit. Yet why should this be so for an agrarian economy based on the transfer of monetarily appraised products? Both Munro and Nightingale presume that balances would be settled in specie (or perhaps in government debt), or that debts in kind originated in payments in specie.[203] Why could labor or goods, albeit appraised in monetary terms, not stand at the origin of and at the liquidation of debts?

Debate around the relationship of prices, credit, and specie centers on which element of the relationship is responsible for sixteenth-century inflation: M, that is, the supply of bullion, or V, that is population growth driving increasing turnover of the money stock. The weight of interpretation currently rests on M, that is, M1. John Munro and others have placed credit under V as simply increasing the velocity of monetary turnover rather than increasing the money stock, asserting that much minor credit was simply not negotiable, given available legal mechanisms.[204] This may excessively minimize the importance of verbal credit in day-to-day transactions. The example of Montivilliers suggests that negotiable verbal debts enforced through the procedures of church courts may have swelled M, the supply of money (if more as M2 than as M1), particularly during the late medieval bullion and *billon* famine.[205] The role of ecclesiastical tribunals in increasing

[201] Schnapper, *Les rentes*, 285.

[202] Most recently, Pamela Nightingale, "Gold, Credit, and Mortality: Distinguishing Deflationary Pressures on the Late Medieval English Economy," *Economic History Review* 63:4 (2010), 1081–1104.

[203] Christine Desan, *Making Money: Coin, Currency, and the Coming of Capitalism* (Oxford: Oxford University Press, 2014), 205–230, adopts this attitude by comparing "the peculiar credit of the English" to continental credit putatively characterized by middlemen and cash loans instead of purchase or sales credit.

[204] See the survey of the literature provided by Briggs, *Credit*, 200–213, and John Munro, "Wage-Stickiness, Monetary Changes, and Real Incomes in Late-Medieval England and the Low Countries, 1300–1500: Did Money Matter?" *Research in Economic History* 21 (2003), 185–297, esp. 216–217.

[205] See the eloquent graph of French mint outputs provided in H. M. Miskimin, "L'or, l'argent, la guerre dans la France médiévale," *Annales ESC* 40:1 (1985), 171–184, at 175. Ian Blanchard has suggested something similar to this, though on the basis of Philipp Schofield's and Chris Briggs's work on manorial courts rather than on the basis

M by enforcing negotiable verbal or privately recorded credit at the end of the Middle Ages may explain why "credit either expanded or contracted with the coined money supply … in a *non-proportional* fashion."[206] Now "credit could not resolve every monetary problem,"[207] because the potentiality of credit to do so depended on the existence of appropriate legal remedies – such as the procedural excommunication of debtors – and on creditors' recourse to these remedies. Indeed, credit may not have had to resolve every *monetary* problem in that, as noted earlier, much exchange concerned purchases or sales of goods evaluated in monetary terms but settled in goods likewise evaluated in monetary terms or through "balance transfers" concerning the same.[208] Alternatively, it is possible that the type of credit secured by church courts increased rather the velocity of exchange.[209]

The activity of church courts in expanding money supply (or in accelerating the velocity of exchange) has perhaps not been fully considered because it began to decline just as new sources of bullion flooded into Western Europe. From the 1460s the Portuguese imported increasing amounts of gold from West Africa, at the same time as new methods of smelting and the invention of pumps permitting the drainage of deeper mineshafts increased the production of silver in Central Europe, quintupling production there between the 1480s and the 1530s. From the 1530s silver from the Spanish New World flowed into Europe in ever-increasing quantities. Over the same period, excommunications in the archdeaconry of Paris fell from an index of 100 in 1426–1439, to one of twenty-two in 1494, and to one of thirteen in 1550. The decline of excommunication for debt may have cushioned the inflationary effect of all of this bullion (and perhaps accentuated price deflation from the

of the civil jurisdiction of ecclesiastical tribunals: "M2: Alternative English Money Supply, 1250–1450," chapter 5 of *Mining, Metallurgy, and Minting in the Middle Ages, Vol. 3: Continuing Afro-European Supremacy, 1250–1450* (Stuttgart: Franz Steiner Verlag, 2005), 1089–1108.

206 Munro, "Wage-Stickiness," 217. My Italics. Of course, Munro and Nightingale focus too much on high-level, elite credit, which may well have been more tied to the quantity of coins. My quibble is not with Nicholas Mayhew's assertion that money supply drove prices more than did population ("Prices in England, 1178–1750," *Past & Present* 219:1 (2013), 3–39) but with what might constitute money supply: Mayhew only accepts that negotiable bills effectively increased M from the later sixteenth century.

207 Mayhew, "Prices," 12.

208 Would we then have to imagine a money supply swelled by goods evaluated in monetary terms? Did a debt of barley valued at 40st exchanged against real goods valued at 40st then function as money? Church courts appear to have facilitated the negotiability of such debts.

209 Evidence from the English registry of coin finds presented by Martin Allen at the 2015 Leeds International Medieval Congress suggests that this may have been the case in England. An apparent decline in the value and frequency of coin hoards after 1450 suggests that credit could have then swelled V, thereby diminishing k, the inverse of V that

1490s to the 1520s) by shrinking one source of M even as new sources of bullion appeared in Europe, Africa, and the Americas. Although the gap between coins in circulation and monetary supply may have been narrower at the end of the Middle Ages than today on account of the legal difficulties in enforcing negotiability, there remained an enormous gap between the supply of coin and the amount of work that money needed to do across late medieval Western Europe, especially as mints tended to overproduce the high-denomination coins that yielded greater seigniorage.[210] The decline of excommunication for debt over the first third of the sixteenth century may help to explain why inflation really only picked up in the 1520s, as opposed to the 1470s.

Returning to the negotiability of verbal debt, when creditors chose to negotiate verbal credit through spiritual sanctions, they deepened its religious valence and more closely aligned its rhythm to that of the liturgical year. Thanks to the presence of ecclesiastical courts enforcing the sacramental, binding nature of simple promises, individuals could transfer verbal obligations with nearly the security of an endorsed bill – and potentially without any other paper record or notarial costs. In two cases from Montivilliers, the register records that the debt at the root of a sanction had been ceded twice. In an age in which the instruments of daily credit were underdeveloped, church courts helped to facilitate the clearing of accounts when they were periodically – quarterly, at Michaelmas, at Martinmas, and so forth – reckoned up by enforcing verbal or unauthenticated issues of credit. Those with sufficient credit could draw upon their wealth of obligations – the resource constituted by their network of debtors – and transfer a debt when their own creditors came calling. Because defaulters, "breakers of faith," could be excommunicated or suspended, creditors could accept their promises with reasonable security. Given that 98.75 percent of the abbess's excommunicated subjects were absolved and that even 79.3 percent of excommunicated

represents the demand for money to hold (where M=kY). The lack of any comparable French registry of coin finds precludes any definitive statement.

210 The US Bureau of Economic Analysis gives the 2013 US GDP as almost $17 trillion. The Federal Reserve Board gives an M2 figure of $11.5 trillion and an M1 figure of $2.9 trillion. Henri Dubois estimated the GDP of France using Paul Bairoch's formula at the end of the reign of Louis XI as 200,000,000£t: "Le commerce de la France au temps de Louis XI. Expansion ou défensive?" in B. Chevalier and P. Contamine (eds.), *La France de la fin du quinzième siècle: Renouveau et apogée* (Paris: CNRS, 1985), 15–29, at 19. Debra Glassman and Angela Redish have calculated the money stock in France to have been nearly 31,000,000£t in 1493: "New Estimates of the Money Stock in France, 1493–1680," *Journal of Economic History* 45:1 (1985), 31–46, at 42. The contemporary relationship between M1 and GDP is not so far from the relationship of Dubois's to Glassman's and Redish's estimates.

nonsubjects were absolved, one is tempted to rate verbal or nonauthentic debt at Montivilliers, if not AAA, then certainly AA+, with a very low potential for default – or, more precisely, little potential for somehow failing to satisfy the creditor (as Durand advised, "satisfaction is whatever the creditor wishes"). By enforcing verbal contracts, the abbess's officiality certainly facilitated local trade. Indeed, the disappearance of this remedy may have encouraged merchants to put more of their capital into land or into inflexible, land-based forms of credit. (Venal offices were often legally treated as real property.)

Officialities provided a means of constraining "foreign" traders, as promises were enforced even outside the territory of the Abbess of Montivilliers: 73.7 percent of all sanctions at Montivilliers in 1499–1530 came in the parishes of Saint-Sauveur (1,528 sanctions or 29.1 percent), Harfleur (1,481 sanctions or 28.2 percent), and the "parish" of the abbess's *extranea jurisdictio* (858 sanctions or 16.3 percent). Those sanctioned or sanctioning under this last category came from the archdiocese of Rouen (629), the dioceses of Lisieux (36), of Bayeux (13), and of Coutances (1), and the exemption of Fécamp (23), and at least as far as Bordeaux (5), as the home territory was not indicated in all extraterritorial cases. The reach of the officiality of Montivilliers ranged along the Atlantic coast from Dieppe to Bordeaux, embracing Gascons, Bretons, Normans, and, it seems, Italians, Spaniards, or English trading within the economic zone defined by its sanctions. Five hundred and eighteen or 60.3 percent of these extraterritorial excommunications were explicitly for debt, somewhat less than the 65.5 percent of all sanctions issued for debt. That 15 percent of total extraterritorial sanctions (62 or almost 20 percent of the excommunications for contumacy and 63 or 12 percent of the excommunications for debt) specified that the sanction came "on account of a [broken] contract (*racione contractus*)" against only 18 sanctions within the abbess's territory mentioning this justification indicates that the extraterritorial reach of the officiality of Montivilliers was at least in part justified by the need to enforce the binding character of promises. The frequency of debts in kind suggests that many promises originated in the delivery of merchandise or in advance payment and were therefore actionable *promissiones acceptatae* rather than simple *pollicitationes* or verbal futures contracts.[211] No less than a pilgrimage church built in fulfillment of a collective vow, the abbess's *extranea jurisdictio* was a monument to the sacred exchange of consent at the root of the vow, the covenant, the promise, and the contract.

We ask again: was the officiality an instrument of social control, repressing lay sexuality and religiosity and disciplining an incontinent

[211] On the distinction, see Decock, *Theologians*, 187–192.

clergy, or was it at once a commercial and a pastoral instrument driven by lay demand, teaching layfolk to observe contracts and vows? We find under the rubric of extraterritorial jurisdiction one case of contempt of court, three cases of defamation or other injury, one case incurred during the visitation of Harfleur, and only eleven marriage cases, of which three specify that they were also on account of the contract of marriage or affiancement ("*in causa matrimoniali, racione contractus*") and of which one concerned defamation relating to the dissolution of a marriage.[212] Because credit was a moral and economic measure, suing one's defamers was a means of preserving one's – or one's economic unit's – credit: at Montivilliers in 1493, for instance, on September 29, 1493 Massiet Combaut was released from prison and absolved of his excommunication upon promising to stand trial "for having sung publicly a certain melody (*quandam cantillenam diffamatoriam*) defaming the marriage of Robinet Quevin and Annette, wife of someone called Viart."[213] The credit of two couples was at stake in prosecuting Combaut for his song. Officers seldom requested extraterritorial sanctions: the receiver of fines did so 27 times, the promotor 11, the official 6, the master of wills 4, and the sealer only 3 times. Of the extraterritorial sanctions, 94 percent had nothing to do with the wishes of court officials. Someone – in fact, a great many someones – must have thought that the abbess's sanctions were worth purchasing. From this perspective, the officiality of Montivilliers was less an instrument of social control by the Church and more the purveyor of a judicial means of negotiating extrajudicial economic disputes in accordance with popular morality.

This brings us to the question of "forum-shopping," that is, to the place of the officiality of Montivilliers in the judicial landscape of Upper Normandy. Church courts were not the only courts operating in late medieval Western Europe, where a plurality of judicial fora offered consumers of justice many if not infinite sites for strategic maneuvers. I can only begin to sketch an incomplete answer here, but it nevertheless appears that individuals sometimes turned to church courts, sometimes to lay courts, and sometimes to both in the pursuit of wrongs, debts, and enmities. Earlier in the fifteenth century, church courts defended their jurisdiction: for instance, in 1427 the promotor of the Archdeacon of

[212] For the last, see ADSM G 5273, Extranea jurisdictio, 1511: "Petrus chouque parrochie de gonffrevilla la orchier jurisdictionis Rothomagensis excommunicatus pro contumacia contra marionam vaultier filiam guillermi vaultier in causa iniuriarum verbalium dissolutionem matrimonii tangentium, racione contractus seu delicti et cetera de die jovis xvij julii."

[213] Should Combaut have failed to heed the terms of his discharge, he would have been returned to prison, excommunicated anew, and fined 20£t: ADSM G 5270, 46v, inserted after the last excommunications for the parish of Rouelles.

Paris excommunicated Andriet de Masières "for citing a priest before a lay judge (*pro eo quod fecit citare quendam presbiterum coram judice seculari*)"; in 1463 the Official of the Abbess of Montivilliers likely encouraged Pierre Brumart to promise not to avail himself of royal *lettres de répit* when he appeared in court to secure absolution conditional on his payment to Jean Beaupains of 17£ 11st in two monthly installments.[214] Later in the century, in contrast, lay courts defended their claims to jurisdiction. No records of litigation before the vicecomital court of Montivilliers survive for the period, so we must turn to the slightly earlier records of a nearby royal jurisdiction. On December 11, 1483, before the *plaids à mace* of the bailiwick of Rouen, Guillaume Pisieu was fined 60st for having had Cardin Mango cited and excommunicated even though Mango's parish priest had affirmed that he was not a cleric.[215] Sixty sous or three livres tournois was a stiff fine. The implication is that only clerics were to come before church courts. And yet, from the evidence at Chartres, Paris, and Montivilliers, plenty of individuals who were not clerics were cited and excommunicated for debt by church courts between 1380 and 1530. If some lay individuals asked the king's courts at Rouen as early as 1483 to order the reversal of excommunications, it was uncommon for cases to go so far as the dispute between Guillaume Pisieu and Cardin Mango.[216] Still after 1500, most excommunicated layfolk did not protest to a royal court either because they chose not to, perhaps fearing the cost, or because their recourse in this matter was not yet assured. What is notable is that the sense that this use of ecclesiastical jurisdiction was inappropriate grew even as fewer and fewer laypeople fell under the spiritual sword in matters of debt. By 1530 most lay debtors must have been brought before the royal viscount of Montivilliers or before another lay

[214] AN Z[1o]17, Saint-Germain, 1435; ADSM G 5271, Harfleur, 1463 (OS): "absolutus per retrusionem dummodo solvat medietatem somme huic ad mensem et aliam medietatem infra alium mensem inde sequentem et promisit se non juvare litteris regiis datum die veneris post letare." The initial excommunication was issued on the Monday after Invocavit.

[215] ADSM 4 B II, 1 bis, f. 4 (Tuesday, December 11, 1483): "Guillaume pisieu de la tillaye / fut mis en amende de ce que non obstant quil l[uy] eust este deffendu non / traictier cardin maingo non clerc en court degl[is]e et quil luy eust este desclaire par le p[re]b[t]re de la parr[oisse] dud[it] lieu de la tillaye que led[it] mango nestoit point clerc Si lavoit icelui pisieu fait citer en lad[ite] court deglise et lavoit fait excommunier / par laquelle amende desclaire fut que led maingo sera desdommage du precedent fait en lad[ite] matiere et contrainct a le faire absouldre. Avec despenses Et fut icelui pisieu baille a jehan que[]lin / Icy pour prendre partie." In the margin is noted "EM[ENDA], lx s."

[216] The Parlements of Paris and of Toulouse had from the 1440s to command the reversal of unjust excommunications through *appels comme d'abus*: Gazzaniga, *Église*; Fevret, *Traité*; Robert Génestal, *Les origines de l'appel comme d'abus. Notes de cours publiées par les soins de Pierre Timbal, avant-propos par Jean Dauvillier* (Paris: PUF, 1951).

jurisdiction.[217] By then, officialities would have mostly seen cases like that of Sire Jean Apris, who had Master Michel Helart suspended for 11st on January 26, 1508 (OS), even though the judgment was based on a debt recorded by a royal tabellion (*litteris tabellionis regis*) and could have been executed against a lay debtor by the viscount of Montivilliers.[218]

Earlier in this chapter, I drew attention to the decline of excommunication for debt at Paris. This decline is more obvious in the more continuous data from Montivilliers. The phenomenon, I would argue, was driven less by economic forces than by religious and political ones. The habit of excommunication for debt arose in response to demand, not in consequence of a standardized, top-down, doctrine-driven movement across Europe. The execution of verbal and privately recorded contracts through excommunication must have resonated with a broadly shared understanding of debt that changed at the end of the Middle Ages. Whether recorded as "for an amount" or "matter" (*pro re*), "for a confessed or adjudged amount" (*pro re confessata* or *judicata*), "for contumacy" (*pro contumacia*), "for a an adjudged sum" (*pro judicato summae*), "for debt" (*pro debito*) as in the province of Reims, as a "breach of faith" (*fidei laesio*) as in England, or with reference to a broken contract (*racione contractus*) as at Montivilliers, procedural excommunications in matters of debt responded to economic needs and religious mentalities shared across the continent. Its decline suggests that the Reformation – again when broadly understood as a phenomenon common to all varieties of Western Christianity and one beginning before the Protestant Reformation – was, as the revolutions of Antiquity had been, a revolution of debtors.[219] I shall elaborate this point in the following chapter, but for now would like to observe that excommunication for debt yoked together late medieval theological and economic trends in a manner that exacerbated the sentiment that believers were insuperably indebted to God for their sins, to Christ for his grace, to their kings for their taxes, to their lords for their lands, and to their neighbors for their livelihood and sustenance. Even though it unsettled many, this mindset of indebtedness was hard to shake.

[217] The *ancienne coutume* of Normandy provided that clerics not apprehended "*à présent mesfaict*" had to be handed over the ecclesiastical justice if required, but did not bar layfolk from appearing before church courts even as it provided that "*toutes personnes layes en peuvent estre querellées*" in disputes concerning debts and contracts. However, for debts over 10st, the cumbrous procedure of "*loy apparissant*" settled by "*loy de recongnoissant ou par bataille, ou par l'enqueste du pays, que len appelle recongnoissant*": C.-A. Bourdot de Richebourg, *Nouveau coutumier général* (Paris: Michel Brunet, 1724), IV: c. LXXXII–LXXXIII, p. 33; c.LXXXVIII–XC, pp. 35–36.

[218] ADSM G 5273, Saint-Sauveur.

[219] I thank Wim Decock for this point, which accords with David Graeber's views on credit.

Elsewhere

The excommunication of layfolk for debt is evident across Europe from the thirteenth to the sixteenth centuries. In the Low Countries, in the maritime Flanders studied by Jacques Toussaert, around 1450 each parish had an average of 35.6 excommunicate parishioners in villages of at the most a couple of hundred residents.[220] The accounts of the Sealer of Tournai published by Monique Vleeschouwers-Van Melkebeek, do not explicitly disclose who was excommunicated for debt and for which amounts. However, the accounts from 1461 onward separate the yield of fines (*Emende*) and of absolutions (the *Parva registra*) to the sealer. The former are penalties for the ordinary canonical offenses of adultery, concubinage, fornication, clandestine marriage, consanguine marriage, and so on. The latter are unmarked, presumably procedural, excommunications: for example, "Willem de le Plancque, excommunicated at the request of Oste Botut, paid 8 s.fl."[221] They make an excellent comparison to the charts of excommunications, absolutions, and sealing fees presented for Rouen in the previous chapter and for Chartres and Montivilliers in this chapter. Figure 3.10 presents the revenues in Flemish *groten* (s. fl.) from the accounting year running from July 1, 1461 to June 30, 1462.[222] I did not count individual absolutions for three reasons: i) to facilitate comparison with the figures that I presented earlier, which do not break revenue down by individual absolved; ii) many individuals were excommunicated "at the request of many individuals (*pro pluribus*)" and therefore had to absolve themselves of multiple, cumulative excommunications, a phenomenon that we have seen elsewhere; iii) such that, while the postmortem absolutions generally cost up to 6 lb.fl., priests were absolved for upwards of 40 s.fl., and the collective absolution of the Abbey of Sint-Andries *juxta Brugis* cost 12 lb.fl.,[223] most ordinary absolutions cost 8 s.fl. for a simple excommunication, 6 s.fl. for a personal interdict, and 5 s.fl. for a relaxation or temporary absolution. For the last reason, because the larger sums were rare, the general figures for revenue do not too greatly distort the business of the officials of Tournai, Bruges, and Ghent.

The two lines mark the beginning and end of Lent, respectively, the weeks beginning on March 1 (*Ebdomada que incepit secunda ante Cyneres*) and on April 19 (*Ebdomada que incepit secunda in Paschalibus*). The annual rhythm of excommunications and absolutions for Tournai in the 1460s,

[220] Toussaert, *Le sentiment*, 442.
[221] Vleeschouwers, *Compotus*, I: 366.
[222] Vleeschouwers, *Compotus*, I: 357–472.
[223] Vleeschouwers, *Compotus*, I: 424.

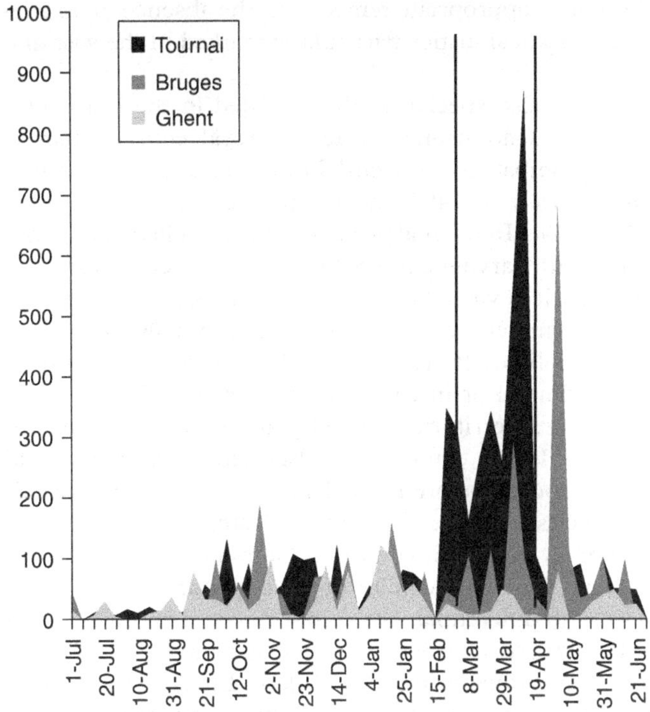

Figure 3.10 Income from absolutions by the Sealer of Tournai in the Archdeaconries of Tournai, Bruges, and Ghent (in s. fl.).
Source: Vleeschouwers, *Compotus*, I: 357–472.

1470s, and 1480s mirrors that evident elsewhere in the study, whereas those for Bruges and Ghent do not.[224] To explain the divergence, I would propose not that the Brugeois or Gantois were more pious than the Tournaisiens. Rather, because the accounts distinguish between fines and what appear to be procedural excommunications, I would propose that most disputed debts in the archdeaconries of Bruges and Ghent came before the municipal aldermen (*schepen*) and that more debt in the archdeaconry of Tournai came before church courts, whether through letters of *nisi*, obligations or condemnations in court, or monitions and citations. It may be that the more flexible legal conditions of consular, "customary" jurisdictions in the Low Countries obviated recourse to ecclesiastical tribunals in matters of debt. Still farther north, lay courts

[224] Beaulande, *Le malheur*, 174–176, discusses the Tournai accounts.

may well have developed appropriate remedies in the absence of an adequate supply of ecclesiastical justice particularly marked in the vast diocese of Utrecht.

The German case is also special, as there existed in the last centuries of the Middle Ages no strong centralized royal court system in the Old Empire to combat ecclesiastical justice until the foundation of the *Reichskammergericht* in 1495 and the institutionalization of the *Reichshofrat* in 1497–1498. Individual princes and cities rolled back ecclesiastical jurisdiction with varying degrees of success.[225] Peter Oestmann has demonstrated that it is virtually impossible to make any systematic statement about the competence of ecclesiastical tribunals in the Old Empire, whether Catholic or Protestant, whether concerning clergy or layfolk, whether in criminal or in civil matters.[226] Although one might think that in ecclesiastical territories where lay and ecclesiastical judges would have likely been less in conflict than elsewhere such cases would have gone before lay courts, before local *Ämter* or such, it is in ecclesiastical or formerly ecclesiastical territories that Oestmann has found the greatest confusion of lay and spiritual justice. Conversely, conflicts such as those of Margrave Albrecht Achilles of Brandenburg (1414–1486) with his clergy served to differentiate the competences of lay and ecclesiastical judges.[227] In any case, late medieval German church courts issued procedural excommunications in matters of debt. Eugen Baumgartner demonstrated the existence of what the Strasbourg synodal regulations of 1318 described as "purely civil cases coming before church courts by custom" in the Upper Rhenish dioceses, a phenomenon outlined by Ferdinand Elsener more generally.[228] For instance, in 1381 Archbishop

[225] Baumgartner, *Geschichte und Recht*; Carlen, "Zum Offizialat"; Elsener, "Exkommunikation"; Justus Hashagen, "Zur Charakteristik der geistlichen Gerichtsbarkeit vornehmlich im späteren Mittelalter," *Zeitschrift der Savigny-Stiftung für Rechtsgeschichte, Kanonistische Abteilung* 6 (1916), 205–292, and Justus Hashagen, "Zur Sittengeschichte des westfälischen Klerus im späteren Mittelalter," *Westdeutsche Zeitschrift für Geschichte und Kunst* 23 (1904), 102–149; Paul Kirn, "Der mittelalterliche Staat und das geistliche Gericht," *Zeitschrift der Savigny-Stiftung für Rechtsgeschichte, Kanonistische Abteilung* 15 (1926), 162–199; Schrader, "Die bishöflichen Offiziale Hildesheims."

[226] Peter Oestmann, *Geistliche und weltliche Gerichte im Alten Reich. Zuständigkeitsstreitigkeiten und Instanzenzüge*, Quellen und Forschungen zur höchsten Gerichtsbarkeit im Alten Reich 61 (Cologne/Weimar/Vienna: Böhlau Verlag, 2012); also Kirn, 191: "ist es kaum möglich, den Gang der Kämpfe in Deutschland zu schildern."

[227] Ernst Schubert, "Albrecht Achilles, Markgraf und Kurfürst Von Brandenburg (1414–1486)," in Gerhard Pfeffer (ed.), *Fränkische Lebensbilder 4* (Würzburg: Ferdinand Schöningh, 1971), 130–172.

[228] Baumgartner, *Geschichte und Recht*, 146–183, at 172: "causae mere civiles ad forum tamen ecclesiasticum de consuetudine spectantes summam quatuor librarum denariorum Argentinensium non excedentes"; Elsener, "Exkommunikation."

Adolf (von Nassau, r.1381–1390) of Mainz provided that the Provost of Jechaburg could judge cases concerning up to 20 marks of silver even though he allowed his archdeacons only to judge cases up to 2 marks, presumably allowing the provost to judge a range of civil cases otherwise reserved to the diocesan official.[229] While Elsener emphasized that there were few complaints about the use of excommunication against debtors, and compared the practice to banishment for debt in late medieval Italy, Baumgartner emphasized the slow nibbling away of ecclesiastical jurisdiction over the debts of layfolk beginning with the issue of privileges of exemption from attendance at the bishop's synodal court (*Sendfreiheit*) for particular archdeaconries or towns.[230] With respect to the archdiocese of Mainz, he noted that in 1372 Landgrave Heinrich (II "der Eiserne," †1376) commanded that any of his subjects bringing secular matters before church courts be fined 3 Hessian pounds and prohibited secular clergy from bringing layfolk before church courts; Archbishop Konrad (presumably II von Weinsburg, r.1390–1396) consequently prohibited his judges from hearing cases concerning annuities (*Zinsen*), ground rents (*Gülten*), or debts except in cases of manifest denial of justice by secular courts and, preserving considerable scope for ecclesiastical tribunals, perjury.[231] That Heinrich II's successors reissued such prohibitions with new sanctions suggests that lay demand and clerical intransigence interpreted the Landgraves' laws in such a way as to preserve the civil competence of Hessian officialities and *Sendgerichte* until Landgrave Philipp abolished the competence of any courts of the archdiocese of Mainz over his territories in 1526.[232] As a result of the persistence of ecclesiastical jurisdiction over the debts of layfolk in 1522, the Diet of Nuremberg complained that "churchmen often bring their lay subjects before ecclesiastical judges on account of monetary debts."[233] In France ecclesiastical competence over debts gradually shrank to cover only the debts of clerics over the first third of the sixteenth century (Febvre's Francophone Franche-Comté was part of the Empire), whereas in Germany it appears on the contrary that church courts kept on excommunicating layfolk

229 Baumgartner, *Geschichte und Recht*, 171–172.

230 Baumgartner, *Geschichte und Recht*, 177–179.

231 Baumgartner, *Geschichte und Recht*, 173.

232 Baumgartner, *Geschichte und Recht*, 178–181.

233 Josse Le Plat, *Momumentorum ad historiam Concilii tridentini … amplissima collectio* (Louvain: Ex typographia academica, 1781–1787), II: 188–189 (reference at Lea, 447): "Praeterea ecclesiastici saepiscule laicorum subditos ob debita pecuniaria coram ecclesiastico judice in jus vocant, ac praegravi eorum judiciorum ordine inibi vexant atque excutiunt."

until the Protestant Reformation drastically, suddenly – and unevenly, as Oestmann has demonstrated – transformed the landscape of ecclesiastical jurisdiction.[234]

In England, the court books of the Dean and Chapter of Lincoln between 1336 and 1349 and those of Deanery of Wisbech between 1458 and 1484 edited by L. R. Poos are littered with cases of debt. Debt matters are more frequent in the later records than the former, reflecting what Chris Briggs has proposed to be a consequence of the decay of manorial courts in the first half of the fifteenth century.[235] One of the loose documents from the jurisdiction of the Chapter of Lincoln records an exemplary condemnation for debt: "We sentence you, William de Brunham of Ourenby in the parish of Seuerby, on pain of immediate, retroactive major excommunication to pay to William de Suthkelsey, chaplain, or his attorney at Outhenby, the ten acres of your best grain or the 50s that you have admitted in our presence to owe him through written obligation and trothplight within five years, that is to say, two acres of grain or 10s at the next feast of St. Peter *ad vincula* (August 1), and so on thereafter until the debt is fully expunged."[236] The records of the Dean of Wisbech contain numerous recognizances of debt analogous to the "obligations" recorded in the registers of the Archdeacon of Paris: for example, "William Priest broke faith with John Caly over 7s. He was suspended on April 20, 1463. He paid. He appeared on May 25 and swore to settle with the party before Michaelmas."[237] In the next entry, in which Caly pursued Richard Parsons over 3s 4d, the

234 The income from the seal of the commissary of the Archbishop of Mainz at Göttingen collapsed from almost one hundred Gulden in 1520–1521 (with the heading in 1524–1525: "Princeps huius terre instituit juditium in sua curia, ubi non solum laici, ymmo abbates, monasteria et alii clerici ut rei respondere coguntur. Perinde cessat iurisdictio domini reverendissimi") to less than 1 in 1528–1529: B. Krusch, "Studie zur Geschichte der geistlichen Jurisdiktion und Verwaltung des Erzstifts Mainz. Commissar Johann Bruns und die kirchliche Eintheilung der Archidiaconate Nörten, Einbeck und Heiligenstadt," *Zeitschrift des Historischen Vereins für Niedersachsen* (1897), 112–277, at 161–162.

235 Briggs, "The Availability of Credit."

236 Poos, *Lower Ecclesiastical Jurisdiction*, 265: "Te Willelmum de Brunham de Ourenby in parochia de Seuerby condempnavimus sub pena majoris excommunicationis exnunc sicut extunc in decem acris melioris bladi tui sive in l solidis sterlingorum <quas vel quos> in quibus coram nobis te fateris teneri per scriptum obligatorium et per fidem mediantem domino Willelmo de Suthkelsey capellano, solvendo eidem Willelmo <vel suo attornato apud Outhenbi> infra v annos proximos futuros, videlicet ad festum Sancti Petri quod dicitur ad vincula proximum futurum duas acras bladi vel decem solidos argenti <ad electionem meram dicti Willelmi>, et sic de anno in annum ad predictum festum donec predicta solutio <dictarum acrarum sive argenti> fuerit eidem Willelmo vel suo attornato plene et congrue persoluta."

237 Poos, *Lower Ecclesiastical Jurisdiction*, 354: "Willelmus Prest violat fidem erga Johannem Caly de eadem detinendo vij s. <Suspensus xx° die Aprilis.> <Solvit.> Comparuit xxv° die Maij et juravit concordare cum parte citra festum Michaelis proximum."

parties agreed to settle "before the next court [day]" and did, according the register.[238] Such practices are evident elsewhere in England. In addition, since no rolls of excommunicates similar to those surviving from late medieval France appear to be extant in England, we might question Poos's assertions that, "in contrast to episcopal consistories, in most English lower ecclesiastical jurisdictions *ex officio* cases comprise the majority of cases" and that *fidei lesio* cases were pursued inquisitorially.[239] What appears to be inquisitorial procedure may represent a jury presentment ultimately based on a creditor's charge: for example, "John Sharp broke faith with John Harvey of Elm over five hundred turves at 14d. He appeared and denied the charge and will have to bring two oath-helpers next Saturday and lawfully purged himself."[240] Had Sharp not appeared, surely he would have been suspended or excommunicated, as was William Eastmund alias Hobson.[241] Perhaps the inquisitorial tone reflects the role of jurors – the *inquisitores* who "presented" charges in the register – who elided accusation and inquisition by transforming a creditor's complaint into the debtor's supposed reputation in the community (*fama*). What on the continent would be an *ad instanciam* case ("X excommunicated at the request of Y") could appear in England to be an *ex officio* case ("X broke faith with Y," that is, "the churchwardens (*iconomi*) or jurors (*inquisitores*) presented that X broke faith with Y"). The Dean of Wisbech's court may have functioned like a court leet, in which the jurors' presentment or accusation had the force of a judgment. As Lord Mansfield explained in 1766, the jury of the leet "accuses and punishes at the same instant."[242] Philipp Schofield has published presentments for oral debts by late-thirteenth-century juries of the leet at

238 Poos, *Lower Ecclesiastical Jurisdiction*, 354: "Richardus Person' taliter delinquit detinendo a dicto Johanne iij s. iiij d. <Suspensus dicto die Aprilis.> <Solvit.> Comparuit dicto die et juravit concordare cum parte citra proximam curiam. Partes concordantur."

239 Poos, *Lower Ecclesiastical Jurisdiction*, xlvi, l.

240 Poos, *Lower Ecclesiastical Jurisdiction*, 371 (October 29, 1461): "Johannes Sharp violat fidem erga Johannem Hervy de Elm detinendo v^{c} terricidiorum precij xiiij d. Comparuit et negavit articulum et habet purgare cum ij manu die Sabbati proximo sequenti et legitime se purgavit. Ideo etc."

241 Poos, *Lower Ecclesiastical Jurisdiction*, 379: "Willelmus Estmunde alias Obson' taliter delinquit detinendo executoribus Johannis Clement xj s. Citatus erga x diem Maij. Quo die non comparuit, ideo suspensus." Here "suspension" is equivalent not to a priest's suspension *a divinis* but to the personal interdictions from entering churches issued on the continent.

242 Cited in John P. Dawson, *A History of Lay Judges* (Cambridge, MA: Harvard University Press, 1960), 256. One might in this context consider that the ecclesiastical judges would have been acquainted with Ulpian's rule (Dig. 50.17.207): "a judgment is to be held to be true" or "to be an accurate reflection of reality (*res judicata pro veritate accipitur*)." Poos also noted with respect to the decanal courts of the diocese of Lincoln that they often had the aspect of manorial courts – in which courts baron and leet may only have been distinguished in the record.

the manor of Hinderclay that suggest exactly this possibility: for example, "Gilbert Chaplin is amerced for 6d because he withheld 6d from R. of Hinderclay."[243] Here the jury of the leet hides what must have been a plaint by R. of Hinderclay. Given that ecclesiastical tribunals everywhere offered equivalent procedural opportunities, whether or not they were recorded in the same manner, the verbal debts inferrable from late medieval business practice by Christopher Dyer and others could have been enforced on pain of personal interdiction from the Church (the "suspension" of English documents) or (major) excommunication. In any case, using Poos's edition of the records of the Deanery of Wisbech, Briggs has counted 528 debt cases between 1460 and 1472, of which 418 were *inter vivos* and the rest testamentary cases. This is an average of 44 per year in a rural deanery comprising seven rural parishes, a level comparable to that seen in contemporary France.[244] More generally, R. N. Swanson has plausibly estimated that fifty percent of the business of late medieval church courts in England concerned various types of debt.[245]

I would not know how to venture a similar figure for France. It is nevertheless clear from my own analysis that cases of debt played a considerable role in the business of the officialities of Chartres, Paris, and Montivilliers, even if they did not constitute the majority of litigated cases leading to definitive sentences. Véronique Beaulande's study of excommunication in the province of Reims, Pierrette Paravy's study of the diocese of Grenoble, and Roger Aubenas's edition of the formulary of the officialities of Aix and Marseille confirm this. At Beauvais, by Beaulande's count, 75 percent of all excommunications and 92 percent of those for which a cause was specified between 1480 and 1487 were for debt. At Corbie, again by Beaulande's count, 82 percent of excommunications in 1531 were for debt, with the percentage rising to 89 percent if citations for unpaid judicial fines or court costs are included.[246] Paravy has estimated that a quarter of the heads of households in some villages were excommunicated for debts.[247] Twenty-five percent of the letters in the formulary published by Aubenas concerned excommunication for debt.[248] Excommunication for debt appears to have been available

[243] Philipp Schofield, "Peasant debt in English manorial courts: form and nature," in Claustre, *La dette*, 55–67, presentments given at 58 n.6: "vid. Gilbertus Capellanus in misericordia quia retinuit R? de Hildercle xii den.'"
[244] Briggs, "The Availability," 21.
[245] Swanson, *Church and Society*, 167.
[246] Beaulande, *Le malheur*, 196.
[247] Paravy, *De la chrétienté romaine*, 462–466.
[248] Aubenas, *Recueil*.

everywhere in late medieval France, even if it was used with decreasing frequency, more and more only against clerical debtors.

The Catholic Franche-Comté is exemplary if late. Although the Regent Mary supported the Parlement at Dôle in its "battle against ecclesiastical jurisdiction" in the 1530s, the battle was only won under the pressure of Philip II forty years later, as Febvre has shown. The Parlement had unsuccessfully resolved in 1532 to forbid excommunications in matters concerning less than 10 *comtois francs* (15£t), reiterating this demand in the 1550s, and coupling it in the 1560s with demands to implement the decrees of the Council of Trent and thereby to limit recourse to such sanctions.[249] The archbisop of Besançon countered that "to suppress to use of excommunication in temporal matters, in matters of debt would be to suppress the officiality itself" and to ruin the town nourished by that spiritual commerce.[250] The officiality did wither after the practice was suppressed in 1572, though not after enriching a few archbishops, scores of legal practitioners, and, Febvre argues, a whole class of expropriating bourgeois who used the officiality of Besançon to execute usurious loans.

In Philip II's native kingdoms, already in 1512 had the provincial council of Seville forbidden officials from issuing monitions or excommunications in blank and for less than one hundred maravedis, a minimal sum equivalent to 10st.[251] This statute suggests that Spanish ecclesiastical judges engaged in the same shady practices as their French colleagues. Summoners selling baskets of blank citations or excommunications for small change may not have been rare in Europe around 1500. Still later, the Council of Trent heard complaints from Italy that "curates sometimes fear to declare who are excommunicates, and who have not confessed and received communion in the parish," implying overuse of excommunication, particularly as another complaint asked

249 Febvre, II: 20.

250 Febvre, II: 21–22.

251 D. Juan Tejada y Ramiro, *Collección de canones y de todos los concilios de la iglesia española ... parte segunda* (Madrid: D. Pedro Montero, 1855), V: 67–109, 107: "LIX. Ne concedantur literae excommunicationis pro rebus parvi momenti. Praecipimus etiam, ut Provisores, et officiales generales, non concedant Literas fulminatorias excommunicationis generales pro rebus levis momenti, et modicae quantitatis, et declaramus, rem esse levis momenti, et modicae quantitatis in hoc casu usque ad valorem centum morapetinorum, et pro minori quantitate non concedendas dictas Literas generales. Quodque super valore, et pretio recipiatur juramentum a parte, quae ejusmodi Literas petierit. Item etiam jubemus, ut praefati judices non dent Literas, nec mandata in albo"; cited tacitly at Lea, 437. Trusting the equivalence in 1530 of 19,364£ 16s 1dt and 3,864,969 maravedis provided by Hilario Casado Alonso, "Les relations entre les foires de Castille et les foires de Lyon au XVIe siècle," in J.-L. Gaulin and S. Rau (eds.), *Lyon vu/e d'ailleurs (1245–1800): échanges, compétitions et perceptions* (Lyon: Presses universitaires de Lyon, 2009), 91–108, 100.

"that the grounds of excommunication be limited."[252] The Italian bishops concurred, petitioning that "the innumerable [causes for] excommunications be reduced to fewer and well-known causes ... [and] that excommunications not be conceded except on account of grave matters."[253] Although other petitions to Trent imply that the movement toward using general monitions primarily in cases of occult theft evident in France was underway elsewhere in Europe, the tenor of the complaints suggest that excommunication for debt persisted in Catholic Europe until the Council effectively eviscerated the lower ecclesiastical jurisdictions.

All this suggests that a non-negligeable minority of the population in many parts of late medieval Western Europe had been excommunicated at one time or another, and that a majority of these had been excommunicated for unpaid debts. The Pre-Reformation Church was in effect selling its salvific magic to creditors on a grand scale. It did this for the most part not because prelates wished but because litigants felt that it was appropriate to avail themselves of the opportunities presented by canonical procedure for executing debts – until around 1500, when they increasingly turned away from church courts in matters of debt. A statistical and qualitative look at the use of spiritual sanctions in the late Middle Ages allows us to see beyond treatises on canonical procedure or learned commentaries on canon law and helps us to view ecclesiastical justice from the perspective of the consumer of justice. We see that church courts were not only instruments of the social control of layfolk by clerical guardians of orthodoxy and morality. They were equally, if not more, demand-driven instruments of the social control of layfolk by layfolk, helping to settle the debts that separated and bound together late medieval members of the Body of Christ. Even as they did this, however, they increasingly incurred the hatred of believers and encouraged hopes for the reform of the institutional Church – even for its effective obliteration. Henry Charles Lea provides a fitting concluding vignette from Scotland: "In a sermon preached at St. Andrew's in 1528, William Arith, a Dominican friar, after premising that cursing 'was the most fearefull thing upon the face of the earth,' proceeded to state, 'but now the avarice of preests and ignorance of their office hath caused it

[252] Le Plat, IV: 759: "Quod limitentur causae, ob quas excommunicationis sententiam fulminet"; 762: "Quoniam curati aliquando timent viva voce declarare qui sunt excommunicati, et quinam non sunt confessi aut non communicaverunt in parochia, statuant, ut in valvis ecclesiarum fixentur eorum nomina, et hoc sufficiat ut vitentur."

[253] Le Plat, IV: 617: "Si possent innumerae excommunicationes ad pauciora et ad certa capita redigi ... Excommunicationes non concederentur nisi pro rebus maximi momenti."

to be altogether vilipended; for the preest, whose duetie and office is to pray for the people, standeth up on Soonday and crieth 'One hath tint a spurtell; there is a flail stollen beyond the barne; the good wife on the other side of the gate hath lost a horne spoone; God's curse and myne I give to them that knoweth of this geere and restoreth it not!' "[254] Who asked the priest to reclaim the spatula, the flail, and the spoon on pain of excommunication?

[254] Lea, "Excommunication," 436.

4 A crisis of credit? The Reformation and the early modern world

Western Modernity has lost the great signposts that once marked its origins. The Renaissance no longer marks the birth of "modern man" or the "state as a work of art."[1] As William Bouwsma observed thirty-five years ago, it is no longer possible to identify the Renaissance as the origin of a secular, liberal, and republican modernity, in spite of the mid-century efforts of exiled European academics and of liberal Anglo-Americans.[2] Likewise, the Reformation no longer marks the birth of modern, liberal religion.[3] Brad Gregory has instead recently proposed in a more pessimistic vein that the roots of the spiritual malaise of contemporary American society lie in the epistemological consequences of the

[1] As proposed in the nineteenth century by Jacob Burckhardt, *The Civilization of the Renaissance in Italy*, S. G. C. Middlemore (trans.), (New York: Penguin Books, 1990), and lately, unconvincingly, by Stephen Greenblatt, *The Swerve: How the World Became Modern* (New York: W.W. Norton, 2011).

[2] William Bouwsma, "The Renaissance and the Drama of Western History," *The American Historical Review* 84:1 (1979), 1–15. Here one thinks inter alia of Hans Baron, *The Crisis of the Early Italian Renaissance: Civic Humanism and Republican Liberty in an Age of Classicism and Tyranny* (Princeton: Princeton University Press, 1955), J. G. A. Pocock, *The Machiavellian Moment: Florentine Political Thought and the Atlantic Republican Tradition* (Princeton: Princeton University Press, 1975), but also of Ernst Kantorowicz's chapter on Dante in *The King's Two Bodies: A Study in Medieval Political Theology* (Princeton: Princeton University Press, 1957), 451–495, or his "The Sovereignty of the Artist: A Note on Legal Maxims and Renaissance Theories of Art," in M. Cherniavsky and R. E. Giesey (eds.), *Selected Studies* (Locust Valley, NY: J. J. Augustin, 1965), 352–365. One thinks too of the vision of legal history tied to the push for a united Europe evident in Paul Koschaker's *Europa und das römische Recht* (Munich: C. H. Beck, 1953) or in Helmut Coing's late *Europäisches Privatrecht: Älteres gemeines Recht (1500 bis 1800)* (Munich: C. H. Beck, 1985).

[3] John Lothrop Motley, *Historic Progress and American Democracy* (New York: C. Scribner and Co., 1869), 71, compares Martin Luther to a well-shaft sunk in the arid Western United States: "half-forgotten Humanity bursts from time to time out of the depths in which it has pursued its joyless, sunless course, moaning and murmuring through long centuries but never quite forgetting its divine and distant origin. Such was the upward movement out of intellectual thraldom which we call the Reformation when the shaft of Luther struck the captive stream." Tom Brady has aptly characterized Motley's Luther as a "metahistorical drill-bit."

Protestant Reformation.[4] All told, it has become increasingly difficult to identify a meaningful connection between our age and the sixteenth century. The spread of the logic of capitalist markets has flattened our sense of European history, reducing its scope to the past two hundred years when the West escaped the slow demographic growth and low standards of living of "motionless history."[5] Yet, just as we cannot ignore the radical demographic, economic, and colonial take-off of the West at the end of the eighteenth century in telling the story of modern consumer society, so we cannot minimize the importance of the sixteenth-century Reformations of Christianity to the development of market culture. Max Weber may not have demonstated the historical connection of Calvinist "innerworldly asceticism" to the emergence of modern capitalism,[6] and Brad Gregory may tend to overemphasize the corrosive effects of Protestantism on the truth claims informing knowledge production and social behavior, but both assert the lasting significance of religious developments at the pivot of the medieval and the early modern ages. Examining the disappearance of excommunication for debt offers a novel perspective on the place of theological and economic debt in the Reformations of Christianity. Market trust originated not in rational calculation but in a notion of moral debt encouraged within late medieval Christian communities that was secularized (but not de-moralized) by early modern states.

The early modern Confessional Age transformed Paolo Prodi's late medieval "society of oaths (*società giurata*)" into Craig Muldrew's "contractual society."[7] The Confessional Age was one in which, for states as for individuals, "contracts must be observed (*pacta sunt servanda*)" and in which the norms of the market came to be ethicized.[8] This "contractual

[4] Brad S. Gregory, *The Unintended Reformation: How a Religious Revolution Secularized Society* (Cambridge, MA: Belknap Press, 2012). How differently Gregory defines the present relevance of Luther than Heiko Oberman!

[5] The term is Emmanuel LeRoy Ladurie's: "Motionless History," *Social Science History* 1 (1977), 115–136.

[6] He may rather have drawn a typological parallel between ascetic Protestant propensity to calculate (*Rechenhaftigkeit*) to prove salvation and capitalist calculation of profits: Peter Ghosh, *Max Weber and the Protestant Ethic: Twin Histories* (Oxford: Oxford University Press, 2014).

[7] Prodi, *Sacramento*, esp. 161–226; on confessionalization, see Heinz Schilling, "The Confessionalization of Church, State, and Society: The Shapes, Successes, Weaknesses, and Prospects of a Historiographical Paradigm," in Wolfgang Reinhard and Heinz Schilling (eds.), *Die katholische Konfessionalisierung. Akten eines von Corpus Catholicorum und Verein für Reformationsgeschichte veranstalteten Symposions, Augsburg, 1993* (Gütersloh and Münster, 1995), 11–49; Wolfgang Reinhard, "Reformation, Counter-Reformation, and the Early Modern State: A Reassessment," *Catholic Historical Review* 75 (1989), 383–404.

[8] The phrase is from Hugo Grotius's *De jure belli ac pacis* (1625); on the ethicization of market norms, see Prodi, *Settimo*.

society," this "age of debt" laid the groundwork for the trust in markets and in credit required for the West's economic take-off in the nineteenth and twentieth centuries.[9] Developing trust in impersonal markets required centuries of pedagogy, for it rested on trust in individuals' contractual obligations. Into the sixteenth century, church courts supplemented confessors' admonitions by excommunicating lay debtors. In the same period, states increasingly concurrenced confessors' admonitions by imprisoning debtors and by executing bankrupts and thieves. The early modern explosion of civil litigation, particularly in matters of debt and contract, exposes how early modern confessional states took on the Church's role in the pedagogy of debt and how early modern believers secularized the notion of credit by depriving church courts of their business. Even in Catholic territories, the enforcement of contracts evacuated church courts for the confessional and for secular courts: Tridentine Christians were bound by their confessors *in foro interno* to honor their promises. Thus Thomas Bozio claimed in the 1590s that Catholics' consequent and exemplary observance of contracts marked them as members of the true Church.[10] Although this "Catholic ethic" was not a capitalist ethic, for it concerned the observance of contracts rather than the sole pursuit of profit, the trust instilled in the confessional was indispensable to Westerners' subsequent transformation into consumers in an impersonal marketplace.

The *società giurata* was constructed after an ecclesial model, in the lay sense of society as a body of believers governed by a morality inculcated by ecclesiastical institutions; early modern contractual society was likewise ecclesially conceived, but in terms of a morality defined by the State's exclusive claim to enforce contracts among its subjects. The splintering of Western Christianity confirmed the incipient sense that transactions occurred less within the Body of Christ than within a commercial space defined by the State. Commerce on credit remained omnipresent, but the secularization of credit relations (not to say their de-moralization[11]) was the first step toward the eighteenth-century conviction that markets

[9] The terms are from Muldrew, *The Economy of Obligation*, 131 and 313–334.

[10] Bozio's thirty-fourth mark of the true Church, cited in Prodi, *Settimo*, 222 and 236 n.64: "Et sane opus est catholicos esse longe iustissimos plerumque in contractibus, quando nulla gens tantae sit constantiae in credendis suae religionis decretis, ut nostros esse inde cognoscimus … Illud vero est praecipuum nostrae doctrinae praeceptum, non remitti peccatum, nisi ablata resituantur … Sic usurae a nullis gentibus severius cohibitae, ut a nostris: contractus eodem modo inaequales, et alia huiusmodi infinita rescissa habita nulla … denique et religionis timore intimo, et poenis extrinsecus adiectis, animi mortalium per nostros ad iustitiae metas revocati, et intra illius confinia conclusi."

[11] Perhaps we had better speak of the ethicization of credit relations, so as to connect the passage of matters of contract from church courts to secular courts to the eighteenth-century tendency to ethicize Christian morality, which John McManners has described as the precondition of Dechristianization: *Church and Society in Eighteenth-Century France*,

were themselves ethical entities. Was it not ethical and moral to enforce the legal claims of purchasers of venal offices, of tax farmers, of clergymen who received benefices in exchange for pensions to the previous occupant, or of landowners who foreclosed upon the lands of indebted peasants? Because "morality was itself a market force,"[12] one can see nineteenth-century virtuous avoidance of debt as a rejection of Old Regime cultures of credit, dependence, and inequality that nevertheless preserved the moral duty to honor one's debts.

The sixteenth-century growth of litigiousness

The frequency of litigation increased across Europe during the sixteenth and seventeenth centuries, before falling again in the eighteenth century. While researching my dissertation, I learned this anecdotally by examining the catalogue of the X Series of the French national archives, the series containing the records of the Parlement of Paris. The registers of morning pleadings before the Parlement shift from one volume to two volumes per judicial year in 1513. The rarer afternoon pleadings make the same shift only in 1543. The *registres du conseil*, that is, of the Grand' Chambre sitting together, split into two per year exceptionally during the active, disturbed year of 1525 and then return to one register per year in 1526. In 1538, however, they shift, this time definitively, to two volumes per year. They expanded to three volumes per year in 1545, four volumes per year in 1558, and five volumes per year in 1566. The movement from one to two volumes does not signify a sudden doubling of the number of folios per register, rather the perception of practical limits on more linearly expanding, unwieldy volumes. The magnitude of the increase in the business of the Parlement of Paris in the middle third of the sixteenth century is clear. Annual business that still in 1537 required only one volume required five thirty years later. This flambée of business before the Parlement occurred despite the creation of new judges, new chambers, and in 1552 a new intermediate appellate jurisdiction across the kingdom. The new appellate jurisdiction, that of so-called *présidial* courts, was intended to relieve some of the pressure on France's parlements: in civil affairs *présidiaux* were to rule in final instance in matters concerning amounts below 250£t and annuities yielding less than 10£t annually; they could judge cases up to amounts of 500£t and annuities yielding up to 20£t annually, though their judgments in such cases could

2 vols. (Oxford: Oxford University Press, 1998), II: 94–118. See too Michel de Certeau, "The Formality of Practices," in *The Writing of History*, 147–205.

[12] Swanson, *Church and Society*, 194.

be appealed to the parlements; in criminal matters presidials judged so-called *cas prévotaux*, cases susceptible to summary judgment by the royal police.[13]

More focused studies have confirmed, through both direct and indirect measures, an increase in litigation from the first third of the sixteenth century as well as an eighteenth-century decline in its frequency. In Dijon, the number of "men of the law" on the tax rolls, a proxy for how many practitioners judicial business might support, multiplied seven times between the mid-fifteenth and the mid-seventeenth centuries; in England the number of attorneys practicing at the central royal jurisdictions of the King's Bench and Common Pleas rose from 150 in 1560 to more than 1,400 in 1650; in Castile as well, suits reaching final judgment at the *chancillería* of Valladolid tripled between 1500 and 1580.[14] At the King's Bench and Common Pleas, Christopher Brooks counts a fourteen-fold increase in cases in advanced stages from 2,100 in 1490, 5,278 in *c.*1560, 13,105 in 1580, 23,147 in 1606, to 28,734 in 1640.[15] In the Empire, the lasting fruit of late-fifteenth-century *Reichsreform* was two appellate courts: the Imperial Chamber Court (*Reichskammergericht*) and the Imperial Aulic Court (*Reichshofrat*), which themselves encouraged the "reception" of Romano-canonical procedures and solutions through their appellate rulings. The number of cases before the highest appellate tribunals in the Holy Roman Empire rose swiftly over the sixteenth century to peak around 1630.[16]

An analogous situation appears in lower jurisdictions. In England, Craig Muldrew has shown litigation in borough courts to have risen swiftly from the middle of the sixteenth century to peak near 1600, before slowly declining into the eighteenth century, whether in Yarmouth, Bristol, King's Lynn, Taunton, Kendal, or Witney.[17] Broken down by actions per household, the increase is from something less than one

[13] Roland Mousnier, *The Institutions of France under the Absolute Monarchy, 1598–1789. Volume II: The Organs of State and Society*, A. Goldhammer (trans.), (Chicago: University of Chicago Press, 1984), 263–266. Inflation soon again inflated the business of the presidials and the parlements (264): "During the sixteenth century [250£t] was equal to the inheritance of a wealthy peasant or the inventory of a small merchant. By 1764, however, it had lost four-fifths of its value. According to the présidial of Lons-le-Saulnier, the marc d'argent was worth 14 livres 5 sols tournois in 1552 but 48 livres in 1764. The setier of Paris (a measure of corn) was worth about 2 livres 5 sols tournois in 1550 but 17 to 18 livres in 1764."

[14] Breen, "Law," 348–349.

[15] C.W. Brooks, *Pettyfoggers and Vipers of the Commonwealth: The 'Lower Branch' of the Legal Profession in Early Modern England* (Cambridge: Cambridge University Press, 1986), 51.

[16] Eva Ortlieb and Gert Polster, "Die Prozessfrequenz am Reichshofrat (1519–1806)," *Zeitschrift für neuere Rechtsgeschichte* 26:3–4 (2004), 189–216, figures at 212–216.

[17] Muldrew, *The Economy of Obligation*, 219, 222, 223, 224, 228, 235.

action per household per year in English towns around 1530–1550 to a peak of nearly three per household per year in 1580–1640, followed by a decline to fewer than one action every other year per household in the eighteenth century.[18] J. H. Baker has identified a similar pattern for the secular immunity of Battle Abbey (which survived the dissolution into the late seventeenth century), where by 1602 the high court faced an "avalanche" of suits, most in matters of debt. Whether pursued as actions of trespass, of debt, or actions on the case, the court's business appears to have centered on debt since the later fifteenth century.[19] Subsequently, debt litigation before secular courts only increased in frequency.

What was behind the sixteenth-century increase in the frequency of civil litigation in secular courts? Muldrew's chronology suggests two answers beyond his proposals about the expansion of trade and growing wealth of the English, the first concerning ecclesiastical jurisdiction and the second concerning the land wars of bastard feudalism. I shall return to the land wars later in the chapter. As to the first, Muldrew's study begins in 1530–1550, when, it is true, the English grew increasingly wealthy, to judge from the evidence of the probate inventories. Yet increasing household wealth was not the only development of the period between 1530 and 1550. The royal assumption of supremacy sealed the fate of English church courts, making them ever more subsidiary and ever more subordinate to legislation and to appellate review by royal courts. It is not unlikely that English borough courts, aided by the increasing frequency of threats of *praemunire* and the expansion of the scope of actions of assumpsit in common-law courts from the 1490s, whether or not (and I suspect it did) this reflected the adoption of canonical habits of mind and legal procedures,[20] assumed the competence over day-to-day debt formerly exercised in part by ecclesiastical tribunals. This would have been the case even in the rural hinterlands of England's numerous small towns. In light of the work of Chris Briggs and Richard Helmholz, one can propose a narrative of the litigation of minor civil matters, particularly verbal debts including sales and purchases on credit, in England

[18] Muldrew, *The Economy of Obligation*, 238.

[19] J. H. Baker, "Personal Actions in the High Court of Battle Abbey 1450–1602," in *Collected Papers on English Legal History* (Cambridge: Cambridge University Press, 2013), I: 442–465.

[20] Strange that the doctrine of consideration was worked out when in the middle of the sixteenth century "special declarations in case … began to throw up endless questions of law that had never been posed before," in, I would add, common-law courts where no remedy previously lay. It is a narrow view of law in England that describes canonical contract doctrine as imported "*ab extra*": Baker, "Origins of the 'Doctrine' of Consideration 1535–1585," in *Collected Papers*, III: 1176–1201, quoted passage at 1200–1201.

between 1400 and 1600: Briggs has proposed that the decay of manorial courts in the first half of the fifteenth century pushed litigants in debt cases toward church courts; this renaissance would have been short lived, for Helmholz and other historians of ecclesiastical tribunals and contract law have shown secular tribunals to have made inroads on their competence from the last decade of the fifteenth century.[21] The chronology would therefore place the rise and fall of ecclesiastical competence over debt between 1400 and 1515 or so, just in time for the rising number of civil actions – on account of economic revival – to initiate the sixteenth-century rise in civil litigation before both borough and royal tribunals.

In France, the story may differ lightly, as ecclesiastical tribunals appear to have had a more important civil jurisdiction earlier than in England, though the question awaits further study on both sides of the Channel. Between the fourteenth and sixteenth centuries, French law increasingly pushed contractants toward the services of notaries and tabellions. Isabelle Mathieu's research into seigneurial courts in Western France illustrates how the massive increase in cases before the courts at the end of the first third of the fifteenth century (to a peak of over 3,000 cases per year in 104 tribunals) was followed by an equally massive decline in cases at the beginning of the sixteenth century (to fewer than 1,000 cases per year).[22] Mathieu interprets this to demonstrate the growth of royal justice at the expense of seigneurial justice through preemption (*prévention*), appeals, and the exclusive right to try so-called *cas royaux*.[23] Even if the increase in cases is exaggerated by the more frequent survival of court rolls and registers from 1400 or so onward, the sixteenth-century decline in business before seigneurial courts does not reflect missing sources. In the first third of the sixteenth century, then, French debt cases would have deserted seigneurial and ecclesiastical tribunals for royal courts at the bailiwick and parlementary levels. These last grew increasingly able and likely to enforce "innominate" or "unvested," "bare," or "verbal agreements (*nuda pacta*)" and debts over the course of the sixteenth century. If Pierre Rebuffi could still in the 1530s write that the seal of a royal court was required for a contract to be immediately executable, by the end of the century Antoine Loisel could extract the sentiment of the ordinary gloss to the Institutes of Justinian, III: 14, and write that "one binds bulls by their horns and men by their words, so a simple promise or agreement is worth as much as a stipulation in Roman law."[24] That is

[21] Briggs, "Availability"; Helmholz, "Assumpsit," and "Probate"; Wunderli, *London Church Courts*.

[22] Mathieu, *Les Justices seigneuriales*, 96.

[23] Mathieu, *Les Justices seigneuriales*, 98.

[24] Pierre Rebuffi, *In consitutiones regias … commentarii* (Lyon: apud heredes Guillelmi Rouillii, 1599), Tractatus de litteris obligatoriis, no.15, p. 56; Antoine Loisel, *Institutes coutumières* (Paris: chez la veuve Abel L'Angelier, 1611), Livre III, Tit. I, no. II, p. 33,

to say, a simple agreement could give rise to legal action. Here the voluntarism of canon law defeats the formalism of Roman law. If the canonists held to the idea that "God wishes there to be no distinction between our word and our contract," civilians argued that pacts had to be "vested" formally, if not necessarily with the archaic stipulation (*Spondesne*? *Spondeo*) of classical Roman law. Specialists in Roman law, like most medieval lay judges outside of village courts, were formalists, demanding respect of contractual forms. Canonists, like theologians or confessors, focused on contractants' wills and on issues of consent, as in their discussions of what made a valid marriage. The increasingly restricted competence of ecclesiastical tribunals, the uneven adoption of solutions to the question of whether parol contracts were legally binding in secular courts, the sixteenth-century increase in material wealth, the growing velocity and importance of regional and supra-regional trade in the lives of relatively humble individuals, the resulting necessity to preserve one's "credit" in both a metaphorical and a real sense, and the difficulty of extending relations of trust to individuals not bound to the creditor by ties of family, locality, clientage, or lordship drove the early modern inflation of litigation. As we contemplate the magnitude of the sixteenth-century increase in litigation, we should not forget that litigation, even when as frequent as the three actions per household per year in late sixteenth-century England, marks only breaches of faith that entered the courts. The majority of contracts, of loans, and of sales on credit did not enter the court record. Although these contracts may not have been observed precisely as agreed at the outset, they were observed sufficiently to satisfy creditors and to prevent them from going to law. Does the sixteenth-century increase in the frequency of litigation before lay tribunals, particularly in civil matters such as debt, then indicate a crisis of trust, a new lack of credence in social relations and in religious institutions?

Law and the Reformation: territory, property, contract

Issues of credit, trust, and belief were central to the Reformation. Late medieval theology and religious practice assimilated believers to debtors such that it is no exaggeration to call the Reformation a revolution of debtors. Theologically, the Protestant Reformation pivoted on soteriology, that is, on the question of how Christ saved believers. Late medieval theologians did not speak with one voice on this question of the mechanism of salvation. Some advocated a nearly predestinarian, Augustinian theology of grace. Some advocated a quasi-Pelagian theology of works.

and in the more accessible edition with the notes of Eusèbe de Laurière (Paris: Durand/Videcoq, 1846), t.1, no.357, p. 359.

Still others tended, from one perspective, to waffle or, from another perspective, to avoid oversimplifying the mechanism of Christ's promise of salvation. Popular perception, however, tended toward a semi-Pelagian "counting piety" focused on whether the quantity of good works performed vicariously or in person would ever be enough to satisfy the sinner's "debt" to God.[25] In the practice of excommunication for debt, church courts yoked together believers' debts to God and to their fellow men. Each unpaid debt, as much as any unjust interest, was a sin against charity – against the divine love that was supposed to animate Christ's body – meriting excommunication.[26] Absolution required satisfaction of the debt to the creditor, satisfaction of the debt to the judge (and to the sealer), and satisfaction of the debt to God via one's confessor.

The language of credit, debt, and obligation were in Christianity from the beginning. Did not the Lord's Prayer, in the Vulgate, admonish Christians to forgive their "debtors (*debitores*)" just as they entreated God the Father to forgive their own "debts (*debita*)?"[27] Did not 1 Corinthians advise Christians: "For ye are brought with a price: therefore glorify God in your body, and in your spirit?"[28] Anselm of Canterbury developed this kernel in the eleventh century into a coherent theory by which God consented to accept his son's atonement for the debts of sinners and by which the Church held the keys to the "treasury of [limitless] merit" earned through Christ's death on the cross. Was not sin, in Anselm's view, failure to pay one's debt to God, the theft of God's due honor?[29] As in the first antiphon of Lauds, the incarnate Christ's atonement was an "*admirabile commercium*," a holy and meritorious transaction by which Christ, the God-man who alone could satisfy God the Father and

25 Thomas Lentes, "Counting Piety in the Late Middle Ages," in Jussen, *Ordering*, 55–91. "Quantifiable religiosity" may translate "gezählte Frömmigkeit" more idiomatically. See too Swanson, *Indulgences*.

26 *Supplementum*, q. xxi art. iii, in *Thomae Aquinatis Opera Omnia*, XII: 43: "Quia poena non debet excedere culpam … dicendum quod culpae quantitas non mensuratur ex nocumento quod quis facit, sed ex voluntate qua quis facit, contra caritatem agens. Et ideo, quamvis poena excommunicationis excedat nocumentum, non tamen excedit quantitatem culpae."

27 Mt. 6:9–13: "Pater noster … dimitte nobis debita nostra, sicut et nos dimittimus debitoribus nostris." Likewise the Greek: "Πάτερ ἡμῶν … ἄφες ἡμῖν τὰ ὀφειλήματα ἡμῶν, ὡς καὶ ἡμεῖς ἀφήκαμεν τοῖς ὀφειλέταις ἡμῶν."

28 1 Cor. 6: 20: "Empti enim estis pretio magno. Glorificate, et portate Deum in corpore vestro." Greek: "ἠγοράσθητε γὰρ τιμῆς· δοξάσατε δὴ τὸν θεὸν ἐν τῷ σώματι ὑμῶν." The Authorized Version chooses "bought for a price" over "redeemed for a great price," somewhat deadening the associative richness of *timé*. I thank Jesse Torgerson for pointing out that God has bought us as high-price slaves.

29 Anselm, *Libri duo cur deus homo*, in PL 158: 360–432. At 376: "Non est itaque aliud peccare quam Deo non reddere debitum? … Hunc honorem debitum qui Deo non reddit, aufert Deo quod suum est, et Deus exhonorat; et hoc est peccare."

Creditor, atoned for the infinite debts of sinful humanity.[30] Late medieval Christians therefore scrambled to access the merit, the salvific credit gained by Christ's *commercium* through the sacraments, through indulgences deriving from meritorious acts ranging from alms-giving to the saying of certain prayers before an image of the Mass of St Gregory (for instance), and through intercessory prayer.[31] It was in this context, of Christians seeking to access Christ's credit so as to repay their debt to God, that Thomas Aquinas could describe the Eucharist in an antiphon for the Feast of Corpus Christi as the "pledge of future glory (*futurae gloriae … pignus*)," a pledge for the repayment of the salvation Christ had promised them.[32] Some, including Martin Luther's teacher Johann von Staupitz, followed the logic of this proposition and transformed Christ into humanity's debtor: "I am yours, save me (*tuus sum, salvum me fac*)." In this way, Luther's proposition that humans were saved not by works but through faith and God's grace alone was a nuancing of the late medieval position. Not good works, not piously totted up prayers but sincere faith in God's promise aided the utterly wretched sinner in accessing Christ's credit with God, that is, saving grace. Lutheran theology implied that semi-Pelagian counters of meritorious actions lacked faith in Christ because they failed to trust his promises. John Calvin departed further in theory albeit less in practice from what Thomas Lentes has called the late medieval "arithmetic of salvation." Calvin's double predestination fully transferred the burden of debt onto God: Christians were less debtors of God than God was the contractant who had covenanted with the Elect to guarantee their salvation. In practice, however, Calvinist "innerworldly asceticism" led to an accounting of the good works that signified one's election perhaps as rigorous as that of any fifteenth-century spiritual athlete.

The political consequences of Luther's, Calvin's, and other reformers' soteriological developments stemmed from the fact that the sacraments – and by extension the institutionalized, juridicized Church that

30 "O admirabile commercium / Creator generis humani / animatum corpus sumens / de virgine nasci dignatus est." On the assimilation of the Incarnation to a gift exchange in this fifth-century antiphon, see Éamonn Ó Carragáin, *Ritual and Rood: Liturgical Images and the Old English Poems of the Dream of the Rood Tradition* (Toronto: University of Toronto Press, 2005), 287–289, and there the quote from the Gelasian sacramentary: "quod pascha nostrum immolatus est Christus … et beati lege conmercii divinis humana mutantur. Quia nostrorum omnium mors cruce Christi redempta est."

31 See Virginia Reinburg, *French Books of Hours: Making an Archive of Prayer, c.1400–1600* (Cambridge: Cambridge University Press, 2012), 154–158; Scribner, "Cosmic Order," 13; and Duffy, *Stripping*, 183–186, on "the contract style" of prayer; Swanson, *Indulgences*, on devotional indulgences in particular.

32 "O sacrum convivium / in quo Christus sumitur:/ recolitur memoria passionis eius, / mens impletur gratia / et futurae gloriae nobis pignus datur. / Alleluia."

administered them – were no longer necessary for salvation. The reformers inverted Cardinal Juan de Torquemada's assertion that submission to the jurisdiction of the Roman pontiff was equivalent to doctrinal orthodoxy.[33] For them, doctrinal orthodoxy demanded repudiation of Rome. Politics flowed from theology such that the Protestant Reformation furthered tendencies toward the encadrement of religious institutions within secular polities evident at least since the Great Western Schism.[34] This encadrement is evident in the realm of law, though most accounts of the Reformation as a legal rupture (*Rechtsbruch*) focus on what would in both classical Roman and in modern terms be called public law.[35] Because orthodoxy was the unquestioned foundation of late medieval polities, the adoption of Protestant theology, forms of worship, and church organization from the 1520s onward necessarily transformed the constitutions of polities across Europe.

Public law determined the established religion or permissible forms of Christianity within a polity. Throughout the Protestant world, beginning in the late 1520s reformed princes issued church ordinances (*Kirchenordnungen*) to govern the liturgies, the clergy, and the churches within their territories. Yet, as famously in England, princes also arrogated competence over doctrine and ecclesiastical property. The Reformation-era extension of the "right to reform (*ius reformandi*)" transformed it from a justification for restoring monasteries to strict observance to a justification for determining the religious content and the religious practices to which subjects would be held. In this sense, the principle of "whose the territory, his the faith (*cuius regio, eius religio*)" consecrated by the religious peace of Augsburg in 1555 was – again – an extension of a trend evident since the late fourteenth century, when Europe's rulers began to beat back ecclesiastical jurisdiction, rejecting some canonical privileges outright and denying ecclesiastical tribunals within their territories the power to enforce such "unreceived" provisions. In England, *praemunire* (acts of 1353 and 1392) justified writs of prohibition against courts christian deployed with increasing frequency at the end of the fifteenth century.[36] In France, the Pragmatic Sanction of Bourges (1438) justified appeals from church courts to royal courts "as

[33] Gabriel, "Qualifications."

[34] If not earlier: Maureen C. Miller, *The Bishop's Palace: Architecture and Authority in Medieval Italy* (Ithaca: Cornell University Press, 2002).

[35] Dig.1.1.1: "Publicum ius in sacris, in sacerdotibus, in magistratibus constitit"; T. A. Brady, Jr., "Reformation als Rechtsbruch. Territorialisierung der Kirchen im Heiligen Römischen Reich im europäischen Vergleich," in P. Blickle and R. Schlögl (eds.), *Die Säkularisation im Prozess der Säkularisierung Europas*, Oberschwaben. Geschichte und Kultur 13 (Tübingen: Bibliotheca academica Verlag, 2005), 141–152.

[36] Swanson, *Church and Society*, 184–190.

if on account of an abuse (*comme d'abus*)" from the 1440s. These appeals grew in frequency in the 1520s and by 1600 had severely curtailed the competence of church courts – in Catholic France![37] This is to say nothing of particular indults, concordats, and privileges granted to secular rulers in matters of clerical taxation, jurisdiction over criminous clerics, or control of appointment to ecclesiastical benefices. In sum, even in the ultra-Catholic Spanish Empire by the end of the sixteenth century it appeared that the Church – however, much "universal" in spirit – existed legally within the Republic.[38] The Reformation, the consequences of which entailed the political circumscription of the Catholic territorial churches, constituted a rupture in what we would call public law and in what we would call private law.

The legal circumscription of the territorial churches within their respective polities visible across sixteenth-century Europe rested not just on Protestant rejection of the Roman church but on properly legal arguments, above all the argument that the Church – hence ecclesiastical courts – had no "territory," that is, no territorial jurisdiction over layfolk or their property. Notable commentators have argued that the main breaks in Western history came around 1200 and 1700, in political theory with the Gregorian Reform and John Locke, respectively, or that the Renaissance, in some sense, may have been more "fundamental" than the Reformation.[39] While it is true that, from one perspective, a notably intellectual one focused on elites, the Reformation can be seen as the continuation of efforts to "spiritualize" the Church inaugurated in the middle of the eleventh century, this is to ignore the very real and practical consequences of the Reformation on the life of European Christians.[40] From the fourteenth century, ordinary believers were subjected to

[37] Génestal, *Les origines de l'appel*; Pommeray, 440–441; Lefebvre-Teillard, 70.

[38] On the phrase, see Jotham Parsons, *The Church in the Republic: Gallicanism and Political Ideology in Renaissance France* (Washington, DC: The Catholic University of America Press, 2004); within France, the Edict of 1695 prescribed (art. 31) that every bishop create an official for each portion of the diocese subject to a different parlement to facilitate appeals *comme d'abus*, in effect redrawing ecclesiastical geography to coincide with royal jurisdictions: J. Declareuil, *Histoire générale du droit français des origines à 1789* (Paris: Recueil Sirey, 1925), 1001; on the *pase real* required for the application of papal dispensations in America, see Benedetta Albani, "Nuova luce sulle relazioni tra la Sede Apostolica e le Americhe. La pratica della concessione del 'pase regio' ai documenti pontifici destinati alle Indie," in C. Ferlan (ed.), *Eusebio Francesco Chini e il suo tempo. Una riflessione storica* (Trent: Fondazione Bruno Kessler, 2012), 83–102.

[39] Brian Tierney, *Religion, Law, and the Growth of Constitutional Thought 1150–1650* (Cambridge: Cambridge University Press, 1982), lectures originally subtitled "from Gratian to Grotius."

[40] For the former, minimalist view of the Reformation's significance, see Constantin Fasolt, "Hegel's Ghost: Europe, the Reformation, and the Middle Ages," *Viator* 39 (2008), 345–386, esp. 383; cf e.g., Duffy, *Stripping*.

recurring waves of evangelization aimed at teaching them the rudiments of the reformed and unreformed faiths, that is, at transforming them from practical to dogmatic Christians.[41] The experience of daily life changed as the intellectual categories and institutional structures shaping that experience shifted. It was only the Reformation – widely understood as the Reformations of Christianity common to Catholic and Protestant polities alike – and the accompanying rejection of ecclesiastical territorial jurisdiction that created the situation that Anne Zink has described in eighteenth-century southwestern France: "above the level of the parish ecclesiastical circumscriptions really concerned the clergy far more than the laity. The *archiprêtrés* had great importance in the Counter-Reformation Church … they served to discipline (*encadrer*) parish priests, to offer them an ecclesiastical sociability that distanced them from layfolk, and to impose upon them an ongoing, continuous education."[42] In the last centuries of the Middle Ages, when archdeacons cited, excommunicated, and absolved, it was entirely otherwise. The early modern de-territorialization of ecclesiastical institutions paralleled and aided the clericalization of the Tridentine Church, in which efforts to reform the clergy tended consciously or not to undermine the conception of the Church as the mystical Body of Christ comprehending clergy and laity alike in favor of the notion that the Church was primarily the institutionally organized body of the clergy directed by the pope and his newly founded congregations of cardinals.

This trend originated around 1300, when the theses of Philip the Fair's publicists and of Marsilio of Padua constitute one response to the contradictions inherent in the application of Aristotelian political concepts to the Church. For Michael Wilks, thirteenth-century visions of universal Christian society were inherently unstable because they implicitly contrasted a "mystical Reality, a Church, whose true personality was expressed by monarchic government" with a "material society, a State, whose will was that of all the members and which had a purely earthly existence."[43] If the Church were a political community, what of the political communities headed by secular princes? The Marsilian solution was radical in theory, the Philippian solution radical in practice. The former subtracted any worldly power from the Church. The latter, at least in the actions of Philip and Guillaume de Nogaret against Boniface VIII, suggested that temporal rulers had a duty to bring errant pastors

41 Bossy, *Christianity*, 170–171, describes the redefinition of Christianity between 1400 and 1700 from a "body of believers" to a "body of belief."

42 Anne Zink, *Pays ou circonscriptions. Les collectivités territoriales de la France du Sud-Ouest sous l'Ancien Régime* (Paris: Publications de la Sorbonne, 2000), 114.

43 Wilks, *Problem*, 526.

including the pope to justice before a council. These developments were less spectacular at lower levels of the ecclesiastical hierarchy. Protests of the clergy of the province of Lyon at the Council of Vienne in 1312 that "ecclesiastical judges have a territory and general competence to hear cases" involving the sealing of contracts provides evidence of the early push to de-territorialize the reach of the Church's administrative apparatus – certainly to restrict its scope only to the clergy of a given territory.[44] It is not coincidental that clerical complaints here concerned limits on ecclesiastical competence over matters of contract, a point to which I will soon return. Reforming clerics also sought to limit the abuses of ecclesiastical tribunals in this matter: the Council of Constance (1414–1418), in a set of reforming decrees arranged by the rubrics of the decretals, forbade prelates to demand a subsidy on their enthronement or for another reason (*charitativam subventionem* or *pro jucundo adventu*), lest "charity be turned into cruelty and joy into punishing sadness." "Because such a penalty is not to be given except for sin," continued the Fathers, "it entirely exceeds the gravity of this sort of crime."[45] This implicitly condemned the regime of papal taxation constructed in the fourteenth century, for papal collectors frequently used excommunication and *molestatio* through ecclesiastical litigation to enforce papal claims and to collect arrears.[46] It was not clear to the Fathers of Constance that failure to pay what is generously ecclesiastical taxation and less generously extortion recalling earlier exactions of "evil customs (*malae consuetudines*, *maltolts*)" was a grave sin meriting exclusion from the community of the faithful.

The legal debate over whether or not prelates with powers of jurisdiction had a "territory" found its center of gravity in the passage of the Codex of Justinian and the appended Latin summary of a Greek law subsequent to the *Corpus iuris civilis*: the law *Episcopale iudicium* and the authentic *Si quis litigantium* (Cod. 1.7.9 et auth.) discussed in Chapter 1. The former provided that "judgment by a bishop is approved for all who choose to be heard by priests, and we command that all authorities respect their judgments as yours, from which there is no appeal." The latter provided that "If the bishop judged at the Emperor's command or in virtue of a judicial commission, between any persons whomsoever,

[44] Ehrle, "Ein Bruchstück," 396, cited at n.26.

[45] Hermann von der Hardt, *Rerum concilii oecumenici Constantiensis de universali ecclesiasticae disciplinae reformatione* (Frankfurt/Leipzig: Christian Genschius, 1697), "Avisamenta secundum aliquas decretalium rubricas pro reformatione congrua facienda," I: 663–755 at lib. V, tit. XI, c.unum, col. 753–754: "charitas in crudelitatem, aut jucunditas in poenalem tristitiam convertatur ... Cum talis poena, non nisi pro peccato infligenda, hujusmodi delicti totaliter excedat quantitatem." Lea ("Excommunication," 443) refers to this passage but extends its significance to debts more generally.

[46] Favier, *Les finances*; here too we await the forthcoming work of Amandine Le Roux.

appeal is to the Emperor or to whomever issued the commission." Whereas the novel at the origin of *Si quis litigantium* initially provided only for the trial of clergy and religious before bishops, in the Middle Ages *Episcopale iudicium* was understood to justify the civil competence not just of bishops but of archdeacons, deans, abbots, and other holders of the power of jurisdiction over matters brought before them, whether by clergy or by layfolk. *Si quis litigantium* was understood to justify that there was no appeal from ecclesiastical judges to secular judges except when they judged as secular lords wielding the king's delegated jurisdiction. As most prelates were also secular lords, this interpretation served as a justification for the separation of their spiritual and their secular courts and submitting the latter to the king's justice. In his parlement in 1287, the king of France therefore commanded, in a precept not always precisely observed, that the officers of secular courts, even those of ecclesiastical lords, were to be lay.[47]

At the end of the Middle Ages, however, the debate concerned less the personnel of courts than their competence. As secular princes chipped away at bishops' territories, jurists joined in. In March 1371 (OS), in an ordinance still debated in the following century, Charles V of France forbade ecclesiastical judges to "judge or involve themselves in any manner with real cases and actions to the prejudice of our temporal jurisdiction."[48] Baldus (†1400) had written "of the sentence of those who do not govern a territory, like bishops according to this law" and that "the bishop had no territory assigned to him by this law."[49] Panormitanus (†1443/5) had written that "the Church ... has no territory except with respect to the clergy; it therefore does not involve itself in the crimes of laymen, even those committed in churches."[50] Baldus apparently rejected any civil competence for bishops over layfolk unless it was secular and had therefore been granted by a secular prince, to whom appeals would

[47] AN J 945 n° 119: "Extractum de registris Curie de parlamento quod fuit anno domini milesimo duocentesimo octogesimo septimo Ordinatum fuit per consilium domini regis quod duces comites barones archiepiscopi episcopi abbates capituli et collegis milites et generaliter omnes in regno finibus jurisdicionem temporalem habentes ad exercendum dictam jurisdicionem temporalem ballivos prepositos et servientes laycos et nullatenus clericos."

[48] Pierre Guénois, *La nouvelle et dernière conférence des ordonnances et edicts royaux distribuée et XII. livres à l'imitation et selon l'ordre et disposition du Code de l'Empereur Justinian* (Paris: Claude Sonnius, 1627), Tome 1, Livre I, titre IV, no.6 p. 71: "de casibus et actionibus realibus in praeiudicium nostra Iurisdictionis temporalis de caetera amplius cognoscere, aut se intromittere quoquo modo"; by 1393 the king's avocats in the Parlement of Paris were trying, unsuccessfully at first, to extend this law to prohibit the bishop from arresting even clerics because "capere de facto et incarcerare est facti actualis, realis et temporalis" or, in French, "prendre est de fait": see Lange, "Birth," 135.

[49] Lange, "Birth," 139; Baldus ad Cod. 1.7.9.

[50] Lange, "Birth," 139; Panormitanus ad X.2.2.8.

then go. Panormitanus rejected any competence for the Church over lay criminals. Neither of these opinions reflected late medieval practice, in which ecclesiastical tribunals heard cases concerning contracts and real property as well as cases of assault or gross immorality involving layfolk.

Only after 1450 did lay judges begin actively to deny ecclesiastical judges cognizance of disputes over the possession of real property and over contracts. In 1451, a barrister argued to the Parlement of Toulouse that "the Church, which has no territory, cannot judge cases concerning the possession of real property," invoking the authority of Panormitanus.[51] This was of course an unwarranted extension of Panormitanus's comment, which concerned the crimes of laymen in churches, not matters of fact and of real property or debts. This statement points to contemporary conflicts in Southern France: in 1456 the Estates of Languedoc complained to Charles VII that royal courts, namely the seneschalsy of Nîmes and perhaps the "*petite chancellerie*" of Montpellier, were enabling debtors obliged before ecclesiastical courts to escape spiritual sanctions by prohibiting parish priests from reading out monitions and excommunications. The king's response to the Estates' appeal to "preserve the Church's competence [in the matter of credit], as he was its guardian," was cool: he wanted more information and would then allow his administration to act "as shall be appropriate."[52] The king and his administrators were likely not unaware of the letters of recision of contract issued at Nîmes or of other inhibitions issued against the execution of ecclesiastical sanctions. Perhaps the king had heard Jean Gerson decry the misuse of excommunication and therefore saw inhibitions and letters of recision in a favorable light? The battle was not lost, however, as the quantity of monitions and excommunications in matters of debt contained in the roughly contemporary formulary of the officialities of Aix and Marseille edited by Roger Aubenas suggests. In the North, the drive to remove civil matters concerning layfolk from the competence of ecclesiastical tribunals was probably slowed by the less frequent recourse to notaries in this region. Nevertheless, soon after the Southerner Bernard Lauret advised in a handbook on prosecuting clerical criminals that "bishops had no territory and thus did not execute their own sentences," the king's attorney argued in 1496 to the Parlement of Paris that "the bishop has jurisdiction in his clergy [but] has no territory," citing Baldus and Lauret.[53] In June 1510, to make it easier for royal officials to suppress the "abuses" of church courts concerning layfolk, Louis XII commanded

[51] Lange, "Birth," 141.
[52] Isambert, IX: 298–299, 311; cited by Lea, "Excommunication," 444.
[53] Lange, "Birth," 139–140.

that "all ecclesiastical judges of our kingdom express the causes of citations in any citations henceforth issued by their courts so that cited laymen might learn whether the matter is within the competence of ecclesiastical judges."[54] Laymen could then address themselves to a royal court, which would issues letters of inhibition against the church court, short-circuiting the procedure and allowing for the invalidation of any improperly assigned spiritual sanctions.

If the practice of ecclesiastical tribunals did not change instantly, it appears (as in England) that royal courts sought increasingly after *c.* 1500 to restrict the competence of ecclesiastical courts by such means. They fined those who used them for what were now deemed improper matters and commanded ecclesiastical judges to reverse what were described as unjust excommunications through appeals *comme d'abus*. For this reason, the Provincial Council of Bourges of 1528 promised to supplicate the king to prevent royal judges from frustrating ecclesiastical jurisdiction "concerning sworn obligations in which the contractants had submitted to ecclesiastical justice, concerning the judgment of personal actions between layfolk, concerning the execution of pious bequests, concerning the inventory of clerics' movable property, and concerning the publication of *monitoires* with the names withheld."[55] At the same time, the statutes regulated excommunication for debt, prohibiting *monitoires* without specific names for amounts of less than 3st and substituting personal interdiction from churches for excommunication in the first instance.[56] This reaction was tardy: by 1528 litigants were walking away from church courts at the same time as royal courts encouraged the contestation of the Church's civil jurisdiction over layfolk. Jean Imbert noted that there were two paths to recourse in secular courts against excommunications in matters of debt prior to 1533: "first, that the excommunicated party formally appealed the publication of such censures in Parlement *comme d'abus*; second, that without appealing he requested of a competent judge cassation of the said [ecclesiastical] censure and that the said annulment (*cassation*) be published at the site of the original censure."[57] Though

[54] Guénois, *Conférence*, Tome I, Livre I, Titre IV, no.4, p. 72. The cited article, number 45 of a long ordinance, is at Isambert, XI: 595; the whole ordinance is 575–603. In the 1530s, Francis I would reiterate the call for more detailed citations before the Ordinance of Villers-Cotterêts eliminated the citation of layfolk in personal matters (which had already been proscribed in real matters).

[55] Mansi 32: 1145–1146.

[56] Mansi 32: 1146–1147.

[57] Jean Imbert, *Les Quatre Livres des Institutions forenses* (Paris: Jean Ruelle, 1552), 446; *Institutiones forenses, Galliae pene totius quae moribus regitur, communes* (Lyon: Sebastian Gryphius, 1552), 301. These remedies were extended to Brittany by the Edict of Valence in August 1536, I: 48; see Guénois, t.I, l.I, t.IV, no.4, p. 72; Isambert, 12: 513–527, omits these provisions.

Imbert mentioned that a ruling when the Parlement of Paris was on circuit at Tours in 1533 forbade royal judges "competence over [ecclesiastical] censures, *querimonies*, and excommunications," this decision went against the tenor of the Parlement's decisions over the past century, for it had ordered the reversal of unjust ecclesiastical sanctions appealed *comme d'abus*.[58] In 1539, the first articles of the Ordinance of Villers-Cotterêts deprived ecclesiastical tribunals of their capacity to cite layfolk in personal actions. By 1550, French church courts had lost competence over the crimes, the real property, and the debts of layfolk. For instance, the 1580 reformation of the custom of Brittany had removed any possibility of the excommunication of a lay debtor. The fourteenth-century, "very old" custom of Brittany provided that "clerics can proceed by citations, inhibitions, and monitions, but cannot constrain any lay debtor to pay his debts on pain of excommunication, unless he has no movable or immovable property on which the creditor may execute the debt." At the instigation, so asserted the commentator, of Anne, Duchess of Brittany (1488–1514) and Queen of France (1491–1498 and 1499–1514), the reformed custom of 1580 deleted the restrictive clause "unless …".[59] By the end of the Old Regime, it was even argued that ecclesiastical judges' lack of "real," property-based, territorial jurisdiction prohibited them from assigning monetary fines except in the form of alms.[60] Depriving the clergy of the capacity to execute even personal debts through excommunication reflected the triumph of the conviction that excommunicating debtors was inappropriate. This was, of course, fatal to the already declining practice of excommunication for debt.

The movement signifies a change in the valence of contracts and contract law, as well as in their site of enforcement. To describe it as the ethicization and secularization of contracts is insufficient, because, even as the enforcement of "naked agreements" retreated from the Church's external forum, it remained important within the internal forum, in the conferences of penitents with their confessors. In the late Middle Ages, as the complaints of the clergy of the province of Lyon in 1312

[58] The Parlement had received appeals from unjust excommunications since the mid-fourteenth century, these had led to temporal sanctions against the guilty ecclesiastical authorities rather than – as henceforth – orders to reverse the unjust excommunication: Vodola, 171 n.155 (citing the *Olim*).

[59] Bertrand d'Argentré, *Coustumes generales du pays et duché de Bretagne reformées en l'an mil cinq cents quatre-vingts. Aitiologia, sive ratiocinatio de reformandis causis* (Paris: Jacques d'Allin, 1610), Titre I, Art. VI, p. 4; cf D'Argentré, *Commentarii in patrias Britonum leges, seu Consuetudines generales antiquissimae Ducatus Britannie* (Paris: Jacques d'Allin, 1611), Tit. I, Art. VI, notae 1–3, col. 13–18. H. C. Lea ("Excommunication," 445–446) cites the *aitiologia*.

[60] J.-B. Denisart, *Collection de décisions nouvelles et de notions relatives à la jurisprudence actuelle* (Paris: veuve Desaint, 1771), 1: 261, 3: 512.

illustrate, jurisdiction over contracts was tied to the "territoriality" of a given court's competence. Ecclesiastical jurisdiction remained territorial into the sixteenth century, extending over the clergy and the laity of a given circumscription. Until then, if lay justice had made inroads in some matters, church courts were still formidable opponents wielding formidable weapons, not least the excommunication with which they enforced respect for their competence and procedures.

This is evident in the sixteenth century drive to define royal judges as the "natural judges" not just of layfolk but of real property in general. In the French version of Imbert's originally Latin *Institutions forenses*, he advises: "furthermore, if one wishes to execute the sentence of an ecclesiastical judge on the property of a priest, one must ask permission and charge to do so of the lay judge within whose jurisdiction the property lies."[61] The terminology of Imbert's Latin version is more revealing: "if the sentence of an ecclesiastical judge is to be executed on the property of a layman or clergyman, it is necessary to request permission of the lay judge who governs the territory (*territorio … praeest*) of the domicile of the condemned."[62] Though clerics arrested by lay officials were immediately to be released to "their judges," that is, the ecclesiastical judges of the "territory" of their domicile, by the middle third of the sixteenth century France's layfolk and France's soil were matters for royal judges. As Imbert's Latin makes clear, royal judges had a territory; ecclesiastical judges had only an exceptional, personal jurisdiction over the persons of clergy. That is to say, as one avocat du roi put it in 1516, "no one is born a cleric"; no one is naturally a cleric.[63] Or, as another avocat du roi is recorded having said in 1545: "the royal judge is the natural judge."[64] Humans, as Aristotle and Aquinas taught, were naturally political animals. They were therefore under the jurisdiction of their "natural judges" – the judges not of their *celestis patria* but of their earthly fatherland. In political practice as in theory, natural, once-born man rather than the man reborn in baptism was to form the subject's primary legal identity. As in the law *Cunctos populos* of Justinian's Codex (1.1.1) and as in the polities not just of German "territorial patriarchs (*Landesväter*)" or "emergency bishops (*Notbischöfe*)" but also of English "Supreme Heads"

[61] Imbert, *Institutions forenses*, 447: "D'avantage si on veult mettre a execution la sentence d'un juge ecclesiastique sur les biens d'un prestre: il fault demander permission et commission de ce faire au juge lay en la jurisdiction duquel sont lesdictz biens."

[62] Imbert, *Institutiones forenses*, 302: "Quin si adversus laicum vel clericum executio sententiae à pontificibus latae in res soli facienda sit, veniam à laico iudice qui territorio domicilii eius qui condemnatus fuit, praeest, indulgeri necesse est." "Territorio … praeest" cites almost verbatim Baldus ad Cod.1.7.9.

[63] Lange, *First French Reformation*, 100–101, 253.

[64] Lange, *First French Reformation*, 252.

or French "popes in temporal matters (*papae in temporalibus*)," religious identity was defined by a sovereign's legislative act rather than by ritual induction into the Church militant. For layfolk, priests and bishops were henceforth judges more often in the *forum internum* of the confessional than in the *forum externum* of ecclesiastical justice. Examples of this development and its legal consequences could be multiplied many times over from sources other than Imbert's handbook.

The spiritualization of the institutional Church demanded a new theorization and a new history of ecclesiastical justice. For half a millenium, the Church's jurisdiction over matters of land, of fact, and of the business of layfolk, defended through "real" sanctions such as banishment, flogging, and imprisonment as well as the fulmination of maledictory excommunications, had been defended as the only proper defense of the freedom of the Church's property and clergy from lay control. Since the eleventh century churchmen had viewed this freedom from lay control as the precondition for a "true," faithful Church and for flourishing spirituality among the clergy and the laity alike. In the sixteenth century, even before the historiographical challenge of the Magdeburg Annals and the Catholic riposte of Cardinal Baronius, we encounter a different story. In his commentary on the custom of Brittany, Bertrand d'Argentré offered a narrative of ecclesiastical history that differed from previous Gallican views. Although conciliarist canonists of the previous century had described the papacy as the source of "deformations of the ecclesiastical polity (*deformationes status ecclesie*)," they had not called into question the existence and competence of the church's court system – far from it! The Catholic d'Argentré offered a new etiological fable of the civil competence of ecclesiastical tribunals. In a section on the need for lay judges to arrest those accused of heresy subtitled "ecclesiastical judges have no territory in virtue of their spiritual power," d'Argentré listed the commentaries of the doctors on Codex 1.7.9 (*Episcopale iudicium*) that by this period justified the denial of civil competence especially over layfolk to ecclesiastical judges.[65] In a comment on the following title of the custom of Brittany, which contained the *ancienne coutume*'s qualified and the *nouvelle coutume*'s absolute incapacity of ecclesiastical judges to excommunicate layfolk, d'Argentré offered his etiology of ecclesiastical justice in a section entitled "ecclesiastical judges long ago usurped much jurisdiction":

[65] D'Argentré, Des Justices, art. 5, nota 1, col. 13: "…cum territorium nullum habeant, ratione spiritualis quidem potestatis, Quod Cy. Bald. Io. Fav. notant, l. Episcopale C. de Episc. aud. Gallus, q.176. in Stylo."

> Long ago there was a great confusion of jurisdictions and competences with respect to the law and its procedures, as the conflicts of Pierre de Cugnières (1297–1345) and Pierre Bertrand (1280–1349) indicate. Ecclesiastical judges set no limit on the growth of their competence, arrogating more and more matters to themselves on the pretext of sin, of the Sacrament, and of evangelical denunciation ... Since the attractive force of such matters is so great that in its broadest sense everything in every way concerns contracts or exchange (*contractus et ... commercia*), ecclesiastical judges used inhibitions and the fear of excommunication against secular judges, lest they try the matter at the root of the inhibition. Only lately have we [Bretons] been freed of this great terror of excommunication, which the French long ago cast aside ... An ecclesiastical judge cannot prohibit a secular judge cognition of a case. Indeed, the relationship having changed, a secular judge may prohibit an ecclesiastical judge cognition of a case ... if he shall have infringed upon the other's competence ... What ecclesiastical judges once did is now wholly abolished, as when they excommunicated secular judges, which today no one would dare.[66]

D'Argentré's history, if not entirely accurate, astutely identifies contracts as the basis of the unmerited expansion of ecclesiastical jurisdiction.[67] Contracts and commerce were everywhere but had in his day been reclaimed by the secular courts. In the following section, d'Argentré turned his focus to the present day, explaining how this unmerited

[66] D'Argentré, Des Justices, art. 6, nota 1, col. 15–16: "Magna olim perturbatio fuit Iurisdictionum et potestatum in exercendo iure et legis actionibus, quod Eduensis et Cunerij conflictationes indicant: nec Iudices Ecclesiastici modum ponebant incrementis cognitionum alias atque alias ad se trahentes, sub obtentu peccati, Sacramenti, et Evangelicae denunciationis, de qua in c. novit ext. de iud. Quare rerum tanta vis ac potestas est, ut infinita comprehensione omnes omnino contractus contineant, et commercia, in eum usum testatas denunciationes, hoc est, inhibitiones repererant, quae iudicibus civilibus intenderentur: ne sibi illi ullam, qua de re visum inhibentibus esset, cognitionem sumerent, addito excommunicationis metu. Magnus is terror, quem tamen iam olim Franci exuerant, nostri serius manumissi ... Nam ut quisque litigator cognitionem Ecclesiastici quaque de re praetulerat, mittebat Ecclesiasticus protinus Apparitorem ad civilem iudicem, qui cognitionem interdiceret, hoc est, inhiberet, donec Ecclesiasticus de potestate aut competentia decrevisset, ille veluti ictus sydere sistebat pavidus cursum coeptae litis, quin ne potestate quidem cognoscendi facta audebat pergere, si erat appellatum ... Sed ea iampridem exolvere, nec ullo modo potest iudex Ecclesiasticus inhibere iudici civili. Contra versa facie inhiberi Ecclesiastico ab civili, si causa postulat, usitatum est, si se alienae cognitioni interserit, quod Lud. Regis Ord. anno 1512. art. 45 est sancitum, et alia Francis. I. anno 1536. art. 50 ... Quare apparet longo ab errore sero reductos in viam iudices civiles, non segniter fines suos ex eo tempore tutatos esse, vereor ne etiam terminum exararent. Nam quod illis olim quoque usitatum erat, plane abolitum, ut iudices civiles excommunicarent, quod iam nemo audet, et extat ea de re irrogatum Regi Franco privilegium Clement. 5. ea extravaganti quae incipit [meruit] Meminit Boër. decis. 114. Feraldus in privileg. regni privileg. 6. ubi complura aresta congerit in eam rem lata adversus Episcopos, Gallus, q.5. Arrestum in Stylo Parlam. 10. part. 7. et part. 6. art. 40. et 69. Degras. lib. 2. iure 9. meminit pragmat. tit. de causis in fin. Guid. Papae, decis. 346."

[67] D'Argentré is more restrictive than Hostiensis, who feared "sic ratione peccati quasi omnis causa coram iudice ecclesiastico agi potest," cited in Landau, "Pacta," 471 n.65.

expansion had been beaten back. To the question of "whether someone might contractually obligate himself on pain of excommunication," d'Argentré responded that "article two of the Ordinance of Francis I of 1539 prohibits a layman from submitting his [civil] matter to an ecclesiastical judge. For this reason the long usurpatory letters of *nisi* are obsolete."[68] For d'Argentré, and for his contemporaries, society was filled with commerce (*commercium*) and transactions or exchange (*commercia*). It was just that they no longer viewed these as matters for ecclesiastical justice, except as at Montivilliers with respect to the debts of those claiming clerical immunity. The following section will examine the "contractual society" in this light. D'Argentré's commentary on one of France's customs exposes the rationale undergirding the sixteenth-century decline of ecclesiastical jurisdiction over contracts, crystallized in France through the Ordinance ofVillers-Cotterêts of 1539: ecclesiastical justice was simply being returned to its proper competence. These developments are but another aspect of the religious, ecclesiastical, and legal reform – the implementations of so many different visions of the primitive Church – that characterized the Age of Reformations.

In the same period, however, the king of France's courts reversed the putative usurpation of ecclesiastical courts by transforming spiritual sanctions into ancillary sanctions for their own courts. Between the two last sections cited from d'Argentré's commentary on the customs of Brittany comes a section that begins "all may use canonical monitions, and excommunicate."[69] For, just as ecclesiastical justice was transformed into the exceptional jurisdiction it would be until the Revolution and indeed afterward, lay courts in France effectively usurped control over the issue of ecclesiastical sanctions. Not only did they order the reversal of putatively unjust excommunications, thereby depriving ecclesiastical courts of any real capacity to defend their jurisdiction against lay infringement, but they began to use ecclesiastical sanctions for their own purposes. The *monitoire à fin de révélations* is a significant institution, revealing the nature of the seismic shift taking place across Europe during the Age of the Reformations from caritative to property-based ethics of exchange. Through this procedure, based on the denunciation of an aggrieved party, royal officials commanded parish priests to warn their flocks to disclose what they knew of a theft or other crime on pain

68 D'Argentré, Des Justices, art. 6, nota 3, col. 17: "an quisquam per contractum sese possit in excommunicationem inducere, stipulatione … nullo modo laicus Ecclesiastici cognitionem prorogare, nec se ei summittere possit, vetante Ord. Francis. I. Regis anno 1539. art. 2. Quare usurpatae pridem obligationes de nisi antiquatae."

69 D'Argentré, Des Justices, art. 6, nota 2, col. 16: "Monere omnes possunt, qui et excommunicare."

of excommunication. By the eighteenth century, "the abuse which had been made of it" brought the *monitoire à fin de révélations* and excommunication more generally into "general discredit."[70] Where the Church had once deployed spiritual sanctions to preserve the confidence on which day-to-day transactions – both trade and, as we shall see, noncommercial social relations – rested, under the Old Regime the Church the threat of excommunication was deployed to reveal the whereabouts of stolen property. Rather than binding society together, the justice of the early modern Gallican church – like the apparatus of the Old Regime State, if one views parish priests as the lowest-level royal officials (which they effectively were) – protected property. As in the example from Scotland with which I ended the previous chapter, Old Regime parish priests denounced from the pulpit not those who broke faith with other believers, but those who stole. Theft, appropriately, rather than mendacity or avarice, was the target of excommunication in early modern France. It was the threat to private property, rather than the breach of faith, that was culpable. The shift from caritative to property-based ethics of exchange meant that charity henceforth referred primarily not to exchange animated by Christian morality than to handouts for the "deserving" poor. At the same time, justice became more formal than equitable, being "increasingly defined only very minimally as the keeping of promises," in Muldrew's description.[71] The finality of the market was being redirected from a supernatural to a this-worldly finality.

By 1600, the medieval situation, in which Europe's secular princes acted (with some exaggeration) as the Church's police departments, had been reversed.[72] Within each polity, the churches functioned as the States' religion departments. This is how ecclesiastical circumscriptions came to concern only clerical education and sociability by the eighteenth century. With the exception of baptisms, marriages, or testaments, their competence was almost exclusively clerical. It did not hurt that the general thrust of Tridentine reforms, late in coming to France, was to ethicize moral deportment and to divorce it from the dogmatic claims and ritual practices of the Catholic Church. Nor was the disdain for worldly, uncommitted, irrelevant prelates and their abuse of their power as gatekeepers to the sacraments in eighteenth-century quarrels over Jansenism unrelated to this development. When in the sixteenth century we see contracts escape ecclesiastical jurisdiction and morals enter the realm of ethics and secular law, we perceive the incipient disembedding

[70] Dupont, *Les monitoires*, 45.
[71] Muldrew, *The Economy of Obligation*, 325.
[72] J. N. Figgis, *Studies of Political Thought from Gerson to Grotius* (Cambridge: Cambridge University Press, 1907), 4.

or privatization of religion, the beginning of its migration out of the economy and into the private lives of believers.

This development was long in coming. The distinction between the Church as a spiritual entity and as a civil authority may have emerged through the incoherence of political and theological elements in late thirteenth-century ecclesiology, and was foreshadowed by Peter John Olivi's comment that "every contract that is contrary to charity and to society's good is illicit."[73] The distinction between the Church as a religious body and a political body was evident in Cajetan's comment that Christians are subject to the pope not "as men (*inquantum homines*)" but "as Christians (*inquantum fideles*)."[74] It was likewise evident to Cajetan's opponent and younger contemporary Jacques Almain that the Church was not a polity. Almain distinguished between spiritual and temporal power so as to deny it to the pope and to the Church more broadly:

> The Church's power to judge (*potestas ecclesiastica jurisdictionis*) ... is the capacity given supernaturally and specially given by Christ to the apostles, disciples, and their legitimate successors for the governance of the Church militant according to the precepts of the Gospel (*leges evangelicas*) to the end of eternal salvation ... But lay or secular power [to judge] is the capacity lawfully given by the people through hereditary succession or by election to one or many for the governance of the community in civil matters according to civil laws to the end of peaceful coexistence.[75]

Almain spoke not of priests' power of order but of popes' power of jurisdiction, defining it in such a way as to make authority within the Church different from any other earthly power. His implication was that the Church had no power over civil matters or with respect to civil laws. This was momentous with respect to civil contracts.

Martin Luther actualized the distinction between the Church's licit spiritual authority and illicit civil authority in matters of contract: "but where there are no [true] Christians, then shall the secular authority force each to pay what he has borrowed."[76] Bad Christians had to be

[73] Wilks, *Problem*; cited in Prodi, *Settimo*, 158: "omnis contractus qui est contra bonum caritatis et societatis est illicitum."

[74] Cited in Prodi, *Settimo*, 213.

[75] Jacques Almain, "De potestate ecclesiastica," in *Aurea clarissimi et acutissimi Doctoris theologi Magistri Jacobi Almain Senonensis opuscula* (Paris: Gilles de Gourmont, 1518), 1r: "Potestas ecclesiastica iurisdictionis: ut dicit de Gersono/ est potestas a Christo/ apostolis/ discipulis/ et eorum legitimis successoribus supernaturaliter et specialiter tradita ad edificationem ecclesie militantis secundum leges evangelicas/ pro consequutione felicitatis eterne ... Sed potestas laica sive secularis/ est potestas a populo ex successione hereditaria vel ex electione alicui vel aliquibus tradita regulariter ad edificationem communitatis quantum ad res civiles secundum leges civiles/ pro consequutione habitationis pacifice."

[76] Cited in Prodi, *Settimo*, 277. Luther, "Von Kaufshandlung und Wucher" (1524), *Luthers Werke*, 15: 302: "So were nu das borgen eyn feyn ding, wo es unter den Christen

coerced to justice by the secular and not by the ecclesiastical authorities. True Christians had no need of coercion, as God's grace permitted them to honor their debts without constraint as a mark of their inner freedom. The Fathers of Trent had (for the most part) different theology, but agreed with Luther that contracts were a matter for worldly authority, even though they still believed that the regulation of contracts lay within the scope of canon law, which was for them a mixed human and divine law. In the discussions over the decree *Tametsi* concerning clandestine marriage and the marriage of minors, Melchior Cano and others argued that the Church could dissolve clandestine marriages without "changing" an unchanging sacrament, as the civil contract, the unbreakable exchange of consent was the material or substance of marriage and the sacrament the form. This would also classify unwitnessed, unblessed exchanges of marital promises as potentially valid contracts if not necessarily valid sacraments.[77] By demanding that couples marry before a priest and witnesses, the Church was therefore simply exercising its legislative capacity in a matter of civil, positive, mutable law. They believed that they were changing not the sacrament of marriage, simply the conditions of the underlying contract. Not all were convinced that the regulation of the marriage contract was a matter for the Council of Trent, though they may have agreed with the Fathers' reasoning that the substance of marriage was a civil contract subject to positive law. In France, the Gallican argument went, that legislative power belonged to the king.[78] As a result, the kings of France reshaped marriage law in the Edict on Clandestine Marriages (1557), the Edict of Second Marriages (1560), and in other laws throughout the early modern period, without formally receiving the decrees of Trent.[79] Protestant monarchs and judiciaries simply ignored *Tametsi*, as in England, which abided by pre-Tridentine marriage law until Lord Hardwicke's Marriage Act of 1753.

The sixteenth-century trend was general: contracts were a matter for civil authorities, not ecclesiastical ones. The Body of Christ was becoming "civil society." Civil society was contractual society. In 1421 Jean

geschehe, da wurde eyn iglicher gerne widdergeben was er geborget hette … Denn Christen sind brueder, und eyner lest den andern nicht … Aber wo nicht Christen sind, da soll die weltliche oberkeyt treyben, das der bezale was er geborget hat."

77 Philip L. Reynolds, "Marrying and Its Documentation in Pre-Modern Europe: Consent, Celebration, and Property," in Reynolds and John Witte (eds.), *To Have and to Hold: Marrying and Its Documentation in Western Christendom, 400–1600* (Cambridge: Cambridge University Press, 2007), 1–42, esp. 17.

78 As Almain said (De pot. eccl., 1): "in dicendo ius debet [ecclesiastica potestas] uti legibus evangelicis ecclesiasticis et non civilibus."

79 Hanley, "Engendering"; Matthew Gerber, "Family, the State, and the Law in Early Modern and Revolutionary France," *History Compass* 7:2 (2009), 474–499.

Gerson lamented exchange as a consequence of original sin, that is, as a consequence of life in post-lapsarian human society: "Woe unto you sons of Adam after his sin, who must live by obligating yourselves in civil contracts!"[80] Civil litigation reflected the fact that humans had to contract to survive and that the law provided one way of measuring the "credit" that determined which credit relationships might be available under which terms to which borrowers. Civil suits over debt and over property made and unmade litigants' credit. As the "land wars" of the late Middle Ages passed from forcible entry and outright battle into courtrooms, and contractual disputes from distraint of chattels or assault into litigation, early modern Europeans sought to build their reputations by successfully pursuing, delaying, and manipulating the civil procedure of secular courts. The fact that more debts and more property transfers were recorded by scriveners or notaries only encouraged this shift in the sites of credit-negotiation that generated (one ventures conservatively to say) a five-fold increase in the amount of civil litigation over the sixteenth century.

Commercium and *mercatio*/*Commerce* and *marchandise*

Parol and privately recorded debts existed within a realm of contract in which certain types of obliging were acceptable – transactions categorized in Latin as *commercium* or in French as *commerce* – and others – those categorized in French as *marchandise* or in Latin perhaps as *simonia* when used in an inappropriate arena by clerics and as *mercatio* or even *venalitas* when used inappropriately by kings, nobles, or nonmerchants – were not. As Émile Benveniste observed, commercial trading is an "occupation without a name" in Indo-European languages: from *ascholía*, *pragma*, *negotium*, *affaires*, to *business* the concept is compounded of negatives or circumlocutions.[81] In late medieval France, *marchandise* was the technical, common term for the activity of merchants.[82] This activity was

80 Cited in Prodi, *Settimo*, 180: "Sed vae filiis Adam post peccatum, quos oportet transire per viam contractuum civilium."

81 Benveniste, "Chapter 11: An Occupation without a Name – Commerce," in *Indo-European Language and Society* (Coral Gables: University of Miami Press, 1973), http://chs.harvard.edu/wa/pageR?tn=ArticleWrapper&bdc=12&mn=3926.

82 Louis XI's attempt to permit nobles, ecclesiastics, and royal officers to trade without losing their status noted "que tous les royaumes, pays ou régions ou le fait de la marchandise est plus commune et plus frequente sont les plus riches et les plus abondans, et par le moyen de la négociation et conduicte tant par mer que par terre des gros et puissans marchands," cited in Jean-Philippe Genet, "L'État de la fin du Moyen Âge et le concept d'espace économique," in B. Chevalier and P. Contamine (eds.), *La France de la fin du XVe siècle. Renouveau et apogée* (Paris: Éditions du CNRS, 1985), 31–49, at 43.

devalued for other social groups, as trading caused nobles to lose their status.[83] In contrast to the word *marchandise*, the word *commercium* or *commerce* was not inevitably tied to the activity of merchants. Still in the 1694 Dictionary of the *Académie française*, the second sense of "commerce" remained "regular conversation and intercourse with someone, whether for company alone or also for some transactions (*communication et correspondance ordinaire avec quelqu'un, soit pour la société seulement, soit aussi pour quelques affaires*)." Jean Nicot's 1606 *Thresor de la langue françoyse* emphasizing the technical activity of merchants in defining "la marchandise" as "merchandise (*merx*)," "commerce (*commercium*)," "dealing (*mercatio*)," "trade (*mercatura*)," or "bargaining (*negotiatio*)."[84]

At the end of the Middle Ages, *commerce* had a far more general meaning along the lines of *permutatio* or *commutatio*, an exchange that may have involved obligation if not commensurate reward. This is apparent from, to draw an example from an author whom we have already encountered, Jacques Almain's explanation of Anselm's theory of Christ's atonement for sinful humanity's unlimited offense – and therefore debt – to God: "it is certain that man incurs guilt – an obligation – for each sin, for he incurs not an obligation toward as good an act as his sin was evil but an obligation toward eternal suffering." Thus, even though "according to [God's] rigorous justice, satisfaction [for sin] is not the performance of a proportionally good act but is had according to God's consent to accept our merits together with that of Christ's passion (*secundum acceptationem Dei ... iuncta passione Christi*)."[85] Indeed, Almain's immediate predecessor Gabriel Biel (†1495) wrote that "for though God can be no one's debtor of necessity, he can nevertheless of his own free will make himself our debtor by promising such a reward for such acts."[86] God's

[83] Mathieu Arnoux has proposed that "l'exclusion du travail de la sphère de l'honorabilité," that is, *dérogation* from noble status for trade signals, along with the reinvention of slavery as an economic instrument, the transition from the Middle Ages to the early modern period: "Croissance et crises dans le monde médiéval XIe-XVe siècle. Réflexions et pistes de recherche," *Cahiers du monde russe* 46:1 (2005), 115–132, at 129. Yet still in 1530 could a bourgeois of Montivilliers be called *honnête homme*: as for Zacharias Petit: ADSM G 5273, Harfleur, 1518.

[84] ARTFL Dictionnaires d'autrefois, http://artfl-project.uchicago.edu/node/17 (26.02.2014).

[85] Almain, "De penitentia," in *Aurea opuscula*, De satisfactione, dist.xv, q.1, f. 20r-v: "Certum est quod per omne peccatum homo incurrit reatum. id est obligationem: et non incurrit obligationem ad actum eque bonum sicut actus est malus: sed incurrit obligationem ad penam eternam: ergo cum ratione talis offense non incurrat obligationem ad actum eque bonum sed ad penam eternam/ ergo secundum rigorosam iusticiam satisfactio non est redditio actus eque boni: sed secundum acceptationem dei ... iuncta passione Christi."

[86] Cited in Bernd Hamm, *Promissio, Pactum, Ordinatio. Freiheit und Selbstbindung Gottes in der scholastischen Gnadenslehre* (Tübingen: J. C. B. Mohr, 1977), 372 n.135: "Nam licet deus nullius debitor esse possit ex natura rei, potest tamen se facere debitorem nostrum ex sua libera voluntate nobis promittendo pro talibus actibus tantum praemium." If

consent to an unequal transaction is not that of merchants treating with each other, but then again even putatively equal transactions often involve asymmetries of power.[87] Far more common at the end of the Middle Ages was the mutual and unequal obligation of lord and subject, patron and client, lessor and lessee, obligor and obligee. Unequal relationships of power lurk in all transactions on credit.

This is because credit was never simply a financial matter. It was strongly moral and irretrievably tied up in hierarchical social relations, as Claire Crowston has demonstrated for the eighteenth-century fashion industry. Laurence Fontaine has proposed that credit in early modern Europe operated according to two logics: the mercantile, egalitarian logic of the market and the aristocratic logic of the gift expressing the innate liberality and honor of the well-born. In either case, obligation established one's membership within a community, whether in laterally oriented communities of traders and consumers or in hierarchically oriented chains of patrons and clients. At the end of the Middle Ages, complicated bead pardons, more frequent quotidian financial accounting, and litigation for debt imply an expansion of numeracy.[88] At the same time, Europeans' horizons expanded: by 1550 Norman ships ranged from Labrador to Brazil to West Africa: it was no longer for merchants only a matter of calculating the values of merchandise in English and French coins. All of this encouraged a more numerate, abstract manner of thinking that tended to strip the veil of aristocratic gift logic (or of Christian gift logic[89]) from social relationships, baring the transactional mentality that united king and peasant, often in opposition to scapegoated populations or individuals seen as bearers of this mentality.[90]

generalized from indulgences to, say, the promise of salvation to believers, this rationale could justify both late medieval "counting piety" and proto-Lutheran Staupitzian fideism.

[87] See Benveniste's examination (*Indo-European Language and Society*, 15: Credence and Belief, see n.72 for the URL) of the etymology of the word "credit," in which he proposes that the Indo-European root **kred* "may be some kind of 'pledge,' or 'stake,' something material but which also involves personal feeling, a notion invested with magic power which all men possess" given with the expectation of a reward and that such relations of "credit" were "first established between men and the gods, and later came to be established between men." Latin "*fides est mihi apud quemquam*"; Sanskrit "*srad te dadhami.*" Fontaine's distinction between aristocratic and mercantile logics of credit may therefore be overdrawn.

[88] Swanson, *Indulgences*, 269–277.

[89] Mt. 10:8: "freely ye have received, freely give (*gratis accepistis, gratis date*)"; Lk. 6: 35: "lend, hoping for nothing again (*mutuum date, nihil inde sperantes*)."

[90] Toby Green has perceptively analyzed this logic at work with respect to the New Christian traders of Portuguese West Africa in the fifteenth and sixteenth centuries: *The Rise of the Trans-Atlantic Slave Trade in Western Africa, 1300–1589* (Cambridge: Cambridge University Press, 2012). In France, which expelled its Jews in 1394, one thinks of the periodic *chambres de justice* set up to harass royal financiers (e.g., Jacques de Beaune,

Mollat has advised perceptively with respect to the famous merchant and privateer Jean Ango the Younger: "We ought to invert the common portrayal of Ango dealing as an equal with kings and say on the contrary that Jean Ango, king of spices, bargained with [the king of Portugal] like a merchant" concerning indemnities for piracy committed by and against Ango's ships.[91] Had Mollat written in the sixteenth century, he might have written that the king of Portugal unworthily merchantized (*marchandait*) with the great merchant from Dieppe. The following section explores the positive aspects of exchange and obligation – *commercium* – and their negative (negative, that is to say, unless this concerned the already "vile" activity of merchants[92]) aspects – *marchandise*.

As Bertrand d'Argentré elegantly noted in the passage cited earlier, "most broadly understood, all matters in every respect involve contracts and exchanges of some sort (*contractus ... et commercia*)." Like Rabelais's giant, d'Argentré described credit and commerce as omnipresent, tying together society. If ecclesiastical jurisdiction extended over all contracts, no aspect of social life would escape it. Was not obligation, was not dependence, was not sworn faith the *vinculum humane societatis*?[93] Without debt, without obligation, according to Pantagruel, who indeed would "wake every morning to pray God for your health and prosperity?" Such ties existed in a world in which good deeds came in response to a sense of obligation, whether for past or for hoped-for, future services. In technical terms, the hope was that non-synallagmatic, nonreciprocal, unilateral contracts (such as a gift or the merits acquired by a repentant sinner) would become synallagmatic, reciprocal, or bilateral contracts. In the religious sphere, this is a clearly noted aspect of late medieval quantitative piety. If baptism wiped out the "debt" of original

baron de Semblançay, executed in 1527) or of the allegations against the Archbishop of Lyon described below.

91 Mollat, *Le commerce*, 505.

92 Albrecht Cordes has pointed out that medieval transnational commercial law was the law of a privileged status or occupational group, "merchants' justice (*ius mercatorum*)" rather than "mercantile law (*lex mercatoria*)": "The Search for a Medieval *Lex mercatoria*," *Oxford Comparative Law Forum* (2003), and in German "Auf der Suche nach der Rechtswirklichkeit der mittelalterlichen Lex mercatoria," *Zeitschrift der Savigny-Stiftung für Rechtsgeschichte, Germanistische Abteilung* 118 (2001), 168–184; see too Dave De Ruysscher, "La *lex mercatoria* contextualisée: tracer son parcours intellectuel," *Revue historique de droit français et étranger* 90:4 (2012), 499–515.

93 It is not otiose to cite Martin of Braga: "iustitia non nostra constitutio, sed divina lex et vinculum societatis humanae" (*Formula honestae vitae, sive de quatuor virtutibus consarcinatio* (Basel, 1545), 26; cited in Hans Kelsen, "Die Staatslehre von Dante Alighieri," in *Hans Kelsens Werke*, Matthias Jestaedt (ed.) (Vienna/Leipzig: Hans Deuticke, 1905; repr. Tübingen: Mohr/Siebeck, 2007), I: 134–300, at 236), for "iustitia est constans et perpetua voluntas ius suum cuique tribuendi" (Dig. 1.1.10). Did not obligations create enforceable rights or *iura*: "obligatio est iuris vinculum" (Inst. 3.13)?

sin, there remained countless debts perhaps omitted from confession or not fully atoned. Chantry priests, the "corpse-eaters" (*Totenfresser*) of Protestant polemic, consequently said masses for the souls of those who had endowed their salaries, for those who had totted up the prospective benefits accruing from anniversary masses, hoping thereby to oblige God to accept this vicarious atonement for the debt of their sins, making a unilateral into a bilateral contract. So, yes, chantry priests "ate" of the dead, offering vicarious atonement in exchange for subsistence wages. Until the sixteenth century, however, very few found this form of sacred commerce to be unacceptable, perhaps because the accounting could never be sure. As the young Luther feared, would God accept his merits? When would the sinner's meritorious acts suffice? When might the sinner cross over from repaying his debt into obliging God to save him?

Such relations are also evident in the secular realm. In the age of bastard feudalism and in the age of clientage, loyalty and service came in exchange for material benefits. If a pious endowment was a contract of a sort, so too were the homages, the alliances, the indentures, and the unwritten faith in somebody or credit with somebody that bound together superiors, peers, and inferiors. Although we might make less of a distinction between "classic" feudal relations as embodied in fiefs in land and those constituted by *fief-rentes*,[94] and money fiefs, which also entailed the exchange of homage and loyalty for a lump sum or annual payment, alliances and pensions are different. Professions of alliance and friendship cannot hide the transactional nature of the relationship created by such agreements. For instance, Jean, bastard of Orléans and Count of Périgord, allied with Jean I, Count of Foix, in 1434 in these terms:

> We, Jean, bastard of Orléans and count of Périgord, make known to all who shall see these letters that, as true love and union are more pleasing than anything to God and are a true good (*perfection de bien*), expecting as well the great good that might come to the king our sovereign lord, his kingdom, and his authority through the good friendship and concord between us and the honored lord, my lord Jean, count of Foix and Bigorre our godfather: of our certain knowledge and consent have today by these letters made with my said lord of Foix and godfather good, durable, loving and loyal friendship, alliance, and confederation to last all our lives and against all persons in the word of whatever estate or condition, save my lord the duke of Orléans and my lord the count of Angoulême my brother in cases which concern them personally, otherwise not. We have sworn and promised, we swear and promise to God our creator on the holy Gospels and true cross because we have touched them and personally sworn faith on our honor and loyalty that from this day forward we shall be to my said lord of Foix and

[94] Dirk Heirbaut, "The *Fief-Rente*: A New Evaluation Based on Flemish Sources: 1000–1305," *Tijdschrift voor Rechtsgeschiedenis* 67:1 (1999), 1–37.

our godfather good, perfect, and loyal relative, friend and ally, and shall have his friends for our friends and his enemies for our enemies, save the persons above excepted.[95]

If the benefit of alliance was not here explicitly monetized, it was nevertheless held out in the promises presumably of military and legal assistance between the Bastard of Orléans and the Count of Foix. The promise of mutual assistance, moreover, applied not just to the persons of the principals, but to their family, their clients, their affinity, their "friends" in the medieval sense. It is further to be noted that this obligation would benefit not just the two parties involved but the king and the kingdom, encouraging "true love," "union," and "concord" among the king of France's subjects. Here we encounter the reality of Prodi's late medieval "*società giurata*," in which subjects were bound to each other and to the king (hence the clauses of exception in this and in the following example). No less than oaths bound together urban communes, alliances and professions of obligation united the king's subjects, particularly his greatest ones, and tied together late medieval kingdoms. It is no coincidence that the struggle of royal governments to suppress bastard feudalism, clientelism, the wearing of livery, or the bearing of arms by nonnobles coincided with the sixteenth-century "naturalization" of membership in the political community. The natural subjection of residents of a territory to their natural lord the king or prince replaced more explicitly contractual obligations. As for Bodin or Hobbes, this natural subjection was presumed, just as the adhesion of the baptized to their confession was presumed – and elided any actual consent.[96] With the exception of resistance theorists, social contract theory justified subjects' natural, civil subordination to the sovereign. Violations of this natural obligation were the capital crimes of treason, of secular heresy or apostasy in polities reimagined on an ecclesiological model.

Some late medieval alliances were more explicitly transactional, as in the following alliance of 1439 between Aymerigon d'Estissac and Gaston IV, Count of Foix:

May all know that I, Aymerigon, lord of Estissac in Périgord, knight, for the great affection that I had in the past for the late high and powerful lord, my lord Jean of good memory count of Foix and Bigorre, and for his house (*son hostel*), had made

[95] P. S. Lewis, "Decayed and Non-Feudalism in Later Medieval France," in *Essays in Later Medieval French History* (London: The Hambledon Press, 1985), 41–68, in Appendix 2: 63–64.

[96] The king of England commanded the keeping of parish registers of baptism from 1538 and the king of France from 1539, signaling how baptism marked entrance into the religious and political communities now defined by more universal subjection to their authority.

with him certain alliances … wishing to continue the goodwill and affection that I had to him and to his house, from today forward of my free will and certain knowledge make myself by these letters your ally, servant, and partisan (*valledeur*), and have promised and sworn to you, high and mighty lord Gaston count of Foix and Bigorre, promise and swear on the holy Gospels of God and on the faith and oath of my body and on my honor that henceforth and for my whole life I shall be the good and loyal ally, servant, and partisan of you and of your house. I shall defend and guard your person and your honor and wellbeing. I shall seek to prevent your misfortune, dishonor, and injury (*dommaige*) with all my power and knowledge; and if any contrary thing should come to my knowledge, I shall inform you of it as quickly as possible by letter or by message. Also, should any person or persons make war or wish to make war or dispute against you, I shall aid you with all my power and with all those who wish to aid me … against all save the king of France my sovereign lord, my lord the dauphin of Viennois his son, and my lord the duke of Orléans. Which things I have promised and sworn for my whole life, as is said, as much of my free will as because you have promised and sworn to be my good and true lord and friend and to aid me, if needed, as is more plainly contained in your letters patent signed with your hand and sealed with your seal, and also because you have given me five hundred *moutons d'or* in a lump sum and promised three hundred *moutons* in annual pension.[97]

These were not trifling and courtly pleasantries. In the southwest of France in the 1430s and 1440s, alliances amounted to promises to go to war along with one's own allies and clients. They put one's person, wealth, family, and possessions at risk. Of course, Aymerigon d'Estissac gained the "good lordship" of the count of Foix, meaning the count's support in war, in litigation, and in whatever other matters might arise. The lump sum payment of 500 *moutons d'or* and annuity of 300 *moutons d'or* (reckoning 32s 6dt per *mouton*) yielded d'Estissac 812£ 10st initially and 487£ 10st each year thereafter. This may well have been equivalent to d'Estissac's annual revenues. (If one considers that the counts of Foix themselves took pensions from the king of France, one can see here how the regressive redistribution of royal revenues helped to firm up the lines of the French polity at the end of the Middle Ages.) In any case, the parties to such alliances – to such contracts of mutual aid – "covenanted," to use the appropriate English term, creating future obligations. Were Aymerigon d'Estissac to hear of a plot against Gaston de Foix, he would be obliged to inform him. In return, the count of Foix would be obliged to him in some unquantifiable way. Aristocrats were as much bound by ties of debt and credit, if not explicitly by monetary obligations – though duties of hospitality and lending were surely included in these contracts of friendship –, as their inferiors were bound by debts and credits in kind and in money. Though these obligations might be couched in what

[97] Lewis, "Decayed and Non-Feudalism," in *Essays*, Appendix 8, 67–68.

Fontaine calls an "aristocratic" language of gift and liberality, these were obligations as serious as any farmer's purchase on credit. At the top of the social hierarchy, the Lord of Estissac's credit required him both to go to war for his "good lord" of Foix and to demand "good lordship" if necessary in return. At a less elevated level, (to take an example we have seen) in the summer of 1521 Jean Boudin excommunicated and then aggravated Guillaume Reboursel for 185 lbs of undelivered summer butter so as to preserve his credit.

Contemporaries were quite clear that one had to give in order to receive: *do ut des, facio ut facias* ...[98] This was the "commerce" that bound together members of the Body of Christ. As anthropologists would remind historians, "gifts" describe relatively open-ended transactions. As Valentin Groebner has observed, "[a]n effective gift was (and is) one that produces ties through ambiguity."[99] In a way, the late medieval king *had* to give pensions in order to claim the loyalty and the taxes – often called "gifts" to their good lord – of his subjects, particularly of his elevated subjects.[100] Mikhael Harsgor's comments on this subject are chronologically and geographically apt:

> Service entailed both obligation and reward. The reward, for the king's councillors, was not, however, represented only by material gifts and offices; it was understood to include the king's protection of these persons. If this royal protection was not as apparent as the councillor expected, he protested. The duke of Albany, member of Louis XII's council, considered himself frustrated because he could not secure the recognition of rights to the lucrative *jugerie* of Lauragais that he had inherited as the result of the king's gift to his father-in-law. As his opponent's *avocats* asserted that the king had had no cause to make such a gift, it is revealing to let the duke of Albany respond in the words of his *avocat* Disomme: 'if kings did not observe their contracts they would be outside of human commerce (*extra commercium hominum*), for they could no longer find anyone who would contract with them.' A general strike of the great lords of the Council would have deprived the Crown of its guiding lights. Respecting and rewarding their services, in this case giving the duke of Albany the *jugerie* of Lauragais, meant that they would serve the monarchy.[101]

[98] Alternately, with respect to colloquy-style prayers: *da quia dedi* or *da quia dedisti*: Reinburg, 152–153.

[99] Valentin Groebner, *Liquid Assets, Dangerous Gifts. Presents and Politics at the End of the Middle Ages*, Pamela Selwyn (trans.), (Philadephia: University of Pennsylvania Press, 2002), 157.

[100] Alain Guéry, "Le roi dépensier. Le don, la contrainte et l'origine du système financier de la monarchie française d'Ancien Régime." *Annales ESC* 39: 6 (1984), 1241–1269.

[101] Harsgor, IV: 2135. The cited passage comes from the plaidoiries matinées of the Parlement of Paris from November 13, 1518 to April 21, 1519: X^{1a}4863, f. 298: "si les Roys n'entretenoient leurs contractz ils seroient *extra commercium hominum*, car ilz ne trouveroient personne pour contracter avec eulx."

This is perhaps a bit naïve, as even the bloodless, incorruptible Weberian bureaucrats who serve as implicit counterfoils to the venal servants of premodern states are rewarded with considerable perquisites. Late medieval magnates were expected to give – and expected to receive – liberally: Philippe de Mezières lamented how magnates approached royal officers, saying: "for your great bravery, virtue, or for our recent acquaintance, and principally so that you preserve me in the grace and love of my Lord the King, and that I be often informed by you of the wishes and commands of my Lord the King, I give you 500, 1,000, or 2,000 *francs* [annually] as long as you shall live; and if you shall serve me well, more still shall I give you."[102]

Peter Lewis has therefore characterized the task of the late medieval monarch in such a situation as one of calculating service and reward within the constraints of his budget: "What does a king think about all day? The answer is his relations with the princes his neighbours and the princes his subjects: treaties, but preferably not battles. Otherwise he presides over a patronage system working through the administrative system: an informal system working through a formal system."[103] Not unreasonably, it appears that late medieval monarchs were careful to sit down with their treasurers to calculate the amount of pensions, 35 percent of Louis XI's net income in 1470.[104] Kings assigned pensions with an awareness of potential obligation, both their own obligations for past services and the hoped-for sense of obligation that would drive pensioners to offer services, or further services. In the former category must surely be placed, for example, "Ysabeau, widow of Pic Farragut from Rousillon, with a pension of 200 livres for the upkeep of herself and her children in 1476–1479," which pension was inherited by her son Fortevent in 1481–1482.[105] In the latter category must be placed the king's contemporaneous pensions to each of France's bailiffs and seneschals. Drawing such distinctions between rewards for service and enticements to service may not be feasible, however. Where does one draw such a distinction for prelates in the king's service who cumulated benefices bestowed upon them by the king? Surely many of them had long been loyal servants. Equally surely the king hoped from further services, in the same way that he may have hoped to receive further services from Fortevent Farragut at the same time as he repaid the obligation presumably created by some service of Fortevent's father. Obligation bound the king to his subjects,

102 Lewis, "Of Breton Alliances and Other Matters," in *Essays*, 69–90, at 69.
103 Lewis, "France and England: The Growth of the Nation State," in *Essays*, 235–239, at 238.
104 Lewis, "The Pensioners of Louis XI," in *Essays*, 91–104, at 93.
105 Lewis, "The Pensioners of Louis XI," in *Essays*, 100.

as it bound them to him. They were as indebted to their sovereign lord as he was to them.[106] The Hundred Years War was in some sense a quarrel about which sovereign had a proper, legal claim on the obedience of his subjects.

What purely legal accounts of State development neglect, and what Peter Lewis's studies of the fifteenth century point out, as William Beik's do for the seventeenth century, is that a crucial part of sovereignty was the creation and cultivation of a sense of obligation through gifts, pensions, and the protective services of good lordship. The latter is notable in how the kings of France "evoked" or transferred lawsuits involving those to whom they were obligated or those whom they wished to obligate before their council or another favorable jurisdiction. However, we must not forget that seventeenth-century monarchs such as Louis XIV thought more – and in more numerical terms – about the potential balance of their obligations to their principal creditors.[107] Late medieval patronage, as Lewis noted, was an "informal system." Written contracts of alliance are only the tip of the iceberg. As for the extensions of credit at humbler levels of the social hierarchy, even much elite obligation must have remained unwritten, inchoate, and imprecise – until one party felt wounded and disputed the obligation. Only then might such commerce have entered the judicial record, if only briefly. It was not always easily to transform immaterial credit into material credit. For instance, because it was difficult to have the provincial receiver on whom a pension was assigned pay out the full amount of hard cash promised by the king, the claims on royal resources constituted by a pension may have been most useful for improving pensioners' credit with lenders.[108] A magnate pensioned by the king, even if he had only paper promises, was surely of greater credit than someone without a claim on the king's revenues.

Exchange creating obligation (*commerce*, *commercium*) was omnipresent in late medieval society. Not everyone was a merchant, but everyone was in commerce and everyone cultivated his or her credit. Kings and lords were in commerce for loyalty and service. Lesser nobles were in commerce for protection and income. Political society rested on trust in reciprocal obligation. Those who rejected this logic or neglected the gratifications and *douceurs* to patrons, judges, and their servants and the sometimes outright

[106] See especially the third part of Jean de Terrevermeille's *Contra rebelles suorum regum* (Lyon, 1526), a vindication of *c.* 1419 of the Dauphin Charles's natural right to his subjects' loyalty even after his father had disinherited him in favor of Henry V of England.

[107] Jacob Soll, "Accounting for Government: Holland and the Rise of Political Economy in Seventeenth-Century Europe," *Journal of Interdisciplinary History* 40:2 (2009), 215–238, esp. 234.

[108] Lewis describes the system in "The Pensioners," in *Essays*, 95–96.

intimidation necessary to form a network of obliged "good lords," allies, and clients came to ruin. J. G. Bellamy gives the example of the stingy and imprudent Robert Pilkington (†1508), who was enmeshed in a decades-long legal contest over the manor of Mellor with a "friend" of Thomas Savage, Bishop of London. Pilkington failed to acquire credit by gratifying "good lords," "friends," and lawyers, going so far in 1500 as to refuse the bishop's offer to purchase the disputed manor because "'for drede of his saule' he would not 'sell nor forbare his ryght and taylyd enheretance." His son continued this fruitless attempt to gain title to the said manor, suffering for his father's failure to engage in the commerce of bastard feudal society.[109] Commerce was simply a word for the necessary interdependence of society.

Such an attitude extended into prayer, as in Eamon Duffy's marvelous example of the autograph notes of Katherine of Aragon, Henry VIII, and Elizabeth of York in an aristocratic lady's Book of Hours: "I think the prayers of a frend the most acceptable unto God and because I take you for one of myn assured, I pray you remember me in yours: Katherine the queen ... Madame I pray you remembre me/ your lovyng maister/ Henry Rex ... Madam I pray you for you forget not me, to pray to God that I may have grace of your prayers, Elizabeth the Queene." Still elevated but not royal "friends" took a different tone: "Thomas Manners, Lord Roos, wrote 'Madam wan you ar dysposyd to pray remember your assured sarvant always, T Roos."[110] The prayers would surely have been salutary for the requestor, but it cannot have hurt the owner to have her "friendship" with the queen, faithful subjection to the king, and the fact that Lord Roos was her "assured servant" on view when she opened her primer. As with *alliances*, these requests could be more explicitly transactional. After the death of Marie de Noyers, Abbess of Montivilliers, on January 12, 1396, her successor circulated a parchment roll eliciting prayers from other monastic institutions, 222 of which subscribed between October 1398 and January 1399. The abbess's letter assured future subscribers that: "you debtors, who are united in brotherhood and association with us, by immediately paying your spiritual debt of prayers and alms shall direct the path of the late Lady Marie, our former abbess, and the said sisters to their [heavenly] fatherland."[111] This evokes a mutual-aid society for prayers among French

[109] J. G. Bellamy, *Bastard Feudalism and the Law* (London: Routledge, 2013; orig. 1983), 73–78.

[110] Eamon Duffy, *Marking the Hours: English People and Their Prayers 1240–1570* (New Haven: Yale University Press, 2006), 51–52. Princess Mary also included a request; the book's owner scratched out her name and her mother's, presumably when the king sought divorce.

[111] ADSM 54 H 23; published by Léopold Delisle, *Rouleaux des morts du IXe au XVe siècle recueillis et publiés par la société de l'histoire de France* (Paris: Veuve Jules Renouard, 1866), 488–507, at 457: "Vos quoque, qui in fraternitate vel societate estis debitores,

clergy in which debts of prayer would never be extinguished, but would continue to circulate, with new debts incurred each time an old debt was repaid. Layfolk had to purchase monks' and nuns' prayers: "on the sixth day of April 1407 my lady Jeanne de Macourt, *pitancière* of the Abbey of Montivilliers received in the presence of the convent a letter from my lady Jeanne Dumont, abbess of the said house, containing 50st that Jean Loiselet called Notelet had given to the pittances to remain in the said convent's prayers."[112] Jean Loiselet did not specify a specific prayer or quantity of prayers. Like the count of Foix, he gave an amount of money without specifying how much service, how many prayers he expected in return. Perhaps he expected the nuns to pray for him when they enjoyed a special delicacy or pittance on the anniversary of his death. Commerce structured society in this world and in the next: late medieval elites obliged themselves and others for military aid, legal aid, gifts of venison, and prayer, as their inferiors were in commerce for aid in brawling, legal support, loans of grain or tools, and prayer.[113] Orders of chivalry created debts of honor, just as confraternities created debts of money, good deeds, and prayer among members. Multiplying creditors of different types provided a form of social insurance and diluted the influence of any one creditor.[114] This last point unnerved late medieval monarchs, who sought to make their powerful subjects' obligation to them primary.

Not yet couched in terms of a market in which equals traded with equals, nonmercantile exchange was envisioned in terms of service and reward, prospective and past.[115] Yet not all commerce was socially acceptable, as noted earlier. In the example cited above the duke of Albany's *avocat* had redeployed the phrase *extra commercium hominum* from the Digest to suggest what would happen to a faithless king who flouted his

spirituale debitum orationum et elemosinarum instanter solvendo, viam dicte domine Marie, quondam abbatisse nostre, dictarumque sororum, ad patriam tendencium."

112 ADSM 54 H 84, Accounts for Mi-Carême, 1406, n.p.: "Le vi^{e} jour d'avril iiij^{cc} et sept rechut madame jehanne de macourt pitanchiere de l'abbaye de moustiervilliers une lettre baillie par la main de madame jehanne dumont abbeesse dudit ostel en la presence du couvent contenant chinquante soulx les quielx jehan loiselet dit notelet a donnes aux pitanches pour demourer es prieres du dit couvent." The pittancer was one of the monastic obedientiaries who managed the benefactions that paid for special allowances of meat, wine, or other delicacies, often on the anniversary of the donor.

113 Felicity Heal has noted that sixteenth-century English tenants often gave "gifts" along with the tithes and rents they paid, most abundantly when the landlords were in residence: "Food Gifts, the Household, and the Politics of Exchange in Early Modern England," *Past & Present* 199:1 (2008), 41–70.

114 Fontaine, *L'Économie*, 70.

115 As Mathieu Arnoux has observed ("Croissance," 128): "Avant d'être un espace où l'abondance d'informations également distribuées entre les acteurs leur permet une économie des frais de transaction, le marché est un lieu d'ordre soumis à un contrôle d'une intensité extrême, où la question de la 'liberté' des échanges ne se pose pas."

promises and those of his predecessors to his subjects.[116] In the Digest, however, "things outside of commerce (*res extra commercium*)" denoted *res publicae*, *sacrae*, *religiosae*, and *sanctae* such as rivers, temples, or tombs.[117] This was not what the Jacques Dixomme had meant. Juristic opinion emphasized that even kings were bound by their contracts. Dixomme had probably in mind the comments made by Ludovicus Pontanus, a jurist who died at the Council of Basel, remarks paraphrased by Jason de Mayno, last of the great Italian commentators of the line of Bartolus and Baldus, concerning contractual relationships between rulers and their subjects. Pontanus had advised in a *consilium* that "If the prince could by a mere act of will break a contract which he makes with a subject, it is probable that no one would make a contract with him, and so he would be deprived of the ability to enter into contractual transactions with other men. But it would be absurd that he who is prince of all should be unable to make transactions (*commercium*) with all."[118] Dixomme may also have had in mind the *Secreta secretorum* attributed to Aristotle:

> You know, then, that faith (or trust: *fides*) brings about the association of human beings, the dwelling-places of cities, the community of men and the government of kings; faith enables strong places to be occupied, cities to be preserved, kings to rule. If you remove faith, all men will revert to their pristine condition, they will be like brutes and beats. Beware, most faithful king, of breaking faith; keep firmly to your oaths and treaties, even if they are burdensome.[119]

Contrast John the Good, captured by the English at the battle of Poitiers in 1356, to Francis I, captured by Imperial forces at the battle of Pavia in 1525: John II paid a ransom in money and in land that crippled his kingdom even after his death; Francis I twisted honor in every way he could to escape his promises to Charles V. In Francis I's response to the Treaty of Madrid we understand just how early modern absolute sovereigns sought to absolve themselves of their contracts and their laws and why they sought to make popular consent ever more tacit, natural, presumed and therefore irrevocable.[120]

116 One thinks here of Arlette Jouanna's *Le devoir de Révolte. La noblesse française et la gestation de l'État moderne (1559–1661)* (Paris: Fayard, 1989).

117 See the texts at Dig. 18.1.6 pr., Dig. 18.1.34 §1, and Dig. 30.39 §10.

118 *Consilia D. Ludovici de Roma* (Parma, 1504), cons.352, 104v: "quod si esset in sola principis voluntate contractum que cum subdito facit infringere nullius verisimiliter cum eo contraheret. et sic hominum commercio careret contrahendo. Esset autem absurdum: ut qui princeps est omnium careret commercio omnium." The passage is cited by Antony Black, "The Juristic Origins of Social Contract Theory," *History of Political Thought* 14:1 (1993), 57–76, at 62–63. This is his translation. For Jason de Mayno's paraphrase of Pontanus's remarks, see Black, 63 n.20, or *Jasonis Maynii in ii. ff veteris partem commentaria* (Lyon, 1572), 136, v[is] Si pecuniam, n°.13.

119 Cited and translated by Black, 60 and n.9.

120 The divergence of early modern attitudes, as absolute monarchs adopted papal claims and as republican polities emphasized contractual rulership, is evident from Mario

Francis I was certainly not *extra commercium*: in 1527 Charles Guillart, one of the presidents in the Parlement of Paris, had criticized him for "putting the commonwealth up for sale (*faire la chose publicque questueuse par argent*)."[121] One might accuse Guillart of exaggeration, yet his description is not inaccurate. The king's obligation to those who lent him or "gave" him money in the form of forced loans, gratifications and gifts, or who purchased venal offices was increasingly open, formal, and precisely calculated. While some voices were raised against venality, most lamented only *excessive* venality. Venality had become so important that in 1523 a new financial office was created to receive such revenues, and in the following year a separate office was created to receive the proceeds of the twenty-five percent tax on the sale of royal offices – this at the same time as royal officials had to swear that they had not purchased their offices upon taking office.[122] Venality of office helped to unify the power centers of late medieval and early modern states. It was not limited to France (though it was most notable there), existing in the Papal State and in England among other places. In the Church, the Concordat of Bologna opened up France's major benefices to overt royal patronage and thus to imbrication in the same circuits of exchange and obligation as secular offices. Elites who did not pay in some way, who had not obliged the king (perhaps even lending to the king through financier *prête-noms*), would be "*extra commercium*." Commerce with the king was necessary to preserve their status by tapping the flows of State wealth.[123] For the king, commerce with elites reinforced his claims to their obedience and service.

As a transactional mentality grew common in the State, it grew less acceptable in the Church, because the Reformation encouraged the demarcation of religion as a special zone exempt from what we call market forces. In 1525, for instance, François de Rohan, Bishop of Angers and Archbishop of Lyon, was accused of improper commerce by the Chapter of Angers. The terms used in pleading his case, which began on February 23 before the Parlement of Paris, are significant. Guillaume Poyet, future *avocat du roi*, president in the Parlement, and Chancellor of France, stated that the chapter's appeal was "a question of the honor of God and of the Church."[124] According to Poyet, this was because the Bishop of Angers had "generally made a business (*marchandise*) of his

Salamonio's statement of 1512–1514 that "the existence of a *societas* requires contracts, which are called laws" (Black, 69).

[121] Lange, *First French Reformation*, 220. The text is from Cicero, *De officiis*, 2.77: "Habere enim quaestui rem publicam non modo turpe est, sed sceleratum etiam et nefarium."

[122] On the significance of this, see Lange, *First French Reformation*, 256–259.

[123] As per Bois, *Crise*, and Fontaine, *L'Économie*, 294, describing the shift from credit as the number of one's clients or friends to credit as "la capacité qu'a le noble à se faire entendre du roi."

[124] AN X[1a]4876, 147v.

diocese" by selling benefices, vending dispensations at outrageous prices, charging mendicants to preach in his diocese, and selling pardons to condemned criminals.[125] Within the Church, such improper commerce was called simony, the sale of spiritual goods and the "first heresy" according to a passage from Gregory the Great included in Gratian's Decretum.[126] Poyet described the bishop not just as venal or simoniac but as a negligent pastor who failed to demonstrate good lordship: the chapter alleged that he had only come to Angers to celebrate mass "four or five times" in his twenty-five year episcopate, that he neither adorned nor repaired his cathedral church, that he had undertaken "one sole visitation," and that he had scandalized his flock with stingy alms-giving.[127] The duties of a good lord, even a spiritual lord, included protection, munificence, and liberality. In other words, good lordship entailed giving gifts that could nevertheless either be or give rise to countergifts. In sum, the tenor of the chapter's accusations was that the bishop was more a merchant than a pastor or good lord. The chapter accused him of engaging in commerce inappropriate both to the matters at hand – the sacraments, ecclesiastical jurisdiction, and his pastoral duties – and to his status as an ecclesiastical lord. While everyone, necessarily and virtuously, engaged in commerce, only merchants engaged in "vile" *marchandise* – the trading or mercantile exchange of equals. If kings, nobles, and peasants gave gifts, rendered service, and swore loyalty *in commercio hominum*, only merchants and bad bishops "bargained and haggled (*marchander et composer*)" over the performance of their obligations. Service and liberality were forms of exchange, just not of mercantile exchange.

It was inappropriate and immoral for nonmerchants to trade for profit alone rather than status or power. The bishop of Angers (so Poyet claimed) overtly flouted the ideal of Christian and noble liberality by failing to disguise adequately his zeal for profit. "It was quite legitimate to demand gifts," Valentin Groebner has written of public officials in this period, but our bishop too greatly violated the rules of the game: "[t]he rules to which gifts were subject were second-order rules, intended to regulate not the acts themselves but rather talk about the rules."[128] To

125 AN X[1a]4876, 148v-149v. "Il a prins et exige grans sommes de deniers … et generalement se fait une marchandise oudict diocese par partie et ses officiers de toutes collacions de sacremens/ tellement que on nen a aucune chose sans marchander et composer et sont choses baillees au plus offrant comme sil estoit question de chose prophane … Qui sont choses illicites et vrayes exactions tant sur le clergie que populaire contre les sainctz decretz et arrestz de la court/ et tout cela est fait par luy pour avoir plus grant prouffict et revenu de sondict evesche."

126 C.1 q.1 c.28: "Fertur simoniaca haeresis (quae prima contra Dei ecclesiam diabolica plantatione subrepsit, et in ipso ortu suo, zelo Apostolicae ultionis percussa atque damnata est) … ".

127 AN X[1a]4876, 148r, 150v.

128 Groebner, *Liquid Assets*, 38, 70.

believe the complaints in his trial, he had been engaging in potentially simoniacal behavior for more than two decades. Yet the language of illicit exactions was deployed only when this court prelate became a convenient target in the quarrel of the Parlement of Paris and the Regent Louise of Savoy: "[i]t was the current political constellations that determined what was public or private in a given case," that is, which demands were appropriate and which inappropriate as well as which gifts created legitimate ties and which gifts created illicit ties.[129] Simony in ecclesiastical matters and venality in administrative or judicial ones were more politically motivated frames of perception than identifiable sets of practices.

Such a cast of mind mitigated uncomfortable contradictions. Tithe-farmers who excommunicated for unpaid tithes would surely have justified their actions as the simple defense of rights that they had purchased – a solid investment, if aggravating to the tithe-payers. No matter that tithes were supposed to support the clergy, they were rights that could be bought, sold, or leased like any other property rights. Since the law was to "render to each his own (*jus suum cuique tribuere*, Dig.1.1.10)," titheholders could gain ready cash by securitizing their revenues, a phenomenon evident in other property-based forms of credit from mortgages to *rentes constituées*. Similarly, venal officeholders would have argued for the legality and the justice of their investments. Yet, however much they sought to serve God, justice, and the king, the occupants of venal offices simultaneously sought to recoup their initial investment and to advance themselves and their families. *Marchandise* was therefore less a separate type of commerce than a qualification of commerce undertaken in a particular spirit. When in 1563 Chancellor Michel de L'Hospital condemned the judges of the Parlement of Rouen for their "lust for vile profit," he condemned the spirit and the nature of their demands for monetary gratification before handing down decisions.[130] L'Hospital told the judges that it would have been better to preserve the ancient custom of receiving only spices, dragées, and gifts in kind. In articulating a second-order rule about how to speak of gift-giving, L'Hospital highlighted the tension between what Laurence Fontaine calls the "gift of love (*don d'amour*)" and the "bargain or transaction of equals (*marché des égaux*)." Even as early modern French judges purchased the obligation to dispense the king's "debt of justice (*debitum justicie*)" to his subjects, they nevertheless viewed this as the "charge (or debt, *deu*) of their offices."[131] Having purchased their offices from the king, but nevertheless indebted

[129] Groebner, *Liquid Assets*, 146–147; Lange, *First French Reformation*, 167–172.

[130] Lange, *First French Reformation*, 257.

[131] AN X^{1a}1529, 29r–v: the Parlement of Paris wrote in 1526 to Louise of Savoy that it could not but disobey her "sans grandement offenser dieu et violer le deu de noz offices."

for those offices, venal officeholders confound our modern notions of public service.

That tension between the logic of the gift and the logic of the purchase, evident in Francis of Assisi's rejection of the world of property that undergirded both logics as well as in profligate nobles' honoring of gambling debts while leaving mundane, dishonorable debts unpaid, was not resolved until the eighteenth century. Amalia Kessler has demonstrated how the rhetoric concerning the Parisian merchants' tribunal transformed from one of expeditious justice for a particular social group or "order" to one of equitable remedies for particular types of transaction, for a function.[132] By 1800, to be a merchant was no longer a hereditary or acquired status but to be involved in trade. Anyone could then be a merchant or consumer. Not only noblewomen could have colored ribbons in their hair, as sumptuary laws vanished. Not only merchants could invest in stocks, as nobles no longer had to hide behind financier *prête-noms* or anonymous limited-liability partnerships (*sociétés en commandite*) to invest in trade without losing their status.[133] Not sumptuary laws or fears of *dérogation* from noble status but financial means would constrain nineteenth-century *homines oeconomici*. Indeed, debt would be increasingly devalued, as indebtedness undermined the image of self-sufficiency at the root of bourgeois society and of the putative market of equals.

The myth of self-sufficiency appeared with the spread of venality. Peter Lewis has described the nonfeudal contract for life service or *alliance* that largely supplanted the money fief or *fief-rente* for term of life in the fifteenth century (as in the examples from his work cited above): "There was, essentially, very little difference between [the *alliance*] and the *fief-rente* for term of life; that difference subsisted in the absence of homage in the *alliance*, the absence of subjection. One was a companion, an ally, a supporter, even a servant of one's lord: one was not his subject, nor his vassal."[134] Which is to say, one was in the lord's debt. The allied debtor did maintain more autonomy vis-à-vis his lord than did the vassal who had sworn homage. Nor did he have to participate in the ceremonies of homage that sixteenth-century nobles found so humiliating.[135] As the commonwealth went up for sale in the sixteenth century and elites

[132] Kessler, *A Revolution*.

[133] Eighteenth-century jurists argued that consular jurisdictions should neither register *sociétés en commandite* nor publish their participants' names, "since people who are not of the mercantile profession would perhaps not want the public to know that they are associated with merchants" (Kessler, 175).

[134] Lewis, "Decayed and Non-Feudalism," in *Essays*, 62.

[135] J. Russell Major, "Bastard Feudalism and the Kiss: Changing Social Mores in Late Medieval and Early Modern France," *Journal of Interdisciplinary History* 17:3 (1987), 509–535.

sought to purchase titles, noble status and securitized seigneurial dues, they grew wary of the dependence implied even by ostensibly innocuous gifts. Natalie Davis has described how by the later sixteenth century French elites were likely to refuse or to return gifts that threatened to create unwanted obligations.[136] Late medieval hopes became early modern fears: in legal terms, early modern nobles feared rather than hoped that non-synallagmatic or unilateral contracts such as gifts would become synallagmatic or bilateral obligations. In this spirit, Michel de Montaigne declared:

> I find nothing so dear as that which is given me, because my will remains mortgaged through gratitude, and would prefer to purchase services (or venal offices, *offices qui sont à vendre*). I truly believe that for the latter I give only money, for the former I give myself. An obligation of honor appears to me more demanding and more weighty than a civil obligation. A notary strangles me more gently than I do myself.[137]

Venality was one remedy for the indefinition of the late medieval culture of debt, because it was a voluntary, specific obligation. Montaigne feared the open-ended nature of debts of honor, an open-endedness clear in late medieval contracts of *alliance*. Fifteenth-century *alliances* or indentures, to speak of an English form, were closer to early modern contracts of indentured servitude than late medieval nobles would have liked to admit, because both sold a potentially total claim on the body. Clearer, notarized obligations could more easily be litigated than, for instance, the duke of Albany's inchoate sense that the kings of France had broken faith. Certain spheres were nonetheless to be free of venality. François de Rohan was criticized for "merchantizing" his episcopal office in 1525 because his behavior implied that neither the sacraments nor ecclesiastical justice were *res extra commercium*. It was quite otherwise for the State: if Cicero's maxim that "to put the commonwealth up for sale is not only shameful but detestable" was cited in the sixteenth century, only in the eighteenth century did State offices begin to be *res extra commercium*.[138] Just as venality in the State became painful when the political sphere came to be conceived as composed of citizens equal in rights and in political voice, excommunication for debt and the abuse of

[136] Natalie Z. Davis, *The Gift in Sixteenth-Century France* (Madison: University of Wisconsin Press, 2000); see too Heal, "Food Gifts"; Sharon Kettering, "Gift-Giving and Patronage in Early Modern France," *French History* 2:2 (1988), 131–151.

[137] *Essais*, III:9, cited in Fontaine, *L'Économie*, 251. Immediately prior: "Je fuis à me soubmettre à toute sorte d'obligation. Mais sur tout, à celle qui m'attache par lien d'honneur."

[138] On the rollback of venality in England, see John Brewer, *The Sinews of Power: War, Money, and the English State, 1688–1783* (Cambridge, MA: Harvard University Press, 1990).

indulgences became painful in the sixteenth century as Christians came to believe that a transactional mentality was inappropriate in religious matters. Commerce belonged to the secular realm of trade and was to be governed by the State's laws. Religion began to be disembedded from other aspects of social life, in which credit as the number of one's debtors remained crucial.

The role of early modern confessional states in this transition was crucial. The triumph of venality in the French state marks new manners of thinking about gifts, contracts, and obligations. Of the role of public finance in state formation, Francesco Boldizzoni has noted that "[f]ar from being a mere superstructure, it emerged that the state contributed to molding the character of economic systems. There was a symbiotic correspondence between the type of political culture and the forms of taxation … The taxation model (such as the prevalence of direct or indirect taxes, exemptions and their amount, the distribution of the tax burden between the social orders) reflected the level of centralization of political power as well as the social structure."[139] Taxation emerged from the "free gifts" and subsidies to the good lord consented by late medieval status groups – clergy, nobles, towns, provinces … – but became in the early modern period the payment of subjects' "debt" to their sovereign.[140] The process by which early modern schemes of taxation emerged from late medieval "caritative" gifts, feudal aids, lay subsidies, crusade taxes, and so on differed across the continent. The exemption of *nobles* and *hidalgos* from most taxation not only created an incentive for the socially ambitious to abandon trade but shaped the political and of course the economic cultures of early modern Spain and France by, to use the Abbé Sieyès's terminology, excluding nobles from the Nation that worked and paid taxes. The lack of such an exemption in England rendered the boundary between simple gentility and yeomanry less important. Because those of gentle birth funded the State, the English political class was at once far broader than on the continent and far less dependent on the monarch to access the regressive redistribution of wealth facilitated by the reliance of early modern states on credit furnished in the end by those very same elites. The low yields on British consols in the eighteenth century in comparison to those on French state debt signals the importance of national and regional cultures of credit and obligation in shaping early modern economic and political societies.[141] French elites reacted so violently to

139 Francesco Boldizzoni, *The Poverty of Clio: Resurrecting Economic History* (Princeton: Princeton University Press, 2011), 164.

140 Guéry, "Le roi dépensier."

141 W. M. Ormrod, M. Bonney, and R. Bonney (eds.), *Crises, Revolutions, and Self-Sustained Growth: Essays in European Fiscal History, 1130–1830* (Stamford, UK: Shaun Tyas, 1999);

the income taxes introduced in the eighteenth century because French aristocrats, as Fontaine has shown, tended to see their tax obligations as gifts and did not understand unpaid debts to compromise their honor.[142]

Whether free gift or *taille*, taxes reflected mutual obligation and, in this sense, founded a community. So too did relationships of credit. As Fontaine has perceptively observed, "in villages debt signified that one belonged to the community."[143] Symmetrically, demanding the repayment of debts signalled a borrower's exclusion from that community.[144] Debt also implied dependence, ordering a community hierarchically. If one's debts were sufficiently diluted among a number of creditors – as with vassals' multiple obligations in the late Middle Ages – this dependence could create a horizontal community, a precondition for both more modern polities and for more modern market relations. Excommunication for debt seems to have served exactly this function, very clearly in the case of the Abbess of Montivilliers's "extraterritorial jurisdiction," by extending the network of credit beyond the family, the neighborhood, the guild, or the exemption of Montivilliers. The disappearance of excommunication for debt in the sixteenth century is therefore part of a far longer movement by which the State made itself the exclusive guarantor of peace, property, and social relations. In the sixteenth century, contracts suffered the same fate that actions concerning real property had been undergoing since the twelfth century. In that century, the English writs of novel disseisin, darrain presentment, and mort d'ancestor had rerouted disputes over property away from private warfare or trials by battle and toward royal courts. In the thirteenth century, the possessory actions of French royal courts served a similar purpose. In the fifteenth and sixteenth centuries, royal jurisdictions developed new remedies and new institutions to counteract anew the centrifugal forces of affinities and clienteles that generated the land wars of bastard feudalism. By the sixteenth century in both France and England, property matters, even those of clerics (at least *in possessorio*), belonged to royal, lay courts. In that century too, contract matters passed to lay courts. The redefinition of Christianity from a community of praxis to a community of doctrine had consequences beyond demands for lay literacy and rudimentary acquaintance with dogma: as religious claims permeated society, the claims of the Church

Jotham Parsons explores the religious sources of economic difference in "Vocation in Seventeenth-Century France: The Catholic Ethic and the Spirit of *Étatisme*," *French History* 28:3 (2014), 322–342.

[142] Fontaine, *L'Économie*, 270; Michael Kwass, *Privilege and the Politics of Taxation: Liberté, égalité, fiscalité* (New York: Cambridge University Press, 2006).

[143] Fontaine, *L'Économie*, 67.

[144] Fontaine, *L'Économie*, 69.

were reduced to teaching those religious claims, claims often determined by the civil authority. If one searches for a hinge on which this transition pivoted, one could do worse than to choose 1539, the year in which the Ordinance of Villers-Cotterêts not only introduced the registration of baptisms by parish priests but forbade the citation of layfolk in personal actions before ecclesiastical tribunals. The registration of baptisms, perhaps in emulation of the English, who required this from 1538,[145] like the introduction of debt registries and the mandatory registration of property transfers, confirms the clear desire of lay courts for competence over matters of contract from property sales to marriage. The "lay spirit" of the late Middle Ages killed excommunication for debt.[146] Secular courts enforced contracts, as states finally overcame Augustinian hesitations that they were little more than bulwarks against human sinfulness. Early modern princes optimistically sought to legislate their subjects to salvation, as civil jurists adopted the ambitious goals of late medieval canonists.[147] Enforcing the observance of contracts was part of this. The early modern French called their enemies not "excommunicates (*excommuniés*)" but "bankrupts (*banqueroutiers*)" excluded not from the sacramental community but from the political and economic community defined by royal courts.[148] Not church courts but royal courts ultimately regulated an individual's credit in the early modern period.

Or perhaps states just reinforced the web of obligation that preserved the social order. With the disappearance of excommunication for debt, those without property – and sometimes those with – could only be imprisoned for debt.[149] From the fourteenth century, monarchs sought to eliminate private distraint of chattels and physical caption of persons

145 Chancellor Poyet had been to England on embassy in 1534 and maintained contacts thereafter: Anne Rousselet-Piment, *Le chancelier et la loi au XVIe siècle: D'après l'oeuvre d'Antoine Duprat, de Guillaume Poyet et de Michel de l'Hospital* (Paris: De Boccard, 2005), 396.

146 Evoking Georges de Lagarde's *Naissance de l'esprit laïque au déclin du Moyen Âge* does not entail the acceptance of all aspects of his thesis.

147 Lange, *First French Reformation*, 25–65.

148 For an example of the former insult, see ADSM G 5270, 26v, entry inserted following the last sanction in Fontenay in 1463 (NS): "Anno domini m°cccc lxxviij° die jovis xxvij[a] mensis augustis johannes breart senior denunciavit quot die dominica novissima cum ipse denunciasset et presentasset mandatum citatorium curie nostre oliverio randou clerico de fontenayo ad exequendum contra dominum johannem seuse presbiterum ipse seuse violenter abstraxit huiusmodi citationem a manibus dicti clerici et idem irato animo proiecit in area ecclesie dicendo quod clericus non erat abilis ad exequendum et denunciavit ipsum breart excommunicatum et sibi dixit quod erat excommunicatus bis ad minus. Presentibus oliverio randou robino randou guerino paige jacobo durant guillermo bernard guillermo vatine et johanne rouse." For an example of the latter, see Fontaine, *L'Économie*, 285.

149 Or hanged, if a vindictive creditor or vendor reclassified the debt as theft.

by offering creditors the chance to have the king imprison debtors. From the 1303 ordinance of reform that permitted the seizure of debtors for private debts in France until the generalization of the clause of *contrainte par corps* for notarized debt in 1566, contractants had the option of obligating either their property only or their property and their bodies. In England, from roughly this period, a series of statutes progressively extended the possibility of imprisonment for debt: in 1285 from debts to the king to actions of account (13 Edw. I); in 1351 from actions of debt to actions of detinue (25 Edw. III); in 1505 to include trespass on the case (19 Hen. VII); and in 1532 to all actions of trespass (23 Hen. VIII). This provided the technical basis for imprisonment for debt, allowing secular courts in England and France to offer powerful remedies for many of the same types of debt formerly provided by ecclesiastical tribunals, but through imprisonment rather than excommunication. Most early imprisonments for private debt were brief, as Julie Claustre has shown for Paris, for a day or two. What changed in the sixteenth century was not just the site of litigation over contracts – both financial contracts and marital contracts – but the moral valence surrounding unpaid debts. The shift from a catechetics of the seven capital sins to one of the decalogue, from the capital sin of greed to theft, a violation of God's explicit commandment, amounts, Paolo Prodi has argued, the ethicization of market behavior. In this sense, both imprisonment for debt and the notion of a criminal bankruptcy (*banqueroute* as opposed to *faillite*) characterize the two centuries that followed the end of excommunication for debt. Indeed, it was legislation of 1536, 1539, and 1561 that shifted the penalty for bankruptcy from spiritual death to corporal death: the Ordinance of Villers-Cotterêts ended the excommunication of layfolk for debts; edicts of 1536 and 1561 prescribed that culpable bankrupts would be punished "extraordinarily and capitally."[150] In this transitional age, the State's guarantee of trust in the performance of contracts was weak enough and the popular sense of the sinfulness of bankruptcy as theft great enough that these violations of market norms merited harsh,

[150] Ordinances of Charles VIII (1490) and Louis XII (1512) forbade cession by procureur and commanded the insolvent to cede his goods "desceint" and "teste nue": *Les edicts et ordonnances des rois de France … divisez en quatre tomes par Antoine Fontanon* (Paris, 1611), I: 762–763. Chancellor Poyet's reforms of 1536 made bankruptcy an extraordinary crime, mandated the imprisonment of bankrupts until they paid, permitted them to be pilloried, and, interestingly with respect to the competence of royal courts, gave "pleine foy" to all documents authenticated with public seals, i.e., notarized: Isambert 12: 527–530, and for the last, 514. The ordinance of January 1560 (OS) registered by the Parlement of Paris on September 13, 1561 established that "Tous banqueroutiers et qui feront faute et fraude, seront punis extraordinairement et capitalement": Isambert 14.1: 63–98, at 96. This provision passed into the 1673 Ordinance of Commerce, Tit.11, Art. 10 (Isambert 19: 105).

even capital, punishment. The end of excommunication for debt marks not the de-moralization of credit but the ethicization of all credit. Pastors enforced market norms in confessionals, as states did in courtrooms, in debtors' prisons, and on scaffolds.

Courts had to enforce market norms less and less often over the course of the eighteenth century, as litigants brought fewer debt cases. In the Empire, the frequency of litigation before the *Reichshofrat* and the *Reichskammergericht*, after subsiding in the mid-seventeenth century, rebounded until *c.*1720, before beginning a decline that slowed in the 1770s and 1780s before falling precipitously in the years immediately prior to the dissolution of the Old Empire in 1804. In numerical terms, there were two cases before the *Reichshofrat* in 1520, 30 in 1530 43 in 1580, 192 in 1630, 60 in 1680, 133 in 1730, 101 in 1780, and 54 in 1800.[151] The decline at the highest levels of justice in the Old Empire from 1720 parallels those evident in France and England at the same time, though more slowly. In England, Christopher Brooks captures the longer term movement: in 1606 there were 1,351 cases initiated per 100,000 inhabitants of England and Wales; in 1823–1827 there were 653 cases per annum; and in 1975 only 560 cases.[152] In eighteenth-century France, the decline in judicial business before the Parlement of Paris made whole chambers of judges financially unsustainable, leading to their wholesale suppression – a suppression not unconnected with royal hopes for the reform of the judiciary through the suppression of repurchased venal offices. In any case, whether it concerns civil matters or minor crimes (*grand criminel* cases are an exception) before French royal courts, decline was evident from 1680 and continued relentlessly until the abolition of the parlements during the Revolution.[153]

What was behind this decline? Colin Kaiser has suggested the ineptitude of young judges in the lower chambers of the Parlement of Paris – who often inherited their offices at age twenty or so – drove litigants away, in commercial matters to the consular tribunals that offered swifter, cheaper, less uninformed justice.[154] Daniel Lord Smail has proposed, drawing on the work of Richard Kagan on Castile and Muldrew on England, that "the eighteenth century marks the age when

151 Ortlieb and Polster, "Prozessfrequenz," 212–216. See too Christian Wollschläger, "Civil Litigation and Modernization: The Work of the Municipal Courts of Bremen, Germany in Five Centuries, 1549–1984," *Law and Society Review* 24:2 (1990), 261–282.

152 Brooks, *Pettyfoggers*, 78.

153 Colin Kaiser, "The Deflation in the Volume of Litigation at Paris in the Eighteenth Century and the Waning of the Old Judicial Order," *European History Quarterly* 10 (1980), 309–336.

154 Kaiser, "Deflation," 315–316.

Europeans finally became accustomed to expressing social competition through manners and material goods, largely obviating the need to use either self-help or the courts for this purpose."[155] The identification of an eighteenth-century "consumer revolution" and, more prosaically, observations such as Daniel Roche's that wealthy Parisians switched from durable, fungible silver plate to fragile, illiquid porcelain dinnerware in the middle of the eighteenth century would seem to add weight to the proposition that the upper reaches of society adopted modes of deportment appropriate to a society in which liquid wealth as opposed to landed wealth grew increasingly important, particularly in cultural terms but also in economic ones.[156] As the horizons of Western Europeans widened over the early modern period, investment, credit, and commercial contracts grew more important to elites than the "land wars" that, whether inside or outside of the courtroom, marked the late middle ages and early modern period. By the eighteenth century, after two centuries of frequent civil litigation had successfully instilled market ethics in European Christians, the frequency of civil litigation declined across the Western Europe.

Violations of market ethics nevertheless remained a crime. Even if creditors initiated civil litigation less frequently from the eighteenth century onward, they could still imprison inveterate debtors. The abolition of imprisonment for debt came late: in 1833 in the United States, in 1867 in France and Austria, in 1868 in the North German Confederation, in 1869 in the United Kingdom, in 1879 in Sweden. The end of imprisonment for debt may mark the strength both of trust in an impersonal market and of awareness of the market's potential unfairness or capriciousness. It certainly points to the development of the sense that debt was an unfortunate blot on one's character rather than a necessity of daily life.[157] Defaulting debtors were to be pitied, and punished economically by seizing their assets, if they had any, and by mortgaging their futures to creditors. In the nineteenth century, the conviction that economic behavior is to be measured by its contribution to national wealth had advanced far enough to push religious qualms about economic behavior back into the confessional and into the increasingly disregarded pulpits, if they were even voiced. Already in 1743, the Bishop of Montpellier urged preachers and confessors "to refrain from speaking of usury so

155 Smail, *Consumption*, 159; also Howell, *Commerce*, 170.

156 Roche, *France in the Enlightenment*, A. Goldhammer (trans.), (Cambridge, MA: Harvard University Press, 1998), 632–634.

157 Margot Finn, *The Character of Credit: Personal Debt in English Culture, 1740–1914* (Cambridge: Cambridge University Press, 2003).

as not to offend or drive away listening usurers."[158] Deirdre McCloskey has asserted of the West's astonishing economic and human development since 1800, "[t]he change was not genetic (as [Gregory] Clark argues) or psychological (as Weber argued) or economic (as Marx argued) or legal (as [Douglass] North argues) but sociological and political."[159] The accommodation of Christian ethics to new forms of domination and of inequality visible in psychology, in economic movements, and in law, was nevertheless a change in human behavior. This is why studying legal practice is so important, for it reveals how new ideals and new behaviors of credit and contract drove the rise and fall of excommunication for debt.

It is true that the disappearance of the canonical remedy against debtors removed a great abuse by which disproportionately grave sanctions were directed against minor offenses. This facilitated the transition from Prodi's *società giurata*, in which human relations were limited by the risk of perjury, to Muldrew's "society of contract" and thence to Bernard Mandeville's, Adam Smith's, or even Milton Friedman's civil society, in which autonomous consumers pursue their own profit. The harshness of early modern punishment of poaching and theft illustrates how profit or the accumulation of property took the moral place truth had once held and how its opposite, theft, took the place of falsehood.[160] Yet serious barriers to freedom of contract, particularly with respect to real property, remained until the French Revolution and elsewhere even after. Until 1790 in France, commerce in nonallodial (i.e., most) real property – including perpetual annuities, classified as real property by the custom of Paris[161] – was limited by, among other things, the *retrait féodal* that gave the lord of a vassal's alienated fief the chance to purchase it and the *retrait lignager* that gave a seller's lineage kin that same opportunity. Though these practices had grown obsolete, their existence, like the continued existence of infeudated tithes and payments to lords upon the transfer

[158] Fontaine, *L'Économie*, 218, citing the *Nouvelles ecclésiastiques*.

[159] McCloskey, *Bourgeois Dignity*, 293.

[160] V. A. C. Gattrell, *The Hanging Tree: Execution and the English People, 1770–1868* (Oxford: Oxford University Press, 1996); Douglas Hay, "Property, Authority, and the Criminal Law," in Douglas Hay, Peter Linebaugh, John G. Rule, E. P. Thompson, and Cal Winslow (eds.), *Albion's Fatal Tree: Crime and Society in Eighteenth-Century England* (New York: Pantheon Books, 1975), 17–63; E. P. Thompson, *Whigs and Hunters: The Origin of the Black Act* (New York: Pantheon Books, 1975); 1 Geo. 1 ser. 2 c.5, the "Riot Act," and 9 Geo. 1 c.22, the "Black Act." In the heartless eighteenth century there was no longer any question of late medieval theologians' approval of theft to preserve life.

[161] Though not by other customs, including that of Burgundy. For the Estates of Burgundy's surprise that the custom of Paris required annuities to be reissued rather than simply ceded, see Mark Potter and Jean-Laurent Rosenthal, "The Development of Intermediation in French Credit Markets: Evidence from the Estates of Burgundy," *Journal of Economic History* 62:4 (2002), 1024–1049, at 1044.

of property or annually in recognition of increasingly theoretical feudal subjection, remained a hindrance to the realization of any concept of absolute property, or at least one capable of absolutely moralizing ownership and immoralizing derogations of that ownership. Nor can we forget that women's freedom of contract and property rights were limited into the last century. The principle of ownership, like the trust that underlies market transactions, is part of the invisible, necessary framework of consumer society. This framework nevertheless has a history.[162]

At the end of the Middle Ages, regressive redistribution rewarded loyal service in a society bound together by an ideology of mutual obligation, today it rewards merit in a society governed by an ideology of irresistible – and just – market forces.[163] Excommunication for debt was excessive, to be sure. Both its abuse and its potential to subvert the social order highlight the potential violence in relationships of credit. Its disappearance marks a step toward the impersonal trust in relations of credit on which our modern economy rests, but only a step. Prodi's "society of the oath" did not instantly become Muldrew's "contractual society." Nor did "contractual society" instantly become consumer society. Instead, the secularization of credit and contract led to a precipitous increase in the frequency of civil litigation across sixteenth-century Europe. In this sense, the Reformation was a revolution of debtors by which European Christians rejected the late medieval culture of debt. Yet, if the mechanisms of debt collection changed in the sixteenth century, the moral obligation of the indebted did not. Only in the eighteenth century did the falling volume of civil litigation confirm the triumph of Fontaine's "mercantile logic" of credit, in which debt was liability rather than asset. Then, one no longer spoke of "merchants' justice (*ius mercatorum*)" but of "mercantile law (*lex mercatoria*)," for, in the modern world, everyone is a merchant of a sort, if only of his or her own labor.[164]

[162] As Joseph Stiglitz has sardonically observed, today we have capitalism for the poor and socialism for the rich: "America's Socialism for the Rich," June 12, 2009, theguardian.com. Or Nouriel Roubini (2008): "We're essentially continuing a system where profits are privatized ... and losses socialized." Or Gaetano Salvemini (1936): "Profit is private and individual. Loss is public and social." The last two examples are from "Capitalism, Socialism or Fascism?" October 25, 2009, washingtonsblog.com/2009/10/capitalism-socialism-or-fascism.html.

[163] e.g., "Increasing inequality and growing immigration are the corollary of technological progress and economic freedoms that most people would not willingly give up" ("Europe's Tea Parties," *The Economist*, January 4, 2014, 7).

[164] Fontaine, *L'Économie*, 314: "Dans l'Europe moderne, tout le monde était plus ou moins marchand." Although Fontaine's "Europe moderne" refers of course to what we call early modern Europe, her book concludes with striking parallels between the early modern and contemporary economies.

Conclusion: from Church to market

Much of our evidence for how medieval peasants imagined their communities is indirect. The Chronicle of Henry Knighton records what are described as the speeches of the leaders of the English Peasants' Rebellion of 1381. However much they may be attributed to fictional or pseudonymous leaders, they bring us close as we can get to the ideology of the French peasants who revolted in 1358. I cite two:

> Iakke Mylner asketh help to turne hys mylne aright. He hath grounden smal smal; the kings sone of heven he schal pay for alle. Loke thy mylne go aright, with the foure sayles, and the post stande in stedfastnesse. With ryght and with myght, with skyl and with wylle, lat myght helpe ryght, and skyl go before wille and ryght before myght, than goth oure mylne aright. And if myght go before ryght, and wylle before skylle; than is oure mylne mys adyght.
>
> ...
>
> John Balle seynte Marye prist gretes wele alle maner men and byddes hem in the name of the Trinite, Fadur, and Sone and Holy Gost stonde manlyche togedyr in trewthe, and helpez trewthe, and trewthe schal helpe yowe. Now regneth pride in pris, and covetys is hold wys, and leccherye withouten shame and glotonye withouten blame. Envye regnith with tresone, and slouthe is take in grete sesone. God do bote, for nowe is tyme amen.[1]

These passages relate to the civil jurisdiction of ecclesiastical tribunals in the late Middle Ages in two ways. First, the letter of "Jack Miller" at once evokes the religious notion of the mystical mill and constructs an image of the polity as an ordinary windmill. The mystical mill, related to the figure of the mystical wine press, originated in depictions of the Gospels as the fulfillment of the Old Testament, with "Moses pouring grain into a mill, and Paul collecting the flour," or with the "[f]our evangelists turning the

[1] Joseph Rawson Lumby (ed.), *Chronicon Henrici Knighton vel Cnitthon Monachi Leycestrensis* (Kraus Reprint Ltd, 1965; repr. of London, 1895), II: 138–140. I have replaced the letter thorn with th and the letter yod with gh and, where appropriate, y. On the speeches, see Steven Justice, *Writing and Rebellion: England in 1381* (Berkeley: University of California Press, 1996).

mill," presumably turning Christ into nourishment for all.[2] The mystical mill would have focused the attention of the believer on how Christ's suffering humanity was shared out equally for all. Miri Rubin has observed that in England and Germany this image was "monastic and clerical ..., not of the explicit nature which we have encountered in other eucharistic developments."[3] Although not as explicit as devotions to the Wounds of Christ, the Man of Sorrows, or the pelican feeding its young with its own blood, one cannot doubt both that the image of the mystical mill was preached to peasants and that English peasants understood how a windmill worked. In 1381 if not earlier, perhaps encouraged by radical priests, English peasants appear to have made a logical interpretive leap toward understanding the Mill of the Host as a symbol of radical Christian equality. Understanding the grain as the saved, as in Christ's parable of the wheat and the tares (Mt. 13:24–30), the grain emerged as the equal specks of flour that would compose the Body of Christ. In contrast to the situation in this life, would not all souls in Paradise be equal? Would not Christ "pay for alle?" Was not Christ's atonement on the cross "payment" for sinful humanity's debt to God?[4] Had not Christ redeemed or purchased believers for a "great price" (1 Cor. 6:20, "*magno pretio*" or "τιμῆς")?

Use of the image does not stop there: "Jack Miller" describes English society as a broken mill, in which the sails and the center-post do not fulfill their functions. "Right" should prevail over "might," and "skill" over "will" for the mill to function properly. Here was a complaint against lords whose force ("might") did not serve law or justice (*directum*, *droit*, "right") and against clerics whose reason (*ratio*, "skill") did not restrain their desire (*voluntas*, "will").[5] Furthermore, whether or not one understands the "four sails" as the estates of the clergy, nobility, burgesses, and peasants, the notion that all the parts of the mill must fulfill their proper tasks makes the image less radical. As in the French Jacquerie, there was probably a sense that the clergy and the nobles had failed the commonwealth. Thus was the mill of society "gone awry or off-kilter (*mys adyght*)." The peasants were not interested in abolishing property or social distinctions but in removing abuses. Even were all members of

[2] Rubin, *Corpus Christi*, 313. An image of Christ's verbal presence in the Gospel has been reified into one of his Real Presence in the Eucharist.

[3] Rubin, *Corpus Christi*, 313.

[4] So Lollards criticized indulgences: if the pope indeed "had autonomous authority to grant remission, he ought in charity to abolish Purgatory by granting [remission] to all, for to allow anyone to go to Purgatory showed lack of charity" (Swanson, *Indulgences*, 306).

[5] On the words: Oxford English Dictionary (oed.com), s.v. right, skill, will; Maurizio Lupoi, *the Origins of the European Legal Order*, Adrian Belton (trans.) (Cambridge: Cambridge University Press, 2000), 420–429.

the Body of Christ equal with respect to their souls, like grains of flour, their functions in the commonwealth were different, like the parts of a windmill. Excommunication for debt rested on the ultimate equality of Christians with respect to their souls. Any man, no matter how powerful, who broke faith with another, could be excommunicated for debt. At the same time as the procedure effectively empowered lenders to damn borrowers for delinquency in minor debts, it afforded those potentially excluded from more expensive, more complicated judicial fora a very real and evidently desired avenue to justice.

My second point is that the letter of John Ball makes it clear that the norms of late medieval exchange were not those of the modern or even early modern market. The morality of rebelling late medieval English peasants and, we may presume, of rebelling late medieval French peasants (though, to repeat, we lack sources for the politico-religious ideas of the Jacques Bonhommes of 1358) focused on capital sins against God and therefore against the community his body. Expectations (if not always practices) of exchange, debt, and restitution reflected norms of charitable rather than profitable exchange, of relations of hierarchy, indebtedness, and reciprocal exchange rather than of purchase, profit, and individual claims to wealth or property. Sir John speaks not of violations of the Decalogue, but of the seven deadly sins: pride, covetise or greed, lechery or lust, envy, gluttony, wrath, sloth. He urges peasants to stand up for truth, and this we may understand less as the theologians' transcendent *veritas* or religious truth than, for example, the *veritas scabinorum*, the inquest of Flemish aldermen, the truth of the local goodmen whose "obvious competitor" was precisely the "clergymen's truth."[6] John Ball's truth was the trustworthiness of the late medieval Christian community, a body of believers bound together in charity by debt and other forms of obligation, rather than the theoretical, remote truth of learned theologians. It was a truth of fidelity, honesty, and fairness in transactions and of equal if proportionate participation in securing the community's good, individual, and collective survival in this world and salvation in the next. Ball's letter accused elites of faithlessness, of being "untrue," untrustworthy men who broke faith with the Christian

[6] R. C. van Caeneghem, "Law and Power in Twelfth-Century Flanders," in *Cultures of Power: Lordship, Status, and Power in Twelfth-Century Europe* (Philadelphia: University of Pennsylvania Press, 1995), 149–171, 159. Geoff Koziol suggested a decade ago in a fruitful seminar that "truth" (in van Caeneghem's case Middle Dutch "*trouwe*") may not have been exactly equivalent to "*veritas*," reflections he has recently elaborated: *The Politics of Memory and Identity in Carolingian Royal Diplomas: The West Frankish Kingdom (840–987)* (Turnhout: Brepols, 2012), 315–399, esp. 349–352 on "truth" and "true men" and on "triuwe and rehtu." See too Lupoi, *Origins*, 379 n.90 on *triuwa* and *treuga*, the truce of true, faithful men.

community. Rebellion is here a more physically violent form of excommunication in that complainants sought to expel violators of the social contract from the community.[7] Promises, implicit and explicit contracts, were the community's foundation, the foundation of the *commercium hominum*. The promise of salvation extended in baptism. The promise of protection and peace extended through taxation or seigneurial exactions. The promise of satisfaction extended in sales or purchases on credit or in loans of materials or tools. The promise to abide by the statutes of a religious order, guild, or town. The promise of justice implicit in omnipresent images of the king as lawgiver and in the daily business of courts who rendered justice in his name. Excommunication for debt pointed to the multiple, manifold obligations that bound together the various communities of late medieval Europe – village or parish, traders at a market, guilds or fraternities, burgesses of a chartered town, the affinity of a lord, lords joined in alliances or by pensions, sworn officers of guilds, towns, and princes, taxpaying subjects of a king, nobles obliged to join in the *ban* or *arrière-ban*, and so on.

By 1500, this whole system of obligation was destabilized by the appearance that "everything could be bought: manors with justice attached, social status, salvation … The commercialised and transferable *rente* loosened the foundation of [seigneurial] dues in bonds of personal dependence and transformed them into nothing more than obligations on a piece of property."[8] The "monetization of all spheres of life," the transformation of "seigneurial" exploitation into "financial" exploitation of peasants demanded a reconception of the notion of community, one based less on moral obligations within a religious community than on nevertheless moralized contractual relations between individuals within a political community.[9] In this way, the secularization of the enforcement of credit complemented the incursions of Europeans in West Africa, the Americas, and Asia: the Atlantic world was made possible in part by new ways of thinking about contracts. Contracts were no longer obligations between members of Christ, but between subjects of different political communities encompassing the Christian and the non-Christian world. Thus, in proclaiming the royal monopoly over the regulation of contracts, the very same Ordinance of Villers-Cotterêts that in 1539 officially barred church courts from personal actions against layfolk devoted its last eight articles (185–192) to the suppression of guilds.[10] At the

[7] Much as Chris Briggs and others have shown communities to have effectively excluded the overly indebted by confiscating their holdings.

[8] Hans-Jörg Gilomen, "L'endettement paysan et la question du crédit dans les pays d'Empire au Moyen Âge," in Berthe, *Endettement*, 99–137, at 137.

[9] The quoted terms are from Gilomen, "L'endettement paysan," 137.

[10] Isambert, 12: 638–640.

same time as the Catholic Church grew suspicious of lay confraternities and sought to recenter religious life around the parish, the king of France sought to repress similarly autonomous social bodies.[11] That he was ultimately unsuccessful does not detract from the significance of the attempt to create Bodinian polities of families united in submission to the sovereign. While it is important not to underestimate the monetization of the earlier medieval economy, the sixteenth-century passage of control over credit from church courts (in part) to secular courts and the accompanying secularization of the language of contract helped to lay the foundations of communities that were horizontal with respect to purchasing potential (hence the Ordinance of Villers-Cotterêts's worries about the "*monopoles*" of craftsmen) if unequal with respect to actual wealth in place of communities that were vertical with respect to chains of dependence and obligation if potentially horizontal with respect to spiritual worth. Even as the market corroded secular hierarchies, indebtedness retained its moral significance. Humanist influences, including the notable popularity of printed editions Cicero's *De Officiis*, convey how the radical suggestion of the potential equality of Christians that erupted for the last time in the sixteenth-century German Peasants War was sublimated into trust that underlay consumer society at the same time as the reckoning of spiritual worth (if not everywhere explicitly tied to one's economic status) was pushed into the private sphere. If still in 1500 debt was a "breach" or "lesion of faith (*fidei lesio*)" that constituted a cause of action against a layman in an ecclesiastical tribunal, by 1600 it was not long before Grotius would propose that "contracts must be honored (*pacta sunt servanda*)," even were there no God.[12] Faith was the foundation no longer of the Church but of the commonwealth and of the community of nations.[13] Soon it would be the foundation of the market, as self-interest took the place of the hope of salvation as the goal of human existence.

The moral burden of debt survived the reconceptualization of Church, State, society, and market in the Age of Reformations. To focus on changes

[11] Natalie Davis provides any number of reasons why Francis might have wanted to do this in "Strikes and Salvation at Lyon," in *Society and Culture*, 1–16.

[12] Grotius, *De jure belli ac pacis libri tres* (Amsterdam: Willem Blaeuw, 1631), unpaginated prolegomena: "quia enim homo supra caeteras animantes non tantum vim obtinet socialem de qua diximus, sed et judicium ad aestimanda quae delectant aut nocent, non praesentia tantum, sed et futura, et quae in utrumvis possunt ducere; pro humani intellectus modo etiam in his judicium recte conformatum sequi, neque metu, aut voluptatis praesentis illecebra corrumpi, aut temerario rapi impetu, conveniens esse humanae naturae; et quod tali judicio plane repugnat, etiam contra jus naturae, humanae scilicet, esse intelligitur … Et haec quidem quae jam diximus, locum aliquem haberent etiamsi daremus, quod sine summo scelere dari nequit, non esse Deum, aut non curari ab eo negotia humana."

[13] Muldrew, *The Economy of Obligation*, esp. 132–141.

relevant to the end of excommunication for debt, the shift from Christianity as a "body of believers" to Christianity as a "body of belief" entailed a reconceptualization of the sacrament of the Eucharist. Rather than being, to use Pierrette Paravy's apt term, a "privilege" conceded by a legal authority as a sign of membership in a community,[14] the early modern encouragement of more frequent communion shows how the Eucharist was increasingly viewed as a helpmeet for individuals in their struggle toward salvation. Likewise, and more generally, Jean Gerson "democratized" and "de-professionalized" theology so that it could serve all pilgrims (*peregrini, viatores*) on the path to God; importantly, Gerson's *Viator* was neither monk nor necessarily a cleric but "everyman."[15] At the same time as religious currents opened the pursuit of holiness or *via perfectionis* to layfolk, the clericalization of the early modern Catholic Church and consequently of canon law entailed a lessening of its overtly jurisdictional nature – in the external forum. Officialities receded from view as the confessor, judge of conscience in the penitential forum, stepped forward. Enshrined in his confessional, this judge "in the internal forum" assigned penances and consoled privately, emphasizing conscience over membership in a community defined by behavior. He might command a believer to restitution, but privately, rather than in a public judicial procedure. Religion began its modern movement inward and out of the public eye.

In terms of politics, the sixteenth century saw both the development of territorial polities defined by stronger princely or governmental control of matters formerly administered by church authorities, town councils, or lords. In France, the *appel comme d'abus* from the 1440s offered royal courts supervision of the activity of church courts. From the 1520s, frequent use of this procedure served to advance the competence of royal courts at the expense of ecclesiastical jurisdiction. As in England and in the Germanies, the advance of secular jurisdiction was justified as the reform of the Church's abuses. Overuse of excommunication had reduced its potency, as Philippus Probus noted in an addition of *c.* 1546 to Cosme Guymier's commentary on the Pragmatic Sanction: "ecclesiastical sanctions are no longer feared, which gives rise to scandals and evils without end … therefore I would hope that the Council of Trent, now that it has gathered, should remedy the situation."[16] Even as the economic incentives for prelates to defend such jurisdiction disappeared and as the civil competence of officialities shrank in response to the reforms

[14] Paravy, *De la chrétienté romaine*, 484, 751.

[15] Mark S. Burrows, *Jean Gerson and De consolatione theologiae (1418): The Consolation of a Biblical and Reforming Theolgoy for a Disordered Age* (Tübingen: J.C.B. Mohr, 1991), 33–36.

[16] Cited in Esmein, "Débiteurs," 241 n.6.

of secular rulers, the Council of Trent reduced the number of clergy who lived from the revenue of ecclesiastical justice by limiting recourse to excommunication and by reducing the autonomy of exempt ecclesiastical institutions, cathedral chapters, and archdeacons.[17] Whereas in 1594 the provincial council of Avignon forbade excommunication for sums less than 20 écus (60£t) and in 1609 the council of Narbonne forbade excommunication for sums smaller than 20£t, in 1601 the Parlement of Paris had declared an excommunication for 33£t abusive.[18] The Church's own reforms came too late. Well before 1600, debt litigation had irretrievably passed to royal or, in the case of consular jurisdictions, quasi-royal justice. A reduced number of church courts survived the sixteenth century, though their competence was essentially restricted to the *état civil* or matters of baptism and marriage, and clerical discipline, including turning criminals in major orders over to royal justice. Their judgments were subject to the review of royal courts. The law by which they functioned was shaped by the king's legislation and by the decisions of his courts. Neither conciliar canons nor canonical doctrine lay behind either the origins or the disappearance of the practice of excommunication for debt: litigants deserted what they increasingly felt to be the abusive civil jurisdiction of church courts at virtually the same time as kings legislated that competence away.

The rise and fall of excommunication for debt therefore marks one aspect of the transition from the medieval to the early modern European world, from a conceptually unified Western Christendom to a Europe of territorial polities riven by religious differences if potentially united by trade. The reformation of the law undertaken by princes during Europe's long Reformation (1400–1700) reconfigured the jurisdictional relationships within their territories. In Catholic lands, canon law stood, but increasingly only insofar as tolerated or modified by the legislation of the local ruler. After the middle of the sixteenth century, canon law was less a competing source of practical law than a restricted body of law governing whichever matters the secular authorities permitted it. This reformation of the law reduced the supply, so to speak, of excommunication for debt. It did so through limits on the amounts for which a Christian could be excommunicated, through the organizational reforms of the Council of Trent that aimed to give bishops greater authority over archdeacons and exempt clergy, and through the efforts of secular courts to offer new forms of civil justice, particularly in matters of debt. By 1600 in France, the king's law was paramount, just as in England the Common Law

17 Lefebvre-Teillard, 25–32; Council of Trent, Session 25, *De Reformatione*, c.3.

18 Dupont, *Les monitoires*, 67.

had secured its predominance over other forms of law. The withering of excommunication for debt signals the emergence of early modern juridical orders across Europe. The threat of excommunication survived in different forms, but primarily in moral cases. Only in France did general monitions persist after the end of the sixteenth century. Until the end of the Old Regime (and in two instances under Napoleon) the State found it useful to have priests threaten witnesses who did not disclose what they knew of a crime with excommunication.[19]

In economic terms, excommunication for debt was only of interest to prelates possessing rights of jurisdiction at a particular, circumscribed conjuncture, for only in great quantities did the practice yield a reasonable profit. Before and after the worst of the late medieval crisis of landed incomes, roughly 1450–1500, it was less important. Whence the demand for the procedure? We can securely identify two potential sources: (i) ordinary people facing credit crises or despairing of recalcitrant debtors and (ii) those like the usurious bourgeois of Besançon. The latter are akin to predatory lenders who purchased annuities from peasants so as to foreclose on their farms. Yet the former appear to behind the proliferation of excommunicated debtors. Because everybody lived by credit, the practice fulfilled an important economic function. In a period when small coinage was scarce, when credit was a social, moral, and economic quantity, and when secular rulers did not concern themselves with minor debt, church courts allowed for the easy exchange of unwritten or privately recorded credit because a man's or a woman's word was always secured, in final analysis, on his or her eternal soul. The practice reveals more about late medieval religion than we might imagine, for the inverse of recognizing that credit was a social, moral, and economic concept is to recognize that the sacramental community was also an economic entity. There was no "market" conceptually separate from society, only the "Body of Christ" within which Christians were saved. There was no Federal Reserve, no FDIC, no Consumer Protection Bureau, only seigneurial, municipal, church, and royal courts.

Excommunication for debt points therefore to another transition, the economic transition that goes by many names: "the transition to capitalism," "the sixteenth-century price revolution," "the age of first empires," even "the Renaissance." The practice stands athwart the medieval and early modern economic worlds, highlighting the integration of local, primarily face-to-face markets into regional economies. In these, relations of trust were less certain and knowledge of one's borrowers was

[19] Dupont, *Les monitoires*, 191-209. Both *monitoires* were requested and fulminated in the autumn of 1806.

difficult to come by, even as relations of credit grew increasingly necessary to commerce and to subsistence. Excommunication for debt helped to extend the community of trust, for in a Christian community all were bound by the hope of salvation. It may have made small-scale credit efficient, since the monetary cost of the practice was small though its emotional and religious cost may have been considerably greater. Its disappearance may therefore have been harmful, particularly as the late sixteenth-century spike in litigation illustrates that sufficient trust in impersonal credit had not yet been established. In contrast to England, even though French "merchants were obliged to convert unrecoverable debts into annuities,"[20] this possibility was not viable for small debts to many different individuals, only for repeated transactions on credit with a single individual. The disappearance of the civil competence of church courts in matters of debt left French subjects easy legal recourse only for expensive, written obligations and may even have driven merchants to invest more in land, so as to secure easily executable credit on the land.

The withering of the practice signals acceptance of the State as guarantor of credit. It is a forerunner of the transition detected by Michel de Certeau in the mid-seventeenth century, when the organizing categories of society shifted from religious to political ones.[21] As the appearance of excommunication for debt in the thirteenth century signals a failure of private guarantees of credit (pledges, shunning, cartel behavior), its virtual disappearance by the end of the sixteenth century signals how new religious ideals encouraged the development of early modern states. Michael Breen has summarized Julie Hardwick: "the early modern French state was less a concrete entity than a claim to authority, one that ordinary French men and women readily borrowed to organize and to maintain the structures of daily life."[22] Excommunication for debt is a transitional institution, superseding private guarantees of debt and being superseded by the State's "public" and exclusive guaranty of debt. In the sixteenth century, changing religious sensibilities turned consumers – consumers of justice – away from the Church as a guarantor of contracts and toward the State. Religious sensibilities drove what Wim Decock has aptly called the "*Verstaatlichung*" of private law, here with respect to contracts.[23] Through the Reformations of Christianity, it seems, the State gained sufficient credit with its subjects to begin its modern role as

[20] Schnapper, *Les rentes*, 284.

[21] Michel de Certeau, "The Inversion of What Can Be Thought" and "The Formality of Practices," in *The Writing of History*, 125–146 and 147–205.

[22] Breen, "Law, Society," 384.

[23] Wim Decock contrasts the present-day *Entstaatlichung* of private law, certainly in the European Union: *Theologians*, 7.

arbiter of the economy. Credit no longer rested on an individual's hope of salvation but on the State's guarantee of his or her property rights.

Even then, the moral economy survived down to the dawn of the nineteenth century. We can see this during the French Revolution in the lynching of bakers accused of defrauding customers, in references to the forced return of the king, queen, and dauphin to Paris as the return of the "baker," "baker's wife," "baker's son," and in the push of the Parisian populace for the law of the Maximum during the Terror. Such language reflected not simply Louis XVI's gravidity but complaints that he – and the Old Regime more generally – was failing to govern properly, that he, like the nobles of France in 1358 or the nobles of England in 1381, was failing to play his part in the moral economy. With the fall of the monarchy, these fears were redirected toward hoarders, toward the "enemies of the people" who merited civil and corporal death. In England, E. P. Thompson has pointed out that "[t]he paternalist model," the moral economy evident well before 1381, "existed in an eroded body of Statute law, as well as common law and custom. It was the model, which very often, informed the actions of government in times of emergency until the 1770s; and to which many local magistrates continued to appeal."[24] This model was directed at allowing the poor their sustenance through the enforcement of laws against forestalling, regrating, and engrossing, of the Assize of Bread, of the laws giving residents priority at grain markets, and even of guarantees of weights and measures.[25] This model crumbled at the end of the eighteenth century, as magistrates – local elites – adopted the ideology of Adam Smith and entrepreneurial grain traders as they moralized market forces. The erosion was slow: still "in 1795 Lord Kenyon, the chief justice, took it upon himself to announce that forestalling remained an indictable offence at common law: 'though the act of Edward VI be repealed (whether wisely or unwisely I take not upon me to say) yet it still remains an offence at common law, coeval with the constitution.'"[26] Lord Kenyon's obsolescent assertion that observing the terms of the moral economy was in some sense a constitutional necessity was cognate to the constitutional views of the peasant rebels of 1381. It no longer appears to have persuaded in the nineteenth century, as the abolition of the Corn Laws or the Irish Famine illustrate.

[24] E. P. Thompson, "The Moral Economy of the English Crowd in the Eighteenth Century," *Past & Present* 50:1 (1971), 76–136, at 193.

[25] Compare Thompson's components of the moral economy to Jean Gerson's rules for merchants (cited in Prodi, *Settimo*, 211 n.14): "Regula mercatorum est ut non in die dominica mercentur. Nec perjurent. Ab illecito sibi caveant lucro; nec ad diem vendant, nec carius propter dilationem. Ut debitum suum tempore promisso solvit; nec scienter mentiantur. Aequam stateram habeant, aequa pondera et aequam mensuram."

[26] Thompson, "Moral Economy," 200.

At the same time as new economic attitudes prepared for the West's economic take-off after 1800, a take-off that brought unimaginable improvement in standards of living and in freedom, laissez-faire killed off a moral economy born of Christian visions of society as the Body of Christ at least four hundred years before. From being one aspect, one "forum" within the Body of Christ, the Market became the organizing principle of society. To expand upon Michel de Certeau's point about the seventeenth-century transition from religious to political principles in the organization of society, we might propose a similar shift from political to economic principles in the nineteenth century. Just as the corrosive effects of the seventeenth-century transition on the European churches only become evident in the following century, so only now are the corrosive effects on sovereign states of the nineteenth-century transition to a globalized economy becoming fully evident.

My aim in this book has been to uncover a nearly forgotten function of ecclesiastical tribunals in the last centuries of the Middle Ages, when their sanctions helped to enforce the trust that underlay market and nonmarket transactions. Given the limited nature of surviving evidence, I cannot say many things about the practice: the average duration of loans at issue, the average amount of the original loan, sale, or purchase credit, the precise landholding of those sanctioned, and so on. I can, however, state confidently that excommunication for debt developed with the bureaucratization of officialities on the basis of their jurisdiction over written contracts. The practice appears to have peaked in the mid-fifteenth-century, when it not coincidentally comprised an important proportion of some prelates' diminished incomes. By 1500, however, it was in decline, as creditors began to turn elsewhere and as reforming secular authorities developed new legal remedies and prohibited church courts from enforcing contracts through spiritual sanctions. I can say that the practice provided an incredibly supple, cheap, and effective means of enforcing the small, verbal or informal contracts on which daily commerce functioned. Since it is not everywhere clear that a similarly effective, cheap remedy emerged everywhere for this type of debt in the sixteenth century, and since the identification of an abuse rests on one's ideal of a particular institution, I cannot say that the disappearance of excommunication for debt was wholly good or bad. Its disappearance may have stimulated credit, because small loans no longer rested on the debtor's potential damnation. Its disappearance may have depressed credit, because small loans may have become unenforceable except through cartel-like behavior or social and commercial exclusion. It may be that the early modern tendency of peasants to burden their land with debt may reflect the absence of any more flexible form of accessible, enforceable credit to smooth the discontinuities of the agrarian year or to bridge years of poor harvests. One suspects that eighteenth-century Champenois peasants had rather, as the Widow Clicquot foreclosed upon their mortgaged lands, been excommunicated.[27] It may be that the moral economy required fear of hell to survive. In a Deist, anticlerical, enlightened age, what was to stand in the way of the pursuit of profit? Excommunication for debt was both an abuse and a relic of Christians' essential equality, a manifestation of exchange governed by Christian morals rather than by moralized market forces. The reassertion of man's essential equality at the end of the eighteenth century might be seen as a recovery of ideas dormant for a century or two in a new register. The era when European states ceased to enforce the moral economy that they had inherited from the late medieval Church is known as the Age of Revolutions.

[27] Thomas Brennan, "Peasants and Debt in Eighteenth-Century Champagne," *Journal of Interdisciplinary History* 37:2 (Autumn, 2006), 175–200.

Select bibliography

I. ARCHIVAL SOURCES

Archives départementales d'Eure-et-Loir, Chartres

G 813, Register, Officiality of the Grand Archdeacon of Chartres, 1400–1402

G 815, idem, 1409–1414

G 816, idem, 1414–1420

G 817, Register of Excommunications and Fines, Officiality of the Sub-Dean of Chartres, 1380–1436

Archives départementales de l'Orne, Alençon

1 G 35, Formulary of the Diocese of Séez, *c.* 1500

Archives départementales de Seine-Maritime, Rouen

4 B II, 1 bis, Plaids à Mace, Bailliage de Rouen, 1483–1484

54 H 3, Legal dossiers for the Abbey of Montivilliers

54 H 23, Prayer Roll, Abbey of Montivilliers, 1398–1399

54 H 84, Accounts for Mi-Carême, Abbey of Montivilliers, 1406

G 1, Catalogue of Archives of the Archbishop of Rouen, 1747

G 8–137, General Accounts of the Archbishopric of Rouen, 1370–1594

G 147, Account of the Clerk of the *Vicairerie*, Rouen, 1465–1466

G 274, Accounts of the Sealer, Rouen, 1433–1537

G 276, Registers of Excommunicates, Rouen, 1453–1529

G 5255, Formulary, Officiality of the Abbey of Fécamp, 1500–1550

G 5268, Register of Court Business, Montivilliers, 1406–1485

G 5270, Register of Excommunicates, Montivilliers, 1433–1463 (part iii: Harfleur, 1438–1463 and remaining parishes)

G 5271, Register of Excommunicates, Montivilliers, 1433–1463 (part ii: Harfleur, 1433–1438)

G 5273, Register of Excommunicates, Montivilliers, 1499–1530

G 5274, Register of Sentences in Matrimonial and ex officio Cases, Montivilliers, 1517–1559

G 5280, Register of Excommunicates, Montivilliers, 1433–1463 (part i: parish of Sainte-Croix)

G 5317, Draft sentences 1506–1519

G 5321, Writ of the Official of Montivilliers, 1386

Archives départementales de l'Yonne, Auxerre

H 2161, Volume M, Cartulary of the Abbey of Saint-Michel, Tonnerre, 1500–1511

Archives nationales de France, Paris

U 419, 182r-185v, Arrêts and Sentences against Louis de Berquin

AN J 945 no. 119, Extract of Registers of the Parlement of Paris, 1287

L 432 n°s 70, Summaries of the Temporal Revenue of Bishop of Paris, 1545, 1596

LL 385 C, Temporal Revenue of the Bishop of Paris 1665–1682

X^{1a}1529, Parlement de Paris, Civil Cases, Registre du Conseil, 1525–1526

X^{1a}4876, Parlement de Paris, Civil Cases, Plaidoiries matinées, 1525

X^{2a}61, Parlement de Paris, Criminal Cases, Plaidoiries, 1494–1497

Z^{1o}4, Archidiaconal Officiality of Paris, Civil Cases,1477–1480

Z^{1o}5, Archidiaconal Officiality of Paris, Civil Cases, 1479–1480

Z^{1o}8, Archidiaconal Officiality of Paris, Civil Cases, 1499–1503

Z^{1o}17, Archidiaconal Officiality of Paris, Excommunications, 1426–1439

Z^{1o}18, Archidiaconal Officiality of Paris, Account of the Sealer, 1550

Z^{1o}41, Diocesan Officiality of Paris, Ex officio Cases, 1624–1625

Minutier Central de Paris, Étude XIX, 67

Bibliothèque nationale de France, Paris, Manuscrits occidentaux:

Latin 1458, Style, Officiality of Saint-Brieuc, *c.*1529

Latin 4812, Formulary, Officiality of Sens, *c.*1500; Officiality of Auxerre, 1583

Latin 10930, Formulary, Officiality of Le Mans, *c.*1429

Latin 17766, Formulary, Officiality of Corbie, *c.*1488

Latin 18371, Style, Officiality of Corbie, late fifteenth century

Nouvelles acquisitions latines (NAL) 426, Formulary, Officiality of Tréguier, *c.*1312–1315

II. PRINTED SOURCES

Almain, Jacques. *Aurea clarissimi et acutissimi Doctoris theologi Magistri Jacobi Almain Senonensis opuscula*. Paris: Gilles de Gourmont, 1518.

Thomae Aquinatis Opera Omnia. Rome: Typographia polyglotta, 1906.

d'Argentré, Bertrand. *Commentarii in patrias Britonum leges, seu Consuetudines generales antiquissimae Ducatus Britannie*. Paris: Jacques d'Allin, 1611.

Coustumes generales du pays et duché de Bretagne reformées en l'an mil cinq cents quatre-vingts. Aitiologia, sive ratiocinatio de reformandis causis. Paris: Jacques d'Allin, 1610.

Aubenas, Roger, ed. *Recueil de lettres des officialités de Marseille et d'Aix (XIVe–XVe siècle)*. Paris: Auguste Picard, 1937.

Baldus super decretalibus. Lyon, 1564.

Bessin, Guillaume, ed. *Concilia Rotomagensis provinciae accedunt diocesanae synodi pontificium epistolae* ... Rouen: François Vaultier, 1717.

Bourdot de Richebourg, C.-A. *Nouveau coutumier général*. Paris: Michel Brunet, 1724.

Denisart, J.-B. *Collection de décisions nouvelles et de notions relatives à la jurisprudence actuelle*. Paris: veuve Desaint, 1771.

Dupont, G., ed. "Registre de l'officialité de Cerisy, 1314–1457." *Mémoires de la Société des antiquaires de Normandie* 30 (1880): 271–662.

Durand, Guillaume. *Speculum judiciale*. Basel: apud Frobenos fratres, 1574.

Favier, Jean, ed. *Les contribuables parisiens à la fin de la Guerre de Cent Ans. Les rôles d'impôt de 1421, 1423 et 1438*. Geneva-Paris: Librairie Droz, 1970.

Fevret, Charles. *Traité de l'abus*. Lyon: Jean Girin, 1667.

Gerson, Jean. *Opera omnia*, ed. Louis-Elliès Dupin. Antwerp: Sumptibus societatis, 1706.

Grotius, Hugo. *De jure belli ac pacis libri tres*. Amsterdam: Willem Blaeuw, 1631.

Guénois, Pierre. *La nouvelle et dernière conférence des ordonnances et edicts royaux distribuée et XII. livres à l'imitation et selon l'ordre et disposition du Code de l'Empereur Justinian*. Paris: Claude Sonnius, 1627.

Guymier, Cosme. *Pragmatica Sanctio cum Concordatis. Cosme Guymier Clarissimi Senatus Parisiensis. Consiliarii solennis et eruditus Commentarius ad Pragmaticam Sanctionem*. Lyon: Benoît Bonnin, 1532.

Dalham, Florian, ed. *Concilia Salisburgensia*. Augsburg: sumptibus Matthei Rieger, 1788.

Éveillon, Jacques. *Traité des excommunications et monitoires. Avec la maniere de publier, executer, et fulminer toutes sortes de Monitoire, et excommunications*. Paris: E. Couterot, 1672.

Fontanon, Antoine. *Les edicts et ordonnances des rois de France … divisez en quatre tomes*. Paris: [Claude Morel], 1611.

von der Hardt, Hermann. *Rerum concilii oecumenici Constantiensis de universali ecclesiasticae disciplinae reformatione*. Frankfurt/Leipzig: Christian Genschius, 1697.

Hostiensis, *Summa aurea*. Venice: heredes Melchior Sessae, 1570.

Imbert, Jean. *Institutiones forenses, Galliae pene totius quae moribus regitur, communes*. Lyon: Sebastian Gryphius, 1552.

Les Quatre Livres des Institutions forenses. Paris: Jean Ruelle, 1552.

Isambert, Jourdan, and Decrusy, eds. *Recueil général des anciennes lois françaises, depuis l'an 420 jusqu'à la révolution de 1789*. Paris: Belin-Leprieur/Verdière, 1825. 29 vols.

Knighton, Henry. *Chronicon Henrici Knighton vel Cnitthon Monachi Leycestrensis*, ed. J. R. Lumby. Kraus Reprint Ltd, 1965; repr. of London, 1895.

La Croix, Jean-François de. *Dictionnaire historique des cultes religieux, établis dans le monde depuis son origine jusqu'à présent*. Paris: Vincent, 1770.

Le Coq, Jean. *Questiones Johannis Galli*, ed. Marguerite Boulet-Sautel. Paris: Éditions de Boccard, 1946.

Le Plat, Josse. *Momumentorum ad historiam Concilii tridentini … amplissima collectio*. Louvain: Ex typographia academica, 1781–1787.

Loisel, Antoine. *Institutes coutumières*. Paris: chez la veuve Abel L'Angelier, 1611.

Luther, Martin. *D. Martin Luthers Werke*. Weimar: Herman Böhlau, 1888.

Lyndwood, William. *Provinciale (seu Constitutiones Angliae)*. Oxford: H. Hall, 1679.

Petit, Joseph, ed. *Registre des causes civiles de l'officialité épiscopale de Paris, 1384–1387*. Paris: Imprimerie nationale, 1919.

Poos, L. R. *Lower Ecclesiastical Jurisdiction in Late-Medieval England: The Courts of the Dean and Chapter of Lincoln, 1336–1349, and the Deanery of Wisbech, 1458–1484*. Records of Social and Economic History, New Series 32. Oxford: The British Academy, 2001.

Pouillé du Diocèse de Chartres. Chartres: Nicolas Doublet, 1738.

Rebuffi, Pierre. *In consitutiones regias ... commentarii*. Lyon: apud heredes Guillelmi Rouillii, 1599.

Tabbagh, Vincent, ed. *Fasti ecclesiae gallicanae. Répertoire prosopographique des évêques, dignitaires et chanoines de France de 1200 à 1500, t. II: diocèse de Rouen*. Turnhout: Brepols, 1998.

Tejada y Ramiro, D. Juan. *Colleción de canones y de todos los concilios de la iglesia española ... parte segunda*. Madrid: D. Pedro Montero, 1855.

Viollet, Paul, ed. *Les Établissements de saint Louis accompagnés des textes primitifs et de textes dérivés, avec une introduction et des notes*. Paris: Librairie Renouard, 1881.

Vleeschouwers-Van Melkebeek, Monique. *Compotus sigilliferi curie Tornacensis (1429–1481)*. Brussels: Commission royale d'histoire, 1995.

Zachariae von Lingenthal, C. E., ed. *Imperatoris Iustiniani Novellae quae vocantur constitutiones extra codicem*. Leipzig: Teubner, 1881.

III. SELECTED HISTORICAL LITERATURE

Albani, Benedetta. "Nuova luce sulle relazioni tra la Sede Apostolica e le Americhe. La pratica della concessione del 'pase regio' ai documenti pontifici destinati alle Indie." In *Eusebio Francesco Chini e il suo tempo. Una riflessione storica*, ed. C. Ferlan: 83–102. Trent: Fondazione Bruno Kessler, 2012.

d'Alteroche, Bernard. *L'officialité de Paris à la fin de l'Ancien Régime (1780–1790)*. Paris: LGDJ, 1994.

Ambühl, Rémy. *Prisoners of War in the Hundred Years War: Ransom Culture in the Late Middle Ages*. Cambridge: Cambridge University Press, 2013.

Arabeyre, Patrick. "Les deux justices. Les deux pouvoirs. La production doctrinale des juristes méridionaux sur les rapports entre justice ecclésiastique et justice royale, de Bernard de Rosier à Guillaume Benoît (deuxième moitié du XVe siècle)." *Les justices d'Église: Cahiers de Fanjeux* 42 (2007): 373–397.

"Un enseignement de science politique dans les facultés de droit canonique françaises de la fin du XVe et au début du XVIe siècle (Paris: Cosme Guymier; Cahors: Guillaume Benoît; Toulouse: Jean d'Ayma)." In *Science politique et droit public dans les facultés de droit européennes (XIIIe – XVIIIe siècle)*, eds. M. Stolleis and J. Krynen: 299–324. Frankfurt-am-Main: Max-Planck-Institut für europäische Rechtsgeschichte, 2008.

Les idées politiques à Toulouse à la veille de la Réforme. Recherches autour de l'oeuvre de Guillaume Benoît (1455–1516). Toulouse: Université des sciences sociales de Toulouse, 2003.

Arnoux, Mathieu. “Croissance et crises dans le monde médiéval XIe–XVe siècle. Réflexions et pistes de recherche.” *Cahiers du monde russe* 46:1 (2005): 115–132.

Arnoux, Mathieu, and Jacques Bottin. “Autour de Rouen et Paris: Modalités d'integration d'un espace drapier (XIIIe–XVIe siècles).” *Revue d'histoire moderne et contemporaine* 48:2 (2001): 162–191.

Arnoux, Mathieu, and Olivier Guyotjeannin, eds. *Tabellions et tabellionages de la France médiévale et moderne*. Paris: École des Chartes, 2011.

Ascheri, Mario et al., eds. *'Ins Wasser geworfen und Ozeane durchquert'. Festschrift für Knut Wolfgang Nörr*. Cologne/Weimar/Vienna: Böhlau, 2003.

Bader, Karl S. “Arbiter arbitrator seu amicabilis compositor. Zur Verbreitung einer kanonistischen Formel in Gebieten nördlich der Alpen.” *Zeitschrift der Savigny-Stiftung für Rechtsgeschichte 90, Kanonistische Abteilung* 46 (1960): 239–276.

Bailey, Mark. *The Decline of Serfdom in Late Medieval England: From Bondage to Freedom*. Woodbridge: The Boydell Press, 2014.

“Manorial Accounts.” In *The English Manor c.1200-c.1500*: 97–116. Manchester: Manchester University Press, 2002.

Baker, J. H. *Collected Papers on English Legal History*. Cambridge: Cambridge University Press, 2013.

Bart, Jean. “La vente a réméré en Mâconnais (1450–1560, environ).” *Mémoires de la Société pour l'Histoire du Droit et des Institutions des anciens pays bourguignons, comtois et romands*, 23 (1962): 137–161.

Baulant, Micheline. “Prix et salaires à Paris au XVIe siècle: Sources et résultats.” *Annales ESC* 31:5 (1976): 954–995.

Baulant, Micheline, and Jean Meuvret. “Les prix des grains à Paris de 1431 à 1788.” *Annales ESC* 23 (1968): 520–540.

Baumgartner, Eugen. *Geschichte und Recht des Archidiakonates der oberrheinischen Bistümer mit Einschluss von Mainz und Würzburg*. Kirchliche Abhandlungen 39. Stuttgart: Ferdinand Enke, 1907; repr. Amsterdam: P. Schippers, 1965.

Bautier, Robert-Henri. “Origine et diffusion du sceau de juridiction.” *Comptes rendus des séances de l'Académie des Inscriptions et Belles-Lettres* (Apr. June 1971): 204–221.

Beaulande, Véronique. *Le malheur d'être exclu? Excommunication, réconciliation et société à la fin du Moyen Âge*. Paris: Publications de la Sorbonne, 2006.

Beik, William. “The Absolutism of Louis XIV as Social Collaboration.” *Past & Present* 188 (2005): 195–224.

Absolutism and Society in Seventeenth-Century France State Power and Provincial Aristocracy in Languedoc. Cambridge: Cambridge University Press, 1985.

Bellamy, J. G. *Bastard Feudalism and the Law*. London: Routledge, 2013; orig. 1983.

Bellomo, *The Common Legal Past of Europe, 1000–1800*, tr. Lydia G. Cochrane. Washington, DC: Catholic University of America Press, 1995.

Bennett, J. W. “The Medieval Loveday.” *Speculum* 23 (1958): 351–370.

Benveniste, Émile. *Indo-European Language and Society*. University of Miami Press, 1973: http://chs.harvard.edu/CHS/article/display/4308.

Berthe, M., ed. *Endettement Paysan et Crédit Rural dans l'Europe médiévale et moderne: Actes des XVIIes Journées d'Histoire de l'Abbaye de Flaran*. Toulouse: Presses universitaires du Mirail, 1998.

Billot, Claudine. *Chartres à la fin du Moyen Âge*. Paris: Éditions de l'École des Hautes Études en Sciences Sociales, 1987.

Black, Antony. "The Juristic Origins of Social Contract Theory." *History of Political Thought* 14:1 (1993): 57–76.

Blanchard, Ian. *Mining, Metallurgy, and Minting in the Middle Ages, Vol. 3: Continuing Afro-European Supremacy, 1250–1450*. Stuttgart: Franz Steiner Verlag, 2005.

Bois, Guy. "Comptabilité et histoire des prix: le prix du froment à Rouen au XVe siècle." *Annales ESC* 6 (1968): 1262–1282.

Crise du féodalisme. Paris: Presses de la Fondation Nationale des Sciences Politiques, 1976.

Bordeaux, Michèle. *Aspects économiques de la vie de l'Église aux XIVe et XVe siècles*. Paris: R. Pichon et R. Durand-Auzias, 1969.

Boldizzoni, Francesco. *The Poverty of Clio: Resurrecting Economic History*. Princeton: Princeton University Press, 2011.

Brady, T. A., Jr. "Reformation als Rechtsbruch. Territorialisierung der Kirchen im Heiligen Römischen Reich im europäischen Vergleich." In *Die Säkularisation im Prozess der Säkularisierung Europas*, eds. P. Blickle and R. Schlögl: 141–152. Tübingen: Bibliotheca academica Verlag, 2005.

Brooks, C. W. *Pettyfoggers and Vipers of the Commonwealth: The 'Lower Branch' of the Legal Profession in Early Modern England*. Cambridge: Cambridge University Press, 1986.

Bossy, John. *Christianity in the West, 1400–1700*. Oxford: Oxford University Press, 1985.

"The Mass as a Social Institution." *Past & Present* 100 (1983): 29–61.

Bottin, Jacques. *Seigneurs et paysans dans l'Ouest du pays de Caux (1540–1650)*. Paris: Éditions Le Sycomore, 1983.

Breen, Michael. "Law, Society, and the State in Early Modern France." *Journal of Modern History* 83:2 (2011): 346–386.

Brennan, Thomas. "Peasants and Debt in Eighteenth-Century Champagne." *Journal of Interdisciplinary History* 37:2 (2006): 175–200.

Briggs, Chris. "The Availability of Credit in the English Countryside, 1400–1480." *Agricultural History Review* 56:1 (2008): 1–24.

Credit and Village Society in Fourteenth-Century England. Oxford: The British Academy, 2009.

Campbell, Bruce. "The Agrarian Problem in the Early Fourteenth Century." *Past & Present* 188 (2005): 3–70.

Carbonnières, Louis de. *La procédure devant la chambre criminelle du Parlement de Paris au XIVe siècle*. Paris: H. Champion, 2004.

Carlen, Louis. "Zum Offizialat von Sitten im Mittelalter." *Zeitschrift der Savigny-Stiftung für Rechtsgeschichte 90, Kanonistische Abteilung* 46 (1960): 222–238.

Caspers, Paul. *Der Güte-und Schiedsgedanke im kirchlichen Zivilgerischtsverfahren. Eine kirchenrechtliche Untersuchung über das Wesen der episcopalis audientia*. Düsseldorf: Triltsch-Verlag, 1954.

de Certeau, Michel. *The Writing of History*, tr. Tom Conley. New York: Columbia University Press, 1988.

Christian, William. *Local Religion in Sixteenth-Century Spain*. Princeton: Princeton University Press, 1981.

Clanchy, Michael. *From Memory to Written Record: England 1066–1307*. Oxford: Blackwell, 1993; orig. 1979.

Claustre, Julie. "Le corps lié de l'ouvrier. Le travail et la dette à Paris au XVe siècle." *Annales HSS* 60:2 (2005): 383–408.

Dans les geôles du roi. L'emprisonnement pour dette à Paris à la fin du Moyen Âge. Paris: Publications de la Sorbonne, 2007.

ed. *La dette et le juge. Juridiction gracieuse et juridiction contentieuse du XIIIe au XVe siècle (France, Italie, Espagne, Angleterre, Empire)*. Paris: Publications de la Sorbonne, 2006.

Clerici, Luca. "Fonctions de la monnaire et formes de paiements en Italie du nord dans la seconde moitié du XVe siècle." *Histoire et Mesure*, 12:1–2 (1997): 5–36.

Colson, Justin. Review of Dyer's *A Country Merchant*, *Reviews in History* nr. 1339 (2012): www.history.ac.uk/reviews/review/1339.

Condorelli, O., F. Roumy, and M. Schmoeckel, eds. *Der Einfluss der Kanonistik auf die europäische Rechtskultur, Bd. 1: Zivil-und Zivilprozessrecht*. Cologne/Weimar/Vienna: Böhlau Verlag, 2009.

Cordes, Albrecht. "Auf der Suche nach der Rechtswirklichkeit der mittelalterlichen Lex mercatoria." *Zeitschrift der Savigny-Stiftung für Rechtsgeschichte, Germanistische Abteilung* 118 (2001): 168–184.

Cromartie, Alan. *The Constitutionalist Revolution: An Essay on the History of England, 1450–1642*. Cambridge: Cambridge University Press, 2006.

Crowston, Claire H. *Credit, Fashion, Sex: Economies of Regard in Old Regime France*. Chapel Hill: Duke University Press, 2013.

Fabricating Women: The Seamstresses of Old Regime France, 1675–1791. Chapel Hill: Duke University Press, 2001.

Davis, Natalie Z. *The Gift in Sixteenth-Century France*. Madison: University of Wisconsin Press, 2000.

Fiction in the Archives: Pardon Tales and Their Tellers in Sixteenth-Century France. Stanford: Stanford University Press, 1987.

Society and Culture in Early Modern France. Stanford: Stanford University Press, 1975.

Dawson, John P. *A History of Lay Judges*. Cambridge, MA: Harvard University Press, 1960.

Decock, Wim. "Leonardus Lessius on Buying and Selling (1605), Translation and Introduction." *Journal of Markets and Morality* 10 (2007): 466–482.

Theologians and Contract Law: The Moral Transformation of the Ius Commune (ca. 1500–1650). Leiden: Martinus Nijhoff, 2013.

De Roover, Raymond. *Business, Banking, and Economic Thought in Late Medieval and Early Modern Europe: Selected Studies of Raymond de Roover*, ed. Julius Kirshner. Chicago: University of Chicago Press, 1976.

Deroussin, David. *Histoire du droit des obligations*. Paris: Economica, 2007.

De Ruysscher, Dave. "La *lex mercatoria* contextualisée: tracer son parcours intellectuel." *Revue historique de droit français et étranger* 90:4 (2012): 499–515.

Desan, Christine. *Making Money. Coin, Currency, and the Coming of Capitalism*. Oxford: Oxford University Press, 2014.

Descimon, Robert. "Les fonctions de la métaphore du mariage politique du roi et de la république en France, XVe–XVIIIe siècles." *Annales ESC* 47:6 (1993): 1127–1147.

"*Nobles* de lignage et *noblesse* de service. Sociogenèses comparées de l'épée et de la robe (XVe-XVIIIe siècle)." In *Épreuves de noblesse: Les expériences nobiliaires de la haute robe parisienne (XVIe–XVIIIe siècle)*, eds. R. Descimon and E. Haddad: 277–302. Paris: Les Belles Lettres, 2010.

Qui étaient les Seize? Mythes et réalités de la Ligue parisienne (1585–1594). Paris: Klincksieck, 1983.

Dessert, Daniel. *Argent, pouvoir et société au Grand Siècle*. Paris: Fayard, 1984.

L'argent du sel. Le sel de l'argent. Paris: Fayard, 2012.

de Vries, Jan. *The Industrious Revolution: Consumer Demand and the Household Economy, 1650 to the Present*. Cambridge: Cambridge University Press, 2008.

Dewald, Jonathan. *Pont-St-Pierre 1398–1789: Lordship, Community, and Capitalism in Early Modern France*. Berkeley: University of California Press, 1987.

Donahue, Charles, Jr. *The Records of the Medieval Ecclesiastical Courts, Part I: The Continent, Comparative Studies in Continental and Anglo-American Legal History 6*, eds. Helmut Coing and Knut Wolfgang Nörr. Berlin: Duncker und Humblot, 1989.

"Roman Canon Law in the Medieval English Church: Stubbs vs. Maitland Re-Examined after 75 Years in the Light of Some Records from the Church Courts." *Michigan Law Review* 72:4 (1974): 647–716.

Dubois, Henri. "Le commerce de la France au temps de Louis XI. Expansion ou défensive?" In *La France de la fin du quinzième siècle: Renouveau et apogée*, eds. B. Chevalier and P. Contamine: 15–29. Paris: CNRS, 1985).

"Drapiers normands aux foires de Bourgogne à la fin du Moyen Âge." *Annales de Normandie, Hors-Série: Recueil d'études offert en hommage au doyen Michel de Boüard* 1:1 (1982): 229–242.

Duffy, Eamon. *Marking the Hours: English People and Their Prayers 1240–1570*. New Haven: Yale University Press, 2006.

The Stripping of the Altars: Traditional Religion in England 1400–1580. New Haven: Yale University Press, 1992.

Dumas, Auguste. "Dieu nous garde de l'"et coetera' du notaire." In *Mélanges Paul Fournier*: 153–169. Paris: Recueil Sirey, 1929.

Dumont, Ernest, and Alphonse Martin. *Histoire de la ville de Montivilliers*. Fécamp: L. Durand et fils, 1886.

Dupont, Pierre. *Les monitoires à fin de révélations dans la procédure séculière*. Paris: Arthur Rousseau, 1930.

Dyer, Christopher. *An Age of Transition? Economy and Society in the Later Middle Ages*. Oxford: Oxford University Press, 2005.

A Country Merchant, 1495–1520: Trading and Farming at the End of the Middle Ages. Oxford: Oxford University Press, 2012.

Lords and Peasants in a Changing Society: The Estates of the Bishop of Worcester, 680–1540. Cambridge: Cambridge University Press, 1980.

Ehrle, F. "Ein Bruchstück der Akten des Konzils von Vienne." *Archiv für Literatur und Kirchengeschichte des Mittelalters* 4 (1888): 361–470.

Elsener, Ferdinand. "Die Exkommunikation als Prozessuales Vollstreckungsmittel. Zur Geschichte des Kirchenbanns im Spätmittelalter." In *Tübinger Festschrift für Eduard Kern*: 69–85. Tübingen: J. C. B. Mohr, 1968.

Esch, Arnold. "Überlieferungs-Chance und Überlieferungs-Zufall als methodisches Problem des Historikers." *Historische Zeitschrift* 240 (1985): 529–570.

Esmein, Adhémar. "Débiteurs privés de sépulture." *Mélanges d'archéologie et d'histoire* 5 (1885): 223–245.

Farmer, Sharon. "Merchant Women and the Administrative Glass Ceiling in Thirteenth-Century Paris." In *Women and Wealth in Late Medieval Europe*, ed. Theresa Earenfight: 89–108. Basingstoke: Palgrave Macmillan, 2010.

Surviving Poverty in Medieval Paris: Gender, Ideology, and the Daily Lives of the Poor. Ithaca: Cornell University Press, 2002.

Fasolt, Constantin. "Hegel's Ghost: Europe, the Reformation, and the Middle Ages." *Viator* 39 (2008): 345–386.

Favier, Jean. *Les finances pontificales à l'époque du Grand Schisme d'Occident, 1378–1409*. Paris: Éditions E. de Boccard, 1966.

Febvre, Lucien. "L'application du Concile de Trente et l'excommunication pour dettes en Franche-Comté." *Revue historique*, 103 (1910): 225–247, and 104 (1910): 1–39.

Fogarty, Gerald P. "The Historical Origin of the Excommunication of Divorced and Remarried Catholics Imposed by the Third Plenary Council of Baltimore." *The Jurist* 38 (1978): 426–433.

Fontaine, Laurence. *L'Économie morale: Pauvreté, crédit et confiance dans l'Europe préindustrielle*. Paris: Gallimard, 2008.

Fournier, Paul. *Les officialités au Moyen Âge*. Paris: E. Plon, 1880.

Fourquin, Guy. *Les campagnes de la région parisienne à la fin du Moyen Âge*. Paris: PUF, 1964.

Gabriel, Frédéric. "Qualifications de la communauté et autorité de la Tradition: l'histoire des dogmes comme construction ecclésiale, de Torquemada à Lethmaet (XVe–XVIe siècle)." *Bulletin du centre d'études médiévales d'Auxerre*, Hors-série n°7 (2013): http://cem.revues.org/12901.

Gazzaniga, Jean-Louis. *L'Église du Midi à la fin du règne de Charles VII (1444–1461) d'après la jurisprudence du Parlement de Toulouse*. Paris: Éditions A. et J. Picard, 1976.

Introduction historique au droit des obligations. Paris: PUF, 1992.

Génestal, Robert. *Les origines de l'appel comme d'abus. Notes de cours publiées par les soins de Pierre Timbal, avant-propos par Jean Dauvillier*. Paris: PUF, 1951.

Le Privilegium fori en France du Décret de Gratien à la fin du XIVe siècle. Paris: Éditions Ernest Leroux, 1921 and 1924.

Genet, Jean-Philippe. "L'État de la fin du Moyen Âge et le concept d'espace économique." In *La France de la fin du XVe siècle. Renouveau et apogée*, eds. B. Chevalier and P. Contamine: 31–49. Paris: Éditions du CNRS, 1985.

Gerber, Matthew. "Family, the State, and the Law in Early Modern and Revolutionary France." *History Compass* 7:2 (2009): 474–499.

Glassman, Debra, and Angela Redish. "New Estimates of the Money Stock in France, 1493–1680." *Journal of Economic History* 45:1 (1985): 31–46.

Graeber, David. *Debt: The First 5,000 Years*. Brooklyn: Melville House, 2012.

Granovetter, Mark. "Economic Action and Social Structure: The Problem of Embeddedness." *American Journal of Sociology* 91:3 (1985): 418–510.

Green, Toby. *The Rise of the Trans-Atlantic Slave Trade in Western Africa, 1300–1589.* Cambridge: Cambridge University Press, 2012.

Gregory, Brad S. *The Unintended Reformation: How a Religious Revolution Secularized Society.* Cambridge, MA: Belknap Press, 2012.

Groebner, Valentin. *Liquid Assets, Dangerous Gifts. Presents and Politics at the End of the Middle Ages*, tr. Pamela Selwyn. Philadephia: University of Pennsylvania Press, 2002.

Guyotjeannin, Olivier. *Episcopus et Comes: Affirmation et déclin de la seigneurie épsicopale au nord du royaume de France (Beauvais-Noyon, Xe-début XIIIe siècle).* Geneva: Librairie Droz, 1987.

"Juridiction gracieuse ecclésiastique et naissance de l'officialitè à Beauvais (1175–1220)." In *À propos des actes des évêques: Hommage à Lucie Fossier*, ed. Michel Parisse: 295–310. Nancy: Presses universitaires de Nancy, 1991.

Hamilton Thompson, A. *The English Clergy and Their Organization in the Later Middle Ages.* Oxford: Oxford University Press, 1947.

Hamm, Bernd. *Promissio, Pactum, Ordinatio. Freiheit und Selbstbindung Gottes in der scholastischen Gnadenslehre.* Tübingen: J. C. B. Mohr, 1977.

Hanawalt, Barbara A. *The Wealth of Wives: Women, Law, and Economy in Late Medieval London.* Oxford: Oxford University Press, 2007.

Hanley, Sarah. "Engendering the State: Family Formation and State Building in Early Modern France." *French Historical Studies* 16:1 (1989): 4–27.

Hardwick, Julie. *The Practice of Patriarchy: Gender and the Politics of Household Authority in Early Modern France.* College Station, PA: Pennsylvania State University Press, 1998.

Harsgor, Mikhael. *Recherches sur le personnel du conseil du roi sous Charles VIII et Louis XII.* Paris: Honoré Champion, 1980.

Haselmayer, Louis A. "The Apparitor and Chaucer's Summoner." *Speculum* 12:1 (1937): 43–57.

Hashagen, Justus. "Zur Charakteristik der geistlichen Gerichtsbarkeit vornehmlich im späteren Mittelalter." *Zeitschrift der Savigny-Stiftung für Rechtsgeschichte, Kanonistische Abteilung* 6 (1916): 205–292.

"Zur Sittengeschichte des westfälischen Klerus im späteren Mittelalter." *Westdeutsche Zeitschrift für Geschichte und Kunst* 23 (1904): 102–149.

Heal, Felicity. "Food Gifts, the Household, and the Politics of Exchange in Early Modern England." *Past & Present* 199:1 (2008): 41–70.

Heirbaut, Dirk. "The *Fief-Rente*: A New Evaluation Based on Flemish Sources: 1000–1305." *Tijdschrift voor Rechtsgeschiedenis* 67:1 (1999): 1–37.

Helmholz, R. H. "Assumpsit and Fidei laesio." In *Canon Law and the Law of England*: 263–289. London/Ronceverte: The Hambledon Press, 1987.

"Debt Claims and Probate Jurisdiction in Historical Perspective." *American Journal of Legal History* 23:1 (1979): 68–82.

"Excommunication as a Legal Sanction: The Attitudes of the Medieval Canonists." *Zeitschrift der Savigny-Stiftung für Rechtsgeschichte, Kanonistische Abteilung* 68 (1982): 202–218.

Roman Canon Law in Reformation England. Cambridge: Cambridge University Press, 1990.

Hoffman, Philip T., Gilles Postel-Vinay, and Jean-Laurent Rosenthal. *Priceless Markets: The Political Economy of Credit in Paris, 1660–1870*. Chicago: University of Chicago Press, 2001.

Holton, R. J. *The Transition from Feudalism to Capitalism*. New York: St. Martin's Press, 1985.

Howell, Martha. *Commerce before Capitalism in Europe, 1300–1600*. Cambridge: Cambridge University Press, 2010.

The Marriage Exchange: Property, Social Place, and Gender in Cities of the Low Countries, 1300–1550. Chicago: University of Chicago Press, 1998.

Hufton, Olwen. *The Poor of Eighteenth-Century France*. Oxford: Clarendon Press, 1988.

Iacobucci, Edward. "On the Interaction between Legal and Reputational Sanctions." *Journal of Legal Studies* 43:1 (2014): 189–207.

Jalabert, Marie-Laure. *Le Livre Vert de Pierre de la Jugie. Une image de la fortune des archevêques de Narbonne au XIVe siècle*. Perpignan: Presses universitaires de Perpignan, 2009.

Jedin, Hubert. "Das Bischofsidcal der katholischen Reformation. Eine Studie über die Bischofsspiegel vornehmlich des 16. Jahrhunderts." In *Kirche des Glaubens. Kirche der Geschichte. Ausgewählte Aufsätze und Vorträge*: II:75–117. Freiburg: Herder, 1966.

Jégou, Laurent. *L'évêque, juge de paix. L'autorité épiscopale et le règlement des conflits entre Loire et Elbe (milieu VIIIe-milieu XIe siècle)*. Turnhout: Brepols, 2011.

Judt, Tony. "A Clown in Regal Purple: Social History and the Historians." *History Workshop Journal* 7 (1979): 66–94.

Jussen, Bernhard, ed. *Ordering Medieval Society: Perspectives on Intellectual and Practical Modes of Shaping Social Relations*, tr. Pamela Selwyn. Philadelphia: University of Pennsylvania Press, 2000.

Kaiser, Colin. "The Deflation in the Volume of Litigation at Paris in the Eighteenth Century and the Waning of the Old Judicial Order." *European History Quarterly* 10 (1980): 309–336.

Kerridge, Eric. *Usury, Interest, and the Reformation*. Aldershot: Ashgate, 2002.

Kessler, Amalia. *A Revolution in Commerce: The Parisian Merchant Court and the Rise of Commercial Society in Eighteenth-Century France*. New Haven: Yale University Press, 2007.

Kettering, Sharon. "Gift-Giving and Patronage in Early Modern France." *French History* 2:2 (1988): 131–151.

Kirn, Paul. "Der mittelalterliche Staat und das geistliche Gericht." *Zeitschrift der Savigny-Stiftung für Rechtsgeschichte, Kanonistische Abteilung* 15 (1926): 162–199.

Koziol, Geoffrey. *The Politics of Memory and Identity in Carolingian Royal Diplomas. The West Frankish Kingdom (840–987)*. Turnhout: Brepols, 2012.

Krusch, Bruno. "Studie zur Geschichte der geistlichen Jurisdiktion und Verwaltung des Erzstifts Mainz. Commissar Johann Bruns und die kirchliche Eintheilung der Archidiaconate Nörten, Einbeck und Heiligenstadt." *Zeitschrift des Historischen Vereins für Niedersachsen* (1897): 112–277.

Kwass, Michael. *Privilege and the Politics of Taxation: Liberté, égalité, fiscalité*. New York: Cambridge University Press, 2006.

Lamoureaux, John. "Episcopal Courts in Late Antiquity." *Journal of Early Christian Studies* 3 (1995): 143–167.

Landau, Peter. "Zum Ursprung des 'Ius ad Rem' in der Kanonistik." In *Proceedings of the Third International Congress of Medieval Canon Law: Strasbourg, 3–6 September 1968*, ed. Stephan Kuttner: 81–102. Vatican City: Bibliotheca Apostolica Vaticana, 1971.

Lange, Tyler. "The Birth of a Maxim: 'A Bishop Has No Territory'." *Speculum* 89:1 (2014): 128–147.

"Droit canon et droit français à travers l'activité du Parlement de Paris à l'époque des Réformes." *Revue historique de droit français et étranger* 91:2 (2013): 243–261.

The First French Reformation: Church Reform and the Origins of the Old Regime. New York: Cambridge University Press, 2014.

"Revisiting the Legacy of Ernst Kantorowicz." *Sixteenth Century Journal* 42:4 (2011): 1003–1026.

Langholm, Odd. *Economics in the Medieval Schools: Wealth, Exchange, Value, Money, and Usury according to the Paris Theological Tradition, 1200–1350*. Leiden: Brill, 1992.

Lardin, Philippe. "Monnaie de compte et monnaie réelle: des relations mal étudiées." *Revue européenne des sciences sociales* XLV:137 (2007): 45–68.

Lea, H. C. *Studies in Church History*. Philadelphia: Henry C. Lea's Son and Company, 1883.

Le Cacheux, Paul. "Le fonds de l'officialité de Montivilliers." In *Travaux de la semaine d'histoire du droit normand tenue à Guernesey du 26 au 30 mai 1927*: 275–305. Caen: Imprimerie A. Olivier et M. Caron, 1928.

Lecroq, Dom Gaston. *L'Abbaye de Montivilliers*. Fécamp: L. Durand et fils, 1936.

Lefas, Alexandre. "De l'origine des juridictions consulaires des marchands de France." *Revue historique de droit français et étranger*, 4ème série, III (1924): 83–120.

Lefebvre-Teillard, Anne. *Les officialités à la veille du concile de Trente*. Paris: R. Pichon et R. Durand-Auzias, 1973.

Le Gall, Jean-Marie. *Les moines au temps des réformes: Frances, 1480–1560*. Seyssel: Champ Vallon, 2001.

Legendre, Pierre. *Leçons IX: L'autre Bible de l'Occident: Le monument romano-canonique: Étude sur l'architecture dogmatique des sociétés*. Paris: Fayard, 2009.

Le Goff, Jacques. *Your Money or Your Life: Economy and Religion in the Middle Ages*, Patricia Ranum (trans.). New York: Zone Books, 1988.

Lemaître, Nicole. *Le scribe et le mage: Notaires et société rurale en Bas-Limousin aux XVIe et XVIIe siècles*. Ussel: Musée du pays d'Ussel, 2000.

Lemarignier, Jean-François. *Étude sur les privilèges d'exemption et de juridiction ecclésiastique des abbayes normandes depuis les origines jusqu'en 1140*. Paris: A. Picard, 1937.

"De l'immunité à la seigneurie ecclésiastique: Les 'territoires coutumiers' d'églises en Île-de-France et dans les régions voisines d'après les diplômes des premiers Capétiens (987–1108). In *Études d'histoire du droit canonique dédiées à Gabriel Le Bras*: I:619–630. Paris: Sirey, 1965.

Lewis, P. S. *Essays in Later Medieval French History*. London: The Hambledon Press, 1985.

Little, Lester K. *Benedictine Maledictions: Liturgical Cursing in Romanesque France*. Ithaca: Cornell University Press, 1993.

Logan, F. Donald. *Excommunication and the Secular Arm in Medieval England: A Study in Legal Procedure from the Thirteenth to the Sixteenth Century*. Toronto: PIMS, 1968.

Lorcin, Marie-Thérèse. "La fraude des décimables: mouvement court ou mouvement long?" In *Prestations paysannes. Dîmes, rente foncière et mouvement de la production agricole à l'époque préindustrielle*, eds. J. Goy and E. Le Roy Ladurie: 599–606. Paris: Éditions de l'EHESS, 1982.

Lubac, Henri de. *Corpus mysticum. L'Eucharistie et l'Église au Moyen Âge. Étude historique*. Paris: Aubrie, 1944.

Luiten van Zanden, Jan, Jaco Zuijderduijn, and Tine De Moor. "Small is Beautiful: The Efficiency of Credit Markets in Late Medieval Holland." *European Review of Economic History* 16 (2012): 3–22.

Lupoi, Maurizio. *The Origins of the European Legal Order*, tr. Adrian Belton. Cambridge: Cambridge University Press, 2000.

Maccarrone, Michele. *Vicarius Christi: Storia del titulo papale*. Rome: Facultas Theologica Pontificii Athenaei Lateranensis, 1952.

Major, J. Russell. "Bastard Feudalism and the Kiss: Changing Social Mores in Late Medieval and Early Modern France." *Journal of Interdisciplinary History* 17:3 (1987): 509–535.

Masson, Pierre. "Le bail à cheptel d'après les actes notariés bourguignons du XIVe siècle jusqu'à la première moitié du XVe siècle." *Mémoires de la Société pour l'Histoire du Droit et des Institutions des anciens pays bourguignons, comtois et romands*, 2 (1935): 77–140.

Mathieu, Isabelle. *Les Justices seigneuriales en Anjou et dans le Maine à la fin du Moyen Âge*. Rennes: Presses universitaires de Rennes, 2011.

Mayali, Laurent. "'Duo erunt in carne una' and the Medieval Canonists." In *Iuris Historia: Liber Amicorum Gero Dolezalek*, eds. Vincenzo Colli and Emanuele Conte. 161–175. Berkeley: Robbins Collection, 2008.

"Procureurs et représentation en droit canonique médiéval." *Mélanges de l'École Française de Rome* 114 (2002): 41–57.

McCloskey, Deirdre. *Bourgeois Dignity: Why Economics Can't Explain the Modern World*. Chicago: University of Chicago Press, 2010.

"The Poverty of Boldizzoni: Resurrecting the German Historical School." *Investigaciones de Historia Económica – Economic History Research* 9 (2013): 2–6.

McManners, John. *Church and Society in Eighteenth-Century France*. Oxford: Oxford University Press, 1998.

Mirot, Léon. "Études lucquoises II. Les Isbarre, monnayeurs royaux, Augustin Isbarre." *Bibliothèque de l'École des Chartes* 88 (1927): 275–314.

Miskimin, H. M. "L'or, l'argent, la guerre dans la France médiévale." *Annales ESC* 40:1 (1985): 171–184.

Mollat, Michel. *Le commerce maritime normand à la fin du Moyen Âge*. Paris: Plon, 1952.

Muldrew, Craig. *The Economy of Obligation: The Culture of Credit and Social Relations in Early Modern England*. New York: St Martin's Press, 1998.

Munro, John. "Deflation and the Petty Coinage Problem in the Late-Medieval Economy: The Case of Flanders, 1334–1484." *Explorations in Economic History* 25:4 (1988): 387–423.

"The Medieval Origins of the Financial Revolution: Usury, Rentes, and Negotiability." *The International History Review* 25:3 (2003): 505–562.

"Money, Wages, and Real Incomes in the Age of Erasmus: The Purchasing Power of Coins and of Building Craftsmen's Wages in England and the Low Countries, 1500–1540." University of Toronto Working Paper No.1 for 2001: www.economics.utoronto.ca/public/workingPapers/UT-ECIPA-MUNRO-01-01.pdf

"The Rise, Expansion, and Decline of the Italian Wool-Based Textile Industries, ca. 1100–1730: A Study in International Competition, Transaction Costs, and Comparative Advantage." University of Toronto, Department of Economics, Working Paper no. 440 (2011): www.economics.utoronto.ca/index.php/index/research/workingPaperDetails/440

"Usury, Calvinism, and Credit in Protestant England: From the Sixteenth Century to the Industrial Revolution." In *Religione e istituzioni religiose nell'economia europea. 1000–1800. Atti della "Quarantatreesima Settimana di Studi" 8–12 maggio 2011*, ed. Francesco Ammannati: 155–184. Florence: Firenze University Press, 2012.

"Wage-Stickiness, Monetary Changes, and Real Incomes in Late-Medieval England and the Low Countries, 1300–1500: Did Money Matter?" *Research in Economic History* 21 (2003): 185–297.

Nightingale, Pamela. "Gold, Credit, and Mortality: Distinguishing Deflationary Pressures on the Late Medieval English Economy." *Economic History Review* 63:4 (2010): 1081–1104.

Oberman, Heiko. *The Harvest of Medieval Theology: Gabriel Biel and Late Medieval Nominalism*. Cambridge: Harvard University Press, 1963.

Luther: Man between God and the Devil. New Haven: Yale University Press, 1989.

Masters of the Reformation: The Emergence of a New Intellectual Climate in Europe. Cambridge: Cambridge University Press, 1981.

Oestmann, Peter. *Geistliche und weltliche Gerichte im Alten Reich. Zuständigkeitsstreitigkeiten und Instanzenzüge*. Cologne/Weimar/Vienna: Böhlau Verlag, 2012.

Oldland, John. "The Allocation of Merchant Capital in Early Tudor London." *Economic History Review* 63:4 (2010): 1058–1080.

Olivier-Martin, François. *L'assemblée de Vincennes de 1329 et ses conséquences. Étude sur les conflits entre la juridiction laïque et la juridiction ecclésiastique au XIVe siècle*. Paris: A. Picard, 1909.

Ortlieb, Eva, and Gert Polster. "Die Prozessfrequenz am Reichshofrat (1519–1806)." *Zeitschrift für neuere Rechtsgeschichte* 26:3–4 (2004): 189–216.

Ourliac, Paul, and Jehan de Malafosse. *Histoire du droit privé, 1. Les Obligations*. Paris: PUF, 1957.

Paravy, Pierette. *De la chrétienté romaine à la Réforme en Dauphiné. Évêques, fidèles et déviants (vers 1340-vers 1530)*. Rome: École française de Rome, 1993.

Parsons, Jotham. "The Catholic Ethic and the Spirit of *Étatisme*." *French History* 28:3 (2014): 322–342.

Pommeray, Léon. *L'officialité archidiaconale de Paris et sa compétence criminelle*. Paris: Sirey, 1933.

Prodi, Paolo. *Il sacramento del potere: il giuramento politico nella storia costituzionale dell'Occidente*. Bologna: Il Mulino, 1992.

Settimo non rubare. Furto e mercato nella storia dell'Occidente. Bologna: Il Mulino, 2009.

Una storia della giustizia: Dal pluralismo dei fori al moderno dualismo tra coscienza e diritto. Bologna: Il Mulino, 2000.

Reinburg, Virginia. *French Books of Hours: Making an Archive of Prayer, c.1400–1600*. Cambridge: Cambridge University Press, 2012.

Roch, Jean-Louis. "Entre draperie rural et draperie urbaine? La draperie foraine de Rouen à la fin du Moyen Âge." *Annales de Normandie* 48:3 (1998): 211–230.

Roche, Daniel. *France in the Enlightenment*, tr. A. Goldhammer. Cambridge, MA: Harvard University Press, 1998.

Royer, Jean-Pierre. *L'Église et le royaume de France au XIVe siècle d'après le "Songe du Vergier" et la jurisprudence du Parlement*. Paris: LGDJ, 1969.

Rubin, Miri. *Corpus Christi: The Eucharist in Late Medieval Culture*. Cambridge: Cambridge University Press, 1991.

Sargent, Thomas J., and François R. Velde. *The Big Problem of Small Change*. Princeton: Princeton University Press, 2002.

Schnapper, Bernard. *Les rentes au XVIe siècle: Histoire d'un instrument de crédit*. Paris: SEVPEN, 1957.

Schrader, Gerhard. "Die bishöflichen Offiziale Hildesheims und ihre Urkunden im späten Mittelalter (1300–1600)." *Archiv für Urkundenforschung* 13 (1935): 91–176.

Scott, Tom. "The German Peasants' War and the 'Crisis of Feudalism.' Reflections on a Neglected Theme." *Journal of Early Modern History* 63 (2002): 265–295.

Scribner, R. W. *Popular Culture and Popular Movements in Reformation Germany*. London: Hambledon Press, 1987.

Seidentop, Larry. *Inventing the Individual: The Origins of Western Liberalism*. Cambridge, MA: Belknap Press, 2014.

Sen, Amartya. "Equality of What?" In *McMurrin S. Tanner Lectures on Human Values*, ed. Sterling M. McMurrin: I:195–220. Cambridge: Cambridge University Press, 1980.

Sirks, A. J. B. "The *episcopalis audientia* in Late Antiquity." *Droit et cultures* 65 (2013): 79–88.

Smail, Daniel Lord. *The Consumption of Justice: Emotion, Publicity, and Legal Culture in Marseille, 1264–1423*. Ithaca: Cornell University Press, 2003.

Swanson, R. N. *Church and Society in Late Medieval England*. Oxford: Blackwell, 1989.

Indulgences in Late Medieval England: Passports to Paradise. Cambridge: Cambridge University Press, 2007.

Theiller, Isabelle. "Comptabilité et réalité financière: quelques observations autour d'un registre comptable de l'abbaye Saint-Amand de Rouen (1387/8-1397)." *Tabularia "Études"* 5 (2007): 51–73.

"Prix du marché, marché du grain et crédit au début du XIIIe siècle: Autour d'un dossier Rouennais." *Le Moyen Âge* CXV:2 (2009): 253–276.

Thireau, Jean-Louis. *Charles du Moulin (1500–1566). Étude sur les sources, la méthode, les idées politiques et économiques d'un juriste de la Renaissance*. Geneva: Droz, 1980.

Thompson, E. P. "The Moral Economy of the English Crowd in the Eighteenth Century." *Past & Present* 50:1 (1971): 76–136.

Timbal, Pierre-Clément. *Les obligations contractuelles dans le droit français des XIIIe et XIVe siècles d'après la jurisprudence du Parlement*. Paris: Éditions du CNRS, 1973 and 1977.

Timbal, Pierre-Clément, and Bernadette Auzary. "Visites décanales faites dans l'Archidiaconé de Paris en 1468–1470." *Revue historique de l'Eglise de France* 62:169 (1976): 361–374.

Toussaert, Jacques. *Le sentiment religieux en Flandre à la fin du Moyen Âge*. Paris: Plon, 1963.

Trexler, Richard. *Synodal Law in Florence and Fiesole, 1306–1518*. Vatican City: Bibliotheca Apostolica Vaticana, 1971.

Trouillot, Michel-Rolph. *Global Transformations: Anthropology and the Modern World*. New York: Palgrave Macmillan, 2003.

Van Bavel, Bas. *Manors and Markets: Economy and Society in the Low Countries, 500–1600*. Oxford: Oxford University Press, 2010.

Van Houdt, T. "Money, Time and Labour: Leonardus Lessius and the Ethics of Money-Lending and Interest-Taking." *Ethical Perspectives* 2 (1995): 11–27.

Venard, Marc. "Les visites pastorales de l'exemption de Montivilliers du XVIe au XVIIIe siècle." *L'Abbaye de Montivilliers à travers les âges (Colloque de 1986), Recueil de l'Association des Amis du Vieux Havre 46* (1988): 85–106.

"Les visites pastorales françaises du XVIe au XVIIIe siècle." In *Le catholicisme à l'épreuve dans la France du XVIe siècle*: 27–63. Paris: Éditions du Cerf, 2000.

Vickers, Daniel. "Errors Expected: The Culture of Credit in Rural New England, 1750–1800." *Economic History Review* 63:4 (2010): 1032–1057.

Villemin, Laurent. *Pouvoir d'ordre et pouvoir de juridiction: Histoire théologique de leur distinction*. Paris: Editions de Cerf, 2003.

Vodola, Elisabeth. *Excommunication in the Middle Ages*. Berkeley: University of California Press, 1986.

Wallinga, Tammo. "*Authenticum* and *authenticae*: What's in a Name? References to Justinian's Novels in Medieval Manuscripts." *Tijdschrift voor Rechtsgeschiedenis* 77 (2009): 43–59.

Wenzel, Éric. "La pratique du monitoire à fin de révélation sous l'Ancien Régime, à travers l'exemple du diocèse d'Autun (1670–1790)." *Mémoires de la Société pour l'histoire du droit et des institutions des anciens pays bourguignons, comtois et romands* 57 (2000): 283–300.

Whittle, Jane. *The Development of Agrarian Capitalism: Land and Labour in Norfolk 1440–1580*. Oxford: Oxford University Press, 2000.

Wilks, Michael. *The Problem of Sovereignty in the Later Middle Ages: The Papal Monarchy with Augustinus Triumphus and the Publicists*. Cambridge: Cambridge University Press, 1964.

Wollschläger, Christian. "Civil Litigation and Modernization: The Work of the Municipal Courts of Bremen, Germany in Five Centuries, 1549–1984." *Law and Society Review* 24:2 (1990): 261–282.

Wunderli, Richard. *London Church Courts and Society of the Eve of the Reformation*. Cambridge, MA: Medieval Academy of America, 1981.

"Pre-Reformation London Summoners and the Murder of Richard Hunne." *Journal of Ecclesiastical History* 33:2 (1982): 209–224.

Yver, Jean. *Les contrats dans le très ancien droit normand (XIe–XIIIe siècles)*. Domfront: Imprimerie du Publicateur, 1926.

Égalité entre héritiers et exclusion des enfants dotés: Essai de géographie coutumière. Paris: Sirey, 1966.

Zink, Anne. *Pays ou circonscriptions. Les collectivités territoriales de la France du Sud-Ouest sous l'Ancien Régime*. Paris: Publications de la Sorbonne, 2000.

Zwalve, W. J. "*Sola scriptura*, An essay in comparative legal history on 'obligacions' in thirteenth-century France and England." *Tijdschrift voor Rechtsgeschiedenis* 80 (2012): 95–128.

Index